W9-AUZ-395

Guarding the Gates

Praeger Security International Advisory Board

Board Co-chairs

Loch K. Johnson, Regents Professor of Public and International Affairs, School of Public and International Affairs, University of Georgia (U.S.A.)

Paul Wilkinson, Professor of International Relations and Chairman of the Advisory Board, Centre for the Study of Terrorism and Political Violence, University of St. Andrews (U.K.)

Members

Eliot A. Cohen, Robert E. Osgood Professor of Strategic Studies and Director, Philip Merrill Center for Strategic Studies, Paul H. Nitze School of Advanced International Studies, The Johns Hopkins University (U.S.A.)

Anthony H. Cordesman, Arleigh A. Burke Chair in Strategy, Center for Strategic and International Studies (U.S.A.)

Thérèse Delpech, Senior Research Fellow, CERI (Atomic Energy Commission), Paris (France)

Sir Michael Howard, former Professor of History of War, Oxford University, and Professor of Military and Naval History, Yale University (U.K.)

Lieutenant General Claudia J. Kennedy, USA (Ret.), former Deputy Chief of Staff for Intelligence, Headquarters, Department of the Army (U.S.A.)

Paul M. Kennedy, J. Richardson Dilworth Professor of History and Director, International Security Studies, Yale University (U.S.A.)

Robert J. O'Neill, former Chichele Professor of the History of War, All Souls College, Oxford University (Australia)

Shibley Telhami, Anwar Sadat Chair for Peace and Development, Department of Government and Politics, University of Maryland (U.S.A.)

Jusuf Wanandi, co-founder and member, Board of Trustees, Centre for Strategic and International Studies (Indonesia)

Fareed Zakaria, Editor, Newsweek International (U.S.A.)

Guarding the Gates

IMMIGRATION AND NATIONAL SECURITY

Michael C. LeMay

PRAEGER SECURITY INTERNATIONAL
Westport, Connecticut • London

Library of Congress Cataloging-in-Publication Data

LeMay, Michael C., 1941–
  Guarding the gates : immigration and national security / Michael C. LeMay.
    p. cm.
  Includes bibliographical references and index.
  ISBN 0–275–99294–2 (alk. paper)
    1. United States—Emigration and immigration—History.   2. United States—
Emigration and immigration—Government policy.   3. National security—
United States.   I. Title.
  JV6450.L46 2006
  325.73—dc22   2006021401

British Library Cataloguing in Publication Data is available.

Copyright © 2006 by Michael C. LeMay

All rights reserved. No portion of this book may be
reproduced, by any process or technique, without the
express written consent of the publisher.

Library of Congress Catalog Card Number: 2006021401
ISBN: 0–275–99294–2

First published in 2006

Praeger Security International, 88 Post Road West, Westport, CT 06881
An imprint of Greenwood Publishing Group, Inc.
www.praeger.com

Printed in the United States of America

The paper used in this book complies with the
Permanent Paper Standard issued by the National
Information Standards Organization (Z39.48-1984).

10   9   8   7   6   5   4   3   2   1

Contents

Tables, Figures, and Boxes

TABLES

Preface

Major or comprehensive changes in the immigration policy of the United States seem to occur about every twenty-five to thirty years. The last such major shift in immigration policy occurred in 1986 and involved enactment of the Immigration Reform and Control Act (known as IRCA). It focused on the problem of illegal immigration and incorporated a new approach to control the flow of undocumented immigrants into the country—the use of employer sanctions. Today, the nation grapples once again with the issue of illegal immigration and what should be done about it? Today, the Congress again considers proposals for comprehensive reform. Today, as in 1986, the media and the political arena is filled with discussion of the need to crack down hard on illegal immigration, to "regain control of our borders," to erect a fence along the more than 2,000 mile southern border, and to militarize the border area. Today, many advocacy groups concerned with the issue of immigration, as do many in Congress, maintain that any approach to comprehensive immigration reform will necessity have to balance harsh or restrictive measures to tighten up our border control and crack down on illegal immigration with some sort of provision to allow for a guest worker program and "earned legalization" for the estimated 11 to 12 million illegal immigrants in the United States. Today, groups for and against any sort of "amnesty" argue that homeland defense concerns demand a thorough revision of immigration policy. Today, as in 1986, Congress is deeply divided on the issue of immigration policy. The Bush administration and many senators favor the use of a guest worker program. The House of Representatives has a majority of members who oppose amnesty, any legalization, the guest worker approach, and favor to the point of having already passed measures that would build a fence and crack down on illegal immigration—a restrictive approach. A majority in the House, and according to many public opinion polls, a majority of the population favor reductions in the total levels of legal immigration in addition to strengthening policy aimed at reducing the illegal flow.

The attacks of September 11, 2001 shook the nation and altered American politics. As this book will explore and show, national security has always played a role in immigration policy, and immigration has always been seen as having an impact on national security matters. The attacks of September 11 merely intensified perceptions of the inherent link between immigration policy and national security policy. As Congress and the nation struggled to find means for immigration policy, various proposals were placed on the agenda of Congress to reform it. Many are more restrictive in direction, including an approach to expand the Border Patrol, to harden the border, and to crack down on the employers of undocumented workers. Others propose including legalization and an expanded guest worker program. Proponents on both sides of these issues address the topic as if their approach was new or would provide a final answer to the problem of illegal immigration in the United States. Having authored previously another book that examined immigration policy from a long-term historical perspective, I knew that these proposals and approaches were far from new. Indeed, all had been tried before with little success and with considerable unanticipated consequences. I felt the need to reexamine the issue, this time with a specific focus on the interrelationship between immigration and national security—now more commonly referred to as homeland security. Hence, this volume, *Guarding the Gates*. Hopefully, the readers will find the long-term perspective on immigration policy and the cycles of immigration policy categorized by this book, insightful when considering what might be the best approach to reform immigration policy in light of the post-September 11 realities of American society and politics.

Acknowledgments

A n extensive book such as this leaves its author with a debt of gratitude
to many persons who went before, to the laborers in the academy of
scholars toiling in the particular field of study that is its focus. This is all the
more the case when the work is one with such a pronounced historical nature.
The contributions of several scholars whose work I drew upon while writing
this book are acknowledged in the extensive bibliography. There are, in addition, several persons whose contributions deserve special recognition here.

The American Political Science Association and the American Historical
Association provided me with a travel grant to attend the Project '87 seminar
on Immigration and the Constitution held at my alma mater, the University of
Minnesota, in the summer of 1986. That seminar—and its roughly two dozen
participants—were very helpful to my focus on this topic particularly for the
earlier chapters of this book. Professor Rudolph Vecoli, the seminar coordi-
nator, and the Immigration History Research Center staff proved to be the most
gracious hosts and very helpful colleagues. I am indebted to Professor Vecoli
for allowing me to use certain material citied herein.

Several colleagues read various drafts of the manuscript for the earlier version
of this book, *From Open Door to Dutch Door* (1987), and offered useful sug-
gestions to improve it: Ronald Hedlund, William McLeod, and John Wiseman.

My colleague and prominent immigration historian, Elliott Robert Barkan,
worked with me in producing another book, *U.S. Immigration and Naturalization
Laws and Issues*, from which I drew material used throughout this revised volume, particularly for the final two chapters. His insights and succinct editing
of material provided invaluable improvements to that and ultimately to this
manuscript.

Students in various sections of my American Public Policy Analysis classes
at Frostburg State University and in the Formation of Public Policy classes at

California State University-San Bernardino served as captive audiences upon whom I could "classroom test" much of the material used herein as I developed them.

California State University-San Bernardino conferred upon me and supports me as "Professor Emeritus." That status afforded me the time to revise and rewrite my earlier book, updating it to this volume and refocusing the discussion to the inherent interrelationship between national security issues and immigration policy. Current events suggested its focus on the perennial linkage between immigration policy-making and national security issues, perceptions, and concerns. Any errors of fact or interpretation contained herein are, of course, solely the responsibility of the author.

Introduction

When President George W. Bush signed into law the act establishing the new cabinet-level Department of Homeland Security (DHS) in 2002, he enacted the most sweeping change in the structures of the national executive branch of government since World War II. He also set in motion the dissolving of the Immigration and Naturalization Service and the merging of its functions and services into the new department. These actions demonstrate the continuing importance of immigration policy-making in the United States. It remains a "hot issue" on the national scene. National security concerns have always played a major role in the determination of immigration policy-making, and immigration policy has always been a factor in how the nation perceived it had best secure the nation's defense. What to do about "the immigration problem" has been a perennial issue in U.S. politics, and cyclical changes in that policy have periodically brought it to the forefront of the nation's policy-making agenda. This book is about immigration policy-making in the United States— what forces have shaped it, how and why various changes have been made in it, and where it seems headed in the immediate future. In particular, it emphasizes the complex interplay between perceptions of and concern for national security and the posture of U.S. policy-making with regard to who and how many are allowed to immigrate here for permanent residence status and eventual citizenship. It is designed to serve as a library reference volume or to be used as a supplemental book for courses dealing with the analysis of public policy. Hopefully, it will also be of particular interest to students of U.S. history who may wish to focus on this particular topic and study how and why that policy has changed over the course of the nation's history. Hopefully, too, it will be of interest to the general reader concerned with this important and timely topic.

The reader might well ask, why study U.S. immigration policy? This is a good question. I believe there are several appropriate responses to it.

First of all, U.S. immigration policy-making is a topic of substantive and timely interest. The United States is the leading country among the nations of the world in the degree to which it has absorbed immigrants. Since 1820, when the government first started keeping count, well over 60 million persons have immigrated here. At any given time in its history, approximately one-quarter of the total population is comprised of persons born elsewhere who have permanently migrated to the United States. The United States is now home to some tens of thousands of residents from some 170 other nations of the world. In recent decades, roughly two-thirds of all the immigration in the world consists of people entering the United States. The influx of these tens of millions of immigrants has in the past and continues today to have profound impact on the nation's culture, economy, and politics. Although now a cliché, it is nonetheless true that we are a nation of nations. We can best understand the impact of that massive in-migration by studying the process of immigration and the policy-making that determines it at any given period of time. The magnitude of the problems associated with regulating the immigration process, especially concerning the estimated millions of undocumented aliens, has compelled renewed scholarly and mass media interest in the subject. Congress is once again in the midst of a periodic review of our immigration policy. As concerned citizens and as students of policy-making, we can best assess these new trends in U.S. immigration policy in the light of an historical review and analysis of our past immigration policy.

A second reason to study immigration policy-making is that it is an *inherently interesting topic*. The story of how the United States came to be "a nation of nations" is one rich in human interest. The vast variety of groups who have mixed and intermingled here, if not "melted into one," compels our focus. It helps us understand our national motto: "E pluribus unum" (Out of many: one). How immigration policy has influenced the composition of our population and how that composition in turn has shaped immigration policy-making is a story that should be of significance to any student of public policy or of the nation's colorful history. This suggests a third reason for this study.

Immigration policy is the type of subject that affords an excellent opportunity to gain insight into the complexity of the policy-making process. As James Anderson defines it in his seminal book, *Public Policy-Making* (New York: Holt-Rinehart and Winston, 1979), public policy is "a purposive course of action followed by an actor or set of actors in dealing with a problem or matter of concern" (Anderson: 3). He distinguishes four types of policies: distributive, regulatory, self-regulatory, and re-distributive. Immigration policy is an insightful example of regulatory policy—that is, one which involves the imposition of restrictions or limits on behavior of individuals and groups (Anderson: 126–128). Not all regulatory policies are as clear-cut as is immigration policy in the dramatic impact that policy has upon the social and political environment. Seldom can a student of the policy process see a more extensive result of a change in policy then is the case with the "gate-keeping" policy examined herein. We cite but two examples here to illustrate the point. In 1881, 11,900 Chinese immigrants entered the country and over 39,000 came in 1882. That number dropped to a paltry 8,031 in 1883 and a mere twenty-three by 1885—after passage of the Chinese Exclusion Act of 1882. In the decade before enactment of the national origins quota system, over 8 million immigrants entered the United States, nearly 71 percent of who came from southeastern European countries. In the decade after passage of the quota system, the United States absorbed the smallest influx of immigrants for any decade since the government began keeping count of such in 1820. Those from southeastern European nations decreased to but 37 percent of that far smaller total flow of immigrants.

Anderson analytically distinguishes a number of functional categories of activity that characterize the policy process—stages in that process, if you will. He identifies them as: problem formation, formulation, adoption, implementation, and evaluation (Anderson: 23–24). This analysis of immigration policy-making exemplifies every stage of that policy process. The story of how that policy has evolved and changed over time is one that usefully exemplifies each category of activity in the public policy process for students of public policy. These activities emerge clearly in the analysis and it makes their interplay apparent, elucidating the dynamic nature of that process for the student.

Yet a fourth reason we might present to answer why one might study immigration policy is that it affords insight into a particularly timely policy problem. This study is a *policy analysis*, not a *policy advocacy*. That is, it is concerned with the examination of the causes and consequences of public policy rather than advocating what government *should* do, promoting some particular policy proposal or response to a problem. Nonetheless, we can learn much from the *long-term* historical perspective to better assess the various pros and cons of recent immigration policy-making. While this book does not advocate any particular policy, it hopefully enables the reader to be better informed in making his/her own judgments as to the various merits of each side of the current debate over U.S. immigration policy.

The approach of this book is to present an historical overview of U.S. immigration policy. Such an analysis identifies a number of *commonalities* in the story of immigration policy-making and how it changed over time. Each period that preceded a significant change in immigration policy, for example, was one in which the United States experienced a major recession or depression, such as the depressions of 1873, 1893, 1920, or the Great Depression of the 1930s, or the more recent recessions of 1981–1983, 1991–1993, and 2001–2003. Every such period was marked as one of social unrest and anxiety. The labor strife of the 1870s led to the immigration restrictions of the 1880s, the first such ever imposed. The "Red Scare" of 1919 immediately preceded the imposition of the quota system of the 1920s. The foreign-policy concerns of the Cold War Era were associated with the changes enacted in the Immigration Act of 1952, just as the social turmoil of the civil rights era and the Vietnam

War were reflected in the Immigration Act of 1965. The near-hysteria in national politics following the attacks of September 11 reverberates in the enactment of the USA Patriot Act and the establishment of the DHS in 2002. Indeed, each postwar period—be it after the Civil War, World War I, World War II, the Korean War, the Vietnam War, the Gulf War, and now the War on Terrorism—saw agitation leading to rather substantial changes in U.S. immigration policy.

Associated, too, with each major shift in that policy is a dramatic shift in the composition of the immigrant population. A change from Protestants from northwestern Europe to Catholics and Jews from southeastern Europe led to the imposition of the quota system designed to limit that latter influx. The need to deal with the "refugees" after World War II compelled yet another substantial change. The massive influx of Chicanos, Haitians, Vietnamese, and other Asian people led to new demands to modify immigration law. The substantial inflow of Arab-Americans in the 1990s and the estimated millions of undocumented aliens preceded a post-September 11 concern to fortify fortress America against the "flood of illegals" and the danger of allowing in foreign terrorists who might serve as "terrorist cells."

Each major shift in immigration policy came only after one or more of the major political parties then dominant in American politics decided to advocate such change as a major plank in their party platform. Likewise, each major shift followed the formation of specific ad-hoc interest groups or interest group coalitions that were advocating or opposing such change: the Know-Nothing party in the 1840s; the Asian Exclusion League in the 1880s and 1890s; and in the 1920s, the Ku Klux Klan, the American Coalition, the Immigration Restriction League, and the American Protective League of True Americans did battle with the Hebrew Sheltering and Immigration Aid Society and the Anti-National Origins Clause League. In the 1980s, the Federation for American Immigration Reform and the Zero Population Growth movements emerged strongly advocating the need for change to a more restrictionist policy stance. Today, groups like the American Civil Liberties Union and the Patriots to Restore Checks and Balances do battle with such groups as the Americans for Immigration Control, Inc., The Minuteman Project, Citizen Outreach, and the Congressional Immigration Reform Caucus.

The long-term view of immigration policy highlights, too, the recurrent arguments, like variations on a theme in a symphony, of proponents for a change in policy. Time and again, concerns are expressed over the impact of immigration on wages and working conditions. Over and over again one hears of the adverse impact of immigration from those advocating increased restrictions. They fear the influx of each new wave of newcomers will damage U.S. culture, social mores, or the way politics are conducted. The recurrent theme of whether or not each new wave of immigrants can, or should, be incorporated into our society is a motif heard throughout the history of U.S. immigration policy. So, too, is the recurring concern expressed over the *method* by which immigrants should be screened, restricted, or managed. Advocates of change suggested new methods: from "excluded categories" containing groups with perceived "undesirable traits" of physical or mental characteristics, to a "literacy test," to the imposition of an elaborated and fixed "quota system," to the development of an equally elaborate "preference system," onto the use of devices to reduce the economic incentives for immigration, and to the current use of "profiling" to prevent terrorists from entering the United States. What is consistent throughout the history of immigration policy-making, however, is that each major shift in policy, what we distinguish herein as each major policy cycle, is associated with the advocacy of some new "method."

The long-term review of immigration history shows that, throughout that history, four main elements of the immigration policy process figure prominently in the formulation of immigration policy: economics, race, nationalism, and foreign policy concerns. Sometimes, these four elements work in relative harmony with one another, reinforcing each other. At other times they work in conflict with one another, and the contending forces seeking to influence immigration policy will each stress differing elements. But in all cases these four elements are the key to an understanding of U.S. immigration policy. Each cycle depicted herein reflects a different array or balance in how those four elements play out in determining the policy position or stance dominating the policy-making approach of that cycle or era.

We see throughout the history of U.S. immigration policy coalitions of stable organized interest groups generally promoting an open-door approach to immigration policy or advocating the need for a restrictionist stance. Time and again, there is evident a coalition of business and ethnic associations in favor of more or less unrestricted immigration doing battle with a coalition of organized labor, the American Legion, and various "patriotic" associations pressing for some new method to restrict the influx.

The decade before each major cyclical shift sees a spate of scholarly books and mass media programs concerned with the then current "immigration problem." Such attempts to mold public opinion are followed by a significant shift in public sentiment in the direction of the new change in immigration policy. A new perception, dare we say a new paradigm, gradually becomes the politically dominant perception as to the nature of the "immigration problem," and signaling the shift to a new "cycle" of immigration policy.

Thus, we come to the basic approach used in this book. Through historical analysis, the book focuses upon the commonalities and themes evident in the story of U.S. immigration policy from 1820 to the present, highlighting the interest groups advocating or opposing major change in immigration policy at any given time, and the coalition of congressional forces they marshal in seeking to implement or oppose such a policy shift. The description of each era has a particular focus on how national security issues and perceptions relate to immigration policy-making—how the two policy-making areas become intertwined. Immigration policy has been referred to as "intermestic policy."

Interest groups are treated herein as organized bodies of individuals who share some goals and try to influence public policy in order to better pursue those goals. The group theory of politics suggests that public policy is the product of a struggle among competing groups. It sees public policy as "the equilibrium point reached in this [group] struggle at any given moment, and it represents a balance which the contending factions or groups constantly strive to weight in their favor" (Earl Latham, *The Group Basis of Politics*, New York: Octagon Books, 1965: 36). While certainly not the case in every public policy arena, analyses of immigration policy underscoring its essential gate-keeping function clearly illustrate that it is one, which reflects the influence of dominant groups. As groups gain and lose power and influence, policy is altered in favor of those gaining influence at the expense of those whose influence is waning (Anderson: 18). In the words of one prominent proponent of group theory:

> The legislature [in this case, Congress] referees the group struggle, ratifies the victories of the successful coalitions, and records the terms of surrender, compromise, and conquests in the form of statutes. Every statute tends to represent compromise because the process of accommodating conflicts of group interests is one of deliberation and consent (Latham: 35–36).

This study demonstrates that a review of the history of immigration policy-making shows a constant struggle for control of the immigration process. It is the story of periodic attempts to achieve a politically stable and acceptable consensus about *procedural justice* in the matter of regulating the influx of permanent residents into the borders. Such analysis demonstrates that ultimately the *disparities in power among competing groups* seeking to influence that balance or consensus is the *key to our understanding of our immigration policy* (Kritz: 363). Clearly, the interplay among those groups is central to understanding the shifts in policy, and the cyclical nature of the periodic reviews and revisions in policy and procedure designed to arrive at a new consensus as to how open or how closed will be the nation's borders at any given time. Such analysis clarifies, too, the inherent interplay between immigration policy and national security—the role of the "eagle" in guarding access to the nation's "gates." The format of the book is as follows: Chapter 1 presents a brief overview of U.S. immigration policy and posits the linkage between national security issues and concerns and subsequent immigration policy-making. It identifies various "waves" in the composition of immigration to the United States. It distinguishes five distinct cycles or phases in immigration policy. Chapters 2 through 6 are each devoted to a discussion of a phase or cycle in policy. The "Open-Door Era" is the cycle when there were virtually no restrictions on immigration. The "Door-Ajar Era" is the cycle that saw the beginnings of restrictions in policy. The "Pet-Door Era" is the cycle when the national origins quota system dominated the policy and severely limited the influx of immigration. The "Dutch-Door Era" is the cycle that established a less restrictionist phase of immigration policy than did the prior era, but one with a decided bias in favor of those who entered "at the top," in that they came in as special refugees from communism or possessed certain characteristics for which the national foreign policy posture enabled them to enter under an elaborate system of "preferences." And finally, the "Storm-Door Era" is the cycle reflecting the renewed need for increasingly restrictive methods to guard the nation against terrorism or the "uncontrolled" influx of "illegal" immigrants.

The final chapter critiques recent laws and proposals in light of the historical overview of preceding chapters. Long-term analysis of policy affords insights into the relative advantages and disadvantages, and some likely impacts, both intended and unintended consequences, of revising immigration policy-making. It suggests that we are just at the beginning of a new cycle or era of immigration policy, a Storm-Door Era. It underscores what will likely be the on-going concern over and the primary concerns of lawmakers for immigration policy that is likely to prevail for the next several decades. As with the previous "cycles," however, it suggests this cycle, too, shall pass to be replaced by some yet unforeseen focus and method that will likely usher in yet another new change in direction and the onset of yet another future cycle.

1

An Overview of U.S. Immigration Policy

THE IMPORTANCE OF IMMIGRATION
IN NATIONAL SECURITY

The restoration of the Statue of Liberty, its centennial celebration, the online opening of the immigration files of Ellis Island, and the recent enactment of the law dissolving the Immigration and Naturalization Service, after nearly a century of service, and the merging of its functions into two new bureaus within the cabinet-level Department of Homeland Security have refocused national attention on immigration policy and its problems. Since 1820, when the nation first formally began to keep track of immigration, more than 60 million people have immigrated to the United States.[1]

As part of what has been called the Great Atlantic Migration, between 1770 and 1890, over 11 million people came from the British Isles alone to North America (the United States and Canada; Guillet, 1937: vii). According to the 2000 census data, the United States is now home to residents born in about 170 other countries of the world. From 1820 to 1920 alone, some 35 million came in, mostly from northwestern Europe. Since the 1980s, the renewed influx of both legal and undocumented immigrants have reached levels commensurate with the first two decades of the twentieth century, until then the high-watermark of immigrant waves. This renewed immigration of historic proportions has generated vexing problems for policy-makers. It has called into question whether the nation could truly control its borders, and has raised issues about how porous the borders are to infiltration by terrorists crossing in from Canada or Mexico. It has also renewed scholarly interest in the topic. Immigration policy is controversial in no small measure because the process it seeks to manage raises fundamental questions about its cultural, demographic, economic, political, and social impacts. Immigration policy is inexorably linked to issues and concerns about national security—highlighted in the public's consciousness and on the government's agenda by the events of 9/11. As Roger Kemp noted:

> After the September 11 terrorist attacks in New York City and at the Pentagon and the hijacking that led to the plane crash in rural Pennsylvania, the federal government coined the phrase "homeland security" to describe all the actions of all levels of government to protect citizens from future attacks of violence by terrorists (Kemp: 52).

The term was defined by President Bush in his National Strategy for Homeland Security plan issued on July 15, 2002, as "a concerted national effort to prevent terrorist attacks within the United States, reduce America's vulnerability to terrorism, and minimize the damage and recover from attacks that do occur" (cited in Relyea: 602).

Both immigration policy and national security (or homeland security) policy are *intermestic* policies—that is, policy areas that inherently and implicitly blend and address both international and domestic concerns. As Morton Halperin notes so well:

> A natural assumption is that governments—including that of the United States—tailors their national security decisions to what is happening abroad or what they hope to achieve abroad. The truth is apparently more complicated. The decisions and actions of governments result from the interplay among executive and legislative organizations, public and private interests, and, of course, personalities. This interplay become a determinant of foreign policy no less than events abroad or at home (Halperin, 1974: 14).

Table 1.1 presents the rank order of persons by claimed ancestry, from selected European nations, taken from the 2000 census, and from Asian countries and their numbers and percentages by region of birth. The massive level of immigration to the United States results from a correspondence between the needs of the overcrowded nations of Europe, the Middle East, Asia, and Latin America, and the needs of a less-populated United States. Indeed during most of the nineteenth century the United States considered itself underpopulated and often actively sought immigrants, inducing their coming by such methods as employers paying for their passage, the governments of western states actively recruiting immigrants, the national government giving free land in the unsettled territories to persons willing to permanently immigrate and reside there. These methods reflected the policy position with regard to national security during the first decades of the new nation's independence. In order to protect that independence from intrusion from European colonial powers, the United States needed to populate its abundant lands. In order to secure the nation against the perceived threat from Native American Indians, it needed to settle the land with Euro-American immigrants.

TABLE 1.1. Rank Order of Immigration to the United States, by Nation of Origin, 1820–2004

(a) Rank Order of Persons by Claimed Ancestry, 2000

Ancestry claimed	2000 population	Percent of total population	Ancestry claimed	2000 population	Percent of total population
German	46,428,321	16.97	West Indian	1,914,410	0.07
English	28,222,890	10.31	Sub-Saharan African	1,530,987	0.06
Irish	33,048,744	12.07	Welsh	1,895,726	0.07
Italian	15,916,396	0.589	Hungarian	1,510,878	0.06
French	9,794,218	0.36	Danish	1,505,450	0.06
Polish	9,029,440	0.33	Czech	1,407,495	0.05
Scottish	5,406,421	0.20	Portuguese	1,315,514	0.05
Scotch-Irish	5,205,335	0.19	Arab	1,237,947	0.04
Dutch	5,203,974	0.19	Greek	1,175,591	0.04
Norwegian	4,524,953	0.17	Swiss	993,552	0.04
Swedish	4,342,160	0.16	Ukranian	857,460	0.03
Russian	2,975,628	0.11	Slovak	817,302	0.03
French Canadian	2,211,688	0.08	Lithuanian	715,039	0.02

(continued)

TABLE 1.1. (*continued*)

(b) Percentage of U.S. Population of Asian Origin by Selected Nation of Origin (Top Ten Asian, Rank Ordered), 2000

Population	Number (thousands)	Percent Asian	Percent U.S. population
Total United States	281,400	—	100
Total Asian	11,899	100	4.22
Chinese	2,735	23	0.97
Philippino	2,365	19	0.84
Asian Indian	1,900	16	0.67
Korean	1,228	10	0.43
Vietnamese	1,224	10	0.43
Japanese	1,149	10	0.40
Cambodian	206	1.7	0.007
Laotian	198	1.6	0.007
Hmong	186	1.5	0.006
Thai	150	1.3	0.005

(c) Region of Birth of Foreign-Born Reporting Same

Total reporting	30,271,370	100%	
Europe	4,758,215	15.7	
Asia	8,263,012	27.2	
Africa	853,636	0.03	
Oceania	170,542	0.005	
Latin America	15,390,419	51.0	
North America	835,546	0.03	

Source: Table by author. Data from U.S. Bureau of the Census, *2000 Profile of Selected Social Characteristics.* Washington, D.C.: United States (accessed online at http://ww.census.gov/).

Source: Table by author. Data from http://www.census.gov/2000/Minority Links/Asian, issued February 2002. Adapted from Table 4, p. 9. Accessed 7/25/03.

The old world was experiencing massive and radical social and economic changes engendered by overpopulation, requiring societal reorganization to deal with resulting problems. The old agricultural order changed from the feudal system's communal and subsistence farming to individually owned farms oriented to supplying an ever-expanding urban market economy. These forces led to the creation of a large mass of landless peasants from the British Isles to Russia. The Industrial Revolution, starting first in England and moving gradually across the European continent, added new strains to the social order as old employment patterns disintegrated. Displaced artisans and farm workers alike joined the waves of immigrants to the United States, the beacon of the new world. They brought in the much-needed population and skills.

Population pressures contributed to economic disruptions and to religious and political persecution. Soon the various governments of Europe and Asia began to encourage emigration. When massive famine was added to such *push* factors, people leaving the old world numbered in the tens of millions a decade. Push factors may account for why tens of millions left Europe, but there were several *pull* factors that drew those millions to the United States.

The United States offered religious freedom to immigrants fleeing religious persecution. Its politically open society drew those escaping political perse-cution. The country's reputation as a land of nearly endless opportunities drew those compelled to flee the economic deprivation and occasionally the near-starvation conditions in their homelands. Open lands attracted the Europeans and Asians (particularly the Chinese) suffering from acute overpopulation. The United States sought to augment its population to defend itself—from "hostile" Indians and from the potential threat of European colonial power and ambitions.

The nation's burgeoning cities needed massive numbers of unskilled la-borers. Many immigrants were drawn to the United States expecting to find the "streets paved with gold," only to find the streets unpaved and to discover that *they* were to do the paving! Their cheap labor made rapid industrialization possible. Massive levels of immigration kept wages down and enabled the ac-cumulation of the large sums of capital necessary for wide-scale industrializa-tion. Immigration provided the pool of needed skilled and unskilled labor at the most opportune time.

THE WAVES OF IMMIGRATION

Traditionally, scholars dealing with this massive influx of immigrants have categorized various periods of immigration into "waves." These distinctions are based on the size and composition of the in-coming groups that comprised each successive wave.

The first wave, from 1820 to 1880, was made up of over 10 million immi-grants permanently entering the United States. People from European na-tions comprised approximately 90 percent of that wave, with northwestern

Europeans predominating throughout the period, on the average comprising about 80 percent of the total influx. The predominance of northwestern European nations is clearly evident in Figure 1.1, which presents graphically the percentages of immigrants to the United States by various regions of birth for selected periods from 1820 to present. Immigrants who came during this first wave are commonly referred to as the *old* immigrants.

The first wave marked a sudden and dramatic increase in total immigration to the United States. From the end of the Revolutionary War to 1819, an estimated 125,000 persons entered, most of whom were Protestants from the British Isles and northern Europe (Vialet: 9). The composition of the influx began to change after the 1830s. Irish and German peasants came by the millions, fleeing the potato famines and the economic depressions of the late 1840s. This sudden shift in the influx of Catholics led to an anti-Catholic *nativist* reaction, which will be detailed more fully later in this chapter.

The next major wave, which, since the time of the Dillingham Commission, has been commonly referred to as the *new* immigrants, occurred from 1880 to

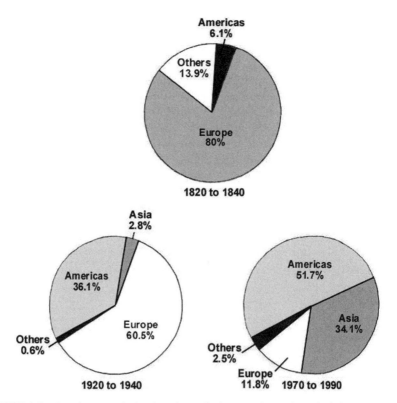

FIGURE 1.1. Immigrants Admitted to the United States, by Region of Birth, 1820–2001
Source: Statistical Yearbook of the Immigration and Naturalization Service (1994), 126.

1920. During this wave, a staggering 23.5 million immigrants flooded the United States. These new immigrants were predominately from Southern, Central, and Eastern (SCE) Europe. The new immigrants were perceived as being even more visibly different from the native stock than were those of the first wave. They set off a renewed xenophobic reaction that culminated in restrictive immigration laws, marking the end of the second wave.

A third wave, lasting roughly from 1920 to 1965, saw the total number of immigrants drop dramatically, from about 23.5 million in the previous forty years to just over 6 million in forty-five year's time. This wave was also marked by changes in the composition of the immigrant influx. Europeans made up approximately 60 percent of the wave, with immigrants from northwestern European nations gradually rising from over 30 percent at the beginning of the period to nearly 50 percent by the end. Immigration from the western hemisphere also rose dramatically, to about 35 percent of the total.

The next wave, from 1965 through 1995, showed a dramatic renewed increase in total immigration, reaching levels similar to the first two decades of the twentieth century. Western hemisphere nations predominated, rising to about half of the total wave. A dramatic increase in Asian immigration also distinguishes this wave.

U.S. immigration policy reflects the perceived needs of the nation as those needs shifted over time and in response to changing economic and demographic conditions. It reflects the changing nature and composition of the immigrant waves. Various national security, economic, ethnic, foreign policy, and Cold War issues have all played key roles in the debates over immigration policy.

The shifts in policy reflect conflicting value perspectives, which tug and pull at one another, causing policy to oscillate in varying degrees between them. On the one hand is the perspective that values the immigrants as a source of industry and renewed vigor, a desirable infusion of new blood into the American stock, enriching the heritage and spurring new economic growth, populating open lands and developing and exploiting the nation's rich natural resources. This development was viewed as necessary to the national defense against foreign threat and intrusion. This perspective forms the traditional base for a more open immigration policy. Almost every president, from George Washington to George W. Bush, has affirmed that we are, indeed, a nation of immigrants, a nation of asylum for which immigration expresses and reconfirms the American spirit of liberty for all. As one leading scholar of immigration put it:

In addition to the historical inheritance of asylum as one of the founding myths, the United States, as a leader of the Western Alliance of democracies against the Soviet Union, has become the champion of the human right to emigrate. Such advocacy, of course, implies the right to immigrate, too, even though it must be limited by practical necessity. In addition, there is the simple political fact of well-organized ethnic constituencies pushing for family reunification and refugee admissions (Professor Lawrence Fuchs, in Kritz: 289).

As another scholar notes: "Political asylum is a defining issue of our time because of its scope and the impact of the refugee crisis, and its roots in deepening global inequities" (Gibney: 2004).

The other perspective calls for varying degrees of restrictions. Its proponents fear an influx of strangers who cannot, or in their view, should not, be assimilated. These forces fear the dilution of U.S. culture. They fear that so vast an influx will destroy the economy or at the very least severely depress wages and working conditions. They contend that refugees and illegal aliens most often lack the skills needed to incorporate into the U.S. economy and society. In the postindustrial era, they fear refugees and undocumented immigrants lack the necessary educational, cultural, and related social backgrounds to contribute to the United States as did the legal immigrants of the earlier centuries. Immigration opponents—those against both legal and illegal immigration, especially give voice to the fear that the very openness of our society and its borders will invite attack from foreign enemies. They advocate changes in policy to restrict immigration levels to avoid such dire effects. It is to an overview of those policy shifts we next turn our attention.

THE FIVE CYCLES OF IMMIGRATION POLICY-MAKING

Immigration policy performs a gate-keeping function. Changes in policy often result in dramatic changes in both the size and composition of the immigrant flow. Who and how many immigrants are allowed to enter the nation implicitly affect a sense of national security. This gate-keeping function suggests the use of a "door" image to characterize various periods or cycles in immigration policy. Just as the immigration influx was categorized into various waves, so immigration policy can be viewed as comprised of five distinct cycles or phases. The first cycle, from 1820 to 1880, may be seen as the "Open-Door Era." During this cycle, policy entailed virtually no restrictions on immigration. Practically all who sought entrance were allowed in, and government policy was to reach out and to seek immigrants. The second cycle, the "Door-Ajar Era," lasted from 1880 to 1920. This cycle saw the beginnings of restrictions, even while the door was still open to most. While total legal immigration levels were still massive, national security concerns played a mixed role. On the one hand, large-scale immigration was economically desirable to feed the growing industrialization of the U.S. economy, viewed then as the most essential ingredient for national security. On the other hand, the "unwashed masses" brought with them the potential dangers of outbreaks of epidemic diseases, feared as "loathsome and dangerous contagious diseases." And many who considered themselves the "native stock" feared that so many people coming from such different cultural and economic backgrounds would be simply unable to assimilate, and could potentially be sources for the disintegration of American society or would transform it in ways they did not desire it to change. The third cycle, which we term the "Pet-Door Era," lasted from 1920 to 1965. This cycle saw the national origins quota system become the basis of national immigration policy. The national origins policy allowed in only the favored few. It coincided with a national security posture based on "isolationism." A fourth cycle or phase can be called the "Dutch-Door Era." It reestablished a more open policy than the previous cycle, allowing for a substantial increase in total immigration, but with a decided bias in favor of those who entered "at the top." Many were allowed in under special provisions or received favored resettlement treatment. Their entry was closely linked to U.S. foreign policy concerns and closely tied to national security needs of the Cold War era. Finally, the most recent cycle, beginning with laws enacted in 1996 and continuing on to even more restrictionist provisions in laws passed in 2002 and 2004, may be termed the "Storm-Door Era," wherein policy reflects a perception of "fortress America" girding itself against an often-hostile world, and an increasingly dangerous "war on international terrorism." Each phase will be examined in greater detail in subsequent chapters, but will here be briefly summarized.

The Open-Door Era

The asylum view determined policy making during the first cycle. With the successful establishment of an independent nation and then its newly revised Constitution in the 1790s, the official policy of the government was to keep its gates open to all. At first, little opposition to this policy was voiced. When the nation took its first census, in 1790, it recorded a population of 3,227,000, mostly the descendants of seventeenth- and eighteenth-century arrivals, or recent immigrants themselves. More than 75 percent were of British origin. About 8 percent were of German origin. The remaining population was comprised of Dutch, French, or Spanish origin, although approximately one-half million were black slaves and about the same number were Native American Indians. This population occupied a land that was vast, sparsely settled, and obviously rich in soil and other natural resources awaiting development and exploitation. The population density in 1790 was only 4.5 persons per square mile (Select Commission, *Staff Report*: 165). There was an obvious need for labor to build the cities, clear the farms on the frontier, and push back the Indians. Additional population was desired to strengthen defenses against Indians and to avoid coming under control of European colonial powers. The U.S. Constitution enshrined the prevailing sentiment among most citizens of the time—that this was a nation of a bold and noble experiment in freedom. They felt that this freedom should be broadly shared by any and all who desired to be free regardless of their former nationality.

President George Washington summed up that prevailing view and the dominant policy of this cycle when he stated:

> The bosom of America is open to receive not only the opulent and respectable stranger, but the oppressed and persecuted of all Nations and Religions; whom we shall welcome to a participation of all our rights and privileges, if by decency and propriety of conduct, they appear to merit the enjoyment (Letter of General George Washington on America as Asylum, December 2, 1783. See LeMay and Barkan, eds., 1999, Document 6: 10).

The Constitution, however, said little about immigration per se. Article 1 prohibited Congress from limiting the states from importing slaves until 1808, but allowed a tax on importation of slaves for up to ten dollars per person. It further granted to Congress the power to set a uniform rule regarding naturalization and to make such laws as were necessary and proper to execute that power. Congress did so rather promptly, in the Act of March 26, 1790 (LeMay and Barkan, Document 7: 11), and amended it several times between then and 1819. The Constitution also contained the commerce clause that gave Congress the power to regulate commerce with foreign nations and among the states. Subsequent Supreme Court cases interpreted that language in ways that significantly impacted immigration policy.

In the 1790s, Congress passed a series of laws regulating naturalization. The first act was quite liberal, requiring only a two-year residency and the renunciation of former allegiances. In 1795, however, turmoil in Europe raised anew fears about foreign influence, national security concerns grew to be a more predominant element in immigration and naturalization policy-making. Congress enacted a more stringent naturalization act that required a five-year period of residency and the renunciation of titles of nobility as well as allegiances. In 1798, Congress, then under control of the Federalist Party, raised the period of residency to fourteen years. They pushed through the Alien Acts, which allowed the president to deport any alien considered to be a threat to the nation (see LeMay and Barkan, 1999, Documents 8–10: 12–16). The Federalist Party acquired an anti-immigrant image that contributed to its decline at the polls. The substantial influx of newcomers who quickly became citizens and joined the ranks of voters rejected the party in large numbers. In 1810, the party made an effort (which proved to be too little, too late) to attract immigrants with the campaign ditty:

> Come Dutch and Yankee, Irish Scot,
> With intermixed relation,
> From whence we came, it matters not;
> We all make now, one nation (cited in Roucek and Eisenberg: 5).

In 1804, Congress passed a law (Act of March 26, 1804) allowing for the naturalization of the wife or children of an alien who died while in the process of naturalization but before his process was completed (LeMay and Barkan: 19).

These acts passed by the Federalists were permitted to expire when the Jeffersonian Democratic Republicans replaced them in power. In 1813, the Jeffersonian Democrats reestablished the five-year provision of the 1795 Act (Act of March 3, 1813, 45 Stat. 1514). In 1819, Congress passed a law requiring a listing of all entering ship passengers, which indicated their sex, occupation, age, and the country to which they belonged. This act, the first effective "immigration act" of the Congress, is briefly summarized in Box 1.1. While it

---

**BOX 1.1.   SUMMARY OF ACT OF MARCH 2, 1819
(RE: IMMIGRATION)**

Be it enacted by the Senate and the House of Representatives of the United States of America in Congress assembled....

Sec. 4. And be it further enacted, That the captain or master of any ship or vessel arriving in the United States or any of the territories thereof, from any foreign place whatever, at the same time that he delivers a manifest of all cargo, and, if there be no cargo, then at the time of making a report or entry of the ship or vessel, pursuant to the existing laws of the United States, shall also deliver and report, to the collector of the district in which the ship or vessel shall arrive, a list or manifest of all passengers taken on board of the said ship or vessel at any foreign port or place; in which list or manifest it shall be the duty of the said master to designate, particularly, the age, sex, and occupation, of the said passengers, respectively, the country to which they severally belong, and that of which it is their intention to become inhabitants; and shall further set forth whether any, and what number, have died on the voyage; which report and manifest shall be sworn to by the said master, in the same manner as is directed by the existing laws of the United States, in relation to the manifest of the cargo, and that the refusal or neglect of the master aforesaid, to comply with the provisions of this section, shall incur the same penalties, disabilities, and forfeitures, as are at present provided for a refusal or neglect to report and deliver a manifest of the cargo aforesaid.

Sec. 5. And be it further enacted, That each and every collector of the customs, to whom such manifest or list of passengers as aforesaid shall be delivered, shall, quarter yearly, return copies thereof to the Secretary of State of the United States, by whom statements of the same shall be laid before Congress at each and every session.

Source: Manifest of Immigrants Act of March 2, 1819 (3 Stat. 489).

clearly defines an "open-door" policy for U.S. immigration, the enumeration and description of the immigrant flow likewise reflects a sense of the impact immigration has on the national identity and on national security.

The wave of Catholic immigrants coming during the 1830s and 1840s set off a dramatic antiforeign reaction. They were easy scapegoats upon which to lay the blame for the problems facing a rapidly changing U.S. society as it began to urbanize and industrialize. They were alleged to be importing crime, disease, poverty, and drunkenness. Social reformers, who desired "to preserve the nation's institutions," and Protestant evangelicals, who sought to "save the nation's purity," joined forces to form such anti-immigrant associations as the Secret Order of the Star Spangled Banner and the Know Nothing political party (Jones: 147–276).

These groups advocated restrictive immigration policies and more stringent naturalization laws. The xenophobic fever even led to violent anti-Catholicism. Inflamed by a spate of virulent anti-Catholic literature, violent attacks on churches and convents took place during riots in places such as Baltimore, Boston, Cincinnati, Hartford, Louisville, Philadelphia, Providence, New Orleans, New York, San Francisco, and St. Louis (see Carleton Beals, 1960; Ray Billington, 1974).

This wave of nativist sentiment, however, did not control public policy-making. The more economically and politically powerful of the native stock continued their more potent support for open and unlimited immigration. The need for cheap labor to supply the explosively expanding cities and factories was the determining factor in public policy. Economic needs, coupled with the philosophical idealism regarding America as the land of opportunity and freedom, prevailed over the narrow views of the anti-Catholic movement. The need to develop the country economically was seen as essential to secure the national defense.

The discovery of gold in California, in 1848, drew a vast population to the West Coast. Conditions during the post-Civil War period created a virtually insatiable need for immigrants. The transcontinental railroad building boom opened up vast lands to settlement. Massive numbers of unskilled laborers were needed to mine the coal and ore, and to work in the mills spurred to new levels by Civil War-generated production. U.S. military prowess developed exponentially as a result of the Civil War and the expanding industrialization of the U.S. economy.

These very forces, however, drew an influx of Chinese immigrants to the West Coast and the composition of European immigrants started to change, with those from south/central/eastern Europe beginning to outnumber north-western Europeans. These changes in the flow of immigration, coupled with economic recessions and a depression during the 1870s, engendered new political pressures for restriction. The banning of the immigration of convicts and prostitutes was passed in 1875 (see "The Page Law," Act of March 3, 1875,

LeMay and Barkan, 1999, Document 28: 33–34). The 1880s ushered in a new cycle in immigration policy-making.

The Door-Ajar Era

Ironically, at the very time when the Statue of Liberty was first erected, symbolizing nothing else but the fact that the nation is open to all the "poor and oppressed" of the world, the *new* immigrants engendered fear and dislike among many in the native stock. Their more "alien" characteristics—strange color, physiques, customs, and languages—aroused anew fears that these strangers would be unable to assimilate. A spate of pseudoscientific studies by historians, sociologists, and biologists attacked them as biologically and racially inferior. Such racist fervor led to the first open restrictionist immigration law, the Chinese Exclusion Act of 1882 (Act of May 6, 1882, 22 Stat. 58; 8 U.S.C.).

Nativist arguments that the new immigrants were racially inferior and more inherently likely to become criminals or diseased were given popular credence. Such arguments undercut the earlier and prevailing tradition of welcome to "all the poor and oppressed." Restrictive immigration policies reflected four historical trends that culminated in the 1880s and 1890s: (1) the burgeoning cities and rapid industrialization, which led to visibly corrupt urban political machines catering to the immigrant ethnic voters; (2) the official closing of the U.S. frontier; (3) the persistence among the new immigrants to maintain their culture and traditions longer and more visibly than did the old immigrants; and (4) the greater religious divergence from Protestantism among the new immigrants who, unlike the old, were more overwhelmingly Catholic, Jewish, or Greek Orthodox.

The Immigration Act of 1882 (Act of August 3, 1882, 22 Stat. 214: 8 U.S.C.) further barred the immigration of "lunatics, idiots, convicts, and those liable to become public charges." This act added new categories of exclusion that reflected to some extent the hysteria of the nativist movement: those suffering from "loathsome or contagious diseases" and persons convicted of crimes involving "moral turpitude" were denied entry. The law also provided for the medical inspection of all new arrivals (see LeMay and Barkan, 1999, Document 34: 55–56). This policy became even more important as a series of epidemic diseases broke out in Europe and Asia and threatened to become pandemics in an era of mass migration unseen previously in world history. Among the more notable epidemics (discussed in more detail in Chapters 2 and 3) were small pox, scarlet fever, Asiatic cholera, Yellow fever, cholera, tuberculosis, bubonic plague, the Spanish influenza, and meningitis.

Even passage of this act, however, did not satisfy the restrictionists. The continued and increasing influx during the 1880s led to further efforts to amend the immigration policy. Restrictionist forces advocated and Congress passed, in

1892, an extension of the Chinese Exclusion Act to ten years (the Geary Act), and then began to focus on a new method and area of regulation—literacy. The first literacy bill was introduced into Congress in 1895, where it quickly passed both houses but was vetoed by President Grover Cleveland. In 1906, another comprehensive immigration act was proposed that included both a literacy test for admission and an English language proficiency test for naturalization. Forces favoring restriction were joined by labor unions in advocating this new policy. Unions were increasingly wary of the economic threat to their wage scales and working conditions implicit in unrestricted immigration. Business leaders, however, opposed the new law. They wanted to avoid any limitations on new and cheap labor sources.

Forces for restriction succeeded in all but the passage of the literacy requirements for entry or naturalization. English language proficiency was accepted for citizenship. In 1907, Congress passed a law creating a joint Congressional/Presidential Commission to study the impact of immigration. Begun in 1909, the Dillingham Commission operated under the pseudoscientific, racist theories prevalent at the time. The commission's recommendations, published in 1911, called for a literacy test and other restrictive legislation.

The war in Europe, however, generated economic growth and increased labor demands in the U.S., both of which ran counter to restrictive policy. The growing political power of the new immigrant groups, coupled with business demand for new labor, preserved a more "free-entry" policy. In 1912, after Congress once again passed a literacy test bill, President William Taft vetoed it. In 1915, another literacy bill was passed and this was successfully vetoed by President Woodrow Wilson.

After the United States entered World War I in 1917, Congress finally passed another bill and successfully overrode yet another veto by President Wilson. The 1917 law finally made literacy an entrance requirement. It codified a list of aliens to be excluded, virtually banning all immigration from Asia. This xenophobic reaction enhanced by the fears that arose during the war years contributed significantly to the success of the restrictionists. A frenzy of anti-German activity culminated in an "Americanization" movement to educate the foreign-born in the U.S. language and customs. Between 1919 and 1921, twenty states passed laws creating Americanization programs. Even industry, for the first time, joined the movement. The completion of the industrialization process and the "closing of the frontier" led to a consensus that national security no longer required heavy immigration levels. This resulted in a new phase or cycle of immigration policy-making, the establishment of the national origins quota system.

The Pet-Door Era

When industry, exemplified by groups such as the National Association of Manufacturers, and industrial giants like the International Harvester Company, and prominent business leaders such as Henry Ford, joined labor unions and the nativist groups all calling for restriction in immigration, a change in policy became inevitable.

Two prorestriction groups—organized labor and a group known as the "100 Percenters"—called for the suspension of all immigration. The Labor supported the suspension as it feared the competition for jobs that occurred with the entry of aliens enhanced by the realignments occurring in the postwar economy. But, the 100 Percenters were simply nativists who feared that European ideas, most notably the "red menace" of Bolshevism, would contaminate U.S. institutions, customs, and society. U.S. foreign policy, in the aftermath of World War I, became increasingly "isolationist."

The Senate led the way with a law designed to reduce total immigration and change the composition of those who enter. A bill, the Quota Act of 1921, was similar to the one originally sponsored by Senator Dillingham of the earlier immigration commission. It was designed to ensure access for immigrants from northwestern Europe while restricting those from south/central/eastern Europe. In 1921, Congress passed, and President Harding signed into law, a measure introducing the concept of national origin quotas (Act of May 19, 1921: The Quota Act of 1921 and also called the "Emergency Quota Act," 42 Stat. 5; 8 U.S.C. 229). In 1924, this approach was expanded upon the enactment of the Johnson-Reed Act, more commonly known as the National Origins Act (Act of May 26, 1924, 43 Stat. 153; 8 U.S.C. 201). This law provided for an annual limit of 150,000 Europeans, a total ban on Japanese, the issuance of visas against set quotas rather than on arrival, and the creation of quotas based on the contribution of each nationality to the overall U.S. population, rather than on the foreign-born population. The bill provided for the admission of immigrants, until 1927, by annual quotas of 2 percent of the nationality's proportion of the U.S. population in 1890. It was amended in 1929, when the national origin quotas themselves were firmly set. They lasted until 1965.

The Immigration Act of 1924, which remained in force until 1952, when it was amended to a certain extent, and mostly in force until 1965 when the quota system was replaced by a preference system, essentially rejected the long-standing "open-door" tradition of U.S. immigration policy. The effects of the quota laws, plus the decline in emigration during the period of the worldwide Great Depression, dramatically reduced overall immigration to the United States for three decades. In 1925, Congress further acted by creating the border patrol as an effort to halt illegal aliens, an estimated half-million of whom entered during the 1920s (Chiswick: 13). This was designed to "secure the nation's borders," especially those to the south, and began an aspect within immigration policy-making that continued to be of major concern for the remainder of the century and in the twenty-first century.

It was not until the 1940s that any pressure for change in the restrictionist nature of immigration policy began to be felt and voiced. A slight relaxation in such policy was induced by needs generated by World War II. The need for the labor of aliens after the United States entered the war led to the establishment of the "Bracero" program. This temporary work program imported workers, mostly from Mexico, to fill war-time needs (Act of February 14, 1944, 58 Stat. 11; 50 U.S.C., App. 1351. See Craig, 1971; LeMay and Barkan, Document 108: 197–198). Also in response to the war-time alliance with China, Congress repealed the sixty-year ban on Chinese immigration. Finally, as news of Nazi atrocities became widespread at the end of the war, President Harry Truman issued a directive admitting 40,000 war refugees, including many European scientists considered especially desirable to the U.S. military as the nation emerged from the war as a worldwide "superpower." Congress further responded to the problems of soldiers who had married overseas by passing the War Brides Act in 1946. This law allowed 120,000 alien wives, husbands, and children of members of the armed forces to immigrate to the United States separate from the quota system.

The postwar years witnessed the emergence of the executive branch in taking a more active role in all policy-making, including a substantially greater role in shaping immigration policy. President Truman initiated the nation's first refugee law, the Displaced Persons Act of 1948 (62 Stat. 1009). It was pushed for by groups such as the American Jewish Committee, the Citizens Committee on Displaced Persons, and even supported by the American Federation of Labor. Its most outspoken opponent was the American Legion. It passed Congress in 1948 and ultimately allowed for the admission of over 400,000 displaced persons through the end of 1951 by "mortgaging" their entry against future immigration quotas.

Congress formally set the Bracero program by the Agricultural Act of October 13, 1949 (63 Stat. 1051). This act codified prior laws and provisions for temporary agriculture workers and established (until it was ended in 1964) the Bracero program. It permitted the legal immigration of temporary agricultural workers (see LeMay and Barkan, Document 117: 217–220).

In 1952, Congress passed the McCarran-Walter Act (66 Stat. 163). It reflected a growing awareness for the need to revise the quota system and it enacted the first "relaxations" to the quota system. While the law reaffirmed restriction and the national origins system, it established the Asian-Pacific Triangle, allocating small, token quotas to the nations within its boundaries (essentially from Afghanistan to Japan and from Mongolia to Indonesia and the Pacific Islands). This act included the idea of a preference system within the quotas, based upon the idea of family reunification and economic considerations. It repealed the last racial and national-origin barriers to U.S. citizenship, in effect, establishing for the first time a uniform standard for the naturalization of all applicants. In did not impose any quotas on western hemisphere nations, allowing for the general provisions against persons "likely to become public charges" to limit immigration from that region (see LeMay and Barkan, Document 118: 220–225). President Harry Truman vetoed the bill, objecting to what he termed as unfair racially biased quotas, but Congress overwhelmingly overrode his veto by 278-113 in the House and 57 to 26 in the Senate.

Cold War-induced foreign policy considerations led Congress to enact a special refugee act, the Refugee Relief Act of 1953. Three years later, President Dwight D. Eisenhower "paroled" 5,000 "freedom fighters" of the failed Hungarian revolution. Congress sanctioned this strategy and permitted 30,000 more Hungarian refugees to enter in 1957 and canceled the quotas "mortgaged" under the Displaced Persons Act.

The Cuban revolution led to yet another wave of refugees from communism, and the parole option was employed yet again to allow ultimately some 800,000 Cuban refugees to enter, making them the largest long-term refugee movement of that time (see LeMay and Barkan, Document 130: 248–249; Chiswick, 1982: 32). President Eisenhower invoked the parole status yet again to admit Chinese immigrants from Hong Kong. In all, from the end of World War II to 1980, nearly 1.6 million refugees from all over the world were admitted to the United States. These admissions were directly linked to U.S. foreign policy concerns and needs (McClellan, 1981: 45).

Another method of skirting the fixed quota system was the use of the private bill. Under this procedure, an alien sought exemption to the quota system through private legislation. A member of Congress introduced a bill for his or her relief. Use of this procedure expanded greatly in the 1950s, and while the total number was not large, it illustrated the need to bypass the inflexibility of the quota system. It led to a new cycle of immigration policy-making—that was perceived of as managing immigration in an age of globalization (see LeMay and Barkan: 251–300).

The Dutch-Door Era

Just as the quota approach to immigration policy-making reflected the racial ideas and concerns of that cycle, the new period ushered in with the Immigration Act of 1965 reflected the concerns of the civil rights era. The election of President John F. Kennedy in 1960 eased the way for a frontal attack on the quota system. While serving as U.S. Senator from Massachusetts, Kennedy wrote *A Nation of Immigrants* (1958). In this work, he made obvious his favorable attitude toward increased immigration and his distaste of the racial and ethnic biases that are obvious in the national origins quota system. The civil rights movement, moreover, was pushing the nation and its leadership, and indeed the public opinion of the American population, to question and seriously evaluate the racial bias of much of its laws. Immigration law did not escape that review. The post-World War II decades had chipped away at the quota system; the passage of special acts, nonquota immigration, and refugee–escapee enactments had all demonstrated that the national origin system was simply too inflexible and biased to be continued.

The success of the first years of the Kennedy administration in basic economic policy, moreover, resulted in the ending of recessions that had plagued most of the Eisenhower period and worked to undercut opposition to immigration reform. The healthy economy of the early- through mid-1960s enabled even organized labor to favor a more liberal immigration policy. By that time, the traditional supporters of the national origin system were unorganized and largely inactive. Senator Edward Kennedy (D-MA), the youngest brother of the president, led the Senate forces seeking to change the law fundamentally. He met with leaders from the American Coalition, the American Legion, the Daughters of the American Revolution, and the National Association of Evangelicals. In his words, "No significant opposition to eliminating the national origins quota system was organized by any of their organizations" (LeMay, 1987: 110). He argued persuasively for the enactment of the bill that the Kennedy administration submitted to Congress in 1963. The assassination of President Kennedy and the election of President Lyndon Johnson by an impressive majority in 1964 gave President Johnson the "mandate" to push Congress to enact the Kennedy immigration bill in honor and memory of the "martyred" president.

Congress did so by passing the Immigration and Nationality Act of October 3, 1965 (79 Stat. 911). Co-sponsored by thirty-two senators, the law sought to balance a number of goals: (1) to preserve family unity and reunite separated families; (2) to meet the need for some highly skilled aliens; (3) to ease problems created by emergencies, such as political upheavals, Communist aggression, and natural disasters; (4) to assist cross-national exchange programs; (5) to bar from the U.S. aliens who might present problems of adjustments due to their physical or mental health, past criminal history, or dependency or for national security reasons; (6) to standardize admission procedures; and (7) to establish limits for the Americas.

The new law not only effectively abolished the national origins quota system, but also emphasized terms other than quota and nonquota immigrants. Perspective immigrants did not meet the preferences, or met one of the preferences, or were not subject to new per country limits because they were the immediate relatives of U.S. citizens or were special immigrants, including persons born in the western hemisphere, former U.S. citizens seeking to resume their citizenship, ministers, and former or current employees of the U.S. government abroad. The law was a reassertion and return to the nation's more liberal tradition in immigration policy.

The nation continued to struggle with the refugee problem and Congress passed a law in 1966 that adjusted the status of Cuban refugees. In addition to dealing with Cuban refugees, Congress responded to the Vietnam War, with its increasing involvement of U.S. soldiers, by enacting a law allowing for the easier naturalization of Vietnam War servicemen, as it had done so for nearly every other major war in which the United States was involved during the preceding century. President Johnson responded to the refugee-flow problem, fed by both the continuation of a massive flow of Cuban refugees and by the exodus of Southeast Asians following the Communist victories in 1975, by issuing a proclamation in 1968 regarding the U.S. adherence to the UN Protocol on the

Status of Refugees. Confronted with the fall of South Vietnam, Cambodia, and Laos to Communist forces and to the resulting hundreds of thousands of refugees, Congress enacted the Refugee Act of 1980. In addition to making the regulation of refugees more systematic as well as increasing the numbers of such persons who could be admitted, the law recognized the new category of asylum seekers (94 Stat. 102; see LeMay and Barkan, Document 139: 272–275).

The changing composition of the flow of immigration, however, coupled with a troubled economy suffering from *stagflation* throughout much of the 1970s—a combination of high unemployment and high inflation due in part to the OPEC-induced oil crisis of the early 1970s—led to a growing political movement to again restrict immigration. President Kennedy had agreed to the ending of the Bracero program (1964) as a compromise to move Congress to increase overall immigration. This policy contributed to a dramatic increase in the number of undocumented aliens (referred to in the mass media simply as "illegal aliens") crossing the nation's borders, mostly from Mexico. In addition to this flow, simultaneous with the massive Mariel boatlift of Cubans in mid-1980, was the influx of "boat people" fleeing Haiti. This combination of events led to a strong political movement in the Congress to close the backdoor of immigration by dealing with the "illegal immigration" problem. President Ronald Reagan responded by setting up a special presidential task force in 1981.

Congress helped the president by setting up the Select Commission of Immigration and Refugee Policy (SCIRP). Like the Dillingham Commission of the Pet-Door Era, SCIRP made a number of specific recommendations that shaped immigration policy-making for the next decade. Its recommendations included a new device and approach to control illegal immigration—the employer-sanctions approach (see LeMay and Barkan, Document 141: 278–279). That approach was adopted in the Immigration Reform and Control Act of 1986 (Act of November 6, 1986, 100 Stat. 3360; see LeMay, 1994). This act included provisions for amnesty for certain illegal aliens and special provisions for Cubans and Haitians, as well as for a special category of immigrants for countries adversely affected by the 1965 reforms.

IRCA, as it became known, had but a very temporary influence on the flow of illegal immigrants, however, and Congress felt that there was continued pressure to deal with the problem of immigration reform.[2] In 1990, it passed another major immigration act, IMMACT, 1990 (see LeMay and Barkan, Document 145: 288–296).

Although hailed as the most extensive reform of immigration law since 1965, IMMACT hardly solved all the problems nor marked an end to demands for immigration reform. Annual studies mandated by the 1990 act further documented the effects of the push side of the immigration process. Attempts to cope with drug smuggling and human trafficking added to the sense of a need for bilateral and multilateral agreements and pressured U.S. immigration policy, briefly, toward a more multinational approach.

The failure of IRCA and IMMACT to effectively stem the tide of undocumented immigrants, and continued festering of asylum problems creating huge backlogs of asylum cases that the INS simply could not handle, led to state governments in the primary receiving states of both legal and illegal immigration, to agitate for the federal government to take action on immigration. California, for example, passed an initiative, Proposition 187, in November of 1994, popularly called the "Save Our State" Initiative (see LeMay and Barkan, Document 146: 296–300). Although many of its provisions were overturned when challenged in federal court (*LULAC et al. v. Wilson et al.*, November 20, 1995), this and other related state pressures sent a message to Congress to perform something dramatic. Proposition 187 passed with more than 60 percent of the vote and its principle champion, Republican Governor Pete Wilson, was easily reelected as governor of California. These pressures resulted in legislation marking the next cycle of immigration policy-making— the Storm-Door Era.

The Storm-Door Era

The renewed visibility of the influx of illegal aliens and some highly publicized cases of attempts to smuggle asylum seekers into the U.S. fueled public opposition to immigration. Congress and the administration made some attempts to beef-up the Border Patrol and prosecute alien smuggling rings under the racketeering laws.

When the federal court overturned much of Proposition 187, Congress and President Bill Clinton reacted by passing two measures that essentially enacted many of the provisions of Proposition 187.

The 1996 welfare reform measure, the Personal Responsibility and Work Opportunity Act of August 22, 1996 (HR 3734—PL 104-193), contained several immigration reform provisions similar to those of Proposition 197 (see LeMay, 2004: 168–170). It restricted federal benefits (health and welfare) for which illegal immigrants and legal nonimmigrants could qualify, made most legal immigrants ineligible for supplemental security income (SSI) and food stamps until they became citizens and strengthened reporting and verification provisions.

Congress then cleared a measure dealing with illegal immigration and some aspects of legal immigration by folding its provisions into the omnibus fiscal 1996 spending bill, the Omnibus Spending Act of September 30, 1996 (HR 3610-PL104-208).

It had roughly two dozen provisions related to immigration and designed to "beef-up" the ability to manage and control the borders and better cope with illegal immigrants, human trafficking, and expedited removal provisions, as well as improvements to the employee verification system and increased public benefit restrictions (see LeMay, 2004: 172–174).

Fortress America really replaced a more open-door America as the nation's stance on immigration after and largely as a response to the attacks of 9/11. The terrorist attacks on the World Trade Center (the Twin Towers) in New York City and on the Pentagon in Washington, D.C. spurred Congress to enact the USA Patriot Act (HR 3162). This lengthy bill of 288 pages contained immigration-related provisions that broadened the definition of terrorism, expanded grounds for inadmissibility to include aliens who were suspected of terrorist activity or who publicly endorsed such, and required the attorney general to detain aliens whom he certified as threats to national security.

About a year later, on November 19, 2002, Congress enacted the Homeland Security Act of 2002 (HR 5005), which established a new Department of Homeland Security. It is a massive law of more than 400 printed pages. It merges twenty-two federal agencies, reorganizes 170,000 federal employees and affects another 80,000, and resulted in the most extensive reorganization of the federal bureaucracy since the creation of the Department of Defense after World War II (1947). In relation to immigration policy, it creates within the new department two bureaus, each headed by an undersecretary: The Directorate of Border and Transportation Security; and a Bureau of Citizenship and Immigration Services (see its major immigration-related provisions in LeMay, 2004: 178–179).

These laws signal the onset of the "Storm-Door Era" in immigration policy. Congress is considering still further provisions to amend immigration, especially regarding states issuing driver's licenses to undocumented aliens. Continued calls to beef-up the Border Patrol and to strengthen immigration control are contained in the law, passed in December 2004, to revise the U.S. intelligence operations.

CONCLUSION

This brief review of the history of immigration policy since 1820 illustrates American society's nearly constant struggle with the immigration process. The cycles identified and discussed more fully in the chapters that follow show the periodic attempts to achieve a new balance in politically acceptable procedural justice as related to the immigration issue. Ultimately, the key to understanding immigration policy is the disparities in power among the competing groups seeking to influence that balance. The interplay among such groups has determined how open or closed will be the doors at any given time. The desirability or lack of the openness or more closed nature of the immigration policy is seen as directly linked to a sense of national security. Immigration policy reform is viewed as necessary to regain "control of the nation's borders."

The interplay among such competing groups is the central theme of this study. Each subsequent chapter will examine, in greater detail than this brief overview allows, a phase or cycle of U.S. immigration policy. They will

TABLE 1.2. Immigration to the United States, Fiscal Years 1820–2001

Year	Number	Year	Number	Year	Number
1820–2001	67,153,749	1858	123,126	1897	230,832
1820	8,385	1859	121,282	1898	229,299
1821–30	143,430	1860	153,640	1899	311,715
1821	9,127	1861–70	2,314,824	1900	448,572
1822	6,911	1861	91,918	1901–10	8,795,386
1823	6,354	1862	91,985	1901	487,918
1824	7,912	1863	176,282	1902	648,743
1825	10,199	1864	193,418	1903	857,046
1826	10,837	1865	248,120	1904	812,870
1827	18,875	1866	318,568	1905	1,026,499
1828	27,382	1867	315,722	1906	1,100,735
1829	22,520	1868	138,840	1907	1,285,349
1830	23,322	1869	352,768	1908	782,870
1831–40	599,125	1870	387,203	1909	751,786
1831	22,633	1871–80	2,812,191	1910	1,041,570
1832	60,482	1871	321,350	1911–20	5,735,811
1833	56,640	1872	404,806	1911	878,587
1834	65,365	1873	459,803	1912	838,172
1835	45,374	1874	313,339	1913	1,197,892
1836	78,242	1875	227,498	1914	1,218,480
1837	79,340	1876	169,986	1915	326,700
1838	38,914	1877	141,857	1916	298,826
1839	68,069	1878	138,469	1917	295,403
1840	84,066	1879	177,826	1918	110,618
1841–50	1,713,251	1889	457,257	1919	141,132
1841	80,289	1881–90	5,246,613	1921–30	4,107,209
1842	104,565	1881	669,431	1920	430,001
1843	52,496	1882	788,992	1921	805,228
1844	78,615	1883	603,322	1922	309,556
1845	114,371	1884	518,592	1923	522,919
1846	154,416	1885	395,346	1924	706,896
1847	234,968	1886	334,203	1925	294,314
1848	226,527	1887	490,109	1926	304,488
1849	297,024	1888	546,889	1927	335,175
1850	369,980	1889	444,427	1928	307,255
1851–60	2,598,214	1890	455,302	1929	279,678
1851	379,466	1891–1900	3,687,564	1930	241,700
1852	371,603	1891	560,319		
1853	368,645	1892	579,663	1931–40	528,431
1854	427,833	1893	439,730	1931	97,139
1855	200,877	1894	285,631	1932	35,576
1856	200,436	1895	258,536	1933	23,068
1857	251,306	1896	343,267	1934	29,470

TABLE 1.2. (*continued*)

Year	Number	Year	Number	Year	Number
1935	34,956	1958	253,265	1979	460,348
1936	36,329	1959	260,686	1980	530,639
1937	50,244	1960	265,398	**1981–90**	**7,338,062**
1938	67,895			1981	596,600
1939	82,998	**1961–70**	**3,321,677**	1982	594,131
1940	70,756	1961	271,344	1983	559,763
		1962	283,763	1984	543,903
1941–50	**1,035,039**	1963	306,260	1985	570,009
1941	51,776	1964	292,248	1986	601,708
1942	28,781	1965	296,697	1987	601,516
1943	23,725	1966	323,040	1988	643,025
1944	28,551	1967	361,972	1989	1,090,924
1945	38,119	1968	454,448	1990	1,536,483
1946	108,721	1969	358,579		
1947	147,292	1970	373,326	**1991–2000**	**9,095,417**
1948	170,570			1991	1,827,167
1949	188,317	**1971–80**	**4,483,314**	1992	973,977
1950	249,187	1971	370,478	1993	904,292
1951–60	**2,515,479**	1972	384,685	1994	804,416
1951	205,717	1973	400,063	1995	720,461
1952	265,520	1974	394,861	1996	915,900
1953	170,434	1975	386,194	1997	798,378
1954	208,178	1976	398,613	1998	654,451
1955	237,790	1976, TQ[a]	103,676	1999	646,568
1956	321,625	1977	462,315	2000	849,807
1957	326,867	1978	601,442	2001	1,064,318

[a] Transition quarter, July 1 through Septembr 30, 1976.
Note: The numbers shown are as follows: from 1820 to 1867, figures represent alien passengers arrived at seaports; from 1868 to 1892 and 1895 to 1897, immigrant aliens arrived; from 1892 to 1894 and 1898 to 2001, immigrant aliens were admitted for permanent residence. From 1892 to 1903, aliens entering by cabin class were not counted as immigrants. Land arrivals were not completely enumerated until 1908.
Source: From "Table 1. Immigration to the United States: fiscal years 1820–2001," in *2001 Statistical Yearbook of the Immigration and Naturalization Service*. U.S. Department of Justice, Immigration and Naturalization Service, Washington, D.C. (February 2003; online at http:// www.immigration.gov/graphics/shared/aboutus/statistics/Yearbook2001.pdf; accessed June 30, 2003).

highlight more of the proposals, laws, and relevant court cases that collectively "make policy" for any given cycle and that determine the character of the policy for that era. Each chapter will highlight the linkage between immigration policy-making and national security issues and concerns that predominated the respective eras. As one noted scholar of U.S. foreign policy-making quotes:

Since the Union's founding era, three central debates shaped the country's internationalism and the grand strategy that has followed from it: whether realism or idealism should guide statecraft; how to reconcile the competing cultures and interests of the country's different regions in formulating grand strategy; and how to manage partisan politics and limit its effects on the conduct of foreign policy. Debate among the founding fathers on these three issues cast an enduring mold— one that continues to this day to shape a uniquely American brand of internationalism (Kupchan: 161).

And just as we can distinguish eras or periods of immigration policy-making, scholars have done so with respect to national security policy as well. Three historical periods provide a particularly good window on the relationship between America's domestic politics and the evolution of its grand strategy:

The founding era and its aftermath, the close of World War I and the country's deliberation in 1919–1920 over its participation in the League of Nations, and World War II and the onset of America's global role during the 1940s (Kupchan: 163).

We close this chapter with Table 1.2, which provides an overall summary of U.S. immigration, by fiscal years, from 1820 to 2001.

NOTES

1. This chapter draws heavily from five sources: Vialet, 1980; The Select Commission on Immigration and Refugee Policy, *Staff Report*: 161–220; LeMay, 1994; LeMay, 2004; LeMay and Barkan, 1999.

2. A Bureau of Census study for the Select Commission put their number at 3–6 million; while a *New York Times* article in 1980 set it at 11 million. A 1985 National Academy of Sciences Report estimates it at 2–4 million. For a thorough summary of the 1986 Law, see LeMay, 1994: 51–74. The amnesty provisions enabled nearly 3.5 million undocumented immigrants to legalize their status. That number probably more accurately reflects the true number of illegal aliens in the country at the time—closer to 5 million than to 6–11 million.

2

The Open-Door Cycle, 1820–1880

INTRODUCTION: NATIONAL SECURITY NEED FOR INCREASED POPULATION

During the foundation era of American history, the leaders of the nation viewed what has come to be known as national security as best preserved by keeping the new nation uninvolved in European conflicts. As noted patriot Thomas Paine proclaimed:

> Any submission to, or dependence on, Great Britain, tends directly to involve this continent in European wars and quarrels... America's calling is in commerce rather than war and that, well attended to, will secure us the peace and friendship of all Europe (cited in Kupchan: 164).

Alexander Hamilton was the more prominent of the founding fathers to advocate stronger central government, and development of the nation's commerce as a source of national strength. "Hamilton had the wit to see the rising power of commercial capitalism" (Tindall: 310). There were, however, quite a number of people who were drawn into opposition to Hamilton's new engines of power: in part southerners, in part backcountry settlers, and in part a politically motivated faction opposing him in his home state of New York. Chief among them was Thomas Jefferson and his Republican alternative and his emphasis upon an agrarian view—the value of the "yeoman farmer."

> Philosophically, Hamilton and Jefferson represented polar visions of the character of the Union in the first generation under the Constitution, and defined certain fundamental issues of American life which still echo two centuries later (Tindall: 312).

Despite these profound philosophical differences among the founding fathers, they found themselves in close agreement on one particular issue of foreign policy: that the United States could *most effectively* safeguard its security by isolating itself from Europe's geopolitical rivalries. During the 1790s, France and England were again at war. On April 22, 1793, Washington issued a neutrality proclamation that avoided even the word neutrality. It rather simply declared that the United States would remain "friendly and impartial toward the belligerent powers" and warned American citizens that "aiding and abetting hostilities" or other unneutral acts would be prosecuted (Tindall: 315).

In 1794, Indians in Ohio reinforced with some Canadian militia attacked General Wayne's force at the Battle of Fallen Timbers. General Wayne's troops won the skirmish, resulting in the Treaty of Greenville in which the United States bought from twelve tribes the rights to the southeastern quarter of the Northwest Territory (now Ohio and Indiana) and enclaves in Vincennes, Detroit, and Chicago. Similarly, Spanish intrigues among the Creeks, Chicksaws, and Cherokees kept up the same type of turmoil that the British stirred up along the Ohio. These raised national security fears about Indian tribal coalitions with European colonial powers.

In his farewell address to the nation, dated September 17, 1796 and not given as a speech but rather published in the Philadelphia's *Daily American Advertiser* two days later, President Washington all but enshrined the grand strategy of isolation from Europe's wars and turmoils as "the Great Rule of conduct for us, in regards to foreign nations" (cited in Kupchan: 165). Washington noted that America's "distant and detached position," and "respectable defense posture" allowed the nation to remain disengaged from European affairs (Eland: 2). As Washington put it: ". . . our true policy is to steer clear of permanent alliances with any portion of the foreign world" (Tindall: 325). The nation's vital interests, and therefore its national security policy, depended upon its geostrategic position. The favorable geography of the United States, with vast oceans on both the east and the west, and with abundant land with rich natural resources, meant that the founders of the republic realized that they had the luxury of staying out of other nations' wars (at that time, Europe's wars). They also realized that if the United States refrained from meddling in the business of other nations, those powers would have no excuse to intervene in its affairs (Eland: 2). In part in reaction to the excesses of the French Revolution, the Federalists enacted the Alien and Sedition Acts of 1798 that empowered the president, in the Alien Enemy Act, to expel "dangerous aliens" on pain of imprisonment (Tindall: 331).

When Thomas Jefferson became president, he initiated policies to expand the nation, principally the Louisiana Purchase. These brought him solid support in the south and west, and even some New Englanders were drawn to his side. The War of 1812 and the rise of Tecumseh and his coalition of tribes renewed national security fears. The Battle of Tippecanoe reinforced suspicions that the British were inciting the Indians. The Treaty of Ghent ended the

War of 1812. It was negotiated by the then Secretary of State James Monroe and its settlement was reached on Christmas Eve, 1814. The War of 1812 generated a new feeling of nationalism and came to be viewed as the Second War of Independence. It launched a period of economic nationalism that affected both economic policy and cultural life (Tindall: 374–380).

Differences between Hamilton and Jefferson and their personal battles eventually developed into political partisan rivalry between the Federalists and the Republicans and by 1794, foreign policy became ensnared in partisan politics. Throughout the early- to mid-nineteenth century, however, U.S. military involvement abroad was sporadic, relatively short-lived, and typically involved sending small raiding parties to protect U.S. traders and citizens abroad: Tripoli (1801–1805, 1815), Algiers (1815), Greece (1827), Sumatra (1832, 1838–1839), Liberia (1843), China (1843, 1854, 1856), Angola (1860), Japan (1863–1864, 1868), and Korea (1871) (Kupchan: 170).

During the 1820s, then Secretary of State, John Quincy Adams, cautioned that the United States should avoid intervening in foreign conflicts even in the interest of "exporting liberty abroad." With the exception of World War I, the politics of military restraint overseas served the United States well for over a century and a half—until World War II and the Cold War ended the isolationist policy (Eland: 2).

The Tariff of 1816 raised federal finances to the point that the national government could support internal improvements, including the building of canals and the national road (1811–1838). James Monroe was elected president and issued the Monroe Doctrine on December 2, 1823 (Tindall: 399). General Andrew Jackson took Florida in a military campaign against the Seminole Indian tribe and by 1819, Spain ceded all of Florida to the United States.

Foreign policy focused mostly on the western hemisphere and the nation's desire to keep European powers from interfering within the "natural sphere of influence" of the nation. The founding fathers saw the nation as an expanding empire—but one in which the American continent belonged by right to those who could colonize it (Jordan et al.: 47). Andrew Jackson swept into office in 1828 and initiated the Indian Removal policy, which Congress endorsed in the Indian Removal Act of 1830, and by 1840 the removal of virtually all tribes from the east to west of the Mississippi, a process begun in the 1820s, was complete (Tindall: 423–427).

President Polk, in 1840, cautioned European nations, such as Britain, France, and Spain, from standing in the way of America's westward expansion. As President Polk put it: "We must ever maintain that the people of this continent alone have a right to decide their own destiny" (cited in Kupchan: 171).

Traditional military force to "secure the nation" remained small—averaging about 10,000 men in arms, and varying between 8,200 in 1817 and 47,867 in 1898 (Jordan et al.: 47). The new nation depended on the vast oceans separating it from Europe and Asia to ensure the grand strategy of isolation. As the nation expanded across the continent, national security policy refrained from emulating the empire-building typical of the major European colonial powers.

> As before in the 1840s, this [U.S.] expansionary impulse was restricted to North America, with the size of the U.S. Army and Navy remaining quite limited despite the country's growing territory. Until the outbreak of the Civil War, the regular army was serving primarily as a domestic police force focusing on the Indian threat. In 1861, this force consisted of only 16,000 men, most of them serving at posts on the Indian frontier. Despite the existence of a large merchant marine, the United States was without a significant battle fleet. Some 7,600 men served in the navy, about one-tenth the manpower of the British navy (Kupchan: 172).

But isolation from European affairs in foreign policy alone could not ensure national security, or as it was referred to then, "domestic tranquility." As early as 1790, students at Yale university debated the question, "Does the national security depend on fostering domestic industry" (Relyea: 611). John Jay, in Federalist Paper 3, wrote about "national safety . . . as it respects security for the preservation of peace and tranquility, as well as against dangers from foreign arms and influence, as from dangers and the like kind arising from domestic causes" (Relyea: 611). To secure such domestic tranquility, the new fledging nation would need increased population to settle the land, defend against hostile Indians, and develop the abundant natural resources that in the long term would secure the United States among the nations of the world. After the Panic of 1837 (a national depression), the country experienced a period of dynamic growth. This spurt of growth could be seen in the agricultural industry, with the invention of the cotton gin and latter the steel plow to tame the prairie sod; in population density and the rapid development of cities; in transportation, with development of river traffic, canals, and especially the railroads; with the expansion of ocean transport; and with the beginnings of the industrial revolution with the development of factories (Tindall: 447–485). The ability of the nation's commerce to assure it of world power status likewise depended upon a growing population. And so it sought to draw immigrants to itself and its self-perceived grand experiment in liberty that would be the beacon to the world for a democratic republic.

In 1845, John Louis O'Sullivan, editor of the *United States Magazine and Democratic Review*, gave a name to the nation's spirit of expansionism when he wrote: "Our Manifest Destiny is to overspread the continent allotted by Providence for the free development of our yearly multiplying millions" (cited in Tindall: 535). And it did expand. President Polk, elected in 1844, encouraged expansion and urged Congress to annex Texas, which joined the union on December 29, 1845. The northern borders with Canada were settled with the establishment of the Oregon Territory in 1846. War with Mexico in 1847–1848 was ended with the Treaty of Guadalupe-Hidalgo in 1848 and resulted in the annexation of California (Tindall: 557).

The United States is, indeed, foremost among the nations of the world in the degree to which it has absorbed immigrants from other nations. No other nation has experienced as many and as varied an influx of various ethnic groups. The nation's original policy was to keep an open door, welcoming all who would come. Indeed, many of the state governments comprising the nation actively sought to draw immigrants to them. They sent agents to European countries recruiting and assisting farmers and artisans to settle in those states and territories. By 1862, with the enactment of the Homestead Act, they offered free land—an incredible pull factor to an overpopulated Europe. The Act provided free land of 160 acres by staking a claim and then living on the land for five years, or by paying $1.25 an acre after six months. This coincided with an agricultural revolution. John Deere of Illinois developed the steel-faced plow and moldboard that conquered the sod of the great prairie in 1838. In 1868, James Oliver of Indiana made a successful chilled-iron plow. By 1880, one single farm in South Dakota was spread over 13,000 acres of wheat (Tindall: 773).

Perhaps equally important to the settlement of the interior was the series of Indian Wars lasting from the 1860s to the late 1870s, with even some intermittent outbreaks into the 1880s. The "pacification" of the Indian tribes of the west and their removal to "reservation" lands, speeded up the settlement of the western plains by Euro-American settlers.

IMMIGRATION AND NATURALIZATION POLICY

As stated in Chapter 1, the Constitution said little about immigration policy. It granted to Congress the power to establish a policy for naturalization. The key phrase in that provision was that Congress "could make such laws as were necessary and proper to execute that power." Section 8 granted to Congress the power to regulate commerce, which was later interpreted to include immigration matters (see, e.g., *Yick Wo v. Hopkins*, May 10, 1886). The Supreme Court generally has been expansive in interpreting the powers of Congress to regulate immigration and restrictive when it comes to state or local government laws or actions with respect to immigration and the rights of aliens (for a more recent example, see *LULAC et al. v. Wilson et al.*, November 20, 1995).

The Constitution's nonexistent or vague language on citizenship, naturalization and immigration followed the tradition of the Articles of Confederation, which left to the states the right to determine citizenship. It took the development of further laws and Supreme Court cases to elaborate upon the meaning of the vague language.

Congress acted quickly on its Constitutional authorization. On March 26, 1790 it passed "An Act to Establish a Uniform Rule of Naturalization" (1 Stat. 103). Congressional use of the phrase "being a free white person," in the law illustrates the racial bias or orientation that became explicit throughout much of the history of U.S. immigration and naturalization law. By the standards of the time, however, it was an extremely liberal or generous policy, requiring only a two-year period of residency and renunciation of former allegiance (see LeMay and Barkan, Document 7: 11–12). In 1795, Congress revised the law slightly, increasing the period for naturalization to five years, but still maintaining an overall liberal approach to immigration and naturalization (Act of January 29, 1795, 1. Stat. 414).

On June 18, 1798 Congress amended the 1795 act. It was intentionally more restrictive; changing the time of residency from five to fourteen years, assessing fees, and stipulating in greater detail the process for naturalization, including a fee for surety of peace and stipulating penalties for various failures to comply with the law (1 Stat. 566). This policy change was motivated by a national security concern. Fear that French "radicals" who had immigrated here might instigate turmoil similar to what the Federalists feared would be akin to the excesses of the French Revolution led Congress to pass the first act concerning "aliens"—the famous "Alien and Sedition" Acts of 1798. Although never enforced, the law gave President John Quincy Adams the authority to deport any alien found guilty of seditious activity. This was the first example of xenophobia, portending subsequent legislation that was more effectively restrictive and often aggressively implemented. The act stated:

> That it shall be lawful for the President of the United States at any time during the continuance of this act, to order all such aliens as he shall judge to be dangerous to the peace and safety of the United States, or shall have reasonable grounds to suspect are concerned with treasonable or secret machinations against the government thereof, to depart out of the territory of the United States (1 Stat. 570).

It expired after the two-year limitation of the law and was not reenacted. Its importance is more for the precedent it set whereby Congress would later enact laws controlling immigration and grant rather sweeping enforcement powers to the executive branch concerning immigration matters (e.g., as it does currently in the USA Patriot Act of 2001 and the Homeland Security Act of 2002).

In 1802, the Jeffersonian Democrats controlled Congress and passed a series of laws about naturalization that further specified who could be naturalized, reinstating the five-year provision on length of residency required, and elaborating more the process of naturalization (see Acts of April 14, 1802, 54 Stat. 1172). In 1804, Congress passed a law allowing for the naturalization of the wife or children of an alien who died while in the process of naturalization but before his process was completed (34 Stat. 603).

As was seen Box 1.1, in 1819, Congress passed the law requiring the enumeration of all immigrant passengers according to the country from which they came (only later do the laws stipulate identification of "country of birth or origin"). The nation, for the first time, began keeping track of the immigration flow. It was still with the government of the various states, however, where primarily responsibility for the actual processing of immigrants remained. The two most important immigration-receiving states at that time were New York and Massachusetts, and specifically, the ports of New York City and Boston, respectively. The Commonwealth of Massachusetts and the state of New York specified shipmasters to declare immigrants, established fees and persons for processing immigration, and placed restrictions on individuals who might immigrate into the state, such as bans against lunatics and paupers (see, e.g., Act of the Commonwealth of Massachusetts, February 25, 1820; Alien Passengers Act of the Commonwealth of Massachusetts, April 20, 1837; and An Act Concerning Passengers in Vessels Coming to the City of New York, May 5, 1847 summarized in LeMay and Barkan, Documents 15, 17, and 18: 20–25).

Figure 2.1 presents the origins of immigrants, by region, for the decades from 1820 to 1880. The next section briefly sketches the immigration patterns of this cycle, the primary groups who comprised the so-called *old* immigrants of this wave of immigration.

Throughout the era, the overarching aim of immigration policy was to attract immigrants to the nation. This provided support to the national security policy of the era, which, as stated in Chapter 1, sought population from Western Europe to fill and develop the abundant lands of the nation. This was seen as necessary both to protect the newly founded nation from European colonial ambitions and to serve as a buffer against Native American Indian resistance to the Euro-American expansion across the land in their ever-expanding western push.

One contrary pressure, however, which figured into a concern for a national security issue that fed support among some in the nation to restrict immigration, arose from the periodic epidemics of contagious diseases that became prevalent in the nineteenth century. Table 2.1 lists notable epidemics that broke out in Asia and Europe in the nineteenth and early twentieth centuries, and then lists some corresponding epidemics that broke out in some parts of the United States. As is seen in the table, these led to specific immigration legislation intended to protect the nation from such outbreaks.

THE OLD IMMIGRATION WAVE

The old immigrants, as we have seen, came mainly from the northern and western countries of Europe and include Germans, Irish, and Scandinavians. Arriving in heavy numbers during the period from 1820 to 1880, they came in two distinct surges. The first, between 1845 and 1854, was dominated by the Irish and Germans. During the second, from 1865 to 1875, the British and Scandinavians also figured heavily along with the continued influx of the Irish and German groups.

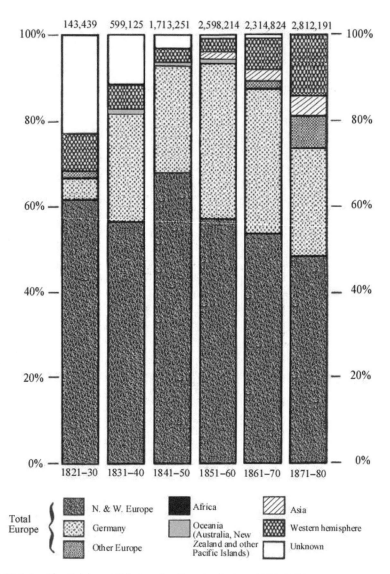

FIGURE 2.1.   The Origins of U.S. Immigration, by Region, 1821–1880

Source: U.S. Bureau of Census, *Historical Statistics of the United States, Colonial Times to 1970*, 2 Vols. Washington, D.C.: U.S. Government Printing Office (1975).

TABLE 2.1.   Notable Epidemic Outbreaks—Nineteenth and Early
Twentieth Centuries

Disease	Years of Outbreak
Small pox	1824, 1851, 1854, 1866, 1868, 1875–1876, 1880–1881, 1887, 1891, 1895, 1901, 1902
Scarlet fever	1822, 1847, 1857, 1880
Asiatic cholera	1832, 1834, 1849, 1854, 1866, 1873
Yellow fever	1805, 1822, 1870
Cholera	1817, 1823, 1830, 1831–1833, 1846, 1849–1850, 1865–1866, 1874, 1884, 1887, 1892
Tuberculosis	1800–1850, mortality rates of 300–500 per 100,000 population; this disease was the greatest epidemic killer of the nineteenth century
Bubonic plague	1900
Spanish influenza	1918–1919; killed an estimated 20 million people worldwide
Meningitis	1920

Some key epidemic outbreaks in the United States

Yellow fever	1820–1823; United States, spreading from the Schuykill River
Asiatic cholera	1831–1832; United States, brought by British emigrants
Cholera	1832; New York City and other major cities
Cholera	1833; Columbus, Ohio
Cholera	1834; New York City
Typhus	1837; Philadelphia
Yellow fever	1841; United States, especially in the South
Yellow fever	1847; New Orleans
Cholera	1848–1849; North America
Yellow fever	1850; United States
Influenza	1850–1851; United States
Cholera	1851; Coles County, Illinois; The Great Plains, Missouri
Yellow fever	1852; United States (New Orleans—8000 died in summer)
Yellow fever	1855; United States
Small pox	1860–1861; Pennsylvania
Small pox	1865–1873; Philadelphia, New York City, Boston, Massachusetts, New Orleans
Cholera	1865–1873; Baltimore, Maryland; Memphis, Tennessee, Washington, D.C.
Typhus, typhoid Scarlet and yellow fevers	1865–1873; recurring epidemics throughout United States
Influenza	1873–1875; North America and Europe
Yellow fever	1878; New Orleans
Typhoid	1885; Plymouth and Pennsylvania
Yellow fever	1886; Jacksonville, Florida

Source: www.wikipedia.com—accessed July, 2005.

German Immigration

German immigration reached 7 million, making it the largest single source of immigration to the United States after that which came initially from all the British Isles. According to the 2000 census, nearly 46.5 million people in the U.S. reported German ancestry, ranking them first among all Euro-American ancestry groups (see LeMay, 2005: 91). Although they immigrated steadily and in heavy numbers throughout the nation's history, three major currents within that flow are commonly distinguished: the colonial, when they came mostly for religious and economic reasons; from 1848 to the Civil War, when they came largely for political and economic reasons; and the post-Civil War period, when they came mostly for economic opportunity, often having been recruited by one of several major industries, various state governments, the railroads, or friends and relatives already living here. Although the native stock (Anglo) treated them as one group based on the fact that they all speak the German language, they were quite a diverse group splintered by regional strife and often along religious lines.

During the colonial era, German immigration was distinguished by the movement of entire communities bounded together by religious creeds unaccepted in their homelands. They came in groups as Mennonites, Dunkers, Lutherans, Calvinists, and a few Jews. Geographically, they were Palatines, Salzburgers, Wurttenburgers, and Hanoverians. They sought out and cultivated some of the richest farmlands in colonial America. Their granaries served as the "breadbasket" of the Revolution. Initially scattered thinly among the native population (i.e., Anglos from the British Isles), they were united only by their common language. They exercised little political clout and showed little interest beyond their local and private affairs.

The Revolutionary War changed all that. Although widely scattered, they still comprised the largest single nationality group after the British. They felt no special loyalty toward the crown and were often unfriendly toward the Tories who favored continued union with England. While initially reluctant to become involved, they were easy converts to the cause for independence. Several German regiments were raised and fought prominently and well in the war. Their war-time service was widely recognized and helped accelerate their political and social incorporation. The war became the first major step toward their assimilation. As their general social and economic conditions improved, they began to take a more active role in public affairs. Politically, they tended to affiliate with the Democrats, reflecting their small-farmer backgrounds. They were less at home with the "eastern seaboard establishment."

During the 1830s and 1840s, Germans immigrated for different reasons. The agricultural revolution hit Central Europe, and inheritance laws requiring land to be equally divided among all children (the effects of *divesture and primogeniture laws*) led to small subsistence farms that became too small to support them in rough times, forcing many off the land. They turned to manufacturing—clocks, tools, and the like—but even this development left them overly vulnerable to economic change. When the potato famine struck, their choice was to emigrate or starve. Fortunately, this coincided with the opening of the American Midwest. State governments, railroads, shipping lines, and manufactures began to entice immigration. The development of steamship lines made the journey far cheaper and less arduous. Texas, the Great Lakes region, and the Ohio River valley all became home to these new settlers. As mid-western cities exploded in population, they attracted large numbers of German immigrants. Chicago, Detroit, Milwaukee, Cincinnati, and St. Louis led the way to a swath of land some 200 miles wide, stretching across the northern tier of states from New York down to Maryland and across to the Mississippi River, known as the *German belt*.

Political turmoil in Germany, culminating in the 1848 Revolution, caused many German intellectuals to flee to America. The "forty-eighters," as they became known, contributed significantly to the liberal movement in states where they settled in large numbers. Even though they numbered only about 10,000, this cohort of immigrants wielded influence far beyond their numerical strength. They started German newspapers, reading societies, theaters, and other cultural activities. Though the full extent of their influence is debated, the forty-eighters provided important leadership in the American labor movement. In the newly emerging conservation movement, the forty-eighter Carl Shurz led the drive to save virgin forest land and became the first Secretary of the Interior, in 1877. Further, they were prominent in the antislavery movement and instrumental in the foundation of the Republican Party, where they took credit—undoubtedly an inflated claim—for the election of President Abraham Lincoln, who shrewdly had invested in a German newspaper.[1]

During and after the Civil War, German immigrant labor filled desperately needed slots in the northern industrial labor force opened up by the war. Industrialization was seen as essential to national security and the cheap labor force that German, among other immigrants, provided, as well as their skilled labor, was viewed as essential to industrialization. The booming economy drew them to areas of high demand, and this became a major factor in their rapid absorption into mainstream American life. The largest wave of German immigrants came after the Civil War period. The Homestead Act of May 20, 1862 offered cheap land that was especially attractive to the overcrowded population of Germany. Box 2.1 briefly summarizes this important *pull-factor* act. Western states advertised for German farmers, who had a reputation of being hardworking and highly productive. State governments joined the railroads in sending agents to induce German immigrants to settle and develop the abundant lands. An additional draw was that America became a haven from the military conscriptions during the German wars of unification.

In addition to the cheap land, those willing to serve in the Civil War were rewarded by the Act of July 17, 1862 (40 Stat. S46), which granted

---

**BOX 2.1.   SUMMARY—ACT OF MAY 20, 1862,
TO SECURE HOMESTEADS**

Be it enacted..., That any person who is the head of a family, or who has arrived at the age of twenty-one years, and is a citizen of the United States, or who shall have filed his declaration of intention to become such, as required by the naturalization laws of the United States, and who has never borne arms against the United States Government or given aid and comfort to its enemies, shall, from and after the first of January, eighteen hundred and sixty-three, be entitled to enter one quarter section or a less quantity of unappropriated public lands, upon which said person may have filed a preemption claim, or which may, at the time the application is made, be subject to preemption at one dollar and twenty-five cents, or less, per acre; or eighty acres or less of such unappropriated lands, at two dollars and fifty cents per acre, to be located in a body, in conformity to the legal subdivisions of the public lands, and after the same shall have been surveyed; Provided, That any person owning and residing on land may, under the provisions of this act, enter other land lying contiguous to his or her said land, which shall not, with the land so already owned and occupied, exceed in the aggregate one hundred and sixty acres... Approved.

Source: Chap. LXXV, Thirty-Seventh Congress, Session II, Ch. 75 (1862), 392–393.

---

naturalization to honorably discharged soldiers. This became an important inducement to recruit aliens to serve in the Union Army during the Civil War, and large numbers of German immigrants so fought.

German immigrants did face some opposition, most notably from the Know-Nothing Party of the 1850s. German Catholics competed with the large wave of Irish Catholics, who quickly dominated the hierarchy of the Catholic Church in America until the early 1900s, when German clergy began to fill some leadership roles in that important social institution.

Irish Immigration

At 33,048,744, residents claiming Irish-ancestry in the 2000 census rank second to German Americans in the number and percentage of the total U.S. population. Today they are evenly balanced in their regional distribution throughout the country: 24 percent reside in the northeast, 25 percent in the midwest, 33 percent in the south, and 17 percent in the west. Among them, less than 200,000 are foreign-born, making up about 1.2 percent of the foreign-born population. Yet about 18.2 percent of them came to the United States between 1980 and 1990. Among those more recently immigrated Irish Americans, 63.8 percent were naturalized.

Like the Germans, Irish immigration can also be traced back to the colonial period, when they settled mostly in Pennsylvania and Maryland. By 1790, the Irish comprised roughly 2 percent of the population of just over 3 million. Their numbers and Catholicism generated the first strong and overt discrimination.

Irish immigrants figured prominently in the cholera outbreak that hit Canada in 1832 and the United States in 1831–1833. Asiatic cholera first broke out in India in 1826. By 1831, it had reached Moscow, and then spread rapidly across Europe, and went to Britain by the end of 1831. Fear of its spreading to Canada by English or Irish immigrants led to Canada's establishing, in 1832, their first island quarantine station at Grosse Ile, in the St. Lawrence River just below Quebec. Ships leaving Liverpool and other ports of the British Isles were then sailing vessels, often overcrowded, with poor to no sanitation procedures, and bringing a 100 to 200 or more passengers in voyages that typically lasted from thirty-six to eighty days. In June, 1832 epidemics of small pox and cholera hit Quebec. At Grosse Ile, seemingly endless lines of people were brought to the unfinished hospitals there for shelter and care. Weekly reports of death grew from 150 to 400 to 475 and then to 500. In August, as many as 600 died between 8:00 a.m. of August 15th and 8:00 a.m. of the 16th (O'Gallagher: 25). With the trek of immigrants up-river, the terror and death spread to Montreal and the surrounding countryside, with a reported 1000 dead there by July 3. By the end of September, Quebec City newspapers reported 3,292 "official burials" because of the epidemic, which was more than the death at Grosse Ile. Although U.S. officials were reluctant to accept passage of immigrants through Canada, they were unable to avoid similar outbreaks in New York City and other seaports in 1831–1833 (refer Table 2.1).

After 1830, when the Irish began fleeing the political and religious persecution under British rule, Irish immigration swelled to a flood. The potato famine precipitated a truly massive migration. For many Irish, the choice was simply to emigrate or starve to death. Between 1847, a year in which 100,000 Irish immigrants arrived in the United States, and 1854, approximately 1.2 million Irish arrived in the United States. That surge peaked in 1851, when nearly a quarter-million arrived (221,000) (Tindall: 447). This famine-induced immigration was important because it meant a deluge of poor Irish immigrants settled on the East Coast, which activated existing prejudice. Their sheer numbers, religion (Catholicism), and open anti-British sentiment contributed to the antipathy toward them evident in the native stock. Perhaps equally important for understanding their incorporation patterns was their poverty. It trapped them within the nation's explosively expanding eastern seaboard cities. Their concentration in the tenement slums of cities like Boston and New York enhanced their ability to use bloc voting.

Their vast influx fed the overall stream of immigration that marked the period. By the mid-nineteenth century, land remained plentiful and cheap and

labor was still relatively scarce and dear. Thus, the 1840s saw 1.7 million immigrants arrive. During the 1850s, 2.6 million more came. By the 1880s, that
number had risen to 2.5 million. In the decade from 1845 to 1854, 2.4 million
came, about 14.5 percent of the total population in 1845 (Tindall: 474). By
1860, one person in eight residing in the United States was foreign-born. At that
point, the Irish were the largest group, at 1.6 million, followed by the Germans,
at 1.3 million, and somewhat dwarfing those who were British-born, at 538,000.
    Their overcrowding on emigrant vessels and the defective diet and lack of
medical supervision experienced during the long voyage proved to be the best
of conditions for the spread of contagious diseases among those whose power
of resistance was so greatly lessened by their poverty and destitution. The crop
failure, disease, and famine in Ireland in 1846–1847 led to mass migration
of the destitute in such numbers that almost all restrictions on ships bound
for Canadian and American ports were withdrawn (O'Gallagher: 47–48). Of
slightly more than 100,000 persons who left the British Isles for America
in 1847, a total of 17,445, or over 16 percent, died during the passage, in
quarantine, or in hospital (Guillet: 91). A typhus outbreak hit Grosse Ile in
1847 that was horrific. The ship, "Syria," left Liverpool with 241 steerage passengers on board, nine of whom died at sea of typhus and forty in the quarantine hospital at Grosse Ile. From then on, the horror mounted throughout
the summer. Ships arrived in ever-growing numbers. Immigrants numbered
12,000 on June 1st and 14,000 by June 8th, with the sick in the hospital
reaching over 1,000 by June 8th, and with forty to fifty deaths per day. From
May 10 to July 24, 1,458 men, women, and children died in the hospital, and
4,572 died on ships or in tents near the healthy quarantined on the island
(O'Gallagher: 52; see also Guillet: 145–154). Medical science at that time knew
little of the causes of these diseases, nor little about how to treat them, other
than quarantine measures, which sometimes spread the outbreak to the
healthy who were quarantined along with or nearby the sick.
    Their high rates of illiteracy and general lack of appropriate job skills forced
them into unskilled labor. They were of lower-class status precisely when the
United States developed class consciousness.[2] They were viewed by many of
the "native stock" as a particular threat, a great concentration of "indigent
foreigners," and a lower class of people who formed the first huge pool of
manual labor (O'Grady, 1973: 65). The Irish were the first ethnic group to face
overt job discrimination. Job advertisements in New York, Boston, and other
eastern cities for some time often included the line, "No Irish Need Apply."
They accepted whatever jobs that were open to them—unskilled work such as
stevedores, teamsters, ditchdiggers, dockers, and terriers. They formed the
construction gangs who razed or erected the buildings of the ever-growing
cities. They built the canals, roads, and railroads connecting the east with the
midwest and beyond. Much to their dismay, not only were the streets of
America not paved with gold; they discovered the streets were unpaved and
they would do much of the paving!

This perceived "flood" of immigrants sparked a nativist reaction. In 1828, the Workingmen's Party began in Philadelphia. It spread west, becoming especially powerful on the West Coast. In 1837, the Native American Association began. It was soon surpassed in influence, however, when in 1849 the Order of the Star Spangled Banner was founded in New York. By 1854, it had evolved into the American Party, more commonly known as the Know-Nothing Party (Tindall: 478).

Box 2.2 presents sentiments reflecting the anti-Catholic, anti-Irish and anti-immigrant attitudes of the Know-Nothing Party. The box summarizes an article, written by an elder, J.R. Graves, published in his *Tennessee Baptist* under the heading "Know-Nothing." It vividly describes the bias of the new political party, which became a leading force for restriction of immigration in the 1850s.

The jobs open to the Irish were seasonal, low-paying, and periodic. This left the Irish subject to constant job threat and labor competition from the Chinese

---

BOX 2.2.   ARTICLE ON KNOW-NOTHING PARTY, 1854

Nothing is more evident than that our political parties have become sadly, deplorably corrupt... Congress has become a most shameful and disgraceful scene of drunkenness, riot, and caucusing for the Presidency and the minor offices of the government. The foreign element is increasing in fearful ratio. Nearly one million per annum of foreign Catholics and German infidels—who, though opposed in all else, are agreed in the subversion of our free institutions—are pouring in upon us and the tide is increasing. These foreigners have already commenced their warfare upon the use of the Bible in our public schools—against our free school system—against our Sabbath—against our laws. They boldly threaten to overthrow our constitution, through profligacy of our politicians; and we see our candidates for political preferment pandering more and more to the Catholic and foreign influence. We see from the last census that the majority of the civil and municipal offices of this government are today in the hands of Catholics and foreigners; an overwhelming majority of our army and navy are foreign Catholics. They hear the editors of Catholic papers, who are endorsed by their Archbishop, threatening in these words: "If Catholics ever gain an immense numerical majority, religious freedom in this country is at an end." So say our enemies. So we believe. [Elder Graves then proceeded to list what he called the sixteen cardinal principles of the new party, and predicted a great future for Americanism.]

Source: S. Darrell Overdyke, *The Know-Nothing Party in the South.* Gloucester, Mass.: Peter Smith Publisher, Inc. (1968), 67.

or blacks. Irish immigrants were often trapped in an existence that was depressingly grim. Social barriers and meager and insecure incomes forced them to live in enclaves in the slums. Many "escaped" such conditions by abusing alcohol, which contributed to the stereotypical image of the Irish as excessive drinkers.

They broke the vicious cycle and moved up the socioeconomic ladder by their involvement in the beginnings of the American labor movement and by use of politics to enter local government bureaucracies. It was the only route realistically open to them. While few Irish had experience in labor union affairs, their precarious economic position led them into labor associations. They were early leaders in the formation of unions from New York to San Francisco, which ran the gamut from skilled craftsmen to longshoremen to simply "unskilled laborers." In the 1850s, unions operated solely at the local level, but by the 1860s they appeared at the national level. In 1861, Martin Burke helped form the American Miners Association. By the late 1870s, a second-generation Irish American, Terrence Powderly, the mayor of Scranton, Pennsylvania by age thirty, gained control of the first truly effective national-level labor union, the Knights of Labor. Peter J. McGuire, the "Father of Labor Day," helped form the American Federation of Labor in 1886 (Tindall: 801–803).

The Irish became politically active and organized mostly after the Civil War, and it took roughly a century (1860–1960) for them to achieve full political incorporation (as demonstrated by the election of John Fitzgerald Kennedy as president of the United States and certifying their arrival at that status) using the political accommodation route.

The extensive urbanization between 1840 and 1860 required rapidly increasing local government workforces, especially police departments. The Irish were quick to join, and some rose rapidly to levels of responsibility. By 1863, a John A. Kennedy (no relation to President Kennedy) led New York City's police force. In 1870, a new detective, Michael Kerwin, became police commissioner. The police job was especially attractive to Irish immigrants. The status of the uniform and the steady employment were magnets, as was the potential power of the position. In Ireland, they had been oppressed by the police— evicted, taxed, seized for questioning, imprisoned, and/or forcibly emigrated to Australia, and even killed. In America, they exercised such power.

> The Irish policeman exercised wide discretion in apprehending violators and as upholders of the law, they interpreted the law with a latitude and flexibility appropriate to their interests and those of the politicians they served, and the political morality they inherited justified this practice (Levine, 1966: 123).

Because politicians controlled appointments to the police force, Irish immigrants quickly realized that job security lay on the success of the growing urban political machine's slate at primaries and on the party's victory on general election day. Irish-dominated police departments became the mainstays of ward and district organizations of the Democratic political party. Politics set the pattern of their relationship to the American society and soon served as a model for most of the later arriving immigrant groups.

Huge numbers of Irish living in enclaves formed an ethnic voting bloc that often provided the margin of victory. Ward leaders and precinct captains of the urban political party machine were often Irish immigrants or their descendents. Using church and related ethnic organizations, they established the machine apparatus that gradually controlled the electoral machinery in many big cities. By the 1870s, they gained control of the Democratic Party machine in Brooklyn. Irish Americans served as mayors in Richmond, Memphis, Baltimore, Wilmington, and Scranton. In 1871, an Irishman entered Congress as a representative from New York; in 1876, another won a seat from Pennsylvania. The highly influential Irish Catholic Benevolent Union (ICBU) sent several of its prominent members to seats on the city council of Philadelphia in the 1870s. One of them, William Harrity, served as chairman of the Philadelphia Democratic City Committee. He went on to serve as chairman of the Democratic National Committee during President Cleveland's 1892 campaign. This set the precedent for a long tradition of Irish Democratic National Committee chairmen. The ICBU sent eight of its members to judgeships during the 1870s, and by 1880 its founder, Dennis Dwyer, won a seat on New York State's Supreme Court.

Their success was duplicated in other parts of the nation, but the early political clout of the Irish reached its zenith in New York City through their fifty-year control of Tammany Hall, the first and the classic example of the urban political machine. As the late Senator Daniel Patrick Moynihan so aptly described it:

> "Dick" Connolly and "Brains" Sweeny had shared power and office with Tweed, as had any number of their followers, but with few exceptions the pre-1870s Irish had represented the canaille. With the dawning of the Gilded Age, however, middle-class and upper-class Irish began to appear; thus ranging across the social spectrum, the Irish appeared to dominate a good part of the city's life for half a century. They came to run the police force and the underworld; they were evident on Wall Street as on the Bowery; Irish contractors laid out the subways and Irish laborers dug them. The city entered the era of Boss Croker of Tammany Hall and Judge Goff of the Lexow Committee, which investigated him; of business leader Thomas Fortune Ryan and labor leader Peter J. McQuire; of reform mayor John Purroy Mitchel and Tammany Mayor "Red Mike" Hylan. It was a stimulating miscellany, reaching its height in the Roaring Twenties with Al Smith and Jimmy Walker (cited in Fuchs, 1990: 79–80).

Scandinavians

According to 2000 census data, 1,505,450 identified themselves as Danish, 4,524,953 as Norwegian, and 4,342,150 as Swedish. Thus, nearly 10.5 million Americans claimed that background.

Scandinavians were among the first European people to explore America, with Viking exploration and minute settlements dating back to the period of 800–1050. In the mid-1600s several settlements of people from the Scandinavian region were established in what is now known as Delaware. A few immigrants continued to come from Norway, Sweden, and Denmark during colonial times, but their numbers were not substantial until after the Civil War. From then on, motivated by push factors such as religious dissension, disenfranchisement, crop failures, and related economic factors, Scandinavians emigrated in large numbers, and most of them came to the United States. Total Scandinavian immigration to the United States now totals approximately 3 million. The Swedes hit their peak in 1910 and the Norwegians in the 1920s. Although the Norwegians, Swedes, and Danes came from countries with diverse governments, traditions, and spoken languages, their physical similarities and a tendency to settle together here led to the use of the term "Scandinavian" to refer to all the three groups.

On the whole, Scandinavians were a very successful group of immigrants. They were willing to work hard. They arrived in better shape than most groups, which enabled them to escape the poverty, slums, and resulting stereotyping and social stigma of the eastern seaboard cities with their "teeming immigrant masses." By 1880, the average Scandinavian immigrant arrived with sixty to seventy dollars. Such sums allowed them to reach the midwest and its abundant and cheap land on which their farming skills could be put to good use. Farming was not their only trade. They went into business, commerce, manufacturing, finance, and the professions. In the frontier settlements, they succeeded in setting up their own stores, shops, factories, and banks. By the 1890s, they were concentrated in the midwestern states whose soil and climate so reminded them of their homelands, and where their successful settlements attracted others. Minnesota, Wisconsin, Iowa, Illinois, and the Dakotas all saw dramatic increases in their populations due to the Scandinavian influx. By the 1890s, they were increasingly attracted to the industrial opportunities in the northeast and to the lumber industry of the Pacific Northwest.

Scandinavian incorporation proved comparatively easy. They entered the country when there were many opportunities to advance through the economic path. Their political involvement generally followed economic and social successes. Several factors account for the relative ease of their assimilation. They did not have to overcome the stigma of some undesirable trait. They were Caucasian and escaped racial prejudice. They were strongly Protestant, avoiding the anti-Catholic sentiment. They came in relatively small numbers over a long period of time, compared to the huge waves of Irish, for example, who came in the millions in a decade. Scandinavians thereby avoided the scapegoat effect. Anti-immigrant hatred was directed toward the Irish (and later the Italians) arriving at the same time and who were feared as job competitors and as "papists." Coming in smaller waves and with sufficient capital and job skills to reach the midwest, they were not viewed as threats to the dominant society's labor force. They worked hard at becoming "Americans." Strongly desiring to assimilate, they mastered English as quickly as possible. Schools were important in their settlements and they insisted on schools that taught English.

Being overwhelmingly Protestant, their religion gave them a common bond with the majority society. They were mostly Lutherans and considered more devout and strait-laced than were the German Lutherans. Their stern faith frowned on drinking, dancing, and levity, and stressed piety and the work ethic. Many were anti-Catholic and thus more accepted by a native stock with whom they shared a common enemy. Scandinavians formed numerous new churches based on American ideas, again easing their incorporation.

Financial success made them more socially accepted. The Homestead Act of 1862 provided cheap land, so they became established without going heavily into debt. Their standard of living soon compared to that of the dominant society located in frontier settlements. Describing Norwegian settlers in the Dakotas in the 1890s, one writer stated: "Most of them came with just enough money to buy government land and build a shack Now they loan money to their neighbors... every county has Norwegians worth $25,000 to $50,000, all made since settling in Dakota" (cited in Dinnerstein and Reimers, 1988: 87–98).

By then, they had a clear understanding of American-style politics with its numerous points of access: elections, representation, constitutions, and frag-mented political power distributed among many local governments. They were patriotic. They organized political groups to get information on laws and elections, and learned American-style politics by organizing new townships, working on town government, levying and collecting taxes, and laying out new roads. Typically by then, more than a fifth of the men participated in town affairs.

The first Scandinavian-born politician to enter statewide politics was a Norwegian, James Reymert, who represented Racine County in the second constitutional convention of Wisconsin in 1847. After the Civil War, Scandi-navians become more visible in state-level politics. Norwegian-born Knute Nelson was the first state governor. He was elected, in succession, to the legislatures of Wisconsin and then Minnesota, to the U.S. Congress, and as governor of Minnesota on the Republican ticket in 1892. Many Scandinavians served in the state legislatures of Wisconsin, Minnesota, and the Dakotas. They tended to be Republicans.

Other Immigrant Groups

Several other groups arrived in significant numbers during the period be-tween 1820 and 1880. The Dutch, French, Scots, Scotch-Irish, and Welsh are commonly grouped among the *old* immigrant groups. They generally exemplify patterns similar to those discussed earlier in this chapter. Another group, the Chinese, showed a considerably different pattern.

Total immigration from the Netherlands has been about one-half million. Although more than half of those came after 1880, they are generally grouped among the old immigrants because they came in significant numbers in the earlier period and because their greatest impact on U.S. society was during the colonial and early independence period. Dutch influence was most strongly felt in New Jersey and New York. Brooklyn, the Bowery, and the Bronx, for example, all take their names as derivatives of Dutch words. The famous and extraordinarily influential labor leader, Samuel Gompers, founder of the American Federation of Labor (AFL) who led the movement from 1884 until he died in 1924, was of Dutch-Jewish ancestry.

Religious dissenters from the Netherlands founded colonies in Michigan and Iowa in 1846. Their departure from the homeland coincided with the potato blight and the accompanying economic depression that hit their homeland, as it did much of Europe, in the late 1840s. Their religious separatists established a settlement in what became Holland, Michigan. It served as the prototype for a new wave of immigrants who were settling in Wisconsin and Illinois, as well as Michigan and Iowa, where the soil and climate were so favorable.

The unifying force among Dutch settlements was religion rather than national identity. Subsequent schisms resulted in the formation of the Dutch Reformed Church, the Christian Reformed Church, and the Netherlands Reformed Church. The Holland, Michigan settlement was especially successful, and Dutch settlers there achieved a high social status, in part reflected by their founding of Hope College. The Christian Reformed Church, a more conservative group, emulated their example in founding Calvin College in Grand Rapids, Michigan.

France has been the source of a large and rather continuous flow of immigrants. French-Americans are generally categorized into three distinct subgroups: (1) immigrants from France proper; (2) French Louisianans, or "Cajuns," who were expelled from Acadia French Canada by the British in 1755; and (3) French Canadians who settled primarily in New England. The total number of migrants from France has approached 850,000.

The colonial era immigrants from France were dominated by the Huguenots; Protestants fleeing religious persecution. Most of them readily converted to the Anglican Church here, and that fact, coupled with their rapid adoption of English, eased their assimilation. They did experience some antagonism due to the comparatively frequent hostilities between England and France that spilled over into animosities in the colonies. Such friction, however, was generally short-lived. Their marginal status did encourage them to anglicize quickly by changing their names and customs, and by learning English. Full assimilation was their clear goal. When during the Revolutionary War, France became an ally against Great Britain, their assimilation was greatly facilitated. It was the French diplomat, De Crevecoeur, who first used the concept of the United States as the asylum for the poor of Europe and who first popularized the concept of America as being "the melting pot" (Rischin: 24; Parrillo: 128).

In contrast, the French Revolution led to thousands of French aristocrats immigrating to the United States. Unlike their earlier compatriots, this group kept to themselves and avoided the native stock, whom they felt to be socially inferior. They rejected assimilation and citizenship. Many returned to France after the fall of Napoleon. The French Revolution also briefly aroused anti-French feelings here as Americans began to fear and detest the excesses of that revolution. This sentiment was especially strong among Federalist Party members and contributed, as we have seen, to their pushing through the Alien and Sedition Acts.

The Louisiana French, who became part of the country by absorption in the Louisiana Purchase in 1803, afforded yet another pattern. They had exhibited an exceedingly strong and persistent subculture that has absorbed other ethnic groups in the area, largely through intermarriage and their matriarchical socialization process.

The French Canadians also exhibited a persistent subculture. Overpopulation at home and the diminishing size of the agricultural land, which had been subdivided for generations, finally led many to immigrate to the United States in the 1830s. Their peak periods were between 1860 and 1900, when an estimated 300,000 came, settling for the most part in the mill and factory towns of New England. Other substantial settlements were in New York, Michigan, Illinois, and Wisconsin. Like the Louisiana French, their family and church structures seemed to account for their persistent subculture and slower rate of assimilation (Parrillo: 131).

The Scots, Scotch-Irish, and Welsh showed similar patterns of immigration and assimilation. They started immigration during the colonial period and have generally incorporated rather easily. Their religious preference for Presbyterianism, Episcopalianism, and Anglicanism helped to promote their reputations for following a strict moral code, the development of the "Protestant work-ethic," and a widespread reputation for frugality and honesty, all of which made them readily accepted by the Calvinist New Englanders. They settled in considerable numbers in Pennsylvania, the Carolinas, and New England. They worked frequently as farmers or miners. In the latter occupation, they were often desired as skilled workers who served as superintendents and foremen.

They did experience some anti-immigrant feeling. Since they often settled in large numbers in what were then frontier regions, the native stock feared they might become the dominant group. The native workforce perceived them as an economic threat due to their job skills, which made them highly desired as workers by some of the native elite who controlled business enterprises.

The Chinese

Such was not the case, however, with the Chinese. They are a unique case among the "old immigrant" groups in that they suffered a racial stigma. They alone among the *old* immigrants, for example, were the target of specific restrictive laws.

At nearly 23 percent of all Asian-Americans, Chinese-Americans are the largest Asian-American group. They were the first Asian immigrants to come to the United States in significant numbers. After the discovery of gold in California in 1848, Chinese laborers surged into the state. The largest group came from Kwantung and Fukien provinces in southern China. In part, they fled economic depression and resulting local rebellions, but also floods, famine, and the general social discontent in their homelands. They were also pulled by the demand for labor created by the California gold rush, and by heavy labor recruitment by the railroad and steamship lines.

At first welcomed and viewed as industrious, thrifty, and adaptable to many types of tasks and willing to perform labor unattractive to the majority white males, Chinese immigrants quickly became essential to the Californian economy. They were well organized, so an employer could secure any number of workers by negotiating with a single contractor. This placed them in a comparatively advantageous position. Once employed, Chinese laborers stayed on the job, agreeing to do the most undesirable tasks. With the lack of labor generally, and especially the lack of women on the western frontier, they found work in the mines, building the railroads, as ranch hands, farm laborers, and domestic servants. The Central Pacific Railroad, for example, employed some 9,000 Chinese immigrants a year. By 1860, they made up about 10 percent of California's population and roughly 25 percent of its workforce (Thompson 1996).

Their warm welcome was short-lived. By the mid-1850s, growing hostility was evident. In the mining regions especially, the Chinese were often robbed and beaten and occasionally murdered. By 1849, a Know-Nothing judge of the California Supreme Court had ruled that the Chinese could not testify in courts against white men. Crimes against them went unpunished.

Their problems reflected resentment against them because they were seen as threats to white labor. Chinese immigrants were overwhelmingly males who came to the United States as *sojourners*—intending to work there only for a few years to save money and then return to their native land to buy land. The Chinese male to female ratio from 1860 to 1890 was a few thousands to one. This problem was exacerbated when fourteen states passed *antimiscegenation laws* (forbidding marriage between the white and Asian races). Those laws, coupled with the scarcity of Chinese females, left the men with no alternatives but total abstention or the use of prostitutes. Prostitution was usually associated with the opium traffic, which soon led to a severe image problem of criminality concerning Chinese immigrants. Difficulty in importing Chinese females contributed to the long-lasting nature of the imbalance. By 1882, Chinese labor immigration was greatly reduced. As of 1890, only 2.7 percent of Chinese were American-born.

Miscegenation laws were but one manifestation of the legal constraints they faced. By the 1850s, California expelled them from the mining work camps, forbade their entry into public schools, denied their right to testify against whites in court, and barred them from obtaining citizenship. By 1865, calls for restrictions on their immigration began. In 1867, the Democratic Party swept into California's elective offices running on an anti-Chinese platform. The Panic of 1873 brought on economic conditions that greatly increased the fear of competition from Chinese immigrant labor, and calls to end the "Yellow Menace" broadened. In 1887, the Workingmen's Party, led by Dennis Kearny and running on a blatantly anti-Chinese campaign, scored political success in several cities. The party called for an end to all Chinese immigration. A sample of the rhetoric and views of the Workingmen's Party is contained in Box 2.3, which quotes parts of a speech given by Dennis Kearney in 1877 and published in the San Francisco *Daily Bulletin*.

By the 1870s, then, such sentiment was so strong on the West Coast that it was tantamount to political suicide to take the Chinese side. Concern over immigration from China and Japan was coming to a head. The Chinese

---

**BOX 2.3.   KEARNEY'S WORKINGMEN'S PARTY
SPEECH (DECEMBER 28, 1877)**

We intend to try and vote the Chinamen out, to frighten him out, and if this won't do, to kill him out, and when the blow comes, we won't leave a fragment for the thieves to pick up. We are going to arm ourselves to the teeth, and if these land-grabbers go outside the Constitution, we will go outside the Constitution, too, and woe be to them. You must be prepared. The heathen slaves must leave this coast, if it cost 10,000 lives. We want to frighten capital and thereby to starve the white men so that they will be exasperated and do their duty. This is the last chance the white slaves will ever have to gain their liberty . . . We have the numbers to win at the ballot box, but you will be cheated out of the result, and all history shows that oppressed labor has always to get its right at the point of the sword. If the Republican robber and the Democratic thief cheat you at the election, as I know they will, shoot them down like rats. You must be ready with your bullets. We will go to Sacramento and surround the Legislature with bayonets and compel them to enact such laws as we wish.

Source: Neil L. Shumsky, *The Evolution of Political Protest and the Workingmen's Party of California.* Columbia: Ohio State University Press (1991), 178.

Exclusion League vigorously advocated restrictive legislation at the local, state, and national levels. In 1875, the first federal-level anti-Chinese legislation, aimed at the immigration of women from China and Japan "for immoral purposes," was enacted. Known more commonly as "The Page Law," is was officially the Act of March 3, 1875, to exclude certain Asian women (18 Stat. 477, 8 U.S.C.). The anti-Chinese legal action culminated nationally in the passage of the Chinese Exclusion Act of 1882, which will be discussed in the next chapter.

Such laws were not the only method to restrict Chinese life and work opportunities. Violence and social segregation were common. Many turned to violence. In 1871, twenty-one Chinese were killed in a Los Angeles riot. In 1880, Denver experienced a severe anti-Chinese riot. A typical example of the use of violence was the Truckee Raid of June 18, 1876. Whites burned two Chinese-occupied cabins and shot and wounded residents (one of whom later died of his wounds) as they attempted to flee the flames. White citizens tried for the crime were acquitted. The Order of Caucasians advocated the elimination of Chinese through the use of violence. They raided and burned various sections of Chinatowns. In 1885, at Rock Springs, Wyoming, a mob killed twenty-eight Chinese and drove hundreds of others from their homes. In Tacoma, Seattle, and Oregon City, mobs expelled hundreds of Chinese from their homes. Unionized labor, particularly the Teamsters, became a major force behind the violent anti-Chinese movement. Although violence subsided with passage of the restrictionist immigration laws, strong prejudice and discrimination remained, especially in jobs and housing, well into the 1890s. Newspapers spread stereotypical images of the Chinese with stories about prostitution, gambling, and opium dens in Chinatowns. "Chinks" and "John Chinaman" were names used as racial slurs (LeMay, 2005: 77).

Job discrimination was prevalent. Violence kept many out of the mine fields, but so did legislation. In 1855, the Foreign Miners' Tax was enacted in California. It required foreign miners to pay a four-dollar-per-month tax (an exceedingly heavy rate in 1855). In addition, the tax increased each year that the miner did not become a citizen. Since the Chinese were legally excluded from naturalization, they were forced to pay ever-higher rates. Such legislation and the violence against them soon forced the Chinese to seek other areas of employment.

The general lack of women in the frontier, however, opened up the area of domestic services to the Chinese as one field in which they would not be viewed as a competitive threat to the white male labor force. Laundries, restaurants, and other domestic services required little capital or job skills. The increasing job discrimination and violence encouraged their tendency to cluster together in urban Chinatowns. Even there, however, they could not escape legislative harassment. San Francisco passed ordinances in 1876 and 1880 aimed solely at the Chinese. A special tax was placed on small-hand laundries, all of which were operated by the Chinese at that time. A "Cubic Air

Act" was passed that jailed the occupants of overcrowded housing rather than the landlords, if each person did not have 500 square feet of living space. The city enacted a "Queu Tax," that is, a tax on pigtails—a hairstyle worn exclusively by the Chinese. An ordinance was passed restricting the shipment of human bones, aimed at the Chinese custom of sending the deceased person's bones home for burial. Although these laws were nearly impossible to enforce very widely and were ultimately found to be unconstitutional, they contributed to the atmosphere and the institutionalization of a rigid social and geographic segregation of the Chinese in America (LeMay, 2005: 77–78).

Forced out of many more desirable jobs, the Chinese immigrants' willingness to serve as scabs and strikebreakers increased their difficulties with organized labor. The Chinese refused to join the Knights of Labor. That fact, and their service as strikebreakers for the Union Pacific railroad in Wyoming, led to severe conflicts there in 1875. Fear of the "Yellow Peril" added greatly to the successful movement to implement restrictive legislation and exemplifies the reaction of nativist groups to a perceived threat of the foreign influx. It is to a discussion of the nativist movement we next turn our attention.

NATIVIST POLITICAL REACTION

The successive "waves" of the old immigrants did not go unnoticed by the native majority. Many WASPS (White Anglo-Saxon Protestants) accepted and welcomed the immigrants. As we have seen, several state governments and businesses, particularly the railroads and various manufacturing concerns, which were just beginning to develop, and the transatlantic shipping lines, welcomed or actively recruited immigrants. But not all the native stock reacted so favorably. The American party, founded on July 4, 1845, was a specific anti-immigrant party whose main platform was the total rejection of the foreigner. In its declaration of principles, the party stated:

> The danger of foreign influence which threatens the gradual destruction of our national institutions has not failed to arrest the attention of the Father of His Country. Not only in rendering the American system liable to the poisonous influence of European policy—a policy at war with the fundamental principles of the American Constitution, but also its still more fatal operation in aggravating the virulence of partisan warfare—has awakened deep concern in the minds of every intelligent man from the days of Washington to now (O'Connor: 122).

The most prominent nativist movement became known as the Know-Nothing Party. Originally called the Order of the Star Spangled Banner, the party had its beginnings as a secret patriotic society founded in New York in 1849. It achieved its earliest successes in Massachusetts and Pennsylvania. In the 1854 elections, it added striking successes in Rhode Island, New Hampshire, Connecticut, Delaware, Maryland, Kentucky, and Texas. The party also wielded a strong influence in Virginia, Georgia, Alabama, Mississippi, and Louisiana (Smith, Theodore: 141; Nevins: 329).

As historian John Higham notes, the nativist themselves described their philosophy as "Americanism." He notes:

> "The grand work of the American Party," proclaimed one of the Know-Nothing journals in 1855, "is the principle of nationality...we must do something to protect and vindicate it. If we do not it will be destroyed."
>
> Here is the ideological core of nativism in every form. Whether the nativist is a workingman or a Protestant evangelist, a southern conservative or a northern reformer, he stood for a certain kind of nationalism. He believed—whether he was trembling at a Catholic menace to American liberty, fearing an invasion of pauper labor, or simply rioting against the great English actor William Macready—that some influence originating abroad threatened the very life of the nation from within. Nativism, therefore, should be defined as intense opposition to an internal minority on the ground of its foreign (i.e., "un-American") connections (Higham, 1955: 4).

In the 1856 elections, the Know-Nothing party ran a presidential candidate, former President Millard Fillmore. Its platform was too narrowly based on an anti-immigrant, anti-Catholic stance to succeed nationally. It was silent on the slavery issue altogether. Thus, the party merely played the role of spoiler in the election. Fillmore received 874,534 votes and carried only the state of Maryland. (For a statement by candidate Fillmore of the party's stance, see LeMay and Barkan, Document 23: 28–29).

Deep-rooted feelings caused many of the native stock to oppose immigrants by joining the new militant nativist party. The massive immigration following the potato famine aroused fear and hostility among nativists, which fed the movement and contributed greatly to the party's rapid rise and temporary success. The slavery question, which ultimately led to the demise of the party, loosened ties so that many voters who were unwilling as yet to cast their lot with either the proslavery Democrats or the antislavery forces coalescing in the formation of the Republican Party, found a temporary home in the Know-Nothing party.

In order to join, one had to be a native-born American and a Protestant. The individual had to swear an oath to vote for whomever or whatever the party told him to vote. If asked about their goals or stands on a position, they were told to reply: "I know nothing," which gave rise to the party's popular name. On occasion, some party members would close one eye and place a thumb and forefinger over the nose, which signified "eyes nose nothing" (Bailey: 135).

The movement attracted the working class, who feared their jobs would be taken and the institutions and order of society as they knew it would be undermined by so vast an influx of foreigners. They feared, also, the increasing political threat as the electoral clout of the immigrant bloc vote was becoming increasingly evident in the beginnings of what would eventually emerge as the urban political machine. These fears, of course, were not entirely unfounded. The new immigrants were flocking to the cities, causing unbelievable overcrowding and providing a massive and cheap labor pool. Employers were quick to determine that the new immigrants would do almost any job for very low pay (and thus continued to advocate for a totally open-door policy with respect to immigration). It was widely felt that large-scale immigration led to the overall low-pay rates and deplorable working conditions that characterized the early years of the industrialization era.

Others were attracted to the movement out of a deep-seated fear of Catholicism highly evident among large portions of the immigrants flooding in since the 1840s. They joined the movement and rose up "... to burn Catholic convents, churches and homes, assault nuns, and murder Irishmen, Germans and Negroes" (Beals: 9). A violent hate campaign was unleashed in many cities where immigrants were concentrated. In New York, mobs of Irish and Know-Nothings clashed, leaving two dead (the situation depicted in the film, *The Gangs of New York*). In Newark, an estimated 2,000 Protestants and Catholics squared off, leaving one dead, many wounded, and a Catholic Church burned to the ground. In 1855, Know-Nothings and Germans in Louisville clashed in an intense riot, which left twenty dead and hundreds of others wounded. In Baltimore, where the party was particularly strong, numerous clashes took place and a riot in 1854 resulted in eight dead (Hofstadter and Wallace: 93, 313). A spin-off group of the Know-Nothings, called the "Plug-Uglies," was often responsible for the physical violence of the period.

Obviously, not all U.S. citizens reacted so negatively. The famous writer Ralph Waldo Emerson attacked the xenophobic hysteria and the nativist movement by stressing what he considered to be the advantage of the so-called "smelting pot theory."

> I hate the narrowness of the Native American Party. It is the dog in the manger. It is precisely opposite to true wisdom.... Well, as in the old burning of the Temple of Corinth, by the melting and intermixture of silver and gold and other metals, a new compound more precious than any, called Corinthian brass, was formed; so in this continent—asylum of all the nations—the energy of Irish, Swedes, Poles, and Cossacks, and all the European tribes—of the Africans, and the Polynesians, will construct a new race, a new religion, a new state, a new literature, which will be vigorous as the new Europe which came out of the smelting pot of the Dark Ages, or that which earlier emerged from the Palasogic and Etruscan barbarianism (cited in Orth and Ferguson: 299–300).

Obviously, however, many of the native U.S. citizens feared precisely that development. Those to whom the nativist movement appealed did not want a new race, nor a new religion, nor a new language, state or literature. They, along with the party and the movement, advocated—ultimately unsuccessfully so—a change in immigration policy in order to restrict the influx and force for such changes as Emerson so eloquently described.

Rapid in its rise, the party experienced an equally rapid decline. Its 1855 convention split wide open over the slavery issue. Its northern members were antislavery; its southern wing would not budge from its proslavery stand. Attempted reconciliation failed, signaling serious trouble for the party. After the 1856 election, it essentially disintegrated, with its southern wing going Democratic (and later, secessionist), and the northern members joining the Republicans.

THE CIVIL AND POST-CIVIL WAR YEARS

The prevailing forces in U.S. society who were able to determine what the nation's immigration policy would actually be were not the nativists. A coalition of prior immigrant groups, organized into various ethnic associations and increasingly voting as a bloc, plus the politicians of the major political parties that sought and catered to that vote, and the leading forces in business, particularly the growing segment of northern manufacturing concerns, all advocated continuation of an open-door policy. They saw open immigration as essential for national security. Only an economically strong, industrialized America could secure the nation from European influence. Only the increased population and industrial wealth could enable the nation to provide an army and navy that would secure America's place among the major powers of the world.

When nativist forces succeeded, in New York and Massachusetts, in enacting state laws that imposed restrictions and taxed passenger shipping lines for each immigrant brought in, the Supreme Court struck down the state laws. In the *Passenger Cases* (1849) and the *Henderson v. New York* case (1876), the Supreme Court ruled against these state attempts to restrict immigration. The Court's majority declared that Congress alone had the right to regulate immigration (the precedent which was reaffirmed by the Court as recently as the *LULAC et al. v. WILSON et al.* case in 1994 discussed in Chapter 1).

Some southern, western and midwestern states, of course, did not want to restrict immigration and its resulting cheap labor. On the contrary, they sought immigrants in order to open up and develop their lands. Nearly every state outside of the northeast region hired agents or appointed boards of immigration in order to lure new settlers from Europe. Michigan began the practice in 1845. By the end of the Civil War, southern and western states joined in the practice, each hoping to divert some of the renewed influx their way. By the 1870s, twenty-five of the then thirty-eight states took some sort of official action designed to promote immigration. South Carolina went so far as to grant a five-year tax exemption on all real estates bought by immigrants (Higham, 1955: 16).

The railroads, which were pushing development into the empty west, needed immigrants to buy the railroad lands and ensure future revenues by growing the crops or raising the cattle that would then be shipped by rail to the rapidly growing cities of the industrial belt. The Illinois Central, the Burlington, the Northern Pacific, and other lines sent agents to Northern Europe to attract immigrants. Other real-estate interests promoted comparable campaigns. It was largely immigrant labor that allowed for the rapid increase in the miles of railroad track girding the country. In 1862, there were 30,600 miles, mostly in the East Coast. The first transcontinental line was completed, at Promontory, Utah, on May 10, 1869. Within twelve years, another transcontinental line was finished. By 1870 that had arisen to 53,000 miles. It reached 94,000 miles in the 1880s, 167,000 in the 1890s and was 199,000 miles by 1900. The railroads became the first truly national industry, led by "giants" such as Jay Gould, prince of the railroad buccaneers, and Commodore Cornelius Vanderbilt (Tindall: 779–783).

Indeed, virtually every major business enterprise hoped to make money from the immigrant flow. Merchants looked to the tens of thousands of immigrants entering annually after the Civil War as an ever-growing supply of new customers, and organized various associations to attract them. The San Francisco Board of Trade, for example, formed the Immigration Association of California, which established hundreds of contracts with agents in Europe. The mining industry in Pennsylvania and in the Rockies, out west, was especially dependent upon immigrant labor. By 1870, a third of the workforce in manufacturing was from immigrant labor sources. That proportion remained constant until the 1920s. New England manufacturers recruited labor in Canada, and others did so in Europe (Higham, 1955: 16–17).

The national government, as we have seen, favored open immigration, and during the post-Civil War years considered various ways to assist it. The Republican Party's platform in 1868 and 1872 advocated continued encouragement of immigration, although in the end official promotion was left to the states. As we have seen, the national government did pass one program that greatly induced immigration, although that was not its stated purpose. In order to encourage the opening and settlement of the west, the Congress enacted the Homestead Act. In the words of President Abraham Lincoln, when he signed the law, "so that every poor man may have a home," the act, as we have seen, gave a homesteader (settler) 160 acres of land if he worked on it for five years (*We Americans*: 156). A claim had to have a house with a window. The rule requiring a 12 by 12 house did not specify feet, and a 12 by 12-inch house sheltered many an owner only from the law, not the elements. Ingenious devices such as that of building a cabin on wheels to roll from claim to claim were used to stake claims under the law.

Congress, of course, realized that more than free or cheap land was needed to settle the west, and it chartered two companies to build railroads, one from the east and the other from the west, to meet at a junction point. It granted each company ten to twenty square miles of land for each mile of track built. The Union Pacific hired armies of Irish laborers to work westward from Omaha. Starting in California, 7,000 Chinese laborers built their way across the Sierra Nevada east through Nevada and into Utah. In 1869, the two met in

Promontory, Utah, completing the first transcontinental rail line. Within a decade and a half, four twin bands of steel girded the continent and opened up the vast lands of the Great Plains to settlement. It was these lands, free or cheap, which drew millions, many of whom were immigrants. The population of the country had trebled by the close of the period.

By the 1870s, with the development of agricultural devices such as the gang plow and reapers, mechanical threshers, and well-drilling equipment and windmills to supply water, an invasion of the western lands was firmly underway. Fueled by a population from the east, with many immigrants coming from Germany and Scandinavia, the frontier was pushed westward. The population of Kansas grew by nearly one-half million in the decade from 1880 to 1890, while Nebraska's did so by more than 600,000. The Dakotas grew by more than 400 percent a decade, reaching nearly 600,000 by 1890. Even Wyoming and Montana attracted tens of thousands. The cornucopia of free or very cheap land drew millions to the nation's shores.

In 1864, Congress passed the Contract Labor Law, an attempt to revive an eighteenth-century technique for stimulating the influx of laborers from Europe. It authorized employers to pay the passage and bind the services of prospective migrants. While the law did not long outlive the war that spawned it, it underscored the hunger for population that grew ever more ravenous in the following years. Congress repealed the law in 1868 in favor of a laissez-faire policy. The repeal was pushed by organized labor that feared the lowering of wages encouraged by the importation of contract labor (Higham, 1955: 46).

THE RECESSION OF THE 1870S AND NEW
CALLS FOR RESTRICTIONISM

A movement in the direction of restrictions on immigration began to build in the later post-Civil War years. Labor unrest gripped the coal fields of Pennsylvania between 1865 and 1875. Strikes, lockouts, and suspensions signaled a period of unrest punctuated by violence. Mine owners reacted by importing more docile laborers from Hungary and Italy in the 1870s. That decade saw the beginning of a dramatic shift in immigration population away from northwestern Europe to those coming from South/Central/Eastern European nations. The *new* immigrants seemed to be both the symbol of and the agents for a widening gulf between capital and labor.

A long and severe economic depression, begun by the Panic of 1873 (Tindall: 730) and continuing during much of the 1870s, fueled a renewal of anti-immigrant fervor and a revitalization of the nativist movement. When Italian strike-breakers were hired by the Armstrong Coal Works, in 1874, they touched off riots resulting in the deaths of four Italian immigrants (LeMay, 1985: 60). The nation was hit with the first interstate strike, led by the first national labor union, the Knights of Labor, with the Great Railroad Strike of 1877 (Tindall: 799).

A rekindling of anti-Catholicism was also sparked during the later post-Civil War years. A substantial fear of "Rum, Romanism, and Rebellion," was exacerbated by the renewed influx of heavy immigration. Catholics comprised only 1 percent of the total population in 1790. They were only 7 percent in 1850. By 1900, however, more than 12 million Catholics were present, representing 16 percent of the total population! Their ratio had more than doubled. Nativists feared them, seeing them growing at an alarming rate (LeMay, 1985: 53).

A growing dismay over the corrupt urban machines also fueled anti-immigrant fervor. "Boss Tweed," a great hulking Scotch-Irishman, organized the Tweed Ring that captured the Tammany Hall organization. Controlling New York's Democratic Party through Tammany Hall, the Tweed Ring plundered the city of millions of dollars from 1865 to 1871. An antimachine reform movement called for restrictions on immigration.

Several states began to restrict immigration. The Supreme Court, as mentioned earlier, reiterated its ban on state and local regulations of immigration in the *Henderson v. Mayor of New York* case (92 U.S. 259, 1875). But the heightened public concern over the influx of immigrants, coupled with the Supreme Court's decision emphasizing that Congress had the sole power to regulate commerce (including immigration), culminated in the initial restrictions on immigration passed by the national government. In 1875, Congress passed the law banning the entry of prostitutes and convicts (the previously mentioned "Page Law," 18 Stat. 477, 8 U.S.C.). Although the law was a weak one in terms of any real restriction to the flow of immigration, and did nothing to alter the nature of the composition of the newcomers in terms of their nations of origin, it did signal that the forces advocating restrictions were gaining political strength and effectiveness in Congressional legislative acuity. It clearly presaged the Door-Ajar Era when increasingly restrictive policy-making was evident.

National Security Needs Trump Restrictionists

A coalition of groups favoring restrictionist immigration policy developed but did not prevail during the closing decades of the Open-Door Era, and even during the next era—the Door-Ajar Era. The coalition of groups favoring immigration was financially and politically more powerful. Their view that the nation needed open immigration to support the expansion of industrialization was seen as essential to national security. The nation simply had to have a large pool of cheap labor to enable industrialization. Industrialization was necessary to support a world-class navy and military force. The perception of what was needed for national security increasingly accepted as the valid growing concept of "Manifest Destiny"—that it was the destiny of the nation to fill the land from coast-to-coast, and the destiny of the nation to become the "beacon of democracy from the new world to the old world." Only open immigration

BOX 2.4. THE CASTLE GARDEN RECEPTION STATION, NEW YORK CITY

More than 7,000,000 immigrants entered America through its doors in 35 years. Castle Garden, the gateway to America for millions of immigrants during the last half of the nineteenth century, is soon to be torn down....

Castle Garden's greatest fame, and its existence as a symbol to millions in America and abroad as the "nation's gateway," began in 1855. In that year the State Emigration Commission took it over. Construction workers tore down the entertainment booths and built offices for examining physicians, police, ticket agents, post office clerks, custom officials, immigration officers, baggage agents, a letter-writing service, a labor exchange and bathrooms.

On August 3, 1855, the first group of immigrants was examined at Castle Garden. From that date until 1890, a period of thirty-five years and eight months, 7,690,606 immigrants passed through its doors, about three-quarters of all the immigrants who entered the country during that time....

The labor exchange established in Castle Garden was a great success. In the first six months of 1868 it placed 7,111 male and 5,840 female workers in jobs before they left the immigration station. Farm and railroad labor and domestic help were most in demand. Farm hands were offered from $6 to $19 a month. Fashionable women frequently journeyed to Castle Garden to pick out their own domestic help. In 1869 more than 12,000 girls, mostly Irish, were placed in jobs, almost the moment they landed, as domestic servants, cooks and laundresses. But the flow of immigration was not enough for America's industrial appetite. Employers complained they could use ten times as many workers.

During the Civil War, recruiting officers of the Union Army erected two huge tents adjacent to the immigration station and sought to enlist the newly arrived immigrants into the army by offering bounties if they could not persuade them to sign up by arguments in their own language. Many of them did and helped to make up the 400,000 aliens and foreign-born from twenty different countries who fought on the Northern side....

In 1880 the first contingent of the Salvation Army arrived with drums and tambourines. In 1883 about 2,800 Mormons who had been converted to the faith in Europe passed through the Castle Garden station on their way to Utah and the Mormon colony. Scarcely a day passed during which a steamship or vessel in full sail did not arrive with its cargo of expectant humans.

When Grover Cleveland became Governor of New York one of the first problems he attacked was the conditions at Castle Garden which were subject to much criticism. Due to bad administration, many of the old practices of exploiting the immigrants had crept back and the station was again gaining an unsavory reputation. In his first message, on January 1, 1883, the Governor called for reforms at Castle Garden. A State investigation led to improvement in 1887.

In 1890, however, immigration through the port of New York was taken out of the hands of State authorities and placed under the jurisdiction of the United States Commissioner on Immigration. All other immigration stations in the country passed to federal control eight years before. The federal government began immediate steps to expand immigration facilities in New York City, then as now the largest port receiving immigrants. Castle Garden was closed and in December, 1890, it was converted into an aquarium which it has been ever since. A year later, immigrants were routed through Ellis Island in New York Harbor.

Source: Foreign Language Information Service, New York: Index No. 4939 (February 24, 1941).

would enable the nation to achieve its manifest destiny. And so despite some tinkering with policy at the edges, the major thrust of immigration policy remained supportive of massive, large-scale immigration. Even as some political forces called for a reduction of immigration, the nation moved on to experience its greatest ever influx. Immigration waves reached their zenith in the period 1880–1920.

This chapter closes with Box 2.4, which briefly summarizes an article about the closing of the Castle Garden immigration station. This article, published on the occasion of the tearing down of the station, which prior to Ellis Island, was the busiest of the nation's major immigrant receiving and processing stations, is notable for its description of the role that Castle Garden played during the Open-Door Era of immigration policy-making discussed in this chapter.

NOTES

1. These claims are cited in Parrillo: 133 and Louis Adamic: 181. They are disputed by the research of Shafer: 32–49. Not all German immigrants were enthusiastic supporters of the war. Rippley discusses several rural counties in Wisconsin where the Germans remained loyal to the Democratic Party. He cites the antidraft riots among Germans of Milwaukee, and in Ozaukee and Washington counties nearby.

2. Parrillo: 137. Dinnerstein and Reimers cite the fact that by 1860 some two-thirds of the domestics in Boston were Irish. See also Oscar Handlin's, *Boston's Immigrants* (Cambridge: Harvard University Press, 1979).

3

The Door-Ajar Cycle, 1880–1920

INTRODUCTION: NATIONAL SECURITY CONCERNS AND EXPANDING INDUSTRIALIZATION

Although immigrants from South/Central/Eastern (SCE) European nations had arrived in the United States during colonial times and throughout the period 1820–1880, their numbers and influence were comparatively small until after 1880. Indeed, 1896 represents the turning point; that is, the year at which, for the first time, the number of immigrants from S/C/E Europe exceeded those from northwestern Europe.

The newcomers left Europe in unprecedented numbers, arriving during the forty years of this cycle in a wave that was characterized as a "flood" of immigration. The tide of immigration rose from under 3 million in the 1870s to over 5 million in the 1880s, another 3½ million in the 1890s, to a peak of 8.8 million in the decade 1900–1910, then tapering off to just over 5,100,000 in the 1910s (Tindall: 823–829). The Contract Labor Law of 1864 established the federal government policy of encouraging immigration by providing a lien on an immigrant's wages by paying for his or her passage. They were drawn here by the explosively expanding urbanization and industrialization processes that created a virtually insatiable demand for cheap labor. In the post-Civil War south, "Big Tobacco" and the movement of the textile industry from New England to the south led to a huge labor demand. In the north, manufacturing was spurred by Edison's inventions and industrial entrepreneurs such as John D. Rockefeller, Andrew Carnegie and Pierpont Morgan (Tindall: 784–796). The nation's security was viewed as depending upon the build up of America's industrial might. The Civil War spurred the industrialization process. The inventiveness of American capitalist entrepreneurs provided the "yeast." In the north, the midwest, and even the south, immigrants made the full rising of industrial capacity possible. Before the Civil War, three-fourths of America's population was rural and agricultural. By the end of the period more than half the population lived in cities, many in huge cities. Chicago, for example, grew from an incorporated city of about 5,000 in 1848, to over 1,690,000 by 1900! Massive immigration made that spectacular growth possible. Immigration satisfied the security need for population to fill and develop the land and to man the ever-burgeoning factories. The industrialization of the economy enabled agriculture to be mechanized, providing the abundance of food production to feed the millions filling the cities of the industrial northeast and midwest. Publication of a famous paper by Frederick Jackson Turner, in 1893, marked the "closing of the frontier."

The 1880s witnessed considerable labor strife. Labor unions resurged and nationalized during the period. On May 3, 1884 the International Harvester plant near Chicago was struck, leading to violence attributed to anarchists, many of whom were immigrants. An economic recession in 1892 and a depression in 1893–1894 set off more labor strife, such as the Homestead Steel Strike and the Pullman Strike (Tindall: 807–809, 893).

These developments fed resurgence in the 1880s of nativist groups advocating restrictions on immigration, for example, the resurgent Ku Klux Klan and the American Protective Association (Tindall: 827–829). The Populist Party, begun in 1891 in Cincinnati, Ohio, also advocated reduced immigration (Tindall: 891–897).

The 1890s proved to be an important turning point in U.S. foreign policy. After more than a century of keeping America's strategic sights focused almost exclusively on its own hemisphere, the United States emerged by the end of the decade as a nation with undisguised global ambitions. Its reach stretched well beyond its immediate neighborhood. In 1879, the U.S. navy ranked seventeenth in the world, by 1893 it ranked seventh (Kupchan: 173).

In U.S. foreign policy, the era is characterized by the "new imperialism," which saw such developments as American incursions into Santo Domingo, Samoa, and Hawaii, which became a U.S. territory with the Treaty of Annexation in 1893. The nation developed into a world power by vastly increasing, and increasingly using, its naval power, particularly during the 1890s in Latin America. The nation's appetite for such expansionism was whetted and exemplified by the Spanish-American War, begun after the ship, *Maine*, blew up in Havana Harbor on February 15, 1897. President McKinley delivered a war message to Congress on April 20, 1897 and the Congress declared war on April 25th, making it retroactive to April 21st. John Hay declared it a "splendid little war." Commodore George Dewey took Manila Bay in the Philippines on August 13th. In Cuba, the military campaign there gave prominence to Theodore Roosevelt and his famous "Rough Riders." The Treaty of Paris ended the conflict on December 10th, adding to American territory the islands of Puerto Rico, Guam, and the Philippines. The annexation of Hawaii in 1893 and these acquisitions as a result of the Spanish-American War marked the arrival of the United States as a "Pacific Power," as well as securing its place among the "major powers" of the world—notably, Great Britain, France, Germany, and Russia (Tindall: 899–939; Kupchan: 173–174).

Theodore Roosevelt went on to be elected president. His foreign policy was expansionist and used U.S. naval power to secure commercial access and success. In 1901, his "Roosevelt Corollary" (to the Monroe Doctrine) was used to promote his Dollar Diplomacy. He used U.S. naval power to back up tough diplomacy in 1902–1903 in Venezuela, and in 1904 in the Domincan Republic. He forced rival pacific power, Japan, into agreeing to the "Gentlemen's Agreement" of 1907 that used such economic influence to make Japan agree to voluntary limitation of emigration of its citizens to the United States. Before he left office, he celebrated America's rise to the status of a world power by sending the U.S. fleet—the Great White Fleet—around the world in 1907 (Tindall: 921–937; Kupchan: 173–174).

As scholars of American national security policy noted:

> The size of the army almost doubled from 1898 to 1901 as the United States, almost without knowing it, emerged from the "Splendid Little War" as a great power with a limited imperialist position in both the Pacific and the Caribbean (Jordan et al.: 47).

Such foreign adventure was not without its opposition. In October 1899, the American Anti-Imperialist League was founded. The Socialist and the Socialist Labor Parties vigorously campaigned against the war and United States' imperialist ambitions.

The U.S. economy likewise expanded rapidly. By 1900, the population had more than doubled what it was at the end of the Civil War. The railroad network went from 31,000 miles to 250,000 miles by 1900. Wheat production increased eightfold during this period. Oil production increased by 2000 percent and outputs in iron and steel established America as one of the world's major industrial powers. With the economic downturns of the mid-1890s and the official closing of the frontier in 1893, the nation looked overseas to restore its economic vitality and to search for new markets. James Bassett Moore, Assistant Secretary of State during the late 1890s put it this way:

> The United States had moved from a position of comparative freedom from entanglements into a position of what is commonly called a world power.... Where formerly we had only commercial interests, we now have territorial and political interests as well (cited in Kupchan: 175).

THE CHANGE IN IMMIGRATION FLOWS

The fact that these newcomers were far different in their physical and cultural features than previous groups and, of course, than the majority society, plus the fact that they arrived in sufficient numbers to preserve their cultural and social identities within the various ethnic enclaves of the burgeoning cities of the United States, all worked to increase the prejudice and discrimination they experienced. Professor Stanley Lieberson puts it this way.

> What accounted for the exceptionally unfavorable response to the newcomers from these more distant parts of Europe? Several new forces were operating: religious issues; concentration in urban centers; implicit and often explicit racial notions; anxiety about assimilation; and the threats to existing institutions imposed by the enormous numbers arriving. These concerns, later aggravated by domestic issues during World War I as well as the social and political tumult that followed, eventually led to the end of an unrestricted migration policy in the 1920s (Lieberson: 21).

In addition to the millions of Catholics arriving, many of the newcomers were Greek- or Russian-Orthodox, or Jews. More than 2 million Jews fled Europe during this period, about 90 percent of whom came to the United States. Jewish population here rose from around 250,000 in 1877 to over 4 million in 1927 (Dinnerstein and Reimers: 37–38).

As with the previous cycle, several push and pull factors were at work in this vast migration, which saw some 27 million emigrants leave Europe and immigrate to the United States. One push factor was the urbanization/industrialization revolutions then spreading across Europe. These basic changes in society and the economies brought with them severe political, social, and economic disruptions. The newcomers were often fleeing horrendous conditions in their homelands: high birth rates, overpopulation, and cholera, malaria, and typhus epidemics. Such conditions in turn led to political unrest and resulting repression. European governments, in turn, coping with revolutionary pressures brought on by the forces of overpopulation, chronic poverty, the decline of feudalism and its resulting social and economic dislocations, as well as the economic shift from agrarian to industrial concerns, found emigration to be an expedient policy, and they openly encouraged the waves of immigrants bound for the United States.

Unrest in Czarist Russia contributed yet another strong push factor. Jews became the scapegoats for all that country's ills. Government-sponsored pogroms, begun in 1881 with the assassination of Czar Alexander II and continuing for some thirty years thereafter, forced many Jews to flee for their lives. Those brutal campaigns of beatings, killings, and lootings were exemplified by the 1903 pogrom in Kishineff, Russia. Some 2,750 families were affected: forty-seven people were killed and another 424 were wounded. Scores of Jewish homes were burned down, and their shops pillaged (Dinnerstein and Reimers: 38).

A number of pull factors were also involved. Transatlantic travel via the steamship lines facilitated the journey. Letters from friends and relatives in the United States developed into *chain migrations*, inducing many of their family and former village inhabitants to join them in coming to the United States. Letters from friends and relatives in the United States spoke of the ample opportunities rather than the hardships of relocation. Finally, the promise of the "golden opportunity" afforded by the United States was the beacon that drew millions to its shores.

On arrival, however, they often found themselves trapped in the teeming urban centers. Slum-bred cholera epidemics forced the general mortality rate of the city of New York to rise dramatically. The tenement slum dwellers of the city's East Side comprised the world's most densely populated district. Its 290,000 persons per square mile exceeded by far the 175,800 persons per square mile of Old London. The great influx contributed to a virtual explosion of city population. Chicago's growth, for example, between 1850 and 1900, was equivalent to building a city to house nearly 34,000 persons a year, every year for the fifty-year period! Immigrant newcomers accounted for a significant portion of that explosive growth rate. By 1920, for example, the new immigrant groups comprised 44 percent of New York's total population, 41 percent of Cleveland's, 39 percent of Newark's, and 24 percent of Boston's, Buffalo's, Detroit's, Philadelphia's, and Pittsburgh's.

Out on the West Coast, fear of the Yellow Peril, as we have seen, led to Sinophobia. A number of groups agitating against Chinese immigration, such as the Order of Caucasians, the People's Protective Alliance, the Teamsters, and the Workingman's Party coalesced into the Chinese Exclusion League, and later on, the Asian Exclusion League. Their movement to pass legislation in Congress met with opposition from the executive branch. A Chinese Exclusion Act was passed in 1879, but vetoed by President Rutherford B. Hayes on the grounds that it violated, as it so clearly did, the Burlingame Treaty. This forced negotiations to amend the treaty, which was ratified in October 1881 (22 Stat. L., 726: 1037–1039). Immediately after, Congress passed a second bill, on May 6, 1882, which came to be known as the Chinese Exclusion Act (22 Stat. 58; 8 U.S.C.). The act uses the term "suspension" rather than "exclusion," and in response to President Arthur's earlier veto, it sets the time period for the act at ten years rather than the twenty-year ban of the 1879 bill.

This Act, and the Act of August 3, 1882 on the Regulation of Immigration (22 Stat. 214; 8 U.S.C.), which levied a 50-cent head tax on all immigrants, charged the Secretary of the Treasury to establish contacts with each state's commissioner of immigration and banned the immigration of criminals. It clearly signaled the dramatic shift in direction of immigration policy-making from the unrestricted open-door policy to one that would increasingly impose various types of restriction. In 1887, Congress amended the Contract of Labor Act of 1885 by extending it and increasing the authority of the Secretary of the Treasury to implement and enforce the act (24 Stat. 414; 8 U.S.C.). These acts demark the beginning of the Door-Ajar Era or cycle of immigration policy-making.

As Table 2.1 shows, a number of epidemic disease outbreaks marked the beginning of the era and contributed to fears of the impact immigrants from S/C/E Europe and Asia might have on the nation's health. Fortunately, a number of important medical breakthroughs offered hope of preventing such epidemics from developing into pandemics. In 1882, a German doctor and bacteriologist, Robert Koch, discovered the causative bacillus for tuberculosis, and by 1921 an effective vaccine was developed to prevent it. In 1893, Koch developed a vaccine for typhoid fever and the outbreaks of the disease in 1900–1910 were generally quickly checked. In 1893, the bacillus for diphtheria was discovered and an antitoxin was developed. With the discovery of the bacteria causing many of the most dangerous diseases, effective treatments, sera, and preventative practices were developed as well. Once medical officers realized that fleas, lice, rats, and similar vermin were the carriers that spread the diseases (e.g., cholera and plague) from rats to humans, they disinfected to kill off the carriers and more quickly limited epidemic outbreaks and even prevented outbreaks from developing. Ships' holds and cargo were fumigated, as were wooden structures on the piers and wharfs of ports of embarkation and debarkation. During the 1890s, the United States Marine Hospital Service, which became the Public Health Service in 1912, conducted the fumigations and inspections at ports of entry. The Service also began sending its doctors to foreign ports of embarkation to assist those countries in developing disinfection and inspection procedures and to help combat outbreaks of epidemics of contagious diseases. They certified ships before they began their journey to the United States. The federal government even purchased and shipped "fumigation chambers" to ports where epidemics like cholera and typhus broke out.

Figure 3.1 presents the origins of U.S. immigration, by region, for the decades 1880 through 1920, the Door-Ajar Era. The following section of this chapter highlights the immigration patterns of the major ethnic groups making up the *new* immigrant wave.

THE NEW IMMIGRANTS' PATTERNS

Italian Immigration

Italian immigration is a phenomenon almost exclusively of the period after 1870. As of 2001, their immigration exceeded 5,430,000 in total. In the 2000 census, 15,916,396 people claimed Italian ancestry. Today they remain concentrated in the east, where over 51 percent reside. The remaining Italian-Americans were distributed at 17 percent, respectively, in the midwest and the south, and 15 percent in the west. Italians continue to come. Among them, over a half-million people (643,203) acknowledged being born in Italy, among whom nearly 10 percent came between 1980 and 2000. Among those foreign-born, 72.6 percent were naturalized citizens and 27.4 percent were not yet citizens (see LeMay, 2005: 130).

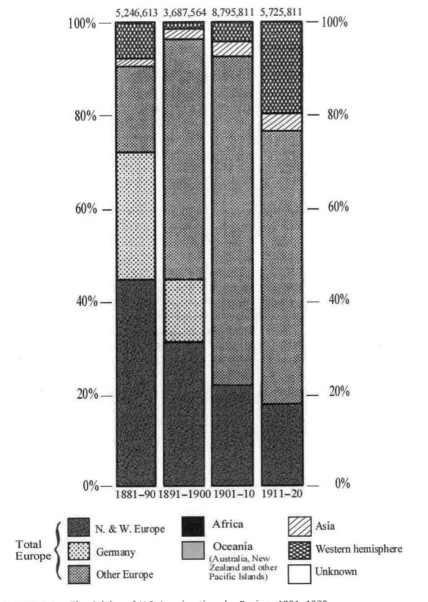

FIGURE 3.1. The Origins of U.S. Immigration, by Region, 1881–1920
Source: U.S. Bureau of Census, *Historical Statistics of the United States, Colonial Times to 1970.* Washington, D.C.: U.S. Government Printing Office (1975).

There was some colonial and pre-Civil War immigration from Italy. As early as the 1620s, the Virginia colony had a few Italian wine growers. Pre-Revolutionary War immigration from Italy was lightly scattered among Virginia, Georgia, the Carolinas, New York, and Florida. Repression in Europe in the 1870s forced a number of Italian intellectuals and revolutionaries to emigrate. Although small in number, those pre-1880 immigrants, mostly from the northern provinces of Italy, had considerable impact on the areas where they settled. They founded the opera in the United States during the 1830s and 1840s. From the 1820s to the 1870s, Italian artists were brought in by the federal government to create commissioned public artwork. By 1848, two Italian immigrants had been elected to the Texas state legislature. A year later, in New York, Sechi de Casali founded *L'Eco d' Italia,* a prominent Italian newspaper that supported the Whig Party and later the Republicans.

By the 1850s, there was an Italian settlement in Chicago, where they served as saloonkeepers, restaurateurs, fruit venders, and confectioners, as well as common ditch-diggers and commissioned artists. They were lured to California by the gold rush. Instead of mining, however, most became wine growers, vegetable farmers, and merchants, giving rise to "the Italian American folklore that 'the miners mined the mines, and the Italians mined the miners'" (Iorizzo and Mandello, 1971: 13). Early Italian-Americans were often skilled craftsmen who were of middle to upper class in background and who came seeking better economic opportunity. These characteristics and motivations, however, changed radically after the 1870s in response to new forces at work, to both push and to pull factors.

The Risorgimento, resulting in the unification of Italy in 1870, sparked a mass exodus of nearly 9 million Italians who crossed the Atlantic to both North and South America seeking better economic conditions denied them by the very movement they had supported at home. The trickle of northern Italians became a flood from the south. From 1881 to 1910, more than 3 million Italians entered the United States. Most settled in the cities of the industrial northeast. By 1930, New York City's Italian-Americans numbered over 1 million and they comprised 15.5 percent of the population (Federal Writer's Project, *The Italians of New York*: viii.)

This flood of immigrants was by no means a static bloc. There was considerable mobility after their arrival, as they moved back and forth between Italy and America. They lived here in enclaves known as "Little Italys." Data from 1910 to 1914 showed that about half of those who arrived here returned to Italy to winter there, working the remainder of the year in the United States (Nelli, 1970).

Several push and pull factors influenced Italian immigrants to undertake the arduous uprooting migration to the United States. Most left Italy because of economic factors, fleeing the shackles of dire poverty. During the 1890s, agricultural workers in Italy earned between 16 and 30 cents per day, and during the winter season that fell to 10 to 20 cents per day. Italian miners received from 30 to 56 cents per day. General laborers received $3.50 for a six-day workweek, compared to $9.50 for a fifty-six-hour workweek in the United States. Carpenters in Italy earned 30 cents to $1.40 per day, or $1.80 to $8.40 for a six-day workweek. That same worker in the United States received an average of eighteen dollars for fifty hours of work per week (Iorrizo and Mondello: 48). Floods, volcanic eruptions, and earthquakes plagued the country and contributed to its bleak agricultural outlook, especially in the south. That region was also especially hard hit by phylloxera, a disease that killed off agricultural plants on a scale similar to the potato blight of the 1840s. Southern Italy was further troubled by frequent and severe epidemics of malaria. Others fled the compulsory military service.

Far more important were the pull factors. The development of the steamship lines made the journey cheaper, faster, and easier. The glowing reports of relatives and acquaintances about the wealth of opportunity drew others. Returning "Americani," some of whom made the trip back and forth, had sufficient money not only to return to Italy temporarily for brides, but also to attract many others to emulate their success in America. State governments, such as those of Illinois, New York, Pennsylvania, California, and Louisiana hired agents to work in Italy to contract for laborers. And they came—from 1890 to 1914 they arrived in excess of 100,000 per year. Between 1900 and 1914, a total of 3 million came. So massive was the out-migration that:

> One author told the humorous and probably apocryphal tale of a mayor who greeted the Prime Minister of Italy then touring the provinces: "I welcome you on behalf of five thousand inhabitants of this town, three thousand of whom are in America and the other two thousand preparing to go (Iorrizzo and Mondello: 48).

Like the Chinese discussed in Chapter 2, the southern Italian was often a *sojourner* in his mentality, undoubtedly associated with the cultural and social background of the peasant, as opposed to the background of the earlier northern Italians. For historical reasons, the *Mezzogiorno* (the south) was more traditional, more backward, and poorer than the north. The *contadini* (peasants) were at the bottom of a still largely feudal society. Oppressed and exploited by *signori* and *borghesi* alike, they were despised as *cafoni* (boors). Illiterate, unschooled, lacking in self-confidence, the peasantry was preindustrial in culture and mentality—not a very good preparation for life in America's teeming tenement slums.

The peasants' motive to immigrate was not only to escape the grinding poverty but also to improve his family's lot by earning money to buy land in his village in Italy. Many came intending to work, save, and return after several years with a few hundred dollars. Like the Chinese, to whom they were often unfavorably compared, the Italians were sojourners, predominately young males. Of the millions who emigrated, about half did in fact return to their villages, having accomplished their mission or having met with defeat. Even those who remained in America often nourished thoughts of the day they could return. Why learn English, why become a citizen, why Americanize, if one were going back to the old country, if not this year, then the next? Italians settled into the teeming cities where they managed to find jobs in a variety of occupations: common laborers on the railroads, digging canals and waterways, digging the sewer systems and laying pipes for the water supply, and digging the subways. Many took up vending and vegetable farming. In contrast to their experience in the homeland, truck farming in the United States was a good investment. Match and shoe factories recruited laborers and soon found that chain migration was so effective that they no longer needed agents to recruit the laborers.

Some settled into more rural areas and occupations. In San Francisco, they dominated the fruit- and vegetable-farming business. They were so prominent in that market in California that "Del Monte" became a household word. In 1881, the Italian-Swiss colony established at Asti in Sonoma County sparked the development of the wine industry there. A smaller but comparable role was played in the wine industry in upstate New York. Other important agricultural settlements included Vineland and Hammonton, New Jersey, and Geneva, Wisconsin. In 1850, Louisiana had more Italians as laborers in the cotton fields than any other state, and New Orleans had a larger population of Italians than any other city. By 1920, however, New York City led the nation with its more than one-half million Italian residents.

They arrived by the hundreds of thousands precisely when the United States was experiencing an economic downturn. The turbulent socioeconomic unrest following the Panic of 1873 and the subsequent crippling depression led to rising anti-Semitism, the emerging Jim Crow movement, and growing antipathy toward European immigration, especially those coming from SCE Europe. The latter were viewed by the native stock as radicals and criminals who filled the ever-growing slums, fueled class conflicts, and contributed to the development of urban political machines and their blatant political corruption.

They did seem to be filling the cities. According to the 1910 census, Italian immigrants accounted for 77 percent of Chicago's foreign-born population, 78 percent of New York's, and 74 percent of Boston's, Cleveland's, and Detroit's. In the late 1880s and 1890s, depression-induced violence swept the country and was frequently directed at the Italians.

Intense discrimination against Italian-American immigrants affected their living conditions. Nearly 90 percent lived in "Little Italy" enclaves of the major cities where conditions were grim. Jacob Riis, the famous "muck-racking journalist," describes the slums in and around "The Bend," "Bandit's Roost," and "Bottle Alley." These characterized the Mulberry Street-Mulberry Bend area composing New York City's first Little Italy section. He says about the area as:

> Half a dozen blocks on Mulberry Street there is a rag-pickers settlement, a sort of overflow from "the Bend," that exists today in all its pristine nastiness. Something

like forty families are packed into old two-story and attic houses that were built to hold five, and out in the yards additional crowds are, or were until very recently, accommodated in shacks built of all sorts of old boards and used as drying racks by the Italian stock (Riis, 1971: 49).

Conditions such as those described by Riis were all too common. Many other studies documented similar conditions. One survey found that 1,231 Italians were living in 120 rooms in New York. Another report stated that they could not find a single bathtub in a three-block area of tenements. In Chicago, a two-room apartment often housed an Italian family of parents, grandparents, several children, cousins, and boarders. A 1910 survey in Philadelphia noted that Italian families had to live, cook, eat, and sleep in the same room, and many tenants shared outhouses and a water hydrant—the only plumbing facilities available—with four or five other families. In addition, many kept chickens in their bedrooms and goats in their cellars (Dinnerstein and Reimers, 1988: 48).

Perhaps ironically, concentration into such enclaves helped them to cope. One way was the *padroni* system. Although probably exaggerated as to its exploitive nature and extensiveness, this form of a "boss" system was an important mechanism for the immigrant. The padroni knew individual employers, spoke English, and understood American labor practices. They were invaluable to American business in need of gangs of laborers. Newcomers depended on them for finding jobs and other services, collecting wages, writing letters, acting as a banker, supplying room and board, and handling dealings between workers and employers.

Congress reacted to such conditions and exploitation of immigrant labor when it passed what became known as the Foran Act in 1885. This law prohibited the immigration of contract labor and imposed fines on the masters of vessels bringing such immigrants to the United States or the employers of any such laborer imported under a contract. Its major provisions are summarized in Box 3.1.

Despite the Foran Act, the "golden era" of the padroni system was from 1890 to 1900. Conditions of poverty drove many families to work long and hard and forced their young to forego school to work at very early ages. In 1897, an estimated two-thirds of the Italian workers in New York City were controlled by padroni. Though exploitive, the system nonetheless helped them to find jobs and eased the acculturation and incorporation processes. After 1900, it declined rapidly when others provided social services previously given out by the padroni. Railroad and construction officials investigated and became aware of the worst abuses. They found laborers without the padroni. Finally, the sheer massive numbers of immigrants pouring into the settlements exceeded what the padroni could handle. Later, immigrants were less dependent on bosses for housing, jobs, and persons to assist them with English or with contacts with government or labor officials.

BOX 3.1. ACT OF FEBRUARY 26, 1885: PROHIBITION OF CONTRACT LABOR (THE "FORAN ACT")

Be it enacted by the Senate and House of Representatives of the United States of America in Congress assembled, That from and after the passage of this act it shall be unlawful for any person, company, partnership, or corporation, in any manner whatsoever, to prepay the transportation, or in any way assist or encourage the importation or migration of any alien or aliens, any foreigner or foreigners, into the United States, its Territories, or the District of Columbia, under contract or agreement, [sic] parol from or special, express or implied, made previous to the importation or migration of such alien or aliens, foreigner or foreigners, to perform labor or service of any kind in the United States, its Territories, or the District of Columbia.

Sec. 2. That all contracts or agreements, express or implied, parol, or special, which may hereafter be made by and between any person, company, partnership, or corporation, and any foreigner or foreigners, alien or aliens, to perform labor or service or having reference to the performance of labor or service by any person in the United States, its Territories, or the District of Columbia previous to the migration or importation of the person or persons whose labor or service is contracted for into the United States, shall be utterly void and of no effect.

Sec. 3. That for every violation of any provision of section one of this act the person, partnership, company, or corporation violating the same, by knowingly assisting, encouraging or soliciting the migration or importation of any alien or aliens, foreigner or foreigners, into the United States...shall forfeit and pay for every such offense the sum of one thousand dollars....

Sec. 4. That the master of any vessel who knowingly brings within the United States on any such vessel and land, or permit to be landed, from any foreign port or place, any alien laborer, mechanic, or artisan, who, previous to embarkation on such vessel, had entered into contract or agreement, parol or special, express or implied, to perform labor or service in the United States, shall be deemed guilty of a misdemeanor, and on the conviction thereof, shall be punished by the fine of not more than five hundred dollars for each and every such alien laborer, mechanic, or artisan so brought as aforesaid, and may also be imprisoned for a term not exceeding six months.

Sec. 5. That nothing in this act shall be so construed as to prevent any citizen or subject of any foreign country temporarily residing in the United States, either in private or official capacity, from engaging, under contract or otherwise, persons not residents or citizens of the United States to act as private secretaries, servants, or domestics for such foreigner temporarily residing in the United States as aforesaid; nor shall this act be construed so as to prevent any person, or persons, partnership, or corporation from engaging, under contract or agreement, skilled workmen in foreign countries to perform labor in the United States in or upon any new industry not presently established in the United States; Provided, That the skilled labor for that purpose cannot be otherwise obtained; nor shall the provisions of this act apply to professional actors, artists, lecturers, or singers, nor to persons employed strictly as the personal or domestic servants, nor to ministers of any recognized religious denomination, nor persons belonging to any recognized profession, nor professors for colleges and seminaries; Provided, That nothing in this act shall be construed as prohibiting any individual from assisting any member of his family to migrate from any foreign country to the United States for the purpose of settlement here....

Source: 23 Stat. 332; 8 U.S.C.

One mechanism that helped Italian immigrants to move up on the employment ladder was involvement in the American labor movement. Their role was rather a mixed one. Initially Italians were used as scabs and strikebreakers. This gave rise to the commonly accepted view that they were antiunion or hard to organize because they were very conservative. In places where they were barred from union membership and activity, they often did play such a role. But where unions were open to them, and where such organization looked likely to succeed, Italians provided a significant number of members and even local leadership. By the early 1890s, Italians ranked second only to Poles in percentage of white ethnics belonging to blue-collar, working-class, organized labor unions.

Unlike the Irish, Italians found the church less useful in assimilation. Their anti-Irish attitudes spilled over into their relationship with the church whose hierarchy was usually Irish-dominated. Gradually, however, Italian-American priests were ordained who better met their needs, and inroads into the upper levels of the hierarchy were achieved by the 1930s. After that, the church did prove useful as a means of their assimilation.

Also aiding them to adjust to life in America was a wide variety of mutual aid or benevolent societies. These self-help associations began early in the Italian-American experience. San Francisco, for instance, had an Italian Mutual Aid Society in 1858. The Italian Union and Fraternity started in New York in 1857. By 1912, there were 212 such societies in New York City alone; by 1919, Chicago had eighty societies. They often began as burial societies or as groups to help their members find jobs and housing. They soon developed into organizations providing insurance, a host of social services, and the basis of the social life of many immigrants.

Mafia and crime-related organizations emerged in a similar fashion. The mob violence and discrimination directed against Italian immigrants contributed to the rise of criminal activities, in part as self-protective associations. Careers in crime became a "curious ladder of social mobility" (Vecoli and Lintelman, 1984: 205). When the urban machines and crime organizations linked in the 1910–1930 period, crime organizations provided leaders to political clubs and party activity, especially in Chicago, where Colosimo, Torrio, and Al Capone emerged. Crime became a source of derogatory stereotyping of all Italians as criminals. That image, plus the 1913 depression, undoubtedly played a part in the revival of anti-Italian immigrant fervor by groups such as the Ku Klux Klan in the early 1900s and to the resurgence in the use of perjorative terms like "wop" and "dago."

War influenced Italian-American assimilation as well. Although to a lesser degree than was the case with the Irish, Italian-Americans saw an initial, if short-lived, benefit to their image and acceptability to Anglo America by their service in the Civil War. New York sent a regiment, the Garibaldi Guard, to fight with the Union forces. Their war record was substantial. In addition to the Guard, 100 Italians from New York served with Union forces, three of whom reached the rank of general. The effects of World War I, in which some 300,000 Italian-Americans served, were also profound.

In politics, the Italians used the Irish model, but arriving in substantial numbers three to four decades after the Irish, they did so much less successfully. They moved into the political arena more slowly and sometimes came into conflict with the Irish politicians who had arrived before them and were reluctant to share power or to move over to make room for the newcomers. Such Irish–Italian conflict was common, sometimes severe, and occasionally violent. Italian-American politicians emerged from the various associations, clubs, and societies. They ran as Democrats, Republicans, Socialists, Independents, and Progressives. The Progressive and Republican parties, however, were the most popular among them. Before the 1920s, most of their political activity was at the local level and they typically supported machine candidates. In New York, their political activity included the creation of the Italian Federation of Democratic Clubs.

In 1919, anti-Wilson views swung many of them away from the Democrats. In New York, Republican Fiorello LaGuardia emerged as their political leader. He was elected to the U.S. House of Representatives in 1915 and, after a distinguished war service, again in 1918. In 1920, he won the seat vacated by Al Smith, the Irish-American who was the Democratic Party nominee for president that year.

Greek Immigrants

Americans claiming Greek ancestry numbered 1,175,591 in the 2000 census. Greeks have been coming to the United States since colonial times. A scattering came as explorers, sailors, cotton merchants, gold miners, and as settlers of the ill-fated Smyrna colony in Florida in 1768. They did not arrive in significant numbers, however, until after 1880. Between 1900 and 1920, they reached their peak immigration when 350,000 arrived. Although they came from all parts of Greece, the majority were young, unskilled males from the villages in the south.

As with other S/C/E European nationality groups, various push factors led to their emigration from the Greek islands. Although political persecution played a part, economic conditions in Greece were the most compelling push factor. The rapid rise in population led to overpopulation that the islands simply could no longer support. By 1931, for example, even after several decades of extensive emigration, there were 870 persons for every square mile of cultivated land (Thernstrom 1980). Another significant push factor was the ongoing state of war between Greece and Turkey. The Balkan War of 1912–1913 caused the peak period of Greek immigration to the United States, when many fled the compulsory military service in what they considered to be a Turkish tyranny. Many Greeks, like the Italians and Chinese, came as sojourners, young men intending to earn enough money to provide a substantial dowry for the prospective brides in their families. The fact that about 95 percent of the early Greek immigrants were young males meant that many returned home for brides.

The opportunity for better jobs was the single most important factor drawing Greeks to the United States. Those who arrived in the 1880–1920 period settled in one of three major areas: the west, to work on railroad gangs and in the mines; New England, to work in the textile and shoe factories there; and New York, Chicago, and other large cities, to work in factories, as busboys, dishwashers, bootblacks, and peddlers.

Like the Italians discussed earlier, Greeks used and were exploited by a *padrone* system. The padrone found jobs for the immigrants, assisted with language problems, and settled disputes. Often the clients of the padrone were young boys sent directly to him, who arranged for their room and board and a small wage. The wage was prearranged and agreed to by the parents. Unfortunately, they did not know the conditions under which the boys lived—squalid and crowded basement rooms in the heart of the tenement slums. They typically worked eighteen hours a day with no time set aside for lunch. The system was highly profitable for the padrone, who made an average of $100 to $200 and in some cases as much as $500 per year per boy. The boys themselves would receive about $100 to $180 annually in wages. The padrone system has been described as a modernized version of the indentured servant system of the late seventeenth and early eighteenth centuries (Soloutos, 1964).

Although a majority of Greek immigrants were young and unskilled, some educated and skilled Greeks also immigrated. They met with unforeseen problems there. Greek lawyers could not practice law until learning English, studying for one year in an American law school, and then passing the bar exam. Greek physicians had it somewhat better; they were able to take a qualifying exam in Greek. Unless they were able to master a reasonable amount of English quickly, however, their practice was limited to serving other Greek Americans. Many college graduates caught the emigration fever, but few had opportunities to proceed with their various interests. For the educated Greek, it was difficult to find employment commensurate to their educational qualifications, and they felt it was beneath their dignity to work as unskilled laborers.

A sizable number managed to start their own businesses. They concentrated on confectioneries, candy stores, and restaurants. After World War I, for example, there were an estimated 564 Greek restaurants in San Francisco alone. By the end of World War II, there were 350 to 450 Greek American confectionery shops and eight to ten candy manufacturing concerns in Chicago alone (Moskos, 1980; Parrillo, 1985).

Similar to the Italians, many Greeks went back and forth several times before finally staying in the United States. This back-and-forth pattern slowed their assimilation rate. It fed a mutual lack of understanding with the majority society, and occasionally, severe conflict. In 1904, for instance, a strike broke out in the diesel shops of Chicago. Heated union management conflict left the city in a bad situation. Unaware of the conditions of the strike, inexperienced Greek immigrants served as strikebreakers. Since they broke the strike, they were considered to be the enemy by local unions. A period of severe anti-Greek press followed. Eventually the strike ended with the regular employees returning to work, but by then a strong anti-Greek sentiment developed. In the west, a virulent nativist reaction directed at Greek immigrants erupted. In McGill, Nevada, three Greek immigrants were killed in a 1908 riot. In Utah, where Mormons seemed particularly antiforeign and anti-Greek, they were characterized in the press as a vicious element unfit for citizenship, and as ignorant, depraved, and brutal foreigners. In 1917, a riot in Salt Lake City almost resulted in the lynching of a Greek immigrant accused of killing Jack Dempsey's brother. In Price, Utah, local citizens rioted and attacked Greek stores, forcing American girls who worked in them to return home. The Ku Klux Klan was particularly active in Utah, and they singled out the Greeks as a special target (Moskos, 1980). In Omaha, in 1909, a sizable Greek community of seasonal workers led to a strikebreaking situation resulting in an ugly riot that caused thousands of dollars of damage to the Greek section of that city. Even supposedly scholarly work, such as that of sociologist Henry Pratt Fairchild, reflected anti-Greek sentiment. His work stereotyped Greek and Italian immigrants as being disproportionately "criminal types," and despaired their ever being able to assimilate (Fairchild, 1911).

Greek immigrants tended to settle in small enclaves where they could socialize with one another and practice their religion. Since the church and state were not separated in Greece, almost every Greek immigrant was a member of the Greek Orthodox Church. An unwillingness to practice their faith with others, even with other branches of the Eastern Orthodox Church, tended to isolate them from the mainstream of American religious life, also slowing their assimilation rate.

Greek social life further tended to isolate them. In the Greek enclaves, the community council and the coffeehouses played a major role:

> In the Greek community, the *kinotitos*, or community council, was the governing body of the people. It provided for the establishment of churches and schools, hired and fired priests and teachers, and exerted a constant influence on Greek affairs. One could always gauge the feelings of the group by the actions of the *kinititos*. For recreation, the Greeks flocked to their *kuffenein*, or coffee houses. These served as community social centers where men smoked, drank, conversed, and played games in what became literally a place of refuge after a hard day of work or an escape from the dank and dreary living quarters. No Greek community was without its *kuffenein*, and one chronicler reported that in Chicago before World War I, "every other door on Bolivar Street was a Greek coffee house" (Dinnerstein and Reimers, 1988: 54).

The Greek Church, the Greek-language press (such as the *Atlantis*), and the more than 100 Greek societies all encouraged cohesiveness and slowed their social and political incorporation. The largest and most notable of the many Greek societies was the American Hellenic Educational Progressive Association (AHEPA). It was founded in 1922 to preserve Greek heritage and help immigrants understand the American way of life. Greek family life was close-knit and stressed education, particularly higher education. Law and medicine were especially valued. Greek education impacted the entire family. Greek children went to two schools: the public school and the Greek-language school. Mandatory for most children, the purpose of the latter was to maintain communication between the parents, the child, and the church and thereby to preserve the Greek heritage in the new land. These schools were usually taught by priests to ensure the church's life-long influence on the new generation. Children went to public school until mid-afternoon, then the Greek-language school until early evening. This process of dual education made it nearly impossible for Greek immigrant children to participate in the after-school activities of the public school, slowing their own assimilation and that of their families.

Slavic Immigrants

Immigrating overwhelmingly in the late nineteenth and early twentieth centuries, East European groups traditionally discussed as the Slavic peoples were often treated alike and experienced many similarities in their emigration, acculturation, and assimilation patterns. Like the Irish, Italian, and Greek immigrant groups discussed earlier, they used politics as a means of accommodation and incorporation into the American society. Since they came later and generally in poorer conditions, they are among the white ethnics who have incorporated more slowly.

They can be grouped into three regions: the Eastern Slavs, the Western Slaves, and the Southern Slavs. Eastern Slavs include the Russians, White Ruthenians, and Ukrainians. Western Slaves include the Poles, Czechs, Slovaks, and Lusatin Serbs. Southern Slavs, located in southwestern Europe, primarily in the Balkan Peninsula, are Slovenians, Croatians, Montenegrins, Serbs, Macedonians, and Bulgarians.

Their migration to the United States is almost completely a phenomenon of the post-1870s. Their largest numbers came between 1890 and 1921, when the immigration act sharply curtailed them. During colonial times, a few Slavic settlers reached the New Amsterdam and New Sweden colonies, and some Moravians joined the Quaker colony in Pennsylvania. The earliest Russian colonists date back to 1747, when a colony settled in Alaska's Kodiak Island. Some Ukrainian immigrants of the colonial era were missionaries in California. Polish Americans proudly stress the role of Generals Pulaski and Kosiusko as heroes of the American Revolutionary War.

Slavic immigrants who came after 1880 tended to settle in the industrial centers of the northeast, some 80 percent of whom were in an area bounded by Washington, D.C. in the southeast, St. Louis in the southwest, and the Mississippi River, Canada, and the Atlantic Ocean. Two-thirds of them can be found in New York, New England, Pennsylvania, and New Jersey. Sizable numbers are also located in Illinois and Ohio. The major cities in which they settled were: New York, Chicago, Detroit, Cleveland, Boston, Philadelphia, Milwaukee, Buffalo, Baltimore, Pittsburgh, Providence, San Francisco, and Los Angeles.

Slavic immigrants tended to replace German and Irish immigrants in the mines and factories of Pennsylvania and the midwest and in the slaughterhouses of Chicago. Like the Chinese, Italians, and Greeks already discussed, Slavic immigrants were also sojourners, making up the majority of the 2 million aliens who returned to Europe between 1908 and 1914. They also experienced severe segregation, frequently manifested in ghettoization, and considerable economic exploitation. The fact that their young boys began work at an early age, typically for a six-day, ten hours per day work a week, meant that they climbed the socioeconomic ladder very slowly. Their peasant backgrounds, longer periods of economic deprivation, which led to child labor and, therefore, less formal educational achievement among the second generation, are all factors that contributed to their slower incorporation rates. This section will discuss the three largest subgroups among the Slavs, the Hungarians, the Poles and the Russians, in greater detail and as exemplars of the Slavic immigrants more generally. By 2001, a total of 1,678,456 immigrants had come from Hungary. In the 2000 census, 1,510,878 persons claimed Hungarian ancestry, 9,029,440 persons claimed Polish ancestry, and 2,975,628 identified themselves as Russians (accessed online at http:www.census.gov/).

Hungarian Immigrants

An estimated 2 million Hungarians came between 1871 and 1920, although about half returned home before World War I. By 1920, for example, New York had 76,000 Hungarian immigrants residing there. Cleveland's Hungarian population was so large that it was referred to as "an American Debucan," and it grew remarkably fast. In twenty years, they increased from 8 to 18 percent of that city's foreign-born population (Weinberg: 174–175).

Wherever they settled, they created strong ethnic enclaves with a persistent subculture. Their community, called Buckeye, encouraged the retention of their cultural identity. They clustered together, creating their own shops and small businesses: butcher shops, confectionaries, bakeries, hardware, clothing stores, taverns, pharmacies, and the like. They also concentrated on the nation's iron, steel, and rubber works. Like the Greeks, they too employed a padrone system, especially for getting work in work-gangs employed as stone cutters in the quarries, or as farm laborers in the south. Conditions were often bad. In the 1920s, they worked an average of sixty hours per week for $10.50 (Weinberg, 1971: 177). They were also mistreated by their bosses. In Georgia, for example, where they worked in the lumber camps, they were whipped. One particular situation led to the bosses being charged under the antipeonage laws, with ironic results.

As the Hungarian peon recalled, a peculiar kind of justice was enacted. "Of all things that mixed my thinking of America," the Hungarian later wrote, "nothing was so strange as to find that the bosses who were indicted for holding us in peonage could go free on bail, while we, the laborers who had been flogged and beaten and robbed, should be kept in jail because we had neither money nor friends" (Dinnerstein and Reimers: 45).

In those areas where they settled in sufficiently large numbers to be visible and seen as a threat, anti-Hungarian feelings developed. The perjoritive terms of "Hunky" and "Bohunk" resulted. They, too, and especially those working in the mines, were involved in the labor agitation of the 1890s. A violent incident in Hazelton, Pennsylvania, occurred in 1897. A posse, headed by a sheriff who was a former mine foreman, opened fire on a group of unarmed strikers, most of whom were Hungarian, killing twenty-one and wounding another forty. There was a general agreement among other mine foreman that, had the strikers not been foreign-born, there would have been no bloodshed (Parrillo: 131).

After World War I, when immigration restrictions were enacted in the quota acts, it became clear to Hungarians that their transient status was detrimental to them, and they ended their sojourner pattern. With the 1920s, those seeking naturalization rose dramatically, and they also became involved in politics, typically voting Democratic.

Polish Immigrants

Estimates as to the number of Polish immigrants vary widely since official records were not always counted separately and the area itself varied, at times being part of Germany, Austria-Hungary, or Russia. Thomas and Znaniecki estimated their number at 875,000, while others placed their number at over 1 million.[1] In the 2000 census, 6,542,844 people claimed Polish ancestry, among whom over 400,000 (6.2 percent) were foreign-born.

Historically, about three-fourths of Polish immigrants were farm laborers, unskilled workers, and domestic servants. Less than 12 percent were classified as skilled. One-fourth of them were illiterate, and virtually all came with less than fifty dollars in their possession. Polish immigrants tended to be young male sojourners. Their attachment to the homeland was perhaps enhanced by the fact that the ills of life in Poland could be blamed on foreign occupations. Resentment of the Polish upper class seemed less than was typical among other Slavic groups.

Some Polish immigrants got into farming in the northeast and midwest, concentrating in truck farming in Long Island and the Connecticut Valley, and in corn and wheat farming in the north-central midwest and in the Panna Maria settlement in Texas, which was founded in 1854 entirely of Polish immigrant families. Most of them settled in big cities, such as Buffalo, Chicago, Milwaukee, Pittsburgh, Detroit, and New York. Chicago ranks after Warsaw and Lodz as the third largest Polish center in the world.

Men and boys shared common labor jobs, such as working in the coal mines for ten-hour days, six days per week, for less than fifteen dollars a week. It was common for children to complete only two years of high school before working full time. That pattern perhaps explains why first- and second-generation Polish Americans were slower in upward mobility than so many other immigrant groups. It was not until they reached the third- and fourth-generations that Polish Americans closed the gap. They still are heavily blue-collar workers, 40 percent of whom are unionized.

By far, the most influential social mechanism in the Polish American community is the church. Numerous scholars have noted it as the unrivaled instrument for the organization and unification of the Polish American community.[2] In that, it served an incorporation function for the Poles as the Catholic parish structure did for the Irish. As with Italians and the other Slavic groups, Polish immigrants had difficulty adjusting to the Irish-dominated Catholic Church. Protests against that power structure took several forms: parish mutual aid societies joining with the Polish Roman Catholic Union (PRCU), which was organized in 1873; the Polish National Alliance, founded in 1880; and the Polish National Catholic Church (PNCC), begun in 1897 and reformed in 1904. Today there are fifty independent Polish parishes unified into the PNCC, plus an unknown number of isolated parishes that have split from Rome but have not formally joined the PNCC. The majority of Polish Americans, however, remain faithful to the Catholic Church, and since 1970 inroads into the hierarchy have been made with a number of bishops and archbishops of Polish descent. And, of course, a Pole served as the Roman Pontiff.

Polonia is the term used to designate the total Polish American population. There are an estimated 800 Polish American Catholic parishes. Closely linked to the church are the parochial schools. In the late 1950s, an estimated 250,000 elementary students were being taught by Polish American Catholic nuns, and over 100,000 more students were in catechism classes. In the 1980s, there were still more than 600 Polish parochial schools.

Polish American political activity developed slowly. In the 1920s, for instance, only about 25 percent of Polish Americans turned out to vote. Their voting impact was diluted, moreover, by splitting it rather than voting as a cohesive voting bloc. Since World War II, however, they have remained consistently and highly Democratic, reflecting their blue collar and unionized status.

By most measures of political incorporation, Polish Americans are today nearly fully incorporated, but exhibit a pattern of slower assimilation than many other "white ethnic" groups.

Russian Immigrants

The earliest Russian immigration to the United States goes back to Alaska and California in the mid-1700s. In 1792, the first Russian Orthodox church was built in America, and as early as 1812 a sizable settlement was founded in Sonoma, California, which lasted about thirty years before the entire group of several hundreds returned to Russia at the request of the Czar. The headquarters of the Russian Orthodox Church in America moved to San Francisco in 1872. It was after the 1870s, however, before the first sizable wave of Russian immigrants came. Those coming in the early 1870s were Mennonites who fled to the Great Plains area and numbered some 40,000. From 1900 to 1913, some 51,500 Russian immigrants arrived, about 45 percent of whom were Jews fleeing persecution in Russia. They will be discussed more fully later in this chapter. The peak period of Russian immigration was between 1880 and 1914. Most were peasants seeking better economic opportunity. The 1917 Russian Revolution virtually stopped emigration until about 1970. In the 2000 census, 2,975,628 residents claimed Russian ancestry. They were heavily concentrated in the northeast. A 1998 study found 2,114,506 claiming Russian ancestry, among whom 9.2 percent were Russian-born, and 34.2 percent of those arrived during the 1980–1990 decade, and 65.8 percent of whom came before 1980.

Earlier Russian immigrants worked in coal and other mines and in the iron and steel mills of Pennsylvania and the slaughterhouses of Chicago. In New York City, they worked in the clothing industry and in cigar and tobacco manufacturing. They held unskilled jobs in construction and with the railroads. Except for the United Mine Workers and the Industrial Workers of the

World, they tended to be nonunionized, and their pay was typically low-scale. In 1909, they worked for an average of twelve hours per day for just over two dollars. As late as 1919, Russian immigrants in Chicago earned only twelve to thirty dollars per week.

A few Russians did establish agricultural settlements, which tended to be small and scattered. Most lived in enclaves in the cities and were crammed into substandard housing. Conditions for construction gangs were grim; typically thirty-six men slept in three-tier bunkhouses. In the congested Slavic ghettos in the mining and iron and steel mill towns, health problems were especially severe.

Like other Slavic subgroups, Russian immigrants sought refuge in church and mutual aid associations. By 1916, the Russian Orthodox Church in the United States had nearly 100,000 members in 169 parishes in twenty-seven districts. They had nearly 7,000 students enrolled in 126 schools. Like the Poles, they split off as independent churches to escape the strong control, in their case of the archbishop, who in this case resided in Russia. By 1920, there were such independent church establishments in Chicago, Detroit, New York, Boston, Philadelphia, Baltimore, Bayonne City, New Jersey, and in Lawrence, Massachusetts. The Russian Orthodox Society of Mutual Aid, founded in 1900, grew to over 3,000 members by 1917. These groups provided health insurance, death benefits, and helped the immigrant secure jobs. After the 1917 Revolution, however, the avowedly political association, the Society to Help Free Russia, was formed. It was anti-Bolshevik.

Russian immigrants were active in several unions, most notably the clock-maker's, men's and women's garment workers, the Society of Russian Book-makers, and the Society of Russian Mechanics. As important as the unions, maybe even more so, were the more than 200 Russian socialistic, anarchistic, and radical clubs that began in 1917, the largest of which was the Union of Russian Workers. These latter groups inflamed anti-Russian and anti-Bolshevik attitudes among their new countrymen, and contributed to a wave of prejudice, discrimination, and sometimes violence. In 1919, when the American Communist Party was formed, and a splinter group, the American Communist Labor Party, began in 1920, a hysterical reaction was set-off, leading to the infamous "Palmer Raids," named after Attorney General Palmer, begun on November 7, 1919. Groups like the 100 Percent Americans agitated public opinion over the fear of Bolshevism arising in the United States. These led to the arrest of thousands and the deportation of some 500 immigrants, many aboard the transport ship, *Buford*, that left December 22, and was dubbed "the Soviet Ark." The several hundreds deported to Russia were forced to depart without benefit of public hearing—condemned, if you will, merely for their nationality and their political ideology (Tindall: 1024).

Ironically, the process of rounding up and summarily deporting Russian immigrants contributed to an outbreak of the Spanish Influenza in New York City in 1919. This highly contagious disease took an estimated 20 million lives worldwide. The outbreak in New York followed the detention of the Russian immigrants at the Ellis Island quarantine station as they awaited their forced departure:

> The outbreak preceeded in point of time the recudenscence of the epidemic throughout the country. There was no evidence that the infections came from abroad. In fact, the bulk of the cases were among so-called radicals who had just previously been collected together from many parts of the country. By doing so, conditions analogous to those prevailing in the military camps during 1917 were approximated when large numbers of non-immunes were assembled in crowded quarters. An outbreak of respiratory disease was the inevitable result, the infection having in all probability been brought to the station by them (NARA, RG-90, Central File, 1887–1923, File 219, Box 38, Ellis Island).

This was a year for which activity at Ellis Island was heavy as postwar immigration began to build up. A report of July 22, 1920 recounting the previous year's activities noted that a total of 333,733 aliens were processed at Ellis Island, along with 85,520 citizens and 310,666 crew members, for a grand total of 729,914 persons who had to go through the inspection process. The outbreak of influenza in December 1919 was not as deadly as the earlier outbreak of the disease, but it kept the Ellis Island quarantine station busy. Suspected cases sent to the quarantine hospital numbered one per day in November, increasing to fifteen per day in December, and peaking at fifty-two per day in January 1920, before dropping off to ten per day in February, eleven per day in March, and back down to two per day in April. Aliens, immigration officers, and other employees were all sent to detention. The hospital treated (for all causes) 5,978 patients that year, and its lab examined 10,550 specimens and studied 1,577 x-rays. Two hundred and sixty-four class A-II medical certificates (i.e., of a "dangerous contagious disease") were issued. Of those, 1,152 were deported, and 78 were allowed to land.

A related reaction was the suppression of the Russian language press. From 1900 to 1920, a total of fifty-two Russian-language papers were published. By 1921, only five such Russian dailies were still being published, the oldest having begun in 1902. The fifth daily, the radical *Novi Mir* (The New World), was suppressed by the U.S. government in 1921. These suppressions led many immigrants to return to Russia and it cut-off future immigration here. It also slowed the acculturation and incorporation of those who remained. The anti-Bolshevik attitude spilled over, moreover, and affected other Slavic groups, such as the southern Slavs.

Their involvement in American politics is primarily a post-World War II development, initially focusing on influencing U.S. foreign policy vis-à-vis Russia and the Soviet bloc. In more recent years, they have become more like the Poles and other Slavic subgroups, voting predominantly Democratic. They can best be described as in the beginning stages of political incorporation.

They have not yet elected a prominent Russian American to higher level positions in state- or national-level government.

Eastern European Jews

Data regarding immigration of Eastern European Jews to the United States are sketchy. An estimated 40 to 45 percent of all SCE Europeans entering the United States from 1870 to 1930 were Jewish. One source estimates their immigration from 1899 to 1973 at nearly 2.5 million (Dinnerstein and Reimers: 172–174). They immigrated here for many of the same push and pull factors that motivated the other Slavic groups, plus the added push factor of religious/political oppression, which ultimately became the most compelling cause of their emigration.

By the 1860s, the serfs, or peasant class, attained a degree of freedom and slowly began to develop a small middle class. By 1860, about 5 percent of Russia's labor force was Jewish. Of that segment, 11 percent were employed in industry and 36 percent in commerce. By law, Jews were forbidden to own land, so they became merchants, tailors, administrators, and other commerce-oriented businessmen. Consequently, many Eastern European Jews were urbanites. Ironically, their very persecution made them more suited to the environment they found here than were the other Eastern European immigrant groups. In addition to the urban experience, generally they had better job skills. They were accustomed to organize for self-protection. This eased their acculturation into American life. Sixty-seven percent of Jewish males immigrating here were classified as skilled workers, compared to an average of 20 percent for all other groups (Dinnerstein and Reimers: 44).

They were soon active in the union movement, especially in the garment industry. The Amalgamated Clothing Workers (ILGWU) was predominantly Jewish and Italian. By World War II, about 60 percent of the ILGWU members were Jewish. About half of the city's Jewish labor force worked in the trade. Other occupations they filled included cigar manufacturing, bookmaking, distilling, printing, and skilled carpentry. A 1900 census study found Jewish immigrants in the professions to be the highest of all non-English-speaking immigrants (Leventman: 40; Bayor: 14–15; LeMay, 1985: 92).

The Czarist government used the Jews as scapegoats for long-festering social, economic, and political grievances. They openly encouraged ethnic minorities, particularly the Jews, to emigrate. Jewish immigration to the United States can be directly correlated with historical events in Russia, particularly the pogroms that swept Russia during the 1880s up to World War II. In the Pale of the Settlement area of Russia—the land between the Baltic and the Black seas—those *pogroms* were especially violent, involving looting, pillaging, riots, murders, and in some cases, the total destruction of Jewish ghettos. Government troops would sit idly by or even join in these ventings of frustration upon the hapless Jews. Such pogroms were often followed by educational restrictions and eventually by expulsion. One such pogrom in 1941, in the city of Lasi, resulted in 10,000 fatalities and the victims being buried in a mass grave (LeMay, 2005: 148).

Since the Jews fled both religious and political persecution, leaving Eastern Europe and especially Russia was not as traumatic an experience for them as for many other Russian immigrants. Indeed, to remain in the homeland was to risk life and limb.

Anti-Semitism was experienced in the United States, of course, but it was nothing compared to the pogroms from which they fled. In colonial America, they were commonly disenfranchised, such voting restrictions lasting until 1877 when New Hampshire became the last state to end them. Anti-Semitic attitudes were prevalent, however, and were reflected in the popular culture, which commonly stereotyped Jews as avaricious scoundrels. Such anti-Semitism was generally easily dealt with by the German-Jews, while their numbers remained small. They were typically middle-class. They initially feared the influx of Eastern European Jews, seeing their vast migration as the cause for a new and more violent outbreak of anti-Semitism. They were correct in their assessment, as the new wave did so. As the prejudice escalated, however, they closed ranks with their religious compatriots and helped the newcomers to adjust.

In the 1870s, the largely latent anti-Semitism broke out into the open. In New York, in 1877, Jews were blackballed from the New York Bar Association. In 1878, New York college fraternities followed suit. The Saratoga Springs resort began to bar them and soon a host of private clubs, resorts, and private schools were doing likewise. The Ku Klux Klan revived during the early 1900s and became a leading anti-Semitic force.

Pogroms broke out in Russia in 1903 and 1906, inspiring the Jewish community in the United States to organize to help their brethren. The American Jewish Committee began to raise money for those still suffering in Europe. In 1913, the B'nai B'rith's Anti-Defamation League (ADL) was formed. By 1909, more than 2,000 Jewish charities in the United States spent over $10 million in that year alone. They organized orphanages, educational institutions, homes for unwed mothers, and for delinquent children. They set up hospitals and recreational facilities, and supported the Jewish Theological Seminary. They began a host of Yiddish-language newspapers. Between 1855 and 1915, 150 such newspapers were begun, including the highly influential *Daily Forward*, and a number of Yiddish radio programs in New York (Howe: 518–551).

In both their religious institutions and their strongly cohesive family life, Jewish immigrants stressed formal education. Advanced learning was especially emphasized for males. Professional jobs were held up as the ideal, highly valued for their secure incomes and their social prestige, not only within the Jewish community but in the broader culture as well. By 1915, they made up 85 percent of the student body of New York's City College, one-fifth of those attending New York University, and one-sixth at Columbia University.

Education became *the* route to middle-class status and *the* means of accultur-ation and assimilation.

THE FIRST RESTRICTIONIST LAWS

The effects of the new and massive wave of immigration and its changing composition were significant and rather quickly manifested. A strong move-ment to restrict immigration was underway by the mid-1870s. Marion Bennett summarizes the shift in policy-making during this period as follows:

> The developments of the era 1880–1920 . . . turned national policy from attempts to adjust immigration problems by treaty and executive agreement back to leg-islation, from attempts to restrict immigration by qualitative restrictions alone to restriction of numbers as well, and continued the established policy to discrimi-nate among potential immigrants on the basis of other considerations if it ap-peared to Congress that a particular race or class of immigrants offered less chance of readily assimilating into the dominant pattern of American life (1963: 39).

The first direct targets of the restrictionist movement were the Chinese. As we have seen earlier, their first national legislative success was the Chinese Exclusion Act of 1882. That same year they also banned "lunatics and con-victs." Some state and even local governments (e.g., Boston, New York City, and San Francisco) began imposing a tax on immigrants as a means of re-stricting their influx. Those taxes were declared unconstitutional by the U.S. Supreme Court in the *Henderson v. Mayor of New York* case of 1875. That court ruling set off a six-year campaign agitating for a federal tax. Such a bill was opposed by the steamship lines and the various proimmigration businesses and manufacturing concerns and associations, and the representatives from the various western and midwestern states still desiring and needing open immi-gration to attract the population increases they so desired. In the early 1880s, New York State threatened to close down Castle Garden, then the major re-ception station for immigrants entering the country, if Congress did not act (Maldwyn Jones, 1960: 250–251).

The movement to pass legislation in Congress met with opposition from the executive branch. The imperial designs of the U.S. foreign policy at the time dictated our relations with China. This brought the executive branch to the position of opposing California's efforts to ban Chinese immigration. When Congress passed a Chinese Exclusion Act in 1879, it was vetoed by President Rutherford B. Hayes, on March 1, 1879 (see his veto message in LeMay and Barkan, Document 30: 35) on the grounds that it violated the Burlingame Treaty of 1868. Pressure to restrict their continued immigration kept building.

In the Senate, Charles Sumner of Massachusetts sponsored an amendment to the Fourteenth and Fifteenth Amendments that would have allowed for the naturalization of Chinese. It was defeated 14 to 30, with 28 abstentions

(Ringer: 628). A new treaty was ratified by the Senate in May of 1881 and formally proclaimed by President Chester A. Arthur on October 5, 1881. Immediately upon ratification of the new treaty, Congress passed a new law suspending all Chinese immigration for twenty years. President Arthur vetoed that bill as well (see veto message of April 4, 1882; LeMay and Barkan, Document 32: 50). As we have seen, Congress then passed a new bill, on May 6, 1882 (22 Stat. 58) that virtually stopped all Chinese immigration for ten years, although it did allow some brides to be brought in to "reunite families." Its impact, as we have seen earlier, was dramatic, decreasing the 40,000 Chinese immigrants who entered the year of the act's passage to 8,031 in 1883, and a mere twenty-three by 1885. It specifically prohibited their naturalization as well (Marion Bennett: 17).

The restrictionist forces were not satisfied with this limited ban on one aspect of immigration and one major immigrant group. In August of 1882, they passed the first general immigration law with an avowedly (though still quite limited) restrictionist intention, the Immigration Act of August 3, 1882 (22 Stat. 214; 8 U.S.C.), which excluded "any convict, lunatic, idiot, or any person unable to take care of himself or herself without *becoming a public charge.*" That public charge clause, as we shall see next, became an administrative tool to significantly restrict immigration during periods of recession and depression. The 1882 law assigned responsibility for implementation of the law to the Secretary of the Treasury but left its implementation and enforcement to state boards or officers designated by him (Maldwyn Jones: 251).

In 1885, Congress enacted the Alien Contract Labor Law (23 Stat. 332), the Foran Act. The Knights of Labor, following up on their success with the Chinese Exclusion Act, led organized labor to work hard to get Congress to enact a national law prohibiting contract labor. The Order of American Mechanics, along with patriotic, veteran, and fraternal associations joined in the strident anti-immigration campaign (Divine: 3). The American Protective Association, formed in Clinton, Iowa, in 1887, developed into the largest and most powerful of the Protestant secret anti-Catholic societies. It adopted a strong restrictionist stance. The late 1880s saw social scientists, such as Richmond Mayo-Smith and geologist Nathaniel Shaler, questioning the economic value of or need for immigration. They advocated using the desirability of immigrants groups to assimilate as the criterion for assessing such groups (Maldwyn Jones: 257–258). Their writings presaged the more blatantly racist arguments of the early 1900s.

Ironically, the Statue of Liberty was dedicated in October 1886, precisely when the anti-immigration mood was rising so sharply and when organized nativism was reviving. That mood contrasted sharply with the sentiment expressed in the famous poem, *The New Colossus*, written by Emma Lazarus and dedicated to the Statue of Liberty. It was inscribed on her base:

Not like the brazen giant of Greek fame,
With conquering limbs astride from land to land; Here

At our sea-washed, sunset gates shall stand
A mighty woman with a torch, whose flame
Is the imprisoned lightening, and her name
Mother of Exiles. From her beacon-hand
Glows world-wide welcome; her mild eyes command
The air-bridged harbor that twin cities frame.
"Keep, ancient lands, your storied pomp!" cries she
With silent lips. "Give me your tired, your poor
Your huddled masses yearning to breathe free,
The wretched refuse of your teeming shore,
Send these, the homeless, tempest-tossed to me.
I lift my lamp beside the golden door!"
(as cited in Vecoli and Lintelman: 99).

The mid-1880s was a period of extensive labor strife, radical agitation, and renewed nativism. The Molly McGuires used a violent campaign against the mine owners of Pennsylvania. The Haymarket Riot in Chicago, in May of 1886, preceded by, but a few months, the formation of a new nativist party—the American Party—in California. The passing of the frontier, officially declared closed with the census of 1890, and the growing class conflict of the 1880s, contributed to a growing xenophobia. Congress amended the Chinese Exclusion Act in 1884 by tightening up its provisions as to bringing in brides of resident Chinese aliens and it required all such permanent residents to acquire a "reentry certificate"—that period's version of the infamous green card—before travel to China to get brides, bury family members with their ancestors, and the like. In 1888, Congress rescinded the right of Chinese immigrants who had traveled back to China to return to the United States unless they had obtained certificates of reentry in advance (Act of September 13, 1888, the "Scott Act," 25 Stat. 476; 8 U.S.C., 261–299.) That practice was fairly common among Chinese resident aliens. In 1887, the famous journalist, Joseph Pulitzer, after whom the Pulitzer Prize is named, led the *New York World* newspaper's campaign that vigorously attacked the management of Castle Garden as one of his many crusading ventures. In the summer of 1888, Congressman Ford of Michigan offered a resolution calling for a select committee to investigate the administration of immigration in New York and elsewhere. Castle Garden was officially closed on April 18, 1890 (Pitkin: 10–13). Clearly, sentiment was growing that the nation really did not want the "huddled masses of wretched refuse of their teeming shores, the homeless and tempest tossed" to enter our shores. Tarnish was growing on the golden door.

In October 1888, Congress again amended the Chinese Exclusion Act barring Chinese laborers and rescinding, ex-post-facto—the validity of any certificate of reentry previously granted (25 Stat. 540; 8 U.S.C. 270). This set up a Supreme Court challenge to the Chinese Exclusion Act and dealt with the legal status of the Chinese immigrant as a permanent alien; *Chae Chan Ping v. United States* (130 U.S. 581-611, 1889). Chae Chan Ping was a laborer who had resided in San Francisco for twelve years. He returned to China in 1887. He had in his possession a certificate for reentry as required by the law of 1884. A year later, when he was attempting to return, he was blocked, due to the passage of the October 1888 Act. He sued taking his case to the Supreme Court. The majority opinion of the court ruled against the plaintiff, rejecting his argument of due process (against the ex-post-facto nature of the October 1888 law) and of the treaty rights, and found for the government. It based its decision on the concept of sovereignty. The racial attitudes of the justices and of the period and the "Yellow Peril" theme are reflected in the words of Justice Field, author of the majority opinion, which explicitly linked a more restrictive immigration policy to national security when it stated:

It was the highest duty of every nation to preserve its independence, and give security against foreign aggression and encroachments. [This was true] . . . no matter in what form such aggression and encroachment come, whether from the nation acting in its national character or from the vast hordes of its people crowding in upon us. The government, possessing the powers which are to be exercised for protecting its security, is clothed with authority to determine the occasion on which its powers shall be called forth; and its determination, so far as the subjects affected are concerned, are necessarily conclusive upon all its departments and officers (130 U.S. 1889: 606).

Despite the ex-post-facto nature of the policy and the obvious lack of due process for all Chinese laborers thus affected by the act (many of whom as long-standing aliens had significant property investments here that were in essence being taken from them without due process), the Court ruled in favor of Congress' right and power to make such immigration laws as it saw fit. Aliens did not have the rights of citizens and were, therefore, not governed or protected by the due process clause. In the words of Professor Benjamin Ringer, "In the final analysis, then, the Chinese immigrant—no matter how long he was in the United States—had no vested right of return once he left this country, and could be barred from re-entry by an Act of Congress as could any first arrival" (Ringer: 673).

THE DEPRESSION OF THE 1890S AND SUBSEQUENT LAWS

A depression in 1891 spurred renewed efforts to restrict immigration. An even more severe depression in 1893 contributed to a natural falling-off in immigration. The decade of 1891 to 1900, for example, saw only 3,687,564 immigrants enter compared to the 5,246,613 persons who had come the previous decade (Marion Bennett: 24). These depressions strengthened the spectrum of support and the arguments being marshaled by the restrictionist movement.

In 1891, Congress established the position of Superintendent of Immigration by the Act of March 3, 1891 (26 Stat. 1084; U.S.C. 101). It expanded the classes of individuals excluded from admission, forbade the advertisement for and soliciting of immigrants, increased the penalties for landing an illegal alien, and strengthened the enforcement process. Some regard this act as the crucial one whereby the federal government established its decisive role in immigration affairs. It prohibited the immigration of "paupers, polygamists, and those with contagious diseases," and stipulated the supervision of immigration to be "wholly under federal authority" (Maldwyn Jones: 263).

This act was soon challenged in the courts as well. The U.S. Supreme Court ruled that the law was constitutional in *Nishimura Ekiu v. United States*, 1892 (142 U.S. 651, January 18, 1892). Its majority opinion again stressed the *sovereignty* issue and the power of Congress both to set immigration policy and to delegate such powers to those immigration service officers as it chose to establish.

Senator McPherson of New Jersey had introduced a resolution to establish a station for immigration on Ellis Island. It was passed in the House after but brief debate, and signed into law by President Harrison on April 11, 1890, replacing Castle Garden as the nation's major reception station depot (Pitkin: 13–19). At that time, the Port of New York (i.e., Castle Garden) was the only one at which immigration was handled directly by the Treasury Department. At other ports—Boston, Baltimore, Galveston, Key West, Philadelphia, Portland, New Orleans, and San Francisco—the federal government contracted with state authorities to administer immigration matters through those respective ports. The 1891 law, however, placed immigration matters solely under federal authority by creating the Office of Superintendent of Immigration within the Treasury Department, and charging the superintendent to report to the Secretary of the Treasury, and through that office to the Congress, annually on the work of the office. The Bureau of Immigration was established within the department on July 12, 1891 (Pitkin: 15).

Organized labor blamed the Depression of 1893 on immigrants. A new fervor to extend restrictions was manifested. The Geary Act of 1892 (Act of May 5, 1892, 27 Stat. 25; 8 U.S.C.) extended the Chinese Exclusion Act another ten years. It has been described as the "most repressive legislation ever experienced by the Chinese in America . . . [An act] which violated every single one of the articles of the Treaty of 1880" (Ringer: 658–659; Maldwyn Jones: 263).

Critics of open immigration were no longer content to merely charge that the *new* immigrants had some shortcomings that prevented their adjustment to life in the United States, they began to demand, with increasing vigor, that the entire process of immigration be greatly curtailed, or, indeed, to be brought to an immediate halt (Handlin: 3). In 1892, Senator Henry Cabot Lodge advocated the use of a literacy test to bar immigrants, and, in 1894, a congressional committee on immigration first recommended a bill that proposed the use of a literacy test (Bernard: 13). In 1894, Congress again amended the Exclusion Act and established a Bureau of Immigration (28 Stat. 390; 8 U.S.C. 174). If the open door to immigration was not yet slammed shut, Congressional policy-making was clearly moving in that direction.

The Supreme Court, in 1896, issued its watershed decision in the case of *Plessy v. Ferguson* (163 U.S. 537, May 18, 1896). This decision underscored a racial interpretation of the law that gave a constitutional approval to *de jure* segregation laws in the south (which came to be known as Jim Crow laws). It established the "separate-but-equal" doctrine that lasted until the Court overturned *Plessy* in 1954. The judicial doctrine was important in restricting the rights of all citizens of color in the United States—Blacks, Asians, Hispanics, American Indians—by allowing state governments to pass laws segregating them from white schools, places of public accommodation, and so on.

The restrictionist movement was greatly aided during the 1890s by the development of "scholarly" studies supporting the need for restrictionism by elaborating on the concept of race. A number of eastern intellectuals joined the movement. In 1890, for instance, General Francis A. Walker, President of M.I.T. and incoming President of the American Economic Association, delivered his presidential address to the association in which he called for the sharp reduction of immigration on economic grounds. In 1894, John Fiske, Nathaniel Shaler, and Senator Lodge organized the Immigration Restriction League (Divine: 3). The League spearheaded the restrictionist movement for the next twenty-five years, advocating the need for a literacy test and emphasizing the differences between the *old* and the *new* immigrants as to their assimilation capabilities. This movement began to link anti-immigration and racial ideas to a sense of national security. In their eyes, in order to preserve the "purity" of the American race, immigration had to be restricted. National identity and national "preservation" were intertwined with restrictive policy.

The mid-1890s saw an increase in the strength of the American Protective Association. Its membership peaked in 1894 before declining by the end of the decade due to internal factional splits (Maldwyn Jones: 256). The Knights of Labor contributed their strength to the growing advocacy against the new immigrants and endorsed the use of the literacy test in 1897. Violent outbreaks against Italians and then other Eastern Europeans became almost commonplace from the mid-1890s to the early 1900s. As one scholar put it:

> From the 1890s to the First World War, and in the succeeding decade, a large number of American scholars, journalists, and politicians devoted their talents to elaborating the doctrine of "racism" as the basis for immigration and population policy. In this country the varied and considerable literature which they produced had a profound effect in preparing the public for the National Origins Law before it passed and in creating a set of rationalizations to justify the law after it was passed. We might add that these writings not only molded American attitudes but proved extremely useful in the propaganda of the leaders of Nazi Germany in later years (Bernard: 16).

The creation of the federal immigration bureau was especially important in that, as we have seen, the Supreme Court deferred to those administrative officers all the power granted to Congress over immigration matters. By the

mid-1890s, those immigration officers could and did operate with wide latitude, and their actions reflected the growing racist ideas of the period.

Japanese Immigration

Another trend adding momentum to the restrictionist movement was the
wave of Japanese immigration. At 10 percent of Asian Americans, Japanese
Americans are now the sixth largest Asian group, according to the 2000 census. Their migration to the United States began in 1868, when 148 contract
workers came to Hawaii as plantation workers. Most, however, came during
the period 1890–1924, and then again since 1965. It was not until the Meiji
Restoration in 1868 that Japanese were allowed to emigrate. Initially they were
encouraged to do so by their government and were well received in Hawaii.
They first came expecting to stay only temporarily under a three-year contract
that had been arranged by the Hawaiian territorial government. They were
viewed as a source of cheap labor and an alternative to the Chinese "coolie"
labor force.

After the initial three-year period, some migrated to the mainland, concentrating on the West Coast, particularly in California. In 1870, there were
only fifty-six Japanese on the mainland, but by 1890 they exceeded 24,000 and
totaled just over 72,000 by the 1910 census. In 1920 they exceeded 110,000, at
which level they basically stabilized because of the Immigration Law of 1924,
which specifically barred them until that provision was rescinded in 1952, giving
them a very small quota.

They adapted well to working conditions in the United States. The majority
were young males (the ratio of male to female was about 4 to 1) from the farming
class, which in Japan placed them within the middle-class. They were highly
literate; nearly 99 percent being able to read, exceeding by far the literacy of the
majority population and clearly distinguishing them from their West and East
European immigrant counterparts. In Hawaii, most Japanese immigrants worked
in farming, usually in all-male work gangs under the supervision of an agent.
Those who made it to the mainland established a more diversified occupational
pattern. Their most typical job was working on the western railroads, but they
were also employed in canneries, mines, as domestic servants, cooks, and waiters, and in grocery and dry goods stores. Their low wage scale troubled them as
they evidenced a strong desire for upward mobility. They soon turned to agriculture on the mainland, particularly truck farming, and they became strong
economic competitors prior to World War I, although Japanese immigrants
farmed less than 1 percent of the agricultural land of California—and that often
on the most marginal land—they produced 10 percent of the state's total crop
(Kitano, 1976; Parrillo, 1985; McLemore, 1982).

Japanese immigrants faced immediate hostility and some violence on the
mainland when anti-Chinese sentiment was extended to them. The shoe-
makers' union attacked Japanese cobblers in 1890. Similar attacks by cooks'

and waiters' unions followed in 1892. Fears of the "Yellow Peril" grew markedly after the success of Japan in the Russo-Japanese War of 1905. In May 1905, the Japanese and Korean Exclusion League were formed. It was soon renamed as the Asiatic Exclusion League. Organized labor and the *San Francisco Chronicle* led the protest movement against them in 1905.

As with the Chinese, legal action against them soon followed. In 1906, San Francisco adopted an ordinance segregating them into "Chinese" schools. In 1907, President Theodore Roosevelt issued an order, lasting until 1948, which barred their entry into the United States from a bordering country or U.S. territory (i.e., from Canada, Hawaii, or Mexico). Opposition to their immigration rose.

In 1908, the Roosevelt administration used diplomatic and economic pressure on the Japanese government to accept the "gentlemen's agreement" to restrict emigration voluntarily. The import of Japanese wives was excluded from that agreement, so the peak year for Japanese immigration was 1907–1908, after which it sharply declined except for the "picture-bride" marriage system that brought in brides. From 1911 to 1920, 87,000 Japanese were admitted, but 70,000 returned home to Japan, for a net gain of a mere 17,000 for that entire decade.

Legal action continued against them. In 1913, the Webb-Henry Bill, better known as the California Alien Land Act, was passed. This law restricted Japanese aliens from owning land. It limited their leasing of land to three years, and forbade land already owned or leased from being bequeathed. California Attorney General Webb frankly described the law he authored as follows:

The fundamental basis of all legislation . . . has been and is, race undesirability. It seeks to limit their presence by curtailing their privileges which they may enjoy here, for they will not come in large numbers and long abide with us if they may not acquire land. And it seeks to limit the numbers who will come by limiting the opportunities for their activities here when they arrive (cited in Kitano, 1976: 17).

Most Japanese got around the law by placing ownership in the names of their native-born (and thus citizen) children. The citizenship status of native-born persons of Asian descent was upheld in *Wong Kim Ark v. United States*, March 28, 1898 (169 U.S. 649). Although the plaintiff in that case was Chinese, the ruling was that a native-born person of Asian descent was indeed a citizen of the United States despite the fact that his or her parents may have been resident aliens not eligible for naturalization. In cases where there were no such children, the immigrants often held the land in the names of Caucasian friends. The racist nature of the 1913 law foreshadowed the troubles to come, and several neighboring states adopted similar laws.

Thomas Sowell refers to their success and the reactions it brought about among the native population.

No matter what their first jobs, most Japanese wanted to acquire a plot of land, and many accomplished this goal piecemeal through a succession of different types of tenure. By 1909, according to the Immigration Commission's estimate, throughout the West some 6,000 Japanese were farming a total area of more than 210,000 acres. The success of their farms derived in part from an unusual degree of specialization, but more fundamentally from the hard work and extraordinary efficiency of their owners or tenants. To block this advance, California enacted the first anti-Japanese land law in 1913. Even though President Wilson sent his Secretary of State to Sacramento to argue against it, the bill passed by 35 to 2 in the Senate and 72 to 3 in the House. Under its terms, persons ineligible for citizenship could not own agricultural land or lease it for more than three years (1978: 77–78).

In 1891, the U.S. Supreme Court ruled on the power of the federal government immigration officials to deny entry into the country (*Nishimura Ekiu v. the United States*, 142 U.S. 651, 1891). Similarly, the Court ruled on a case involving the power of the federal government to *expel* an alien, in *Fong Yue Ting v. United States*, 149 U.S. 698, 1893). The petitioner in that case, a Chinese laborer, challenged the immigration bureau's authority to expel him for failing to have a "certificate of residence." Justice Gray delivered the majority opinion, ruling such matters were of *civil* law, not criminal law, and those operated with far fewer due process protections. The majority opinion stressed, once again, that immigration policy was a matter of *sovereignty*, not merely commerce. The decision again linked explicitly national security with immigration policy when it stated:

The right to exclude or to expel all aliens or any class of aliens, absolutely or upon certain conditions, in war or in peace, being an inherent right of every sovereign and independent nation, essential to its safety, its independence, and its welfare, the question now before the court is whether the manner in which Congress has exercised this right . . . is consistent with the Constitution . . . Congress, having the right, as it may see fit, to expel aliens of a particular class, or to permit them to remain, has undoubtedly the right to provide a system of registration and identification of the members of that class within the country . . . .

The order of the deportation is not a punishment for crime. It is not banishment, in the sense in which that word is often applied to the expulsion of a citizen from his country by way of punishment. It is but a method of enforcing the return to his own country of an alien who has not complied with the conditions upon the performance of which the government of a nation, acting within its constitutional authority and through the proper departments, has determined that his continuing to reside here shall depend. He has not, therefore, been deprived of life, liberty or property, without due process of law, and the provisions of the Constitution, securing the right of trial by jury, and prohibiting unreasonable searches and seizures, and cruel and unusual punishment, have no application.

Later, courts reaffirmed the majority position that Congress had sole and virtually absolute discretion in deciding whom to admit, ban, or allow remaining in this country and under whatever administrative conditions it desired. Three years later, a majority of the Court, again reflecting the prevailing racism of the time, asserted:

> No limits can be put by the Court upon the power of Congress to protect, by summary methods, the country from the advent of aliens whose race or habits render them undesirable as citizens, or to expel such if they have already found their way into our land and unlawfully remain therein (*Wong Wing v. United States*, 163 U.S. 228, 237, 1896).

The immigration bureaucracy became an increasingly important part of the policy and process of admission or denial. Boards of Special Inquiry, established in 1893, began to hear tens of thousands of cases annually—in 1910 alone, for instance, they heard 70,829 such cases (Pitkin: 45–46). Critics assailed the boards for being arbitrary, inefficient, and often politically corrupt. In the spring of 1896, following a lingering depression, the immigration bureau used the special inquiry process to detain hundreds of Italian immigrants by invoking the "pauper" clause. Conditions on Ellis Island became so bad that the Italian émigrés rioted. Dr. Senner, the then Commissioner on Ellis Island, had openly worked with Prescott Hall, Robert DeCourcey Ward, and Senator Henry Cabot Lodge of the Immigration Restriction League.

Inspectors were hired on the basis of a political spoils system and throughout the 1890s, inspections were badly administered and politically corrupt. The money-exchange service, baggage handling, and food concessions were a source of wealth and an inducement to corruption. The flood of immigrants taxed the system as well. Ellis Island processed some 6,500 immigrants daily.

In 1896, Terrance Powderly became the new head—entitled Commissioner-General of Immigration—of the Bureau of Immigration in Washington, D.C. Factions in the Treasury Department developed between Powderly in D.C. and Fitchie and McSweeney in New York (Pitkin: 28). Reforms under President Theodore Roosevelt, after 1902, cleaned up the worst aspects of the political corruption of the bureau. The agency began to tighten administrative procedures as well from 1903 to 1907. Watchorn, a career immigration service officer handpicked by Roosevelt, took over Ellis Island in 1907. His administration of the station was highly praised (Pitkin: 42).

FURTHER ATTEMPTS AT RESTRICTIONISM

During the early 1900s, the restrictionist movement pushed ahead, using several approaches. It pushed for the exclusion of the Japanese and the Chinese, advocated the extension of excluded groups, and pushed for adoption of a literacy test. The major proponents of these increasingly restrictive policies were the Immigration Restriction League, many officials of charitable and law enforcement agencies, leading sociologists and biologists, organized labor, and a variety of patriotic societies. Opposing them as well as any further restrictions were an assortment of ethnic societies, the steamship and railroad lines, manufacturers, and the National Liberal Immigration League, formed in 1906 to counter the Immigration Restriction League (Pitkin: 36).

The restrictionist forces renewed attempts to pass a literacy bill after President Cleveland, who had vetoed the first such bill, left office. Bills were introduced in 1898, 1902, and 1906, all of which were defeated. The proliteracy effort failed enactment prior to World War I because an effective coalition developed against that provision. Business groups remained in favor of an open-door policy as a means to ensure the continued supply of cheap labor. The National Union of Manufacturers and the National Association of Manufacturers helped defeat these early literacy bills (Pitkin: 46; Maldwyn Jones: 260–262). A coalition of southern senators helped maintain President Cleveland's veto in 1896, as representatives of those states wanted the continued influx of cheap labor (Divine: 4). During the period between the Spanish-American War and World War I, overall nativism declined to some extent as the nation experienced a period of economic expansion and social buoyancy. The imperialistic outburst drained off some of the xenophobic impulses. Then too, a growing number of ethnic associations were fighting proposals to restrict immigration. The German–American Alliance, the Ancient Order of Hibernians, the B'nai B'rith, the Hebrew Immigration Aid Society, and the Council of the Union of American Hebrew Congregations all fought the literacy and related restrictionist attempts.

The Republican Party platforms from 1904 through 1912 had no restrictionist planks, as they had in the preceding decade. Speaker Joe Cannon led the effort strenuously and successfully to defeat the literacy bills (Maldwyn Jones: 261–262).

In 1903, two immigration bills passed, however, which signaled a movement in the direction of restrictionism. One act moved immigration policy control from the Treasury to the newly established Department of Commerce and Labor (Act of February 14, 1903, 32 Stat. 825; 8 U.S.C.). In March 1903, as part of its major codification of immigration laws, Congress increased the head tax on the immigration of aliens and also prohibited entry to and the naturalization of anarchists—the first such ban on the entry or the naturalization of any person based on their political or ideological beliefs. This legislation also provided for the extensive recording of data on all immigrants arriving in the United States (Act of March 3, 1903; Re: Codification of Immigration Laws, 32 Stat. 1213; 8 U.S.C.; and 32 Stat. 1222). The 1903 act strengthened the immigration service by giving the Commissioner-General of Immigration greater control over the personnel and activities involved in the machinery of enforcement. By 1906, the new commissioner took pride in claiming his bureau was being converted into an efficient and depersonalized bureaucratic instrument of social policy. But the sheer volume taxed the ability of the service to provide adequately for the processing of so many. Ellis Island, in 1905, handled 821,169 aliens—with each inspector examining 400–500 immigrants per day! Critics maintained that the policy was inhumane, inequitable, and cruel in its treatment of hapless human beings. At Angel Island:

> Aware of their strategic role as gatekeepers, a number of these officials soon took advantage of the situation in which so much was at stake for the Chinese, particularly the merchants. They extorted bribes and engaged in other corrupt practices. Compounding these problems . . . was the fact that many of these officials were drawn from California with its pathological dislike of the Chinese. As a result, they resorted to technicalities to reject the credentials of Chinese, detained many others unnecessarily while their credentials were being checked, and demanded payoffs from still others (Ringer: 670).

The move of the bureau to the Department of Commerce and Labor did afford business interests greater access to the immigration bureaucracy in continuing their advocacy of a more open-door stance, thereby maintaining the tradition of a relatively free supply of cheap labor. The 1903 law also extended the class of excluded aliens to include anarchists, inspired no doubt by the assassination of President McKinley by the avowed anarchist Leon Czolgosz (Bennett, 1963: 24).

During the decade from 1900 to 1910, the United States experienced the largest influx of immigrants ever to that time—8,795,386 persons entered during those years. This renewed surge, plus the already discussed concern over Japanese immigration, coupled with the Panic of 1907 and its subsequent economic depression, fueled the fires for a renewed effort at restriction. The results of the Gentlemen's Agreement, once it began to run smoothly by June of 1908, were both dramatic and quick. During that month, for example, total immigration from Japan to the continental United States and Hawaii shrunk to only 35 percent of what it had been for that same month the year before. For the first complete year of operation, ending on June 30, 1909, the total figure dropped to 3,275 from 16,418 for the year 1908. It had been 30,287 in 1907 and 14,243 in 1906. In 1910, it was less than 3,000 (Ringer: 705).

In 1907, Congress amended the immigration act, increasing the head tax and adding to the excluded classes of individuals but essentially restating the comprehensive act of June 6, 1906. The 1907 law also had a provision establishing what became known as the Dillingham Commission (34 Stat. 898; U.S.C.). That same year, Congress added important regulations regarding the issuing of passports, expatriation, and the marriage of American women to foreigners (34 Stat. 1228; 8 U.S.C. 17).

Homer Lea, California's leading publicist of the "Yellow Peril," warned, in 1909, that the United States was loosing its "racial purity" to Asian and S/C/E European immigration. The south joined the anti-immigration movement as those racial arguments struck a responsive cord. The American Federation of

Labor endorsed calls for a literacy test. Samuel Gompers articulated the position of the AFL when he stated:

> The *strength* of this country is in the intelligence and prosperity of our working people. But both the intelligence and the prosperity of our working people are endangered by the present immigration. Cheap labor, ignorant labor, takes our jobs and cuts our wages.
>
> The fittest survive; that is, those that fit the conditions best. But it is the economically weak, not the economically strong, that fit the conditions of the labor market. They fit best because they can be got to work the cheapest. Women and children drive out men, unless either law or labor organizations stop it. In just the same way, the Chinaman and the others drive out the American, the German, the Irishman.
>
> The tariff keeps out cheap foreign goods. It is employers, not the workingmen that have goods to sell. Workingmen sell labor, and cheap labor is not kept out by the tariff. The protection that would directly help the workers is protection against cheap labor itself.
>
> The Nashville Convention of the American Federation of Labor, by a vote of 1,858 to 352, pronounced in favor of an educational test for immigrants. Such a measure would check immigration in a moderate degree, and those who would be kept out by it are those whose competition in the labor market is most injurious to American workers. No other measure which would have any important effect of this kind of is seriously proposed (as cited in Handlin: 186).

Congress passed another literacy test in 1909. It was vetoed by President Taft. His veto message, written by Secretary of Labor Nagel, argued that there still was a need for immigrant labor (Bernard: 13–14).

THE PRE-WAR YEARS

In 1910, Congress amended the 1907 act to remove all limitations on the deportation of alien prostitutes (known as the White Slave Traffic Act, 36 Stat. 825; U.S.C. 397–404). From 1907 to 1911, the special commission on immigration (the Dillingham Commission), met and studied immigration policy. It was composed of nine members—three senators, three representatives, and three presidential appointees. It was heavily stacked in favor of the restrictionist point of view. It issued its massive report—42 volumes—in 1911. The significance of their report was in the fact that it was proported to be an objective and scientific study, although the bias of its members is evident in its findings. The commission, not surprisingly given its membership, recommended the adoption of a literacy test, maintaining that such a test was "demanded by economic, moral, and social considerations" (see Divine: 4). It openly admitted the purpose of the proposed law, which featured a literacy test, was to decrease immigration by 25 percent (Bernard: 13; for a summary of the recommendations of the commission, see LeMay and Barkan, Document 61: 103–106).

The commission accepted the Darwinian theories taken by the Immigration Restriction League from the writings of John Commons, Edward Ross, and especially from William Ripley's *The Races of Europe* (1899). The racial overtones of the commission's report were augmented by the highly popular and influential work of the time, Madison Grant's *The Passing of the Great Race in America* (1916).

Of course, the commission's study and the restrictionist movement's literature did not go unchallenged. Scholars and social workers disputed the findings of the commission—particularly Jane Addams of the Hull House movement in Chicago, and Grace Abbott of the Immigrants Protective League, who later served as head of the Children's Bureau. Sympathetic or proimmigrant works by scholars and journalists included: Jacob Riis' *The Making of America*, who went on to become especially influential with the Roosevelt administration; Mary Antin's *The Promised Land*; Carl Schurz's *Reminiscences*; Eward Steiner's *On the Trail of the Immigrant*; and Louis Adamic's *Two-Way Passages* (Bernard: 17).

In 1913, Congress, following the recommendations of the Dillingham Commission, passed a literacy test bill, which was promptly vetoed by President Taft. That same year, Congress moved the immigration service to the newly created Department of Labor (37 Stat. 737, 1913). The act divided the service into two bureaus known as the Bureau of Immigration and the Bureau of Naturalization. The Bureau of Immigration was headed by a commissioner-general and the Bureau of Naturalization by a commissioner. They were placed under the immediate direction of the Secretary of Labor, who promptly reduced the immigration service staff.

THE POSTWAR YEARS—THE BEGINNINGS OF ISOLATIONISM

When war broke out in Europe in 1914, the United States returned to the foreign policy posture and dictum of the republic's early years—strict neutrality. Public opinion was strongly against any involvement in the war. Keeping America out of the war was one of the campaign themes that contributed to President Woodrow Wilson's success in gaining a second term in 1916. That policy position shifted in 1917, however, when German submarines began attacking U.S. merchant ships crossing the Atlantic. Congress declared war on April 6, 1917. The United States entered the "War to End All Wars" as an "associated power" of the Allied Powers (Relyea: 604; Jordan et al.: 48; Kupchan: 177).

The World War I years were something of an interlude in immigration pressures. Whereas over 1,200,000 entered the United States in 1914, by 1915 that number had dropped off by 75 percent, to just over 300,000. In 1918, less than 30,000 were processed through Ellis Island. This slackening off in the immigration flow reduced restrictionist pressures during the war-time interlude. A 1915 literacy test passed by Congress was vetoed by President Wilson and his veto was sustained. He labeled it a test of opportunity, not of intelligence.

The Russian Bolshevik Revolution, however, aroused anew fears of radicalism in this country and renewed efforts toward restricted immigration. In the postwar years, these forces were more effective. The American Legion, the National Grange, and the AFL all strongly supported the literacy test bill. This time a new law passed by Congress was enacted over President Wilson's veto (39 Stat. 874; 8 U.S.C.; for his veto message, see LeMay and Barkan, Document 62: 107–108; and for a summary of the law, see Document 63: 108–112). The new law doubled the head tax from four to eight dollars, added chronic alcoholics, vagrants, and those suffering from psychopathic inferiority to the list of excluded classes. In 1917, it also passed the Asiatic Barred-Zone, which more forcefully excluded the Chinese and Japanese, virtually excluding all Asian immigration (Maldwyn Jones: 270). Also that year, a joint order of the departments of State and of Labor was issued requiring passports and certain other information from all aliens seeking to enter the United States during World War I. This act also required the issuing of visas from an American consular officer in the country of origin rather than allowing a person to enter the United States and then seek permission to enter having already arrived at the shores or port of entry (order issued July 26, 1917, Washington, D.C., 1042–1044).

Finally, in 1917 Congress passed a law allowing for the repatriation of persons expatriated because of service in an allied foreign armed service during World War I (Act of October 5, 1917; Re: Resumption of Citizenship, 40 Stat. 340). And in 1918, the president issued a detailed executive order of fourteen pages in length specifying the rules and regulations to implement a proclamation concerning the exclusion, entrance, and forced departure of aliens during the war (Executive Order 2932, August 8, 1918). In October 1918, Congress expanded the provision spelt out in the Act of March 3, 1903 and in the Act of February 5, 1917, which added membership in or espousal of communism to the list of excluded classes or those subject to expulsion, which previously had stipulated anarchists (40 Stat. 1012; 8 U.S.C. 137).

Postwar periods have commonly been times of reaction, when fears and concerns about national security increase. National security concerns began to dominate U.S. foreign policy with a decided tilt towards isolationism. The years after World War I fit the pattern of reactionism. Radicals of all types were fiercely persecuted during and immediately after the war. Wobblies, socialists, anarchists, and anyone suspected of holding such views were tarred and feathered, jailed, and sometimes even lynched. The Red Scare of 1919 led to the arrest of thousands and the deportation of over 500.

Palmer's Raids rounded up 6,000 to 10,000 suspected immigrants in thirty-three cities across the country, but only for their political affiliation. They were detained in overcrowded 'bullpens' and coerced into signing confessions. Many who were arrested were U.S. citizens. Five hundred and fifty-six were deported for their political affiliations not for their part in the [anarchist] bombings (Etzioni and Marsh: 36–37).

The period seemed to unleash the darker forces in the American psyche. The Ku Klux Klan revived and grew dramatically, taking on a stridently anti-Catholic, anti-Jew, and antiforeigner outlook. The Klan joined forces with the American Protective League and the True Americans and together launched an incendiary period of anti-Catholicism (Higham: 286–298). It was the triumph of racist ideas providing a rationale for the restrictive laws of the 1920s. "Eugenics," a pseudoscience that supposedly "proved" that certain races were endowed with hereditary superiority or inferiority, provided the basis for the quota system.

These trends fit in with the foreign policy and national security concerns of the post-World War I years:

> Following World War I, America again tried to turn its back on the world outside the Western Hemisphere, rejecting President Wilson's approach to the League of Nations, pushing for disarmament in the Washington and Geneva Naval Conferences in 1922 and 1927, and renouncing war as 'an instrument of national policy' in the Kellogg-Briand Pact of 1928. Americans focused on a return to 'normalcy', i.e., getting on with domestic concerns (Jordan et al.: 48).

The war experience also had an impact on Congressional–Executive relations in making national security and foreign policy. The experience of American participation in World War I provided evidence and greater acceptability for a number of administrative innovations—a more integrated executive branch under overall presidential management, effecting efficiency and economy in government operations, a unified executive budget, and some role for the president in executive reorganization (Relyea: 605).

Following the Allied victory, President Wilson advocated his Fourteen Points Peace Plan and the idea of collective security in joining the League of Nations. The president presented the treaty to the Senate in July, 1919 (Kupchan: 178).

Senate Republicans, William Borah (R-Idaho) and Henry Cabot Lodge (R-Mass), led the fight to defeat the treaty. Campaigning on a theme of a "Return to Normalcy," and advocating the position that "noninvolvement in Old World affairs is not aloofness, it is security" the Republicans elected President Warren Harding over Democrat candidate James Cox (governor of Ohio) with the avowed purpose of returning to conservatism, traditionalism, and a closed society (Kupchan: 183). There was a climate of opinion favoring a reversal of the open-door policy on immigration. In the words of one scholar of immigration history:

> Now for the first time important sections of Big Business, as a result of the fear that immigrants might propagate the ideas of the Russian Revolution, took a

stand for the restriction of immigration. For the first time leaders of industry feared the alleged radicalism of the immigrant laborer more than they desired his services as a worker. Economic depression and unemployment again faced the country, and the immigrants, as had happened many times before in our history, were made a scapegoat for the hard times. More significant, however, were the intensified nationalism growing out of the war and the specter of Soviet Russia on the distant horizon (Bernard, 19).

Republicans portrayed the League as a threat not just to the country's sovereignty, but also to the war-aroused spirit of American nationalism. As President Harding put it: "In the existing League of Nations, world-governing with its superpowers, this Republic will have no part." Senator Lodge, speaking against the Treaty, said: "We are asked to substitute internationalism for nationalism and an international state for pure Americanism" (cited in Kupchan: 184).

The battle over the issue and its resolution in the rejection of the treaty and American involvement in the League of Nations set foreign policy decision-making into a context of Republicans versus Democrats, Lodge versus Wilson, and the south and west versus the east. It ushered in a period in which the United States steered clear of alliances and commitments to collective security, mustering enthusiasm only for anodyne agreements like Kellogg-Briand that condemned war and committed the signature nations to the peaceful resolution of disputes (Kupchan: 187).

NOTES

1. Thomas and Znaniecki put their number at 875,000; Dinnerstein and Reimers: 38; Dinnerstein and Jaher: 232; and Parillo: 174, all put it at over 1 million. Lopata: 38 puts the maximum at 1,670,000 for the number who immigrated here from 1885 to 1972, and estimates the total Polish-American group, referred to as Polonia, at about 12 million. Levy and Kramer's (141–142) estimates of "Slavic Americans" range from 6 to 15 million.

2. See, for instance, Thomas and Znaniecki (1977), Parrillo (1985), Lopata (1976), and Dinnerstein and Reimers (1988). As with the Italians and other Slavs, the Polish immigrants had difficulty in adjusting to the Irish-dominated Catholic Church.

The Pet-Door Cycle, 1920–1960

INTRODUCTION: NATIONAL SECURITY—ISOLATIONISM TO INTERNATIONALISM

The national mood shifted after World War I. Disillusion with European affairs in the immediate postwar years resulted in a change in the perception of what was needed for national security. The country turned inward. Isolationist sentiment dominated U.S. foreign policy-making as public opinion came to accept the fact that the country was protected by the vast oceans separating the United States from Europe and Asia. In Congress, a coalition in both houses moved to drastically restrict immigration policy in order to reduce the influence of foreign immigrants on U.S. society—to keep America "pure." Even immigrants already here were pushed to "Americanize," as several groups promoted political and social movements of Americanization. Immigration policy shifted as a direct result of the changing national mood. It was not until United States engagement in World War II and its subsequent emergence as a world superpower that foreign policy became internationalist, and national security policy emerged as a concept tied to U.S. military might, its projection around the globe, and the Cold War with its policy to "contain" the Soviet Union. Participation in national security policy-making became more complex, with the various participants focusing on a different face of the issue and with a sense of different dangers and opportunities (Halperin: 17; see also Tindall: 1149–1185). As one scholar of post-World War II security policy notes:

> We proceeded then in an inhibating framework of "bipartisanship" built by FDR and Truman—and maintained by Eisenhower in his own fashion—to afford support for a revolution in our foreign relations, breaching the isolationist tradition. Men who had been bred in that tradition before shifting ground

themselves now sought to keep the country with them on the plea that politics "stops at the water's edge (Halperin: 64).

Ethnic minority groups played a stronger role in foreign and national security policy-making during the Cold War years, again providing a link between immigration policy, the presence of so many and such varied an array of ethnic groups within the population, and the nation's perceptions of how best to ensure national security.

A recent study of the origins of the Cold War further suggests that Truman's concern about the growing disaffection for the Democratic party among ethnic minority groups with Eastern European attachments was one of the motives, which led him to take a strong stand against Soviet efforts to establish domination over countries such as Poland, Czechoslovakia, and Hungary (Halperin: 71).

THE IMMIGRATION ACT OF 1917

The ability of Congress to override President Woodrow Wilson's second veto of the literacy bill passed in 1917 was a clear indication that the tide in favor of restrictionism was flowing to irresistible levels. The Red Scare of 1919, with its accompanying xenophobic fear of Bolshevik radicalism, set the stage for the 1920s that in turn ushered in a new era of immigration policy-making. A tradition of open-door policy that went back a century but that was being increasingly closed during the past four decades was to be overturned. In its stead, the United States was about to adopt a policy of avowed restrictionism. Moreover, it was about to enter a policy of *effective* restrictions, one which would essentially close the door to all but a favored few.

When it became clear that the passage of the literacy bill, even if over the president's veto, was not enough to stem the tide of large-scale immigration, the proponents of restriction were forced to advocate a more stringent, and what proved to be a far more effective device: the imposition of an absolute number limiting the influx of immigrants. Some called for the total suspension of all immigration from anywhere from two to as long as fifty years. In terms of both absolute numbers and as a percent of total population, the decade from 1900 to 1910 registered the highest influx of immigration in the nation's history (Figure 4.1). Despite the various restrictive measures passed during the 1880s and 1890s, and despite the literacy test imposed in 1917, the decade from 1910 to 1920 was second only to the preceding one in terms of absolute numbers entering the United States during a decennial period, and third in terms of annual immigration as a percentage of total population size. The proponents of restriction realized that a more drastic step was needed than any previous measure passed if they were to successfully stem the flood of immigration. They rather quickly changed from advocating literacy to the

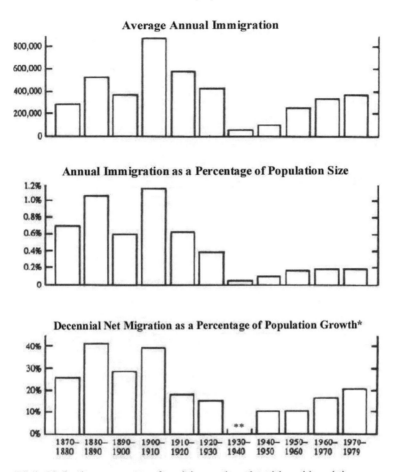

*Decinnial migration as a percentage of population growth equals total decennial population increase minus natural population increase (births and deaths) divided by total population increase.
** Emigration exceeded immigration by 85,000.

FIGURE 4.1.   Levels and Rates of U.S. Immigration, 1870–1979
Source: Select Commission on Immigration and Refugee Policy, Staff Report. Washington, D.C.: U.S. Government Printing Office (April 1981) 28.

imposition of quotas based upon national origins. As shall be seen more fully in the following, they did so with rather remarkably dramatic results.

Figures 4.1 and 4.2 graphically portray the effects of that policy shift. As Figure 4.1 demonstrates, absolute numbers declined sharply in the decade from 1920 to 1930. In the decade from 1930 to 1940, when the Great Depression was added as a factor greatly reducing immigration, the United States experienced the least-ever level of immigration, both in absolute terms and as a percentage of

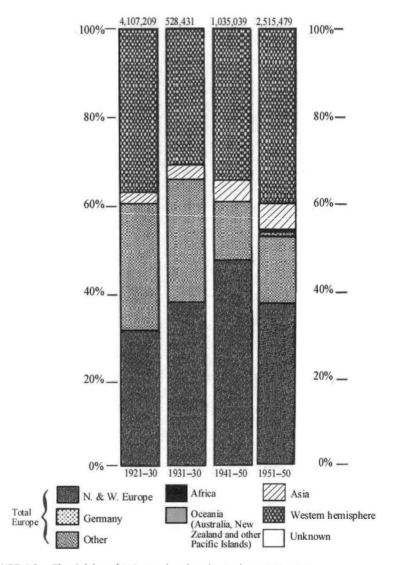

FIGURE 4.2.   The Origins of U.S. Immigration, by Region, 1920–1950

Source: U.S. Bureau of the Census, *Historical Statistics of the United States, Colonial Times to 1970*. Washington, D.C.: U.S. Government Printing Office (1975), 28.

total population. Indeed, as can be seen in Figure 4.1, the 1930 to 1940 decade was one in which emigration exceeded immigration by 85,000, resulting in a *negative* decennial net migration as a percentage of population growth. But the change in numbers was not the only dramatic result of the new policy.

Figure 4.2 shows the origins of United States immigration by region for the decades of the pet-door cycle. The pronounced movement away from SCE European immigration towards that from northwestern Europe is clearly evident in Figure 4.2.

This chapter will briefly discuss how and why those dramatic shifts occurred. It begins the discussion by focusing upon the 1921 emergency immigration restriction law that first introduced the concept of the quota system. The quota system was very heavily weighted in favor of immigration from northwestern European nations. The 1924 National Origins Act somewhat modified the weightings, showing an even greater bias against SCE European immigration and firmly setting the principle of the national origins system as the prevailing policy position, which lasted for the next forty years!

THE QUOTA ACT OF 1921

The years from 1917 to 1920 witnessed the restrictionist fever rise to its highest point. An *Americanization* movement swept the nation in the aftermath of World War I. In the hysteria of the postwar era, people called sauerkraut "liberty cabbage," and hamburgers became "Salisbury steaks." Many cities and towns renamed streets, replacing "foreign-sounding" names with "American" ones. The state of Oregon enacted a law requiring all children to attend public schools [an act obviously aimed at Catholic parochial schools], and California struck out at aliens by ordering every adult male alien to register and pay a special annual poll tax of ten dollars, a not insignificant sum for the time. Although both the Oregon and California statutes were declared unconstitutional by the U.S. Supreme Court, their enactment represented the zenith of the Americanization movement (Higham: 260). The *Dearborn Independent*, Henry Ford's notorious newspaper, launched a massive anti-Jewish campaign and stressed the need for immigration restriction. The revived Ku Klux Klan grew markedly in membership and influence. It, too, advocated strict limits on immigration. The AFL continued its campaign, begun in the 1880s, to limit the influx of "cheap immigrant labor." Both the Democratic- and the Republican-party platforms called for effective limits on immigration.

The fear that the economic chaos which gripped Europe in the immediate postwar years would lead to a flood of new immigration to the United States fed the restrictionist movement. When the United States experienced a slight depression in 1920, the passage of some restrictive immigration legislation seemed inevitable. In 1920, the House voted to end immigration altogether, although the Senate refused to go that far. A number of leading senators, however, advocated a strict restrictionist policy. Among the more prominent were: Senators Danford and Taylor of Ohio, Johnson and Shortridge of California, Lodge and Morse of Massachusetts, Johnson and Watson of Indiana, Reed of Pennsylvania, Corliss of Michigan, Hepburn of Iowa, Caffery of Louisiana, and Wilson of South Carolina. Clearly, the restrictionist sentiment was becoming evident in every region of the country. There were only a few defenders of open immigration vocal in the Senate: Gibson of Maryland, Mahany of New York, Bartholdt of Missouri, and Buch of Louisiana (see Philip Taylor: 244). In the House, Bourke Cochran and Adolph Sabath were the primary voices in favor of open immigration.

The presidency, too, had shifted to an isolationist foreign policy, to support for a restrictionist immigration policy. Vice-president Calvin Coolidge had succeeded President Harding after the latter's heart attack, and then was elected president in his own right in the 1924 election. Both men as president favored isolationism and restrictionism as suggested in the "Return to Normalcy" policy (Tindall: 1072–1081).

The restrictionist forces were gaining not only in numbers, but also in the influence of their positions in Congress. Senator Dillingham, who had chaired the Immigration Commission in 1907, was, by 1917, the chairman of the Immigration Committee in the Senate. Likewise, the chairman of the Republican-dominated House Immigration Committee was Albert Johnson of Washington, a leading restrictionist voice.

In 1919, after the famous Palmer Raids, 500 immigrants suspected as radical anarchists and Bolsheviks, were deported aboard a ship to Russia nicknamed, "The Soviet Ark." Public sentiment aroused by the Sacco-Vanzetti case, and the collapse of Wilsonian idealism, evident in the Senate's rejection of U.S. membership in the League of Nations, gave a new edge to the restrictionist arguments. The postwar isolationist mood was easily tapped by the forces advocating limits on immigration. A new sense of nationalism, distrustful of further entanglements with Europe or imperialistic designs on Asia, was committed to isolationism and disdainful of all foreigners. It echoed through the debates over our joining the League of Nations. It swayed the position taken by the American Legion. It rumbled in the "konklaves" of the Klan. It aroused emotions in the religious revival meetings propelling a wave of fundamentalism in religious fervor and in a nativism movement that grew in number of members and variety of nativist groups. It unleashed a torrent of state legislation excluding aliens from many occupations. Licensing acts barred them from practicing architecture, engineering, chiropractic, pharmacy, medicine, surgery, surveying, and executing wills. Such laws even forbade their operating motor buses (Higham: 271, 301; Tindall: 1028–1032).

The 1919 Red Scare, coupled with the depression, led to the adoption of a prorestrictionist stance by forces one might otherwise expect to have been in favor of a more open policy. The Progressive party voiced concern about the nation's ability to absorb and assimilate many aliens. The New Republic mused that unrestricted immigration was an element of nineteenth-century liberalism fated to end and that a progressive society could not allow social ills to be aggravated by excessive immigration (Higham: 302). Business and economic interests that previously had been strong advocates of continuing an open-door policy were either silent or changed to a restrictionist position. The 1920

Depression meant that there was no labor shortage. Many business leaders accepted the arguments of the "100 Percenters," the American Legion, and similar nationalist groups within the Americanization movement. Kenneth Roberts published a series of articles in the very popular *The Saturday Evening Post*, which became a leading proponent of the restrictionist crusade from 1920 to 1924. Roberts' series popularized a new element in the restrictionist arsenal of arguments—an "ethnic theory" (Divine: 10). The halls of Congress soon echoed with calls to end the "alien flood," "barbaric horde," and "foreign tide." All the stereotypes common in the popular press were used in the Congress. In the words of a congressman from Arkansas:

> We have admitted the dregs of Europe until America has been orientalized, Europeanized, Africanized and mongrelized to that insidious degree that our genious, stability, greatness, and promise of advancement and achievement are actually menaced. Accordingly, I should like to exclude all foreigners for years to come, at least until we can ascertain whether or not the foreign and discordant element now in what many are pleased to term "our great melting pot" will melt into real American citizens (cited in Ringer: 801).

So much for "Give me your tired, your poor, Your huddled masses yearning to breathe free, The wretched refuse of your teeming shore, Send these, the homeless, tempest-tossed to me, I lift my lamp beside the golden door." The sentiments of the congressmen, and so many of his Senate colleagues, could not have been further from those inscribed at the base of the Statue of Liberty.

When the business forces were either silent or switched to a prorestriction position, passage of some sort of legislation-limiting immigration became inevitable. It was virtually unopposed in Congress. As Professor Divine notes:

> Fundamentally, it was the transformation in American economic and political development that set the stage for restriction. The growth of the American economy and particularly the technological changes brought about by the industrial revolution had greatly reduced the need for the raw labor furnished by immigrants. A mature industrial system required a moderate number of trained workers, not great masses of manual labor (Divine: 9).

When the United States emerged from World War I as a true world power, it developed a more intense nationalism in which U.S. citizens increasingly demanded unity and conformity. The new position of the nation on the international scene became the base for the restrictionist policy.

The thrust of advocating the quota approach to restrictionism came from several sources. The return to economic prosperity in 1921 relegated the economic issues to a secondary role in the debates over passage of an immigration law. The National Association of Manufacturers led the proimmigration forces. The AFL attacked them as being interested solely in cheap labor. It argued strenuously that there already was an adequate supply of labor in the nation's workforce. A leading sociologist, Henry Pratt Fairchild, advocated the position taken by organized labor. As a result, the economic arguments became largely deadlocked between opposing pressure groups. This development forced the restrictionists to concentrate their attacks on immigrants from the "ethnic theory" approach. Among the leading voices for these theories were Carl Brigham, a Princeton psychologist famous for developing the "IQ" test, William MacDougall of Harvard, the prominent and extreme "eugenist," who was the "biological expert" for the House Immigration Committee and who went so far as to advocate the sterilization of all inmates of mental institutions (Bernard: 29); and Gino Speranza, a native-born U.S. citizen of Italian descent who wrote a series of articles in *World's Work* that popularized the idea of the need for national unity and conformity by defending racial and cultural homogeneity. These sources helped forge a new concept of "racial nationalism." Undoubtedly, however, the most influential voice and central inspiration in these racial theory writings was that of Madison Grant. In his highly influential book, *The Passing of the Great Race,* Grant wrote that the nation was becoming inundated by a large and increasing number of weak and broken and mentally crippled of all races drawn from the lowest stratum of the Mediterranean basin and the Balkins, together with the hordes of the wretched, submerged populations of the Polish ghettos. He also mentioned that, "Our jails, insane asylums and almshouses are filled with this human flotsam and the whole tone of American life, social, moral and political, has been lowered and vulgarized by them (89–90).

Grant's book was first published in 1916, but new editions in 1921 and 1923 brought its total sales to nearly 16,000 copies. Grant also published a series of editorials in the *New York Times* and the *Saturday Evening Post.* He inspired a number of popular writers and influenced many scholarly ones. He was the leading popularizer of a theory that recognized within the "white race" a three-tiered hierarchy of Mediterraneans, Alpines, and Nordics. According to Grant, white Americans were Nordics, the highest, and should regard any mixture with the other two as a destructive process of "mongrelization" (Higham: 272).

By 1921, congressmen, reflecting this perspective, were arguing that the melting pot had failed and immigration was causing the nation to suffer from "alien indigestion." They feared the country was beginning to contain "intermingled and mongrelized people," and began substituting the idea of racial purity for the melting pot. A Maryland senator called for a "racially pure" country so that we might achieve the greatness of England, France, or Germany. A congressman from Maine stated:

God intended, I believe, [the U.S.] to be the home of a great people, English-speaking—a white race with great ideals, the Christian religion, one race, one country, and one destiny . . . It [the U.S.] was a mighty land, settled by northern Europeans from the United Kingdom, the Norsemen, and the Saxons, the people of a mixed blood. The Africans, the orientals, the Mongolians, and all the yellow races of Europe, Asia, and Africa should never have been allowed to people this great land (cited in *"We the People" and Others*: 801–802).

The House Committee on Immigration was the most prominent voice in Congress for these racial theories. Indeed, by 1921, it was stressing a racial theory as *the fundamental* justification for restriction.

Nor was Congress alone susceptible to the new racist ideology. The Supreme Court, in *Ozawa v. U.S.* (260 U.S. 195, 1922), ruled on a case that challenged the constitutionality of the law that forbade Japanese immigrants to become naturalized citizens. The Court upheld the law, ruling that it was constitutional to restrict them from citizenship. Clearly, the law that made the Japanese "aliens ineligible for citizenship" was blatantly racist (Ringer: 790–791). The Court later ruled, in 1927, to uphold an ordinance of Cincinnati which barred noncitizens from operating pool halls. Although the Court acknowledged the Fourteenth Amendment's prohibition against irrational discrimination, it ruled that the Cincinnati ordinance was not irrational. The Court agreed with Cincinnati's attorney, who depicted pool halls as vile places in need of strong police powers to curb them. Since "noncitizens" as a class were less familiar with the laws and customs of the nation (and in this case, of the municipality), than were the native-born or naturalized citizens, the city argued, it was a reasonable exercise of local police powers to exclude them. The Court agreed that "alien race and allegiance" may be a legitimate object of legislation so as to be made the basis of a permanent classification. This same line of reasoning justified a host of state licensing laws that limited aliens in practicing various professions and occupations (*Clarke v. Deckenback*, 274 U.S. 392, 1917).

The Supreme Court ruled further on what constituted a "white" person insofar as that word was understood in terms that admission to naturalization was open only to a "free white person" in 1923. The Court ruled that in the law, "free white person" meant those persons who appeared and would commonly be viewed as "white" and specifically rejected a person of the Caucasian race who, as an East Indian, did not appear to be white and therefore was judged to be ineligible for naturalization (*United States v. Bhagat Singh Thind*, February 19, 1923, 61 U.S.C. 616).

The principle of allocating quotas on the basis of those already represented by the various nationalities among the U.S. foreign-born population (which became the cornerstone of the quota system), was first introduced by Dr. Sidney Gulick in 1914. He intended it as a liberal alternative to positions being advocated by the strict restrictionists, some of whom had begun calling for total suspension of immigration. Dr. Gulick was a former missionary in Asia. In 1918, he formed the National Committee on Constructive Immigration Legislation. He suggested that each nationality be assigned a quota proportionate to the number of *naturalized* citizens and their U.S.-born children already drawn from that nationality. Annually, an immigration commission would fix a certain percentage—he suggested 10 percent or less—of those first- and second- generation citizens. As he put it: "The proved capacity for genuine Americanization on the part of those already here from any land should be the measure for the further immigration of that people" (cited in Higham: 302).

The "percentage quota principle," as it became known, was soon the central piece of all immigration laws passed during the 1920s. What differed among its advocates was the notion of precisely how the quotas should be set up. After the 1921 law, however, the basic principle that there should be quotas was accepted to the point of being enshrined into law. The pivotal and basic function of the quota system was to limit immigration from Europe. The battles were largely over how to distribute such quotas among the various countries of Europe.

In the final Congressional debate over the bill, and in the later battles in 1923 and 1924, the primary organizational support in favor of the origins bill and concept included: the AFL, the American Legion, the Immigration Restriction League, the National Grange, the Ku Klux Klan, the Junior Order of the United American Mechanics, as well as such patriotic associations as the Sons of the American Revolution, the Patriotic Order of the Sons of America and the Daughters of the American Revolution. The primary opposition to the bill included: the Anti-National Origins Clause League; a New York taxpayers association; several industrial and employer organizations, chiefly the National Association of Manufacturers, the American Mining Congress, the Associated General Contractors, the National Industrial Conference Board, and the U.S. Chamber of Commerce; some farm organizations concerned that agriculture would be denied sufficient manpower; spokesmen for various Jewish, foreign language, and other "ethnic groups," that would be adversely affected by the 1890 base year, such as the Vasa Order of America (Swedish), the Steuben Society, the Danish Brotherhood of America, the Sons of Norway, and the German-American Citizens League (Marion Bennett: 52–53; Divine: 33–37).

The Senate passed a bill, sponsored by Senator Dillingham, which limited European immigration to 5 percent of the number of foreign-born of that nationality present in the U.S. as determined by the 1910 census. The bill exempted Canada and Latin America from the quota system. The Senate version would have limited total annual immigration to 250,000. The bill easily passed in the Senate. Its only real opposition came from southern and western senators who wanted total suspension of immigration. The House abandoned its various suspension plans in favor of the Senate quota system, but reduced the limit from 5 to 3 percent of the 1910 census (Higham: 310–311). It limited total immigration to 350,000 and assigned most of that to northwestern Europe. Congress adopted that version in a conference committee and sent the bill to President Wilson. He killed the bill with a pocket veto during his last days in office—a veto which was quickly to be in vain.

The in-coming president, Warren Harding, called a special session of Congress. In the House, Albert Johnson supported the bill rather than his own total suspension plan. The Johnson Act, also known as the Emergency Immigration Restriction Act of 1921, thus first established the principle of the quota system.

It was heavily weighted in favor of northwestern Europe. It set the total of quotas at 357,803. It passed the House without a recorded vote. In the Senate, it passed 78 to 1 and was signed into law by President Harding as the Act of May 19, 1921: The Quota Act of 1921 (42 Stat. 5; 8 U.S.C. 229). Its annual quota for each country was based upon 3 percent of the foreign-born residents from that country residing in the United States as determined by the 1910 census. It drastically cut down the influx of overall immigration, and shifted its composition by limiting Asia, Africa, and Oceania to less than 1,000 immigrants, northwestern Europe to basically 200,000 immigrants, and southeastern Europe to just over 155,000 immigrants. The act reaffirmed, moreover, all the previous restrictions on "excluded groups" by barring the mentally, physically, and morally "undesirable" classes, including those persons likely to become public charges, as was established in the 1917 immigration act.

THE IMMIGRATION ACT OF 1924

The restrictionist movement was not satisfied with the results of the 1921 act in stemming the flow of immigration into the United States. They pushed for greater restrictions and quotas that would further shift the flow coming in toward northwestern European nations of origin. The quota system that as temporarily set up, imposed some harsh injustices. Ships arriving during the first months after passage of the law often carried more than the monthly quota than that were allowed for entry from that country. Polish, Rumanian, and Italian immigrants especially jammed Ellis Island and steamships in the harbors of Boston and New York. Administrative "exemptions" to the monthly quotas necessitated by these dire (and largely unforeseen consequences) conditions angered the congressional restrictionist forces.

The debate to change the quotas set up in the "emergency" quota act of 1921 to more permanent quotas raged and reached its peak between 1921 and 1924. Albert Johnson's committee in the House, with strong and vocal backing from the AFL and the American Legion, continued urging total suspension. Prescott Hall, of the Immigration Restriction League, Madison Grant, Lothrop Stoddard, Kenneth Roberts, and Harry Laughlin all supported the Johnson Committee and stirred up public debate on the issue.

A prominent New York attorney, John D. Trevor, began to work closely with the Johnson Committee. By the fall of 1922 they were advocating changing the base year for the census from 1910 to 1890, and reducing the quota from 3 to 2 percent. The calculation of the quotas based on 1890 census data, of course, meant that the total annual immigration would be less, and the continued influx from SCE European nations would be reduced from a flood to a trickle— which was their specific intent.

By 1922, the effects of the 1920 Depression were dissipating markedly. As unemployment shrank, business began experiencing a labor shortage. Manufacturers renewed their advocating the easing of restrictions. The National

Association of Manufacturers (NAM) lobbied strenuously to do so. The U.S. Chamber of Commerce lobbied for *adding* 2 percent to the quotas (i.e., from 5 to 7 percent). The president of U.S. Steel labeled the 1921 law as "one of the worst things this country has ever done for itself economically" (cited in Higham: 315). Big farmers, losing their hired hands to the lure of the cities' better-paying jobs in the factories, joined business in protesting the law.

By 1923, the Senate Immigration Committee, at the urging of NAM, introduced a bill retaining the quota system, but allowing for additional immigrants in times of labor shortages. Senator Reed of Pennsylvania sponsored a compromise bill that increased total immigration but reduced the share of SCE European nations. A period of stalemate ensued as the Republican leadership in both houses decided to defer action until 1924.

From late 1923 to early 1924, sentiment began to shift. Increased mechanization in the economy was easing labor shortage pains and requiring more skilled labor rather than more unskilled ones. The National Industrial Conference Board, a research and public relations agency working for thirty-one leading industrial associations, held a conference on immigration in New York in December of 1923. Business resolve for easing restrictions was wavering. NAM and the Chamber of Commerce recommended, early in 1924, that the quotas of 1921 be retained rather than being reduced, but neither organization was willing to strongly lobby the Congress on the matter.

The battleground shifted, then, to various ethnic associations pushing for or opposing quotas as they would affect the immigration status from those countries. A "Nordic theory" gained ground. The newly elected president, Calvin Coolidge, gave the restrictionist cause his blessing by calling, in his first presidential address, for action that would assure that "America might be kept American" (Higham: 318). The Secretary of Labor, James Davis, after touring Europe, submitted the administration's proposal to the house committee. The Johnson Committee overhauled that, however, relying more on its unofficial advisor, John Trevor, who supplied what became the solution to the deadlock.

Trevor designed an attack on the quota system of the 1921 law. He argued that the quotas based on the 1910 census data did not reflect the "racial status quo" of the nation. Use of the 1910 database, he maintained, overly favored southeastern Europeans. Trevor used a "racial breakdown" of the U.S. population published earlier in Clinton Stoddard Burr's *America's Race Heritage*. Trevor's analysis "proved" that, as of 1920, about 12 percent of the U.S. population was derived from southeastern European countries, but on the basis of the 1921 law they were allocated 44 percent of the total immigration quota. If, however, the 1890 census data were used, they would have only 15 percent.

Johnson's Committee, relying on the Trevor brief, introduced a new bill. The Ku Klux Klan launched a massive letter-writing campaign supporting the bill to "preserve" America's racial purity. The AFL also backed the bill.

Representative Carl Vinson of Georgia stated the committee's majority perspective on the proposal in April of 1924 when he stated:

Those favoring unrestricted immigration are wont to harken back to the days of the discovery, colonization and settlement of our country. In respect of this argument, I want to be thoroughly understood. Were the immigrants now flooding our shores possessed of the same traits, characteristics and blood of our forefathers, I would have no concern upon this problem confronting us, because, in the main, they belonged to the same branch of the Aryan race. Americans and their forebears, the English, Scotch and Welsh, are the same people.

These ancestors of the real American people were related one to the other and possessed, to a large degree, similar tastes, traits and characteristics. And in the amalgamation of these peoples and their transition into American life we find the persons who created and now maintain the greatest Nation on the globe.

But it is the "new" immigrant who is restricted in emigrating to this country. The emigrants affected by this bill are those from Italy, Greece, Russia, Poland, Bulgaria, Armenia, Czechoslovakia, Yugoslavia, and Turkey. I respectfully submit, with all the power within me, that the people from these countries do not yield their national characteristics, but retain them practically unimpaired by contact with others (cited in Marion Bennett: 48).

In its report on the bill to the full House, the committee stated:

Since it is the axiom of political science that a government not imposed by external force is the visible expression of the ideals, standards and social viewpoint of the people over which it rules, it is obvious that a change in the character or composition of a population must inevitably result in the evolution of a form of government consonant with the base upon which it rests. If, therefore, the principles of individual liberty, guarded by constitutional government created on this continent nearly a century and a half ago are to endure, the basic strain of our population must be maintained and our economic standards preserved (in Marion Bennett: 49).

Congressional representatives from the West Coast, particularly those from California, and those from the south, emphasized similar racial sentiments in their concerted efforts at restrictionism. California's representatives bore down on the alleged inadequacies of the Gentlemen's Agreement. They stressed its questionable legal validity, its vagueness, and its ineffectiveness. They played on the "Yellow Peril" theme, warning that Japan's overpopulation and thirst for land might lead to a future "race war."

Congressman Vaille, a Republican from Colorado, and a leading proponent of drastic immigration restriction based on both racial and nationalistic grounds, echoed those concerns when calling for a quota based on "established groups," by which he meant those from northwestern Europe. In support of the Johnson bill, he stated, in April of 1924:

The present law, our first numerical limitation on immigration, which has been in effect for three years, admits from any country—with certain exceptions not involved in this inquiry [i.e. those excluded from China, etc.]—3 percent of the number of persons born in that country who were resident in the United States by the census of 1910. The total quota is 357,803.

The Johnson bill, now pending, proposes to admit from any country 2 per cent of the number of persons born in such country who were resident in the United States by the census of 1890, and, in addition, 100 from each country. The total proposed quota is 161,184.

Now, people who have come here from Italy, Rumania, Greece, Czechoslovakia, and other countries in southern and eastern Europe claim that this "discriminates" against their countrymen. Why? The answer is in the fact that, as they themselves admit, the bulk of their immigration came after 1890, whereas the great bulk of the immigration from northern and western Europe came before that year.

We would not want any immigration at all unless we could hope that they would have become assimilated to our language, customs, and institutions, unless they could blend thoroughly into our body politic . . . .

It is a fact, not merely an argument, that this country was created, kept united, and developed—at least for more than a century of existence—almost entirely by people who came here from the countries of northern and western Europe . . . .

Shall the countries which furnished those earlier arrivals be discriminated against for the very reason, forsooth, that they are represented here by from 2 to 10 generations of American citizens, whereas the others are largely represented by people who have not been here long enough to become citizens at all? (U.S. Congress, House of Representative, *Congressional Record*, 68th Congress, 1st sess., April 1–14, 1924, pt. 6, 5643–5645).

And a congressman from Maine, railed against past immigration policies by maintaining that they:

Have thrown open wide our gates and through them have come . . . alien races, of alien blood, from Asia and southern Europe, the Malay, the Mongolian, the oriental with their strange and pagan rites, their babble of tongues—a people that we cannot digest, that bear no similarity to our people, that never can become true Americans, that add nothing to civilization, but are a menace to our form of Government . . . The hour has come. It may even now be too late for the white race in America, the English-speaking people, the laborer of high ideals, to assert his superiority in the work of civilization and to save America from the menace of further immigration of undesirable aliens . . . [to accomplish this] I wish it were possible to close our gates against any quota from southern Europe or from the orientals, the Mongolian countries and the yellow races of men (as cited in "We the People" and Others, 802).

The anti-Japanese provision in the bill was to exclude "those persons who could not become citizens and who must continue to owe allegiance to a foreign country." The debate centered on the theme of nonassimilability and linked Japanese exclusion and minimal quotas for those from southeastern European nations.

Only Representative Burton of Ohio argued for giving Japan a quota, and his views were considered to reflect the administration's position, particularly that of Secretary of State Hughes. In the Senate, Reed of Pennsylvania, the bill's co-author, originally fought against the provision to totally exclude the Japanese. Senators Shortridge of California and Lodge of Massachusetts fought vigorously to include their restriction. When opposition to the ban against the Japanese collapsed, even Senator Reed switched his position, supporting the amendment to the bill that would preclude them. The provision passed 71 to 4 (two opposed, two abstained) (see Ringer: 822). It clearly demonstrated the *racist ideas* behind the restrictionist law.

Senator Colt, however, the chairman of the Senate's Immigration Committee, adamantly opposed changing the census base year. He argued it was discriminatory. Secretary of State Hughes quietly supported the senator's position. The Senate committee reported a bill to keep the census year at 1910, but to lower the percentage from 3 to 2 percent of that base. Senator Reed led the measure through the committee and Senate deliberations, as Senator Colt was in poor health and not enthusiastic about the bill (Divine: 35).

Senator Reed then pushed a proposal through the Senate committee that used the quota based on 1890 census data, receiving valuable support and encouragement from Senator Henry Cabot Lodge of Massachusetts. The full Senate adopted the version retaining the 1910 census base and stipulated that the quota system would not go into effect until 1927, to enable the immigration service ample time to formulate exact quotas. For the interim (i.e., until 1927—although it was actually 1929 before the issue was resolved), the Senate accepted the House version of 2 percent, based on the 1890 census. This compromise version won overwhelming support: 62 to 6 in the Senate, and 323 to 71 in the House (Divine: 17). President Coolidge signed the bill into law on May 26, 1924.

The only opponents of the measure were representatives who served as advocates of the southeastern European groups adversely affected by the law. Jewish leaders secured the vocal support of Senator Sabath of Illinois and Senator Colt of Rhode Island, who labeled the measure and its proponents as un-American and lackeys of the Ku Klux Klan. Senator Underwood, of Alabama, responded to that criticism by stating that his opposition to immigration was economic, not racial.

The law had support from members of both parties: only thirty-five Republicans and thirty-six Democrats opposed it in the House. It had overwhelming support from virtually every section of the country. The only dissent came from some senators and representatives of districts in the northeast where immigrants from SCE Europe were concentrated. The measure was politically popular. It reflected the triumph of the "Nordic majority" in the country over the southeastern minority.

The Immigration Act of May 26, 1924 (known as the "Johnson-Reed Act"), was a lengthy and technical one, running to thirty-five pages in the code of statutes. Its central restrictive features are excerpted in Box 4.1. Its percentage

BOX 4.1.   ACT OF MAY 26, 1924—THE JOHNSON-REED ACT

Sec. 1. That this Act may be cited as the "Immigration Act of 1924."
Sec. 2. (a) A consular officer upon the application of any immigrant ... may ... use to such an immigrant and immigration visa which
shall consist of one copy of the application provided for in section 7,
visaed by such consular officer. Such visa shall specify (1) the nationality
of the immigrant; (2) whether he is a quota immigrant (as defined in
section 5) or a non-quota immigrant (as defined in section 4); (3) the date
on which the validity of the immigration visa shall expire; and (4) such
additional information necessary to the proper enforcement of the
immigration laws and the naturalization laws as may be by regulation
prescribed.
[The act then goes on to prescribe photographs, notation on the
passport of the number of visa, when such visas are not to be issued, the
fees for visas.]
[Sections 3, 4, and 5 then define the terms "immigrant," non-quota
immigrant," and "quota immigrant.]
*Enumeration of Preferences within quotas: time for giving prefer-
ences; percentages of preferences.
Sec. 6(a) Immigration visas to quota immigrants shall be issued in each
fiscal year as follows:

1. Fifty per centum of the quotas of each nationality for such year shall be
   made available ... to the following classes of immigrants, without priority of preference as between such classes: (A) Quota immigrants who
   are the fathers or mothers of citizens of the United States ... or who are
   the husbands of citizens of the United States by marriages occurring on
   or after May 31, 1928 of citizens who are citizens of the United States
   who are twenty-one years of age or over; and (B) in the case of any
   nationality the quota of which is three hundred or more, quota immigrants who are skilled in agriculture, and the wives, and the dependent
   children under age of eighteen years, of such immigrants skilled in
   agriculture, if accompanying or following to join them.
2. The remainder of the quota of each nationality for such year ... shall be
   made available in such year for the issuance of immigration visas to
   quota immigrants of such nationality who are the unmarried children
   under twenty-one years of age, or the wives, of alien residents of the
   United States who are lawfully admitted to the United States for permanent residence ...

Sec. 7. [Gives an elaborate description of duplicate application of visas
and the form of visas, copies to be kept for records, statements required as
to membership in classes of aliens excluded, statements as to exemptions

from exclusion and the various verifications as to signatures, ages, fees paid, etc.]

Sec. 8. [Covers when a consular official may issue a nonquota immigration visa.

Sec. 9. [Covers the issuance of nonquota visas and quota visas to relatives.]

Sec. 10. (a) Any alien about to depart temporarily from the United States may make application to the Commissioner of Immigration and Naturalization for a permit to reenter the United States stating the length of his intended absence, and the reasons therefore.

[Subsections (b)-(g) detail the issuance of reentry permits, their fees, effects, and treaty-merchant reentry permits.]

Sec. 11. (a) The annual quota of any nationality shall be 2 per centum of the number of foreign-born individuals of such nationality resident in continental United States as determined by the United States census of 1890, but the minimum quota of any nationality shall be 100. [Subsections (b)–(g) detail how national origin is determined, presidential proclamation of quotas, monthly issuances of visa limits, and the issue of visas to nonquota immigrants.]

Sec. 12. (a) For the purpose of this Act nationality shall be determined by country of birth, treating as separate countries the colonies, dependencies, or self-governing dominions for which separate enumeration was made in the United States census of 1890 and which is not included in the enumeration for the country to which such colony or dependency belonged . . . .

[Subsection (b) requires the secretaries of state and commerce, with the attorney general, to issue jointly statements as to the numbers of the various nationalities as of the census of 1890. Subsection (c) covers the effects of changes in the political boundaries of foreign countries; (d) and (e) cover the issuance of monthly statements and the proclamation of visas available.]

Sec. 13. (a) No immigrant shall be admitted . . . unless he (1) has an unexpired immigration visa . . .; (2) is of the nationality specified in the visa; (3) is a nonquota immigrant if specified in the visa as such; (4) is a preference-quota immigrant if specified . . . as such; and (5) is otherwise admissible under the immigration laws. [Subsection 13(b) covers such details as readmission of aliens without visas.] (c) No alien ineligible to citizenship shall be admitted to the United States unless such alien (1) is admissible as a non-quota immigrant under the provisions of subdivisions (b), (d) or (e) of section 4; or (2) is the wife, or the unmarried child under 18 years of age, of an immigrant admissible . . . and is accompanying or following to join him, or (3) is not an immigrant as defined in section 3 . . . (e) No quota immigrant shall be admitted under subdivision

(d) if the entire number of immigrant visas which may be issued to quota immigrants of the same nationality for the fiscal year has already been issued....

Sec. 14. [Covers deportation procedures for alien children under age sixteen.]

Sec. 15. [Covers the maintenance of exempt status.]

Sec. 16. [Covers when it is unlawful to bring to the United States by water an alien, including the fines or prison penalties thus engendered.]

Sec. 17. [Covers the Commissioner of Immigration and Naturalization's authority to issue rules and regulations to implement the act.]

Sec. 18. If a quota immigrant of any nationality having an immigration visa is excluded from admission to the United States under the immigration laws and deported, or does not apply for admission to the United States before the expiration of the validity of the immigration visa, or if any alien of any nationality having an immigration visa issued to him as a quota immigrant is found not to be a quota immigrant, no additional immigration visa shall be issued in lieu thereof to any other immigrant.

Sec. 19. No alien seaman excluded from admission . . . shall be permitted to land . . . except temporarily for medical treatment, or pursuant to such regulations as the Attorney General may prescribe for the ultimate departure, removal, or deportation of such alien from the United States. [Subsequent sections and subsections detail the detention of seamen on board vessels, penalties, evidence of failure to detain or deport, deportation procedures, preparation or use of documents and the offenses in connection with forging, counterfeiting immigration visas or permits, false statements, and so on.]

Sec. 23. Whenever any alien attempts to enter the United States the burden of proof shall be upon the alien to establish that he is not subject to exclusion under any of the provisions of the immigration laws.

[Sections 24 to 32 essential repeat prior law as to steamship fines, prevention of alien landings, and so on of the Immigration Act of 1917.]

Source: 43 Stat. 153; 8 U.S.C. 201.

of population quota was revised from 3 to 2 percent, and the census of population upon which the quotas were based changed from 1910 to 1890. As intended, this new quota system shifted the far smaller flow of immigration dramatically from SCE European nations to those from northwestern European origin.

Perhaps as important to the quota system, the provision for requiring visas served as an effective regulating device. Indeed, the *overseas* issuances of visas charged against quotas became the most effective means devised to control the use of quotas and to allow for *administrative screening* of immigrants prior to their entry into U.S. ports. The 1917 provision prohibiting persons "who might become public charges" provided an effective administrative tool to enforce that prohibition. It was used to drastically cut down the amount of total immigration during times of depression by setting strict standards for economic tests to demonstrate the applicant's admissibility.

In order to enforce more effectively the immigration laws and to regulate more effectively the control of illegal aliens entering the United States, mostly through its rather porous borders with Mexico, the Congress established a Border Patrol in 1925 (Act of February 27, 1925, 43 Stat. 1049–1050; 8 U.S.C. 110.)

The effects of the quota act of 1924 were immediate and dramatic. By June 30, 1925 the new act had not only checked the amount of immigration, but had its intended impact on its racial character. In its first year in operation, 294,314 immigrants were admitted, less than one-half of the 706,896 who had entered the proceeding fiscal year. Of those admitted, 75.6 percent were from northern and western Europe (compared to their 25.7 percent in 1920–1921). Only 10.8 percent of those admitted were from southern or eastern Europe, a decrease from 27.2 percent in 1923–1924, and from the 66.7 percent they contributed in 1920–1921. In that same year, 92,278 aliens left to take up permanent residence abroad. Thus, 19,956 more Italians left the United States than entered it. The number of Czechs, Yugoslavs, Greeks, Lithuanians, Hungarians, Poles, Portugese, Rumanians, Spaniards, Chinese, and Japanese who left the country considerably exceeded those of the same nationality who entered (Foreign Language Information Service, FLIS File No. 01211-01212, 1925.)

The increasing use of air travel by the year 1925 required Congress to address the application of laws to air travel, some of which affected immigration procedures. Congress passed an Act of May 20, 1926 regulating Air Commerce (44 Stat. 572; 49 U.S.C. 177(d)).

THE NATIONAL ORIGINS ACT OF 1929

Passage of the Johnson-Reed Act of 1924 did not end the battles, although it settled the major policy positions firmly in favor of restriction. The national origins principle was by then accepted as the basis for our national immigration policy. Future battles focused only on the mechanics of how the quotas themselves would be fixed.

In an editorial in March of 1924, the *New York Times* summed up the fundamental perspective of the national origins system, advocating what it held to be the basic need of a *permanent* quota system, again explicitly linking immigration policy to sovereignty and national security concerns:

> In formulating a permanent policy two considerations are of prime importance. The first is that the country has a right to say who shall and who shall not come in. It is not for any foreign country to determine our immigration policy. The second is that the basis of restriction must be chosen with a view not to the interest of any group or groups in the country, whether racial or religious, but rather with a view to the country's best interest as a whole. The great test is admissibility. Will the newcomers fit into the American life readily? Is their culture sufficiently akin to our own to make it possible for them easily to take their place among us? There is not question of "superior" or "inferior" races or of "Nordics" or of prejudice, or of racial egotism. Certain groups not only do not fuse easily, but consistently endeavor to keep alive their racial distinctions when they settle among us. They perpetuate the "hyphen," which is but another way of saying that they seek to create foreign blocs in our midst (cited in Marion Bennett: 53).

In the years following enactment of the 1924 act, Congress continued debate about a method for determining a permanent quota system. Many of the same battle lines that had formed prior to the act's passage reformed to fight anew the fixed quotas. In the Senate, Reed of Pennsylvania and Heflin of Alabama were leading proponents of restriction. In the House, Albert Johnson of Washington, author of the 1924 law, continued to be a leading restrictionist voice as to fixed quotas, even as he pressed for total suspension of immigration. Southern congressional support was led by Representative John Box of Texas, who advocated extending the quota system to Mexico and Latin America. Representative Vaile of Colorado and Jenkins of Ohio were leading restrictionists. Hearings on the matter held by the House Committee on Immigration received testimony in favor of the national origins system from thirty-five college biology professors, mainly from Ivy League schools such as Harvard, Princeton, and Yale (Divine: 35).

By 1928, John Trevor had formed a new group, the American Coalition, which was comprised of a coalition of earlier "patriotic" groups like the Sons of the American Revolution, the Patriotic Order of the Sons of America, the Daughters of the American Revolution, and so on. It proved to be eminently successful.

The racial nationalism theories popularized in the press added to public opinion support for their cause. Madison Grant published a series of articles in *The Forum* in 1927–1928. Lothrop Stoddard propounded many of Grant's ideas in his influential book, *Reforging America,* published in 1927. Similarly, a Chicago lawyer, Edward Lewis, authored *Nation or Confusion* in 1928. Kenneth Roberts, the historical novelist and a leading advocate for the quota system during the 1920–1924 debates, wrote a series for the *Saturday Evening Post* that ran in 1928 and supported the national origins plan and proposed extension of the law to include Mexico. Other publications advocating the national origins system included Charles Goethe's articles in *Eugenics* (1929), and historian Albert Bushnell Hart's in *Current History* (1929) (Divine: 61–63). As with all proponents of restriction, their advocacy emphasized race and nationalism.

Of course, groups such as the AFL, the Junior Order of United American Mechanics, and the American Legion continued their staunch support on economic grounds and favored any plan that increased northwestern European quotas at the expense of southeastern European quotas. By 1928, the U.S. Chamber of Commerce even came out in support of the system. The political party platforms of both the major parties (Republicans and Democrats) in the 1928 Presidential campaign supported the restrictionist approach (see summaries of their planks in LeMay and Barkan, Document 85: 157–158), as did the acceptance speeches of Herbert Hoover, Republican Nominee and Alfred Smith, Democratic Nominee (see Document 86: 158–159).

The Anti-National Origins Clause League became the leading critic of the plan. It worked with a coalition of various ethnic groups opposed to the plan altogether or favoring revisions of it that would at least lessen its adverse impact on their nationality group. In the House, Representatives Kvale of Minnesota and Newton of Massachusetts were leading opponents. In the Senate, Copland of New York became a leading antirestrictionist. Congressman John O'Conner, a Democrat from New York, made an impassioned speech in opposition to several bills, including what became the 1929 bill to fix permanent quotas. His comments addressing the "pervasive spirit of intolerance and bigotry" that he believed infused the United States to an alarming degree are evident in his speech to the House presented in Box 4.2.

**BOX 4.2. STATEMENT OF CONGRESSMAN
JOHN O'CONNOR, NEW YORK**

Here today I want to discuss [the] spirit [that] I believe pervades our country to an alarming extent, and I want to discuss it without any thought of the past or recent events. I approach it looking to my country's future.

I believe that there are many people in this country today who fear that these United States of ours is the most intolerant, narrow-minded nation on the globe. I am not going to use any bromides about loving my country. That is the gratuitous mouthing of a demagogue. If I think my country is wrong, I propose to criticize it in its own citadel. I will defend it against attack from without, but I reserve the right to criticize it from within. I fear there is a spirit pervading our country today reflected in these immigration bills that is a menace to the country—a spirit of intolerance and bigotry not only to religion but to races.

Take this bill before us today, the Box bill, relating to immigration coming over our borders. It represents a spirit of superior intolerance to our neighbors on the north and the south.

Oh, I do not like the spirit behind all these measures. There seems to be a spirit of bigotry and intolerance in America directed at the races of the rest of the world that surely is un-American. There are certain people in our country who believe that no other race on the face of the globe can be compared in education, in culture, in respectability to the inhabitants of the United States.

Let me state here, gentlemen, not in order to say anything sensational but to bring the truth forcibly before this body: Take a railroad train and go through the South, through the West, through the North, and in the outlying sections of the country. Look at what we call our own people, who have not had the opportunities of the people in the big cities. You will see American people of the Nordic races, you will see people whose forefathers were here 300 years ago, but you will see them in the lowest state of civilization. Is that the type to which you refer when you speak of the "American blood" in America? Yes, you will see them in rags and tatters; you will see them unkempt, uncultured, uneducated, and un-couth.

Then I suggest you take an automobile and ride through the so-called foreign segments of the big cities and see these foreign people whom you hate so vehemently. Look at their children going to school in droves, seeking every opportunity for education, eager to acquire and to assim-ilate all the customs and habits of our country. See them going through the grammar schools, the high schools, to the colleges, from Harvard to Stanford, eager to become part of America and its institutions.

Let me make this assertion here, after due consideration, that I believe that the foreigners of this country today on the whole furnish better material for citizenship than many of the so-called American types living in the outlying sections of the country . . .

How long can demagogues in all political parties continue to preach this doctrine of saying "America for Americans only?" It surely must result in damage to our country. It is a spirit of vindictiveness against anybody whose ancestors were not born here 300 years ago. I do not care that its effects is (sic) in elections, but I do care what effect it is going to have on our country in the future.

Source: Congressional Record, as cited in the Foreign Language Information Service, In-terpreter Release Clip Sheet, 6, 4, February 23, 1929.

The opponents of restrictionism generally emphasized economic arguments, stressing the need for labor and the fact that immigrant labor was willing to do the unpleasant jobs that had to be done and that native workers were unwilling to do.

The debates were more than about racial theories versus an economic supply of cheap labor. The various "formulae" being debated led to significantly different quota limits for the various national origin groupings. Table 4.1, for example, presents a comparison of the variations in immigration quotas for selected—but typical—European countries under the 1890 census and various national origin quota plans. It shows the dramatic differences of the various formulae made in a country's limits, sometimes increasing or decreasing a limit by 200 or 300 percent!

As we have seen here, the consequences of the 1924 act were considerable: European immigration slumped from over 800,000 in 1921 to under 150,000 by 1928. Still the restrictionist movement was not satisfied. The 1924 act exempted countries in the western hemisphere and the Philippine Islands (then a U.S. territory as a result of the Spanish-American War). Restrictionists advocated a limitation of immigration from Latin America, especially Mexico. That movement began in 1926, led by Representative Box of Texas, who as we have seen was an ardent restrictionist and member of the House Immigration Committee. His allies included Hiram Johnson of Texas and Thomas Heflin of Alabama. Leading Senate forces included Harris of Georgia, Willis of Ohio, and Reed of Pennsylvania, all leading restrictionists. They found a convenient slogan for their proposals of a quota for Mexican immigration, one echoed as recently as the 1980s and 1990s: "close the back door" (Divine: 53).

In the congressional debates over the Box bill, Mexican immigrants were depicted as peons who taxed the school systems beyond their capacities and lowered educational standards. The typical Mexican immigrant was portrayed

TABLE 4.1. Comparison of Immigration Quotas under 1890 Census and the National Origins Plan for Representative European Nations

European Nations	1890 Census Plan	1927 Quota Board Report	1928 Quota Board Report	1929 Quota Board Report
Germany	51,227	23,428	24,908	25,957
Great Britain	34,007	73,039	65,894	65,721
Irish Free State	28,567	13,862	17,429	17,583
Italy	3,845	6,091	5,989	5,802
Norway	6,453	2,267	2,403	2,377
Poland	5,982	4,978	6,090	6,524
Russia	2,248	4,781	3,540	2,784
Sweden	9,561	3,259	3,399	3,314

Source: Adapted from Robert A. Divine, *American Immigration Policy, 1924–1952*. Yale University Press (1957). From Government data on page 30.

as a social leper who would contaminate the U.S. way of life. Harry Laughlin, the "eugenics expert," of the House Immigration Committee, testified that immigration from the entire western hemisphere should be limited to "whites." Representative Box described Mexicans as:

> ...illiterate, unclean, peonized masses...a mixture of Mediterranean-blooded Spanish peasants with low-grade Indians who did not fight extinction but submitted and multiplied as serfs. [The influx of Mexicans] creates the most insidious and general mixture of white, Indian, and Negro blood strains ever produced in America (cited in Divine: 57).

His proposal to limit Mexican immigration, however, ran into strong and well-organized opposition from the southwest. An economic coalition of farmers, cattlemen, miners, sugar manufacturers, and railroad interests all favored continued and unlimited Mexican immigration there. Mexican workers were valued as a source of common labor preferred for being docile, nonaggressive people who would do what they were told and accept jobs that white workers simply refused to do.

In addition to this economic perspective, opposition to limits on Mexican immigration founded foreign policy considerations: on "Pan-Americanism." Secretary of State Kellogg was ardently seeking to foster better relations with Latin America. Senator Hiram Bingham of Connecticut and Carl Hayden of Arizona led the fight against western hemisphere quotas. When Senator Harris of Georgia introduced a bill in 1929, which would amend the quota law to include a limit on Mexican immigration, President Herbert Hoover indicated that if the bill passed, he would veto it (Divine: 67).

In 1929, the National Origins Plan was finally enacted and the quota system became fully, and permanently, operational (Act of March 2, 1929, 45 Stat. 1512; 8 U.S.C. 106a). President Hoover then issued a presidential proclamation stipulating the new and permanent quotas for each fiscal year thereafter. Identified as the national origins system, it was based on the proportion of each nationality in the total U.S. population, determined by an analysis of the 1920 census. The overall ceiling for non-western hemisphere immigration was lowered to somewhat over 150,000. Its quota numbers are briefly illustrated in Box 4.3. For comparison purposes, Table 4.2 presents the quota limits for various countries under the three different versions of the quota system used in the 1920s—the 1921 Emergency Act, the 1924 Johnson-Reed Act, and the National Origins Act of 1929 (what became the permanent or fixed quotas).

Reflecting the national mood of nationalism, the U.S. Supreme Court handed a decision on May 27, 1929, in which the Court ruled on a question of whether or not a person could be denied naturalization because of his or her *political beliefs* (in this case, pacifism). In the *United States v. Rosika Schwimmer* (279 U.S. 644), the court decided that a woman who refused to

BOX 4.3. PRESIDENT HOOVER'S PROCLAMATION OF MARCH 22, 1929: ON THE NATIONAL ORIGIN IMMIGRATION QUOTAS

Country or Area	Quota	Country or Area	Quota
Afghanistan	100	Irish Free State	17,853
Albania	100	Italy	5,802
Andorra	100	Japan	100
Arabian Peninsula	100	Latvia	236
Armenia	100	Liberia	100
Australia	100	Liechtenstein	100
Austria	1,413	Lithuania	386
Belgium	1,304	Luxemburg	100
Bhutan	100	Monaco	100
Bulgaria	100	Morocco	100
Cameroon	100	Muscat (Oman)	100
China	100	Naura	100
Czechoslovakia	2,874	Nepal	100
Danzig	100	Netherlands	3,153
Denmark	1,181	New Zealand	100
Egypt	100	Norway	2,377
Estonia	116	New Guinea	100
Ethiopia	100	Palestine	100
Finland	569	Persia	100
France	3,086	Poland	6,524
Germany	25,957	Portugal	440
G. Britain & N. Ireland	65,721	Ruanda/Urundi	100
		Rumania	295
Greece	307	Russia, European & Asiatic	2,784
Hungary	869		
Iceland	100	Samoa	100
India	100	San Marino	100
Iraq	100		

Source: President's Proclamation 1872 of March 22, 1929. *Orders, Proclamations and Treaties:* 1092–1093.

swear that she would fight to defend the Constitution of the United States (even though at the time no women were allowed to fight in the U.S. military), because of her beliefs in pacifism, could be denied her application for naturalization.

TABLE 4.2. Comparison of Quotas Allotted to Selected Countries under Three Different Versions of the Quota System

	1921 Act 3% – 1920 Census	1924 Act 2% – 1890	1929 National Origins (Fixed) Plan
Total	357,803	164,667	153,714
Asia	492	1,424	1,423
Africa/Oceana	359	1,821	1,800
Europe	356,952	161,422	150,491
Northwest Europe			
Belgium	1,563	512	1,304
Denmark	5,619	2,789	1,181
France	5,729	3,954	3,086
Germany	67,607	51,227	25,957
G. Britain/N. Ireland	77,342	34,007	65,721
Irish Free State	77,342	28,567	17,853
Netherlands	3,607	1,648	3,153
Norway	12,202	6,453	2,377
Sweden	20,042	9,561	3,314
Switzerland	3,752	2,081	1,707
Total northwest Europe	197,630	140,999	127,266
Southeast Europe			
Austria	7,342	785	1,413
Czechoslovakia	14,357	3,073	2,874
Greece	3,063	100	307
Hungary	5,747	473	869
Italy	42,057	3,845	5,802
Poland	30,977	5,982	6,524
Portugal	2,465	503	440
Romania	7,419	603	295
U.S.S.R.	24,405	2,248	2,784
Turkey	2,654	100	226
Yugoslavia	6,426	671	845
Total southeast Europe	155,585	20,423	23,235

Source: Bernard: 27. Reprinted from LeMay, 1987: 91 with permission of Greenwood Publishing Group, Inc., Westport, CT.

Nor was the U.S. government the only one concerned with the literacy of the immigrants in the 1920s. New York State, among others in the Northeast, required that new voters prove their ability to read and write English (Foreign Language Information Service, *Interpreter Release Clip Sheet,* 6, 8, April 24, 1929. For a listing of the effects of the test for a six-year period, 1923–1928, see LeMay and Barkan, Document 91: 167–168).

THE GREAT DEPRESSION DECADE

The year 1929 was not only the year of passage of the permanent quota system; it saw the stock market crash that ushered in the Great Depression. This worldwide depression had as great an impact on immigration as did any law. The drop in immigration, already precipitous since the quota acts of the 1920s, was exceptional during the decade of the 1930s. While over 4,100,000 had entered during the 1920s, immigration fell to just slightly over one-half million for the entire decade of the 1930s. Total immigration to the United States was at the lowest level for a decade since 1820. "In national security policy, the depression years further exacerbated isolationism: Americans, absorbed by the problems of the depression, chose to retreat all the more into isolationism" (Tindall: 1161). In 1935, FDR tried to get United States participation in the World Court, but isolationist and unilateralist instincts prevailed in the Senate, which rejected ratification. In August 1935, Congress passed, and President Roosevelt signed the first of a series of neutrality acts (in 1937, and 1939 as well), that barred sales or shipments of munitions to belligerent nations (Jordan: 48; Tindall: 1165; Kuchan: 188). In spring of 1937, isolationism reached its peak. A Gallop opinion poll in that year found that 94 percent of those polled preferred efforts to keep the nation out of war over efforts to prevent war (Tindall: 1167).

Periods of depression have always resulted in a slackening off of immigration, since the economic crisis means the U.S. will be seen as offering less opportunity to perspective immigrants. When the depression is worldwide, moreover, it means the ability and opportunity to migrate is lessened. Periods of severe economic dislocation—recessions and depressions—have been times when the restrictionist movement flowered, instigating new demands for the protection of the native worker against the encroachment of foreign labor. The 1930s were no exception.

In the decade of the 1930s, the major battles over restriction centered on whether to do so by administrative or legislative action, and on the extension of the quota system limitations to the Philippines. Restrictionist groups pushed Congress to decrease quotas as set by the 1929 law by 60 to 90 percent. Opponents argued that more stringent enforcement of the existing laws would be adequate to deal with the issue.

In 1930, Senator Hugo Black of Alabama introduced a bill to suspend all immigration except for immediate family members of U.S. citizens for a period of five years. Although the Senate rejected the Black proposal, the vote was fairly close, 37 to 29.

The State Department reacted to the Black proposal and related restrictionist debate in Congress by enforcing administratively a very strict interpretation of the "public charge" clause to all those seeking a visa. Within five months, it succeeded in cutting European immigration by 90 percent. Consular officers throughout the decade followed the president's order to interpret strictly that provision, and the period 1930–1931 saw a drop of 62 percent in quota immigration, and during the decade from 1931 to 1940 those immigrants coming to the United States exceeded repatriated immigrants for a net total of only 68,693 (Divine: 78).

Nonquota immigration (e.g., from Canada, Mexico, and the Philippines) throughout the decade was nearly as large as quota immigration, and it rose and fell in a manner closely paralleling that of quota immigration. Obviously, the depression conditions were lessening the incentives to migrate. The rigid screening process for visas and the unfavorable economic conditions depressed quota and nonquota immigration alike. Table 4.3 shows the annual quota and nonquota immigration data for the 1930 decade by region of origin.

Having successfully passed the National Origins Act of 1929, the restrictionists moved on during the 1930s to campaign to "plug" what they felt were loopholes in the immigration barriers. One of the major targets was the immigration from the Philippines. Among the first attempts to limit Filipino immigration was a proposal first introduced in 1928 by Representative Richard Welch of California. It had the staunch support of the West Coast labor unions and the AFL. When a deadly outbreak of spinal meningitis in 1929 was traced to a Filipino immigrant, the movement to impose a quota on the Philippines gained momentum.

The prorestrictionist forces used the same hodgepodge of racial arguments and economic fears that had characterized earlier battles. The same organizations were active, once again lobbying Congress. The major prorestrictionist organizations of the 1930s included the American Coalition, the California Joint Immigration Committee, the AFL, the National Grange, the American Legion, and the Native Sons of the Golden West (Divine: 69–70).

The forces opposing Filipino restriction included, of course, various Filipino political leaders, particularly Manuel Roxas, the Speaker of the Philippine Legislature, who argued eloquently that the right to migrate anywhere in the United States and its territories was a moral right of all residents under the U.S. flag. He was supported by the U.S. War Department, the Department of State, Hawaiian sugar planters, and the Pacific American Steamship Association. Senators Hawes of Missouri and Norris of Nebraska, both strong advocates of Philippine Independence, called the restriction proposal "dishonorable" and "amoral." In 1930, the proposal was defeated in the Senate by a vote of 41 to 23 (Divine: 70).

Southern and western state representatives continued to battle for restriction. In addition to Johnson of Washington and Reed of Pennsylvania, Representatives Moore, Johnson and Dies of Texas pushed for limits. In 1931, they urged adoption of a "reduction of quotas" bill that was the high point of their legislative efforts in the early depression years. They were opposed by congressional representatives from the northeast. Leading antirestrictionists in the House were the New York City delegation, Representatives LaGuardia, O'Connor, and Dickstein. In the Senate, Walsh of Massachusetts and Elmer

TABLE 4.3. Quota and Nonquota Immigration to the United Sates, 1930–1940

(a) Annual Immigration Quotas and Quota Immigrants Admitted by Region

	All Countries	Northwest Europe	Southeast Europe	Asia	Africa	Pacific
Annual quotas	153,714	125,853	24,648	1,805	1,200	700
1930	141,497	116,062	24,002	891	273	269
1931	54,118	38,706	14,498	490	206	218
1932	12,983	6,368	6,402	331	72	170
1933	8,220	3,831	4,091	189	20	89
1934	12,483	6,839	5,286	223	33	102
1935	17,207	8,849	7,971	202	41	144
1936	18,675	10,754	8,142	234	40	157
1937	27,762	16,481	10,754	295	64	168
1938	42,404	25,383	16,254	584	74	199
1939	62,492	41,135	20,400	587	78	202
1940	51,997	34,313	16,828	549	99	208

(continued)

TABLE 4.3. (continued)

(b) Nonquota Immigrants Admitted by Region for Years 1930–1940

	All Nations	All Quota Nations	Northwest Europe	Southeast Europe	Asia	Africa	Pacific	All Nonquota Nations
1930	100,203	36,805	38,805	30,350	2,474	117	149	63,308
1931	43,021	21,357	3,101	16,253	1,821	71	111	21,664
1932	22,593	12,884	2,566	8,748	1,390	62	118	9,709
1933	14,848	7,306	1,778	5,223	254	15	36	7,542
1934	16,987	8,307	2,000	6,038	228	8	33	8,680
1935	17,749	9,571	1,760	7,513	241	12	45	8,178
1936	17,654	9,049	1,687	7,068	229	19	46	8,605
1937	22,482	9,776	1,875	7,505	323	18	55	12,706
1938	25,401	10,397	1,891	8,099	334	9	64	15,004
1939	20,596	8,038	1,910	5,675	374	13	66	12,558
1940	18,759	6,405	1,784	4,201	327	20	73	12,354

Source: Table by author; data from M. Bennett: 68–69; Divine: 90.

Thomas of Oklahoma were prominent antirestrictionist voices. In December 1931, Samuel Dickstein of New York, an ardent antirestrictionist spokesman, replaced Albert Johnson as chairman of the powerful House Immigration Committee. The antirestrictionist forces generally had the support of the Roosevelt Administration, particularly that of the Secretary of Labor, Frances Perkins.

In 1932, Representative Moore of Kentucky introduced a new bill to restrict immigration by lowering the quotas and expanding their coverage. It was vigorously opposed by Jewish organizations already attempting to increase the number of immigrants allowed to enter as the persecution of Jews increased in central and eastern Europe in the 1930s. This effort was led by the Hebrew Sheltering and Immigration Aid Society. They also had the lobbying support of the YWCA. In 1932, a new source of antirestriction surfaced as well—the extreme left-wing groups such as the American Communist Party and the Young Communist League. Also active in the early 1930s was the National Council for Protection of the foreign-born. Moore's bill died in Congress.

In 1933, the political forces advocating Philippine independence tried a new ploy. They attempted to gain the support of the prorestrictionist forces in Congress by offering a compromise bill. In essence, the bill provided that if Congress should enact a law fixing a specific date for Philippine independence, the Filipino representatives and their supporters would accept a provision restricting Filipino immigration during the transition period, as long as such restrictions were based on economic grounds rather than racial ones. This bill passed in 1934 was signed by President Roosevelt and approved by the Philippine Legislature in May of 1934. The Philippine Islands were given an annual quota of 50, and the "problem" of Filipino restriction was settled (Divine: 73–75).

With that issue off the agenda of Congress, the mid-1930s were a time of relative inaction. From 1933 to 1938, Congress seemed more friendly, in tone at least, toward the issue of immigration. Representative Dickstein, as chair of the House Immigration Committee, introduced a series of proposals to liberalize the immigration laws on behalf of refugees from Germany. His proposals were supported by the lobbying efforts of the American Jewish Congress, the Hebrew Sheltering and Immigrant Aid Society, and some Catholic and Protestant groups concerned about the refugee problem. In 1933, the League of Nations established a High Commission for Refugees Coming from Germany. It was headed by a U.S. citizen, James MacDonald. In 1938, the league established a single High Commission for Refugees. These efforts added to the public relations push by forces advocating a relaxation of the quota restrictions. By 1938, the Jewish refugee problem was becoming an increasingly critical issue.

As one would expect, efforts to ease restrictions were vigorously opposed by the American Coalition, the American Legion, and the AFL. Representative Jenkins of Ohio and Rankin of Mississippi were leading opponents in the

House. Public opinion was still on the side of the restrictions, and the measures all died in the House.

In 1939, another attempt was made. Senator Wagner of New York introduced a bill to allow the nonquota entry of 20,000 *refugee children*. A Nonsectarian Committee for German Refugee Children was formed that won over organized labor by getting the endorsement of the AFL-CIO. It even had southern proponents in the person of Frank Graham, the president of the University of North Carolina, and Homer Rainey, president of the University of Texas. This proposal, too, had the traditional opposition of the American Legion, the American Coalition, and the like (except organized labor), which had characterized many of the earlier battles. Even this measure, however, died in the House.

Finally, the administration acted, applying its own interpretation. It allowed in some 20,000 children in 1939. In total, some 250,000 refugees entered the U.S. during the 1934–1941 period, but all came in under the existing quota laws (Maldwyn Jones: 281). This refugee problem pointed out a major weakness of the quota system—its inflexibility. Full use of the quota system was often prevented by its procedures. The 1929 law provided that for quotas over 100, no more than 10 percent of a yearly quota could be used in a single month. When transportation conditions or related refugee problems blocked the movement of persons to fill the 10 percent provision, no carryover was allowed. Nor was there any carryover allowed for any unused quotas from one year to the next. In addition, the red tape involved in getting visas, especially during the turbulent 1930s, meant that many quotas were unused.

The quota laws had their intended effect, as can be seen in Table 4.4. It presents the sources of U.S. immigration from 1820 to 1947, showing the distribution by percentages and by decades for the major regional sources of origin. Northwestern European immigration, which had fallen from over 70 percent of the total in the 1880s to less than 20 percent during the 1910–1920 decade, prior to the quota laws, shifted dramatically upward to nearly 40 percent during the 1930s. In contrast, southeastern European immigration fell from nearly 71 percent in the 1910–1920 decade to under 30 percent during the 1930s.

THE WORLD WAR II YEARS AND THE
DISPLACED PERSONS ACT, 1948

In 1940, FDR was re-elected to an unprecedented third term. He began moving foreign policy toward a less isolationist stance. He began the policy by which the United States became known as the Arsenal for Democracy (Tindall: 1175). He was advised by and increasingly involved members of a "kitchen cabinet" in foreign and national security policy-making.

Because they were all internationalist in outlook, generally connected with the East and its bigger schools and foundations, and usually members of the

TABLE 4.4. Sources of Immigration to the United States, 1820–1947, by Percentages, by Decades

Decades	All Europe (%)	N/W Europe (%)	S/E Europe (%)	Canada (%)	Mexico (%)	All Others (%)
1820–30	70.2	68.0	2.2	1.6	3.2	25.0
1831–40	82.8	81.7	1.0	2.3	1.1	13.0
1841–50	93.3	93.0	0.3	2.4	0.2	4.1
1851–60	94.4	93.6	0.8	2.3	0.1	3.2
1861–70	89.3	87.8	1.5	6.6	0.1	4.0
1871–80	80.7	73.6	7.2	13.6	0.2	5.4
1881–90	90.3	72.0	18.3	7.5	—	2.2
1891–1900	96.5	44.6	51.9	0.1	—	3.4
1901–10	92.5	21.7	70.8	2.0	0.6	4.9
1911–20	76.4	17.4	59.0	12.9	3.8	6.9
1921–30	60.3	31.2	29.0	22.5	11.2	6.0
1931–40	66.0	37.4	28.6	20.5	4.2	9.3
1941–47	44.4	34.9	9.5	23.2	8.7	23.6

Source: Bernard: 40. Reprinted by permission of Harper and Row.

Council on Foreign Relations in New York, as the years wore on, the group acquired, from an English counterpart, the name of the establishment. And to a large extent, it can be said that from 1940 through 1965, the United States followed the establishment foreign policy (Halperin, Clapp, and Kanter: 74–75).

As with the case of previous war periods, during World War II immigration dropped dramatically. The war-time era had an impact on immigration-related policy-making far beyond the levels of the influx.

When the Japanese attacked Pearl Harbor on December 7, 1941, they brought on a virtual nightmare experience to the Japanese-Americans living on the mainland. A total of 112,000 persons of Japanese ancestry, some 70,000 of whom were native-born U.S. citizens, were rounded up and sent to "relocation camps" in the interior because of what was termed "military necessity." The relocation camps were, in fact, concentration camps. Conditions, especially in the beginning, were grim. Men and women, grandparents and infants, young children and young adults, simple gardeners and fishermen, were herded behind fifteen-foot high barbed-wire fences in camps guarded by tommygun-armed troops stationed around the perimeter and on spotlight towers. Residents lived in crude barracks, in which stalls of a mere 18 by 21 feet housed families of six or seven. They were partitioned off with seven-foot high partitions with four-foot openings, affording little privacy. A barrack building 90 by 20 feet typically held six families. Residents had to use outside latrines. They were locked in by 9:00 p.m. and had a 10:00 p.m. lights-out curfew. Located in seven states, the camps were governed by a War Relocation

Authority and the War Relocation Work Corps. What follows is a description of Poston in Arizona, whose peak population reached 17,867 by August 1942.

The barracks were flimsily constructed. Sometimes as many as eight people lived in one room. Mattresses were made by stuffing cloth bags with straw. There was hardly any furniture. The heat was intense in the summer, and the minimum temperature during the winter occasionally fell below the freezing mark. And then there were the barbed wire and the guards. It is little wonder that some people felt betrayed at having been sent to such a place and either actively resisted or failed to cooperate fully with the administration's plans (McLemore, 1983: 179).

Table 4.5 lists the internment camps, their dates of operation, and the numbers interned at each camp.

Since we treated even enemy aliens from Germany and Italy far better than we did those native-born U.S. citizens, and since no other ethnic or racial group residing in America during World War II suffered comparable indignities nor was treated in such a cavalier and categorical manner, only *racial prejudice* can adequately explain the internment policy.[1] Its chief author, General John L. DeWitt, commanding general of the Western Defense Command, provided a blatantly racist rationale for the camps:

TABLE 4.5. Japanese American Relocation Camps and their Capacities

Camp Name/Location	Dates of Operation	Numbers/Internees
Gila River, Arizona	Aug. 1942–Nov. 1945	13,400
Granada, Colorado	Sep. 1942–Oct. 1945	7,600
Heart Mt., Wyoming	Sep. 1942–Nov. 1945	11,100
Jerome, Arkansas	Nov. 1942–Jun. 1944	8,600
Manzanar, California	Jun. 1942–Nov. 1945	10,200
Minidoka, California	Sep. 1942–Oct. 1945	9,900
Poston, Arizona	Jun. 1942–Nov. 1945	18,000
Rohwer, Arkansas	Oct. 1942–Nov. 1945	8,500
Topaz, Utah	Oct. 1942–Oct. 1945	8,300
Tule Lake, California[a]	Jun. 1942–Mar. 1946	18,800
Total[b]		114,490

[a] There were two camps at Tule Lake. The second was a high-security prison for the 3,500 Japanese Americans believed to pose individual threats to the war effort. None was ever charged with or convicted of spying or sabotage. Still, this small group was not released until the war was over.

[b] Some prisoners were released before others were interned. The total number of evacuees was more than 120,000.

Source: Peter Wright and John Armor, *Manzanar.* Used by permission of Times Books, a division of Random House, Inc.

In the war in which we are engaged, racial affinities are not severed by migration. The *Japanese race is an enemy race* and while second- and third-generation Japanese born on U.S. soil and possessed of U.S. citizenship have become "Americanized," *the racial strains are undiluted* (cited in McLemore: 184; italics added).

In the succinct words of one scholar, "One hundred thousand persons were sent to concentration camps on a record that couldn't support a conviction for stealing a dog (Rostow, 1945: 184). And, of course, it is ironic that their "racial strains were undiluted" precisely because of U.S. laws that forbade marriages between the white and Asian races.

Although General Mark Clark had earlier informed General George Marshall that there really was not military necessity for the camps, and although this assessment was concurred in by the Director of the FBI, General DeWitt was not dissuaded. Earl Warren, then Attorney General of California, and General DeWitt responded to the fact that no acts of sabotage had taken place with the ingenious reasoning that the very absence of sabotage or any other evidence of fifth column activity "merely showed how disciplined the resident Japanese were . . . they were merely biding their time to strike a well-planned and devastating blow synchronized with attacks by the armed forces of Japan" (cited in Ringer: 863). General DeWitt said elsewhere: "A Jap is a Jap. It makes no difference whether he's an American or not."[2]

The FBI and naval intelligence officers had quickly rounded up everyone who might be regarded as the slightest threat (those held at Tule Lake mentioned earlier). Nonetheless, General DeWitt and the congressional delegation from the coast pressed on with the evacuation plans. Secretary of War Stimson and Attorney General Biddle agreed to support the plan, and Roosevelt issued executive order 9066 on February 12, 1942. The president sought and received congressional approval. It passed overwhelmingly: in the Senate only Taft spoke against it. By October of 1942, approximately 110,000 evacuees were relocated to the various camps.

Because of the relocation, Japanese Americans suffered a huge financial loss. And of course, no price can be placed on the emotional trauma, the broken hearts or the sorrows of separated families, or those in which fathers interned in the camps had committed suicide in response to their shame and despondency. The overall cost to the U.S. taxpayer was an estimated $250,000,000 for a program that history has demonstrated was simply unjustified by military necessity. It was simply put as a hysterical reaction to the war and the Pearl Harbor attack coupled with underlying racism.

Paradoxically, on Hawaii, which was in a much more vulnerable position, authorities did not even attempt a mass evacuation of the 120,552 Japanese American citizens living there. The war passed without a single proven act of espionage or sabotage by any Japanese American there or on the mainland. The army announced that "the shipping situation and the labor shortage make it a matter of military necessity to keep the people of Japanese blood on the island." Yet the army had used those very words of "military necessity" to justify the West Coast evacuation plan (Hosokawa: 457–467; LeMay, 2005: 84).

The Japanese Americans accepted the evacuation and internment surprisingly peacefully. There was one riot at Poston and another at Manzanar during the early period when the conditions at the camps were exceptionally bad. Once the period of hysteria passed, Japanese American evacuees of proven loyalty were allowed to leave the camps and join the U.S. Army. Some 20,000 did so, 6,000 of whom served in the Pacific, but most of whom were in the famed 100th Battalion, 442nd Regimental Combat Team, which went on to become the most highly decorated unit in the European theatre.[3]

In *Hirobayashi v. the United States* (320 U.S. 81, June 21, 1943), and in *Korematsu v. the United States* (323 U.S. 214, December 18, 1944), the Supreme Court upheld the constitutionality of the evacuation and internment programs. In the latter decision, approved by a 6-3 vote, the dissenting justices rendered a sharp dissenting opinion. Justice Francis Murphy labeled the evacuation as "the legislation of racism." Justice Robert Jackson wrote:

> Once a judicial opinion rationalizes an order to show it conforms to the Constitution, or rather, rationalizes the Constitution to show that the Constitution sanctions such an order, the Court for all time has validated the principle of racial discrimination in criminal procedure, and of transplanting American citizens. The principle then lies about like a loaded weapon ready for the hand of any authority that can bring forward a plausible claim of an urgent need. Every repetition imbeds that principle more deeply in our law and thinking and expands it to new purposes.[4]

Fortunately, the principle did not lie about for long. In *Ex parte Mitsuye Endo* (323 U.S. 283–310, December 18, 1944), the Supreme Court reversed itself and revoked the West Coast Exclusion Order. Effective January 2, 1945, the Japanese Americans were no longer under forcible detention. By June of 1946 all the camps were closed.

The war-time sentiments that plagued the Japanese Americans aided another racial group and led to the slight modification of immigration policy-making. The war-time alliance with China against Japan was the main factor in leading to the repeal of the Chinese Exclusion Act. Madame Chiang Kai-shek visited the United States in 1943. A citizen's committee was formed to advocate for repeal. It was passed with little opposition on December 13, 1943 and a small quota was established for China, and allowed for their naturalization (Act of December 17, 1943, 57 Stat. 600; 8 U.S.C. 212(a)). Two months later, President Roosevelt officially added a quota of 105 to the immigration provisions.

During the war, Roosevelt revived the Council of National Defense, which had been dormant since the end of World War I. He used it as an administration instrument to devise, institute, coordinate, and plan defensive activities in the United States. This greatly shifted national security policy-making from the legislative to the executive branch. Similarly, the Office of Emergency Management became a sort of overall tent and service agency for the defense and war establishment. It gave FDR and the administration immense flexibility as conditions in the war effort changed to constitute and reconstitute units of government. Another policy that shifted national security policy power from the Congress to the presidency was the law enacted eleven days after the Pearl Harbor attack—the first War Powers Act. It authorized the president to make such redistribution of functions among executive agencies as he deemed necessary (Relyea: 608). It was at this time that the term "national security" came to be used. It was an amalgamation term viewed as "the ability of the nation to protect its internal values from all external threats" (Relyea: 611).

The United States emerged from World War II as a true "superpower." Isolationism was effectively ended. The United States joined the United Nations on July 28, 1945 by a vote of 89 to 2 in the U.S. Senate! This was such a sharp contrast to the post-World War I experience in which the Senate rejected the treaty to join the League of Nations, a far less powerful international organization than was the United Nations. In part, this reflected FDR's political strategy. Having learned from Wilson's mistakes, FDR co-opted Republican leadership to push for establishing and joining the United Nations. He had included powerful Republicans in his cabinet: Henry Stimson as Secretary of War, Frank Knox as Secretary of the Navy, and as part of his kitchen cabinet, Wendell Wilkie, who had been his Republican opponent for the presidency in 1940, but who had become an ardent internationalist after Pearl Harbor. Roosevelt established a "Committee of Eight," to consult with him regarding administrative plans for foreign policy, the United Nations, and related national security issues. The Committee of Eight was comprised of four Democrats, three Republicans, and one Progressive. Essentially, FDR crafted a bipartisan consensus that served the country in foreign-policy issues for the next half century (Kupchan: 198).

Roosevelt advocated a notion of the Four Policemen—the world's major states; the United States, Great Britain, the Soviet Union, and China. He saw these four powers as able to dominate the United Nations to make it more effective than had been the League of Nations in promoting collective security that would not be detrimental to United States national security.

When Truman assumed the presidency upon the death of Roosevelt, he continued that foreign policy emphasis. He noted that World War II might have been avoided entirely had the democracies of the world banded together to block German and Japanese aggression in the mid-1930s. The experience of World War II and the birth of the Cold War in its aftermath transformed some important aspects of American approaches to national security. Reluctantly at first, Americans came to accept the role of the United States as a world power with worldwide responsibilities. The specter of communism as a challenge to the freedom of people everywhere and the advent of Soviet nuclear capability destroyed Americans' traditional sense of continental security and induced them to look to security well beyond their shores (Jordan et al.: 55).

With respect to immigration policy-making, the immediate postwar years and several war-induced problems increasingly highlighted the difficulties and inflexibilities of the quota system. On December 28, 1945, Congress passed the War Brides Act (59 Stat. 659; 8 U.S.C. 232–236) allowing the spouses and children of members of the armed forces to immigrate to be reunited with their family. It allowed for up to 150,000 wives, fiancées, and some 25,000 children and a few hundred husbands of U.S. citizens serving in the armed forces to be brought in outside the quota limits. A similar act in 1947 allowed in some 5,000 Chinese and 800 Japanese wives of U.S. servicemen outside of the quota system.

In 1946, the U.S. Supreme Court heard a case to reconsider the Schwimmer case decided in 1929. The issue was whether an applicant for admission to citizenship could be naturalized if the individual was a conscientious objector to military service. The Court in this case, *Girouard v. United States* (328 U.S. 61, April 22, 1946), reversed itself and ruled in favor of the applicant despite his objector status, 7 to 1 with one justice not participating. The Schwimmer decision was overturned.

It was the problem of refugees and displaced persons; however, that really showed the greatest need for some modification of the quota system. At the end of the war, there were an estimated 8 million displaced persons in Austria, Italy, and Germany, over 1 million of whom were in displaced-persons camps. President Truman's first response was to issue a presidential directive, in 1945, which admitted 2,500 that year. They were aliens admitted *under* the quota system, brought in as permanent residents at government expense. Preferences were given to orphans and relatives of U.S. citizens. About half were from Poland and nearly 1,000 were from Italy (*Public Papers of the Presidents*, December 22, 1945, 572–578; Marion Bennett: 89). For the next two-and-a-half years, this directive was used to bring in over 41,000 persons, some 38,000 of whom were quota immigrants, over 2,000 of whom were nonquota, and just over 1,000 of whom were nonimmigrants (mostly students). About 12 percent of the displaced persons admitted as quota immigrants had a preference within the quota as blood relatives of U.S. citizens or of admitted permanent resident aliens (Marion Bennett: 89).

It was the millions of refugees in the DP camps in Europe, however, that really demonstrated the need for further action. In June of 1948, Congress passed the Displaced Persons Act (Act of June 25, 1948, 62 Stat. 1009). This act set up a preference category and established a Displaced Persons Commission to administer the act. Besides giving preference within the quotas to certain categories of displaced persons, it allowed some people from some countries to immigrate beyond the country's quotas by "mortgaging" against future quotas. Existing health, literacy, and related requirements of the quota act, however, were *not* set aside for these displaced persons.

President Harry Truman reluctantly signed the act, stating that he did so "with very great reluctance," because he believed the act did not go far enough, that it still discriminated against Catholics and Jews, and that in his view displaced persons should be permitted to enter as nonquota immigrants. In the 1948 presidential campaign, the Progressive party issued a campaign handbook stating the party's position on immigration and naturalization laws. They echoed Truman's concerns in calling for a complete revision of the quota laws and the Displaced Persons Act away from what they termed were the racially biased perspectives, and for granting indemnity to Japanese American citizens who suffered losses during the internment of World War II (see LeMay and Barkan, Document 115: 213–216). Congress amended the law in 1950, admitting higher percentages of Catholics and Jews. Ultimately, over 400,000 refugees came in under the act over a four-year period (Bennett: 76–77).

The growing need for agricultural workers, particularly in the west, led to the Agricultural Labor and Illegal Entry Act of October 31, 1949—the "Bracero program" (63 Stat. 1051). It allowed immigrants to come in as temporary agricultural workers. Legislation was required since under the 1917 Immigration Act, such workers would not have been admissible under the contract labor prohibitions. The act also strengthened the border patrol, since the problem of illegal entrants, along the thousands of miles of the border of Mexico, were becoming increasingly apparent.

In 1949, Congress amended the Philippine Act of 1946 by extending benefits to June of 1951 and it passed another agricultural act for the recruitment of agricultural labor in short supply.

In June 1950, Congress made a special provision for 250 special immigrant visas for alien sheepherders for a one-year period. In the August of that year, Congress declared Guamanians born after April 11, 1899, to be citizens and thus eliminated any immigration restrictions upon them. That same month, it also passed an act that permitted the admission of racially inadmissible alien spouses and minor children of citizen members of the armed forces.

Finally, in the September of 1950, Congress passed the Internal Security Act (64 Stat. 987). This act increased the grounds for exclusion and deportation of alleged alien subversives. Reflecting the Cold War tenor of the times, it required Communist organizations and officers to register. It refined, clarified, and augmented the classes of people considered to be risks to internal security. It banned their admission and strengthened the administrative and enforcement work of the Immigration Service, while revising the deportation authority and procedures as stipulated in the Immigration Act of 1917. It required all resident aliens to annually report their addresses.

In 1950, a special Senate committee, established in 1947 under the chairmanship of Senator Rivercomb and then continuing under Senator McCarran, issued a lengthy report. This report was the most comprehensive study of immigration since the Dillingham Commission Report of 1911 and served as the basis for the debate and proposed legislation that became known as the

McCarran-Walter Act. It was a modest step in relaxing quota system restrictions.

The special problems of dealing with refugees, the human hardship caused by the inflexibility of the quota system, and the growing hysteria and fear of communism associated with the Cold War resulted in the passage of the Immigration and Naturalization Act of June 27, 1952, also known as the McCarran-Walter Act (66 Stat. 163). This massive comprehensive omnibus bill, which comprises 200 pages in the Code of Statutes, codifies all the previous immigration laws into one comprehensive statute. Although it mostly reenacted the various quota laws and many of the 1917 law provisions, it did detail some revisions in those laws as well. It maintained the basic quota system but allowed for some new immigration quotas for a revised Asia-Pacific Triangle. It has remained the basic law for nearly fifty years; most legislation passed since then, such as the acts of 1965, 1976, 1986, 1990, actually amended this act. The act reflects the impact of Cold War-related foreign policy considerations upon U.S. immigration policy with its special considerations for the entrance of "refugees" and "anticommunist freedom fighters" (see excerpts in LeMay and Barkan, Document 118: 220–225). President Truman vetoed the act, but Congress overrode his veto and passed the act over his objections.

In the debates leading up to passage of the 1952 act, antirestrictionist forces were led by Representative Emmanuel Celler in the House, and Senators Lehman and Humphrey in the Senate. They attacked the continuation of the quota system as an incorporation of a philosophy of racism not unlike that of Nazi Germany, the espousal of which led to such tragic consequences for the entire world. Major ethnic associations generally supported the liberalization efforts of the Lehman-Humphrey forces.

Those favoring restriction argued that the postwar economy could not absorb a large-scale immigration which would surely follow any substantial easing of restriction limits. They raised the specter of the cold war, the dangers of communist subversion, and defended the tight security provisions of the bill. Congress passed the act by a voice vote in May of 1952. It overrode President Truman's veto by a vote of 278 to 113 in the House, and 57-26 in the Senate (Chiswick: 28).

The act did not impose a quota for the western hemisphere. It relied on the general categories of exclusion—such as the "public charge" clause—to limit immigration from that region. The act also ignored the Bracero program and the issue of illegal immigration.

President Truman established a special commission to study the whole issue of immigration. Its report, issued in 1953, advocated his positions on immigration. While the report, entitled *Whom Shall We Welcome*, was ignored by the Congress, it did lay the groundwork for much of the revisions enacted in 1965. The issue never caught on, and with President Eisenhower's election, the report and the issue were essentially left to die.

THE REFUGEE RELIEF ACT OF 1953 AND
THE POST-KOREAN WAR YEARS

While Congress chose to ignore the report, the refugee problem did not go away. President Eisenhower soon called for revisions in the immigration laws to admit "escapees" from behind the iron curtain. Among his first proposals to the Congress, it allowed for them to enter "outside the quota system," at 120,000 annually for two years. It based the need to allow them in on both humanitarian grounds and to further U.S. foreign policy.

A House minority report objected to even this modest attempt at liberalizing the immigration law since to do so, in their words, "would destroy the principle of national origins upon which our immigration law is based" (Chiswick: 30). Representative Francis Walter led the House opposition, and Senator McCarren led the Senate forces to amend the administration's plan. The Congress finally agreed to accept 214,000 special immigrants in the Refugee Relief Act of August 7, 1953 (67 Stat. 400). This group contained a large number of German-ethnic expellees, and Poles, Italians, Greeks, and some Arabs and Asians. They were required to obtain U.S. citizen sponsors assuring them of jobs and housing, unless they were close relatives. It also involved elaborate screening to assure that there were no "subversives" sneaking in through the act.

In November, 1954 another important event taking place was the closing of Ellis Island as the nation's primary receiving and processing station.

Debate on the proposal typified the immigration conflicts that went on throughout the decade of the 1950s. Proposals to amend or radically change the national origins system died in committee. Proposals, however, which were tied to foreign policy and national security or which stressed special status under humanitarian grounds fared better. The actual effect of such "special legislation," however, was to undercut the national origins system. Immigrants coming in under special provisions were often from southeastern Europe and their entry resulted in doubling or tripling the numbers from those countries allowed in under the quota system.

In 1956, Congress rejected yet another proposal to overhaul the national origins system. It did, however, allow for another "special" act to deal with a particular refugee problem. The failed Hungarian revolution of that year produced a mass exodus of "freedom fighters," who President Eisenhower wanted to be admitted. He brought in 5,000 under the Refugee Relief Act of 1953, but that number was inadequate to handle the problem. In 1957, the president sought special legislation and some broader changes in the immigration laws. Congress rejected the broad changes, but did grant the president latitude in bringing in the freedom fighters. A special "parole" status enabled over 30,000 Hungarian refugees to enter (Act of July 25, 1958, 72 Stat. 419). Voluntary agencies met the cost of their resettlement, assisting them in finding sponsors, jobs, and housing (McClellan: 21; Chiswick: 32).

Congress also canceled the "mortgage quotas" of the Displaced Persons Act—marking another breakdown in the restrictionist policy of the quota system. While Congress continued to chip away at the system, it became ever clearer that a substantial revision of the system was becoming necessary.

THE RESETTLEMENT OF REFUGEES PROGRAM OF 1960

Late in the Eisenhower presidency, the Castro revolution in Cuba generated another large wave of refugees from communism seeking entrance to the United States. The president again used his "parole-status" powers to admit Cuban refugees. Ultimately, some 800,000 Cuban refugees entered, marking it as the largest long-term refugee movement in U.S. history. The president also used parole status for Chinese arriving from Hong Kong. In the national security atmosphere that characterized the Cold War period, Congress obliged the president.

Indeed, not only did Congress allow the executive branch wide latitude in essentially skirting the quota system within which U.S. immigration policy was enshrined, Congress itself increasingly employed yet another method of getting around the quota system—its use of the private bill. From 1937 to 1964, a total of 33,480 such private bills were introduced. These resulted in 5,635 persons being admitted (LeMay, 1987: 110). While the number was not large, it further indicated the inflexibility of the quota system and fueled concerns to amend it.

CONCLUSION—NATIONAL SECURITY
OF A WORLD SUPERPOWER

By the 1960s, then, sentiment was shifting to amend immigration policy. Increasing importance was given to foreign policy considerations. As the U.S. tied its national security to various military alliances and to the containment of communism during the Cold War, immigration policy was viewed in a new light. The quota system was seen as too inflexible to allow for refugees from our Cold War-allied nations. Given American hegemony as the world superpower, the U.S. "sphere of influence" expanded to include Southeast Asia as well as Europe and the Americas. National security was viewed as being secured by the threat of nuclear retaliation to be delivered by intercontinental ballistic missiles. The Cold War struggle between the two superpowers involved psychological battles between the minds and hearts of peoples around the world. An ideological basis to national security involved promoting democracy around the world. This required amendment of the blatantly racist nature of U.S. immigration policy seen as unacceptable, inflexible, and counter-productive to U.S. foreign policy initiatives. The resulting amendments, in the 1965 Immigration Act, signaled the arrival of the next cycle, the "Dutch-Door Era," which will be discussed in the next chapter.

NOTES

1. See, for instance, Eugene Rostow, "Our Worst Wartime Mistake," *Harper's Magazine* (September 1945): 193–201; Ken Ringle, "What Did You Do Before the War, Dad?," *The Washington Post Magazine* (December 6, 1981): 54–62; Ringer: 884; and LeMay, 1985: 191–206.

2. "One Time Internee Returns to Camp," *Cumberland Evening Times*, Thursday, August 15, 1985: 38.

3. See Hosokawa: 366; McClemore: 180–181.

4. See Justice Robert Jackson's dissenting opinion in *Korematsu v. United States*, 65 *Supreme Court Reporter*, 1944: 206–208; and the arguments in *Ex parte Mitsuye Endo*, December 18, 1944 in LeMay and Barkan, Document 110: 201–204.

———— 5 ————

The Dutch-Door Cycle, 1960–1990

INTRODUCTION: NATIONAL SECURITY
VIA INTERNATIONAL RELATIONS

Just as the quota approach to immigration policy-making and naturalization law reflected the racial ideas and concerns of that era, a new cycle was ushered in with the election of John F. Kennedy as president in 1960 and is best marked as the beginning with the enactment of the Immigration Act of 1965. This law reflected the national security issue and concerns of foreign policy; and, in domestic politics, of the civil rights era. President Kennedy's election in 1960 eased the way for the frontal attack on the quota system. While serving in the senate, as mentioned, Senator Kennedy wrote *A Nation of Immigrants* (1958). His book discussed immigration and showed his favorable attitude toward the notion of America as a nation of asylum. Events on the international scene resulted in successive waves of refugees from nations considered our allies in the Cold War or immigrants from nations with whom we had or desired close ties in the battle for preeminence in the Cold War for whom there was considerable political pressure to open more of our borders. And on the domestic front, events of the civil rights movement pushed the nation, public opinion, and the leadership of the country to question and seriously reevaluate the racial bias underlying much of the law, particularly those relating to the quota system and immigration more generally. The post-World War II and Korean War period had chipped away the quota system. The passage of a series of special acts, nonquota immigration, and the refugee–escapee enactments all demonstrated that the national origin quota system was simply too inflexible and too biased to be continued.

On July 14, 1960, Congress passed an act to enable the United States to participate in the resettlement of Cuban refugees (74 Stat. 504). In 1962, with Kennedy's election and then the mid-term congressional elections, which

resulted in a slightly more liberal Congress, it passed the Migration and Refugee Assistance Act which extended the response to the Cuban refugee problem and strengthened the role of the executive branch in the formulation and
implementation of immigration policy. This paved the way for the enactment
of the 1965 immigration act that essentially ended the quota system. Policy-
making in this cycle can be characterized as having a much more active role
being played by the executive branch; one at least equaling the role of the
Congress. Presidents more often took the initiative in formulating immigration
policy instead of merely reacting to congressional initiatives and formulations.
It is also a cycle in which foreign policy matters evidently weighed in more
heavily than in the previous cycles. The "dutch-door" image is suggested by
legislation allowing special assistance and therefore privilege to selected groups
who "come-in" at the top, if you will, of the immigration flow, largely motivated by foreign policy and national security concerns. The cycle is also notable for policy-making that attempts to rid laws of the openly racial bias of the
earlier era. Foreign policy concerns led the national policy-makers to increasing
relations with and use of the United Nations and other international agreements, pacts, and relations across a host of policy areas, including impacts on
U.S. asylum, refugee, and immigration policy matters.

This period or era also saw a shift in how the population viewed such con-
cepts as nationalism and ethnicity. As a noted scholar of these topics puts it:

> Nationalism and ethnicity are central to the subject of politics, whether in the
> world of action or the realm of study. Countless wars, revolts, and conflicts have
> been the result of the passion which nation and 'kith and kin' have aroused in
> human beings. It has been estimated that more than ten million lives have been
> lost since 1945 alone as a result of ethnic violence. That total has probably risen
> by another million since 1975 . . . Two thousand died in 1989 alone in ethnic
> violence in the Punjab, and as many in Sri Lanka (Kellas: 1).

A *nation* is now commonly seen as a group of people who feel themselves to
be a community bound together by the ties of history, culture, and a common
ancestry. *Nationalism* is both an ideology and a form of behavior. The ideology
of nationalism builds upon people's awareness of a nation to give a set of
attitudes and a program of action. These may be cultural, economic, or political attitudes and programs. As "nation" can be defined in either an ethnic,
social, or official sense, so too can nationalism. *Ethnic group* and *ethnocentrism*
are comparable terms to nation and nationalism. The major difference between
them is that the term "ethnic group" is more narrowly defined than is "nation,"
and likewise, "ethnocentrism" is more rooted in social psychology than is
"nationalism." Ethnic groups are exclusive or *ascriptive* groups, meaning that
membership in such groups is limited to those who share certain inborn
attributes. Nations, in contrast, are inclusive and are culturally or politically
defined (Kellas: 4).

In many countries—including particularly the United States—ethnic groups have an important influence on foreign policy. A multiethnic state based on immigrants is likely to have more involvement in nationalism abroad than a nonimmigrant multinational state. A political system with a nondisciplined party system and dependent upon private funding, such as that of the United States, gives greater scope for ethnic political influence than those such as Britain, or France, with greater party discipline and less private funding. But in nearly all states, ethnic groups have a significant, if often hidden, influence in the making of foreign policy (Kellas: 158).

New groups and new methods for determining and controlling the flow of immigration emerged during this cycle, as well. It is also a cycle in which those new laws and the new approach caused dramatic shifts in the flow—some intended; others were unintended consequences of the laws. They resulted in a marked increase in overall immigration, a drastic shift in the flow of illegal immigration, and a radical change in the composition of the immigration influx that ultimately lead to demands, by the end of the cycle, to change directions in U.S. immigration policy-making once again.

THE IMMIGRATION AND NATIONALITY ACT OF 1965

During his first two years in the White House, President Kennedy's administration was preoccupied with foreign policy (Berlin and the Cuban Missile crises). Although during his campaign he had promised to end segregation with the "stroke of a pen," the concerns over national security and foreign policy put domestic civil rights policy matters on the back burner of the administration's agenda, and President Kennedy failed to propose any specific action on immigration matters. Then, the growing agitation over civil rights turned the administration's and the nation's attention inward. The civil rights movement marked a changing national attitude toward racism that undercut restrictionist immigration policy. The sort of open bigotry contributing to the lopsided majorities in favor of the quota system as recent as the 1952 McCarren-Walter Act were no longer acceptable, at least in public policy advocacy, by the mid-1960s.

The success of the Kennedy administration's economic policy, moreover, resulted in the end of the recessions that had so plagued the nation during six of the eight years of the Eisenhower administration. The healthy economy of the early- through mid-1960s enabled even organized labor to favor a relaxation of restrictionist policy. By the mid-1960s, the traditional supporters of the national origins quota system were unorganized and largely inactive.

When the Kennedy administration did address the issue, late in 1962, it began formulating a proposal, which ultimately became the Immigration Act of 1965, and in the spirit of the Civil Rights Act of 1964, that was a reassertion and return to the nation's more liberal tradition in immigration. It set up individual rather than group criteria for granting immigration visas. The debate in the U.S. Senate over the enactment of the bill reflected the full range of opinion on immigration policy. Senator Edward Kennedy of Massachusetts, the president's younger brother, was a leading proponent and co-sponsor of the measure. He met with leaders from the "opposition"—the American Coalition, the American Legion, the Daughters of the American Revolution, and the National Association of Evangelicals. They offered no significant opposition in eliminating the national origins quota system (Chiswick: 33; see Senator Kennedy's congressional testimony on the bill in LeMay and Barkan, Document 131: 254–257).

President Kennedy sent his proposal to Congress in July 1963. Senator Philip Hart of Michigan and Representative Emmanuel Celler, then chairman of the House Judiciary Committee, introduced companion bills. President Kennedy's assassination and some congressional opposition delayed passage of the bill. Senators Sam Ervin and Everett Dirkson (R-Ill.) fought a rearguard battle to preserve the quota system and won some eventual revisions to the proposal that the administration had not particularly wanted. They insisted on an overall ceiling of 120,000 for the western hemisphere rather than the unlimited status in the original bill. The figure of 120,000 was a compromise representing roughly the flow of western hemisphere immigration for the few years immediately preceding the act. In the House, Representative Michael Feighan of Ohio, chair of the House Subcommittee on Immigration, was also effective in the use of delaying tactics in 1963–1964. In July 1963, he was appointed chairman of the Joint Committee on Immigration and Nationality Policy (Harper: 38).

President Kennedy's assassination, viewed almost immediately as "martyrdom," plus the landslide election of President Lyndon B. Johnson in 1964, set up the dynamics resulting in the end of the quota system and its replacement by a "preference" system. President Johnson, as a former Senate Majority Leader, was one of the best "nose counters" in the business. His landslide victory in 1964 swept into office a large number of liberal Democrats who "rode-in on the president's shirttails." He suddenly had more noses to count than ever before! By 1964–1965, a significant number of congressmen were climbing on the immigration-reform bandwagon. Dozens of bills were introduced abolishing the national origins quota system.

The administration's proposal was resubmitted by President Johnson on January 13, 1965. It was introduced in the House by Representative Celler and in the Senate, on January 15, by Senator Philip Hart, this time with thirty-two senate co-sponsors that included both Senators Edward Kennedy (D-Mass) and Robert Kennedy (D-N.Y.). The measure sought to balance five major goals: (1) to preserve the family unit and reunite separated families; (2) to meet the need for some highly skilled aliens; (3) to help ease population problems created by emergencies, such as political upheavals, communist aggression, and natural disasters; (4) to better understand people's cross-nationally through exchange programs; and (5) to bar from the U.S. aliens who would likely represent problems of adjustment due to their physical or mental health, criminal history, dependency, or for national security reasons (Harper: 56). The major provisions of the act are shown in Box 5.1 (see also the more detailed excerpts of the bill and discussion of the law in LeMay and Barkan, Document 132: 257–261). It passed in the Senate by a vote of 76-18 and in the House by a vote of 320 to 69 (Chiswick: 37).

The act replaced the quota system with a preference system. The preference system allocated immigrant visas within each foreign nation as follows:

1. First preference: unmarried sons and daughters of U.S. citizens;
2. Second preference: spouses and unmarried sons and daughters of permanent resident aliens;
3. Third preference: members of the professions and scientists and artists of exceptional ability;
4. Fourth preference: married sons and daughters of U.S. citizens;
5. Fifth preference: brothers and sisters of U.S. citizens;
6. Sixth preference: skilled and unskilled workers in short supply; and
7. Seventh preference: refugees (Harper: 132–133; LeMay, 1987: 111–112).

President Johnson signed the law on October 3, 1965, in front of the Statue of Liberty, in New York harbor. His remarks upon signing the bill into law are presented in Box 5.2. Senator Edward Kennedy echoed President Johnson's statement as to the basis of the new law: "If there is one guiding principle to this bill, it is that we are going to treat all men and women who want to come to this country as individuals, equal in the eyes of the law. We ask only, in the words of President Kennedy, what they can do for this, their new country" (cited in Gorman, 2004: 382).

In his remarks, President Johnson also referenced foreign policy and national security concerns when he addressed the plight of Cuban refugees, asking Congress to pass supplementary funds to carry out a directive he gave to the Departments of State and Justice and Health, Education and Welfare to immediately make necessary arrangements for an orderly entry of a huge wave of Cuban refugees into the United States. Congress responded with the Act of November 23, 1966 to adjust the status of Cuban refugees to that of permanent residents and to set up a government-financed resettlement program (80 Stat. 1161).

Some significant changes in the immigration flow resulted from the 1965 act. In the decade after its passage, total immigration increased by nearly 60 percent. Immigrants from some countries experienced really dramatic increases: Greek immigration increased by 162 percent; Portuguese by 382 percent; Asian immigration had an overall increase by 663 percent, with some countries showing remarkable gains: India by over 3,000 percent; Korea by 1,328 percent; Pakistan by 1,600 percent; the Philippines by nearly 1,200 percent; Thailand by over 1,700 percent; and Vietnam by over 1,900 percent.

**BOX 5.1. MAJOR PROVISIONS OF THE
IMMIGRATION ACT OF 1965**

It amended the Immigration and Nationality Act of 1952 by doing the
following.

1. It abolished the national origins quota system, after a transition period
   to June of 1968.
2. It abolished the Asian-Pacific Triangle provision.
3. It allowed for the use of quota numbers in the previous year as a pool of
   additional numbers for each year of the transition period, for preference applicants chargeable to oversubscribed quotas.
4. It revised previous preference categories into a new system of preferences strongly favoring (74 percent) relatives of citizens and permanent resident aliens.
5. It required that an alien coming to work in the U.S. and not entitled to a
   preference obtain certification from the Secretary of Labor that he/she
   would not displace nor adversely affect the wages and working conditions of workers in the same field in the United States.
6. It included refugees as one of the preference categories.
7. It set up an annual ceiling of 170,000 on immigration of aliens in the
   preference and nonpreference classifications with a 20,000 limit for
   any single foreign state.
8. It established an "immediate relative" (previously called nonquota)
   status for parents of adult U.S. citizens.
9. It increased the dependent area of immigration (previously classified as
   nonquota) to 1 percent of the 20,000 maximum allowable numbers
   available to the governing country, that is, from 100 to 200 annually.
10. It set the filing date of the petition to determine the chronological order
    of preference applicants.
11. It required that applicants be considered in the order of their prefer-
    ence class (first-come, first-served).
12. It created a Select Commission on western hemisphere immigration to
    study economic, political, and demographic factors affecting immi-
    gration.
13. It set a ceiling of 120,000 on immigration from the western hemisphere
    nations after July 1968.
14. It included all independent countries of the western hemisphere in
    "special immigrant status" (previously called nonquota status).

Source: 79 Stat. 911.

BOX 5.2. REMARKS OF PRESIDENT JOHNSON ON SIGNING 1965 ACT

... This bill that we sign today is not a revolutionary bill. It does not affect the lives of millions. It will not shape the structure of our daily lives, or really add importantly to our wealth or our power. Yet it is still one of the most important acts of this Congress and of this Administration. For it does repair a very deep and painful flaw in the fabric of American justice. It corrects a cruel and enduring wrong in the conduct of the American nation.

This bill says simply that from this day forth those wishing to emigrate to America shall be admitted on the basis of their skills and their close relationship to those already here. This is a simple test, and it is a fair test. Those who can contribute to this country—to its growth, to its strength, to its spirit—will be the first that are admitted to this land.

The fairness of this standard is so self-evident that we may well wonder that it has not always been applied. Yet the fact is that for over four decades the immigration policy of the United States has been distorted by the harsh injustice of the National Origins Quota system. This system violated the basic principle of American democracy—the principle that values and rewards each man on the basis of his merit as a man. It has been un-American in the highest sense, because it has been untrue to the faith that brought thousands to these shores even before we were a country. Today, with my signature, this system is abolished.

We can now believe that it will never again shadow the gate to the American nation with the twin barriers of prejudice and privilege.

Our beautiful America was built by a nation of strangers. From a hundred different places or more, they have poured forth into an empty land—joining and blending in one mighty and irresistible tide. The land flourished because it was fed from so many sources—because it was nourished by so many cultures and traditions and peoples...

Now, under the monument which has welcomed so many to our shores, the American nation returns to the finest of its traditions today. The days of unlimited immigration are past. But those who do come will come because of what they are, and not because of the land from which they spring...

Over my shoulder here you can see Ellis Island, whose vacant corridors echo today the joyous sounds of long-ago voices. And today we can all believe that the lamp of this grand old lady is brighter today—and the golden door that she guards gleams more brilliantly in the light of an increased liberty for the peoples from all the countries of the globe.

Source: Lydon Johnson, "Remarks on Immigration Law," *Congressional Quarterly,* October 1965: 2063–2064.

Among the countries of Europe, those in which there was an overall decline in immigration of over 38 percent and those which registered the largest negative percent change were: Austria, with a decline of over 76 percent; Ireland by over 77 percent; Norway by over 85 percent; and the United Kingdom by a whopping 120 percent (see table in Chiswick: 39).

The 1965 act's provisions for professionals were especially helpful for opening up immigration from Asia. Korean and Philippine health professionals entered in large numbers, who then could use the family preference category later to bring in their family members. By the late 1970s, over 70,000 medical doctors alone had immigrated under provisions of this act. By that time, there were more Filipino physicians in the United States than the native-born black doctors.[1]

These dramatic changes can be seen in Figure 5.1. It presents graphically the numbers of immigrants admitted to the United States by various regions of birth for selected fiscal years, 1960–1990. Figure 5.2 presents graphically similar data, showing the percent distribution by decade from the various regions of last residence of legal immigrants for 1960 to 1990, the decades of the "Dutch-Door Cycle."

An already multiethnic society was rapidly becoming even evermore so. Multiculturalism became a positively valued concept and respect for and appreciation of the nation's remarkable diversity of cultural groups was voiced in the media and in the halls of legislatures across the nation.

The 1965 act was soon outmoded, however, in its provisions for refugees. The act set what at the time seemed a generous provision for refugees—an annual preference limit for refugees at 10,200. Events in Cuba, Vietnam, and Haiti soon outstripped the ability of that limit to begin to cope with the demand for entrance on the basis of refugee status, an integral aspect of the national security element of overall immigration policy.

The question of how one may lose one's citizenship was at issue again in 1967 in an important Supreme Court decision on the matter. In *Afroyim v. Rusk* (May 29, 1967, 387 U.S. 253), the Court decided that a citizen who held dual citizenship with Israel did not lose his citizenship merely by the act of voting in an election of the country in which he held the other citizenship. The case is particularly significant in the strong language used by the justices in stipulating how limited is the government in "taking away" citizenship once granted by birthright or by naturalization.

The continuing problem of mass movements involving tens of thousands of refugees generated by war or natural disasters influenced the United Nations to revise its protocols relating to the status of refugees. The United States, as a nation which was a state party to the agreement and the protocols, was in essence agreeing to changes in its laws dealing with refugees as well. This was accomplished by a proclamation regarding the UN protocols issued by President Johnson on November 6, 1968 (Orders, Proclamations, and Treaties 1208.233–1208.263).

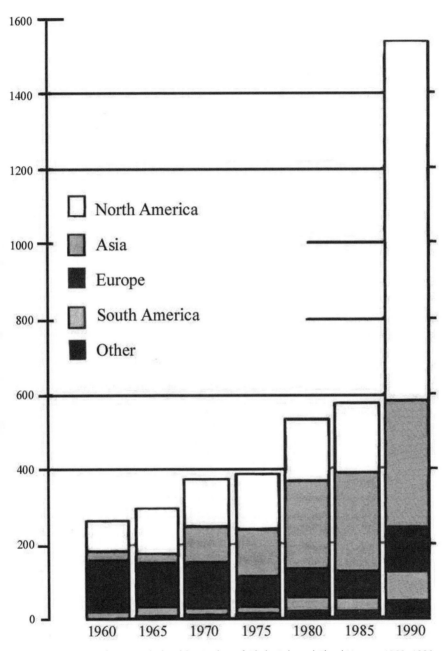

FIGURE 5.1.   Immigrants Admitted by Region of Birth, Selected Fiscal Years—1960–1990
Source: Adapted from "Chart A," p. 13 in *2000 Statistical Yearbook of the Immigration and Naturalization Service,* U.S. Department of Justice, Immigration and Naturalization Service. Washington D.C.: Online at http://www.immigration.gov/graphics/shared/aboutus/statistics/IMM00yrbk/IMM2000.pdf (accessed December 2004).

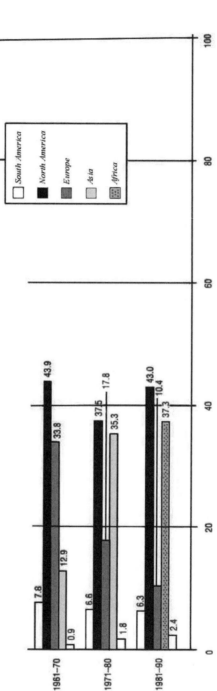

FIGURE 5.2. Region of Last Residence of Legal Immigrants, Percent Distribution by Decade, 1960–1990

Note: Oceania and unspecified region represent no more than 1 percent of legal immigration each decade.

Source: Adapted from "Chart B," p. 16: in *2000 Statistical Yearbook of the Immigration and Naturalization Service,* U.S. Department of Justice, Immigration and Naturalization Service. Washington D.C.: Online at http://www.immigration.gov/graphics/shared/aboutus/statistics/IMM00yrbk/IMM2000.pdf (accessed December 15, 2004).

THE 1976 AMENDMENT TO THE IMMIGRATION AND
NATIONALITY ACT AND THE 1980 REFUGEE ACT

By the mid-1970s, the number of refugees seeking entrance far exceeded the 6 percent set aside for them in the 1965 Act's preference category for refugees. From Cuba alone, from 1960 to 1980, 800,000 refugees came. Since the 1965 law defined refugees as those fleeing communism or from the Middle East, it did not even consider the case of those fleeing from the right-wing dictatorships in the western hemisphere, that is, the Haitians. The collapse of the South Vietnamese government in 1975 created yet another large pool of refugees fleeing communism. From 1975 to 1979, over 200,000 Vietnamese came to the United States.

When the boat people began to arrive in 1979, the administration committed itself to allow in another 168,000 in 1980. In the spring of that year, another wave of Cubans arrived by boat. In all, from 1975 to 1980, some 500,000 refugees from Southeast Asia alone arrived at the shores. Soviet Jews fleeing directly from the Soviet Union contributed another 70,000 from 1969 to 1980. The foreign policy exigencies of the Cold War compelled further changes in the U.S. immigration law. Allowing admission of the refugees fleeing communism, particularly those from countries that had been allies to United States in Southeast Asia, became part of the national security equation. A moral obligation was felt to accept these allies, and their talents and values were viewed as welcome additions to the population in the battle against the spread of international communism.

In 1976, Congress amended the Immigration and Naturalization Act of 1965 by modifying the preference system to include migration from the western hemisphere, along with a 20,000 annual limit for each nation. The Asian and Hispanic influx of the late 1970s, shown so dramatically in Figures 5.1 and 5.2, sharply changed the mix of legal immigrants. European immigration fell to 13 percent of the total. By the mid-1970s, most immigrants came from Mexico, the Philippines, Cuba, Korea, and China/Taiwan.

At first, the president and the attorney general responded to these refugee pressures by using the executive parole power to permit Cubans, Vietnamese, and the others (i.e., Cambodians, Laotians) to enter beyond the refugee category limits. Congress joined by allocating funds to support the parolees and passed legislation to adjust their status—such as the Indochinese Refugee Resettlement Program in 1975.[2]

During the final weeks of the congressional session of 1976, the Congress passed a law to amend the Immigration Act of 1965 to deal with a perceived problem created by that law. The result of the 1965 law was that all would-be immigrants from the western hemisphere were required to apply for visas on a first-come, first-served basis, including those who were close relatives of U.S. citizens and those who were skilled foreign workers, both of whom were groups who received preferences if from the eastern hemisphere. By the mid-1970s, the waiting period for immigrant visas in the western hemisphere stretched over an excess of two years. This waiting period caused hardships for those who otherwise would have qualified for a preferred status and have gained much faster entry into the United States. To rectify these problems, the 1976 amendment law extended the preference system to the western hemisphere nations. It was anticipated that the amendment would reduce the waiting period for immigrants from Mexico, for example, in half (Act of October 20, 1976, HR 14535).

The war in Vietnam and the refugee waves that followed in its wake, however, did impact public opinion regarding foreign policy, national security policy, and immigration policy. The Vietnam War experience cracked the previous consensus on bi-partisan and internationalist foreign policy. For example, at the start of the war only 18 percent of the public agreed with the statement, " The United States should mind its own business internationally," but by 1974 over 41 percent agreed with the statement (Kupchan: 200).

Domestic tranquility was likewise disrupted by social tensions arising from such a diverse, multiethnic society. The mid-1960s witnessed a series of urban riots quickly referred to as "a national security crisis" inside American cities. During the long, hot summers from 1965 to 1968 more than 300 episodes of civil disorder erupted. Boundaries between military and civil affairs began to blur as quelling urban riots became domestic jobs fit for the armed forces (Jennifer Light, 2004: 401).

Moreover, these refugee pressures and the growing anxiety over the estimated one-half to 1 million undocumented aliens entering the United States illegally by the end of the 1970s decade prompted Congress to establish a Select Commission on Immigration and Refugee Policy in 1978. It issued its report in 1981 and its work influenced policy provisions in a 1980 act.

By the end of the decade, then, Congress, the president, and the various relief agencies dealing with the assorted and increasingly numerous refugee crises all realized that the limit on the refugee category was simply too low and too rigidly defined. Older refugee law tended to deal with the refugee as a single individual "escaping" communism. But the 1960s and 1970s saw flows in which refugees arrived in mass asylum movements: 400,000 from Cuba, 340,000 from Vietnam, 110,000 from Laos, nearly 70,000 from the Soviet Union and a similar number from Kampuchea (formerly Cambodia), 30,000 from Yugoslavia, nearly 25,000 from mainland China and Taiwan, nearly 20,000 each from Rumania, and Poland, and about 10,000 each from Czechoslovakia, Spain, and Hungary. Such events swamped the 20,000 per-country limit of the 1965 act.

Congress acted in the form of the Refugee Act of 1980. This was a concerted effort to systematize refugee policy. It incorporated the UN definition of a refugee as one who had a "well-founded fear of persecution" owing to race, religion, nationality, or membership in a social group or political movement. It initially allowed for 50,000 people annually to enter the United States as refugees. The president could notify Congress if he determined that events warranted an increase in the number and, after fiscal year 1982, he would have the responsibility for presenting to Congress a recommended total annual figure. Thus, for example, 72,000 were authorized for 1984 and 67,750 actually arrived. Another 11,600 were granted asylum (LeMay, 1987: 123). The Act of March 17, 1980 was simply entitled, "The Refugee Act" (94 Stat. 102). In addition to raising the refugee limit to 50,000 annually, it raised total legal immigration from 290,000 to 320,000. It strengthened the refugee procedures and gave the president greater and more flexible powers to deal with emergency situations.

The plight and the problems of the Haitian influx, who as "economic refugees" and who, not incidentally were black, raised additional perplexing issues. The Vietnamese refugees were political allies to whom the nation felt a moral obligation and it was therefore more willing to help them. Then too, the Vietnamese were by and large well-educated, middle-class persons. Two-thirds of them had held white-collar jobs in Vietnam. About one-fourth were from professional, technical, and managerial occupational backgrounds. Only 5 percent were farmers and fishermen (Montero: 23). The Vietnamese have acculturated more rapidly than any previous Asian group, undoubtedly due in part to their middle-class background status and to the generous assistance programs not afforded to regular legal immigrants coming in under preferences other than the special refugee status. The Haitians, in contrast, were first treated simply as illegal immigrants. As "economic" refugees fleeing dire economic conditions, not political repression (although there was plenty of that, just not admitted to in formal foreign policy as Haiti was not a communist country), they were not allowed in under the refugee category. They began arriving in steadily larger numbers in 1972. For years, their legal status was clouded as the State Department and the country grappled without knowing ways to handle them.

Being economic refugees, they were not accorded the aid or public support given to the Cubans, the Vietnamese, the Hungarians or the Soviet Jews. They were overwhelmingly unskilled and illiterate. They were held in detention camps for years. Once released from those camps, they were not aided, as were the other refugees, in finding jobs and housing or otherwise acculturating to U.S. life. Their illiteracy, low job skills, and language problems made them easily exploitable, and they lived in near slave-like conditions as migrant workers. They were often viewed as a special threat to the local labor market. The problem of what to do about "economic refugees" and other undocumented aliens mounted during the late 1970s as their numbers rose to an estimated 3 to 6 million.[3]

Table 5.1 shows worldwide response to the massive refugee movements of the 1970s. It shows the number of refugees accepted by the country, from 1975 to 1980. Note that those accepted by the United States constituted over 45 percent of all refugees accepted worldwide and nearly triple that of any other

TABLE 5.1. Refugees Accepted, by Country, 1975–1980

Country	Number	Country	Number
United States	677,000	Austria	4,300
China	265,000	New Zealand	4,100
Israel	105,700	Belgium	3,900
Malaysia	102,100	Argentina	2,800
Canada	84,100	Norway	2,700
France	72,000	Denmark	2,300
Australia	51,200	Romania	1,200
Germany (FRG)	32,100	Spain	1,100
United Kingdom	27,600	Italy	900
Tanzania	26,000	Chile	800
Hong Kong	9,400	Japan	800
Switzerland	7,500	Cuba	700
Sweden	7,300	Mexico	700
The Netherlands	4,700	**Total**	**1,498,000**

Source: Michael J. Sherbinin, ed., *1981 World Refugee Survey.* New York: U.S. Committee for Refugees (1981); cited in Papademetriou and Miller, 1983: 284.

nation. Figure 5.3 shows, in graphic form, the continued refugee influx into the United States from the end of World War II to 1990. As we have seen, that flow was increasingly comprised of those coming from Asia and South and Central American countries. Refugee and asylum flows are the result of "push factors." These differ from the pull factors discussed previously which can be directly addressed in U.S. immigration policy-making. Push factors inducing waves of immigration may have a more significant long-term impact on the flow than any other factor.[4]

The entire era saw U.S. foreign policy relying on multilateral approaches involving security alliances, and multinational efforts to tackle global problems. One such area relating to national security depending upon that approach concerned nuclear proliferation.

In the 1950s and 1960s, there was a widespread fear that within a few decades some fifteen to twenty states would have acquired nuclear weapons. In light of these early, gloomy, speculations, it could be argued that the nonproliferation efforts have been quite successful. Apart from the five acknowledged nuclear weapon states (China, France, the United Kingdom, the United States, and the former Soviet Union), there are currently only three additional *de facto* nuclear weapon states: India, Israel, and Pakistan ... After several years of negotiations, a more comprehensive approach was adopted with the Treaty on the Non-Proliferation of Nuclear Weapons of 1968 ... The NPT came into effect in 1970, and by that time ninety-seven countries had signed the treaty. At the first Review Conference in 1975, there were 111 member countries (Ham: 11–13).

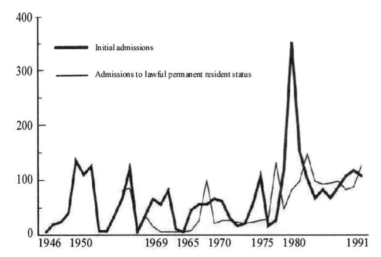

FIGURE 5.3.   Refugee and Asylee Admissions to Permanent Resident Status, Fiscal Years 1946–1991
Source: Adapted from *Immigration and Naturalization Service*, 1992: 75 in LeMay, 1994: 20.

U.S. military force was also used during this period to effectively bolster foreign policy initiatives that were nonconflict-related. Between 1945 and 1978, the U.S. military was used in literally hundreds of incidents that were without violence to underscore verbal and diplomatic expressions of American foreign policy and/or to create a general climate of goodwill for America by responding to natural disaster relief situations. No other nation in the world rivals the United States in the use of its military resources for disaster relief abroad (or for that matter, domestically as well).

Armed forces, being well-organized, highly disciplined, well-equipped, mobile, and *existing* national resources, can be quite useful in various contingencies not involving conflict, particularly disaster relief or prevention. Ground troops have been used to fight fires, remove snow, clear up after tidal waves, and search for survivors after floods, earthquakes, storms, and other natural calamities. Aircraft can rapidly transport skilled military and civilian personnel, field hospitals, medicine, shelter, and even food. Ships can deliver large amounts of supplies more efficiently over a longer period of time. On occasions, moreover, ships closer to a disaster have provided immediate aid of great significance (Blechman et al.: 3–4).

In a society as vastly multiethnic as is the United States, the use of such nonviolent military force in so many nations abroad impacts domestic politics among ethnic groups who perceive a stake in such policy due to their multiple ethnic loyalties.

IMMIGRATION POLICY-MAKING IN THE 1980S

The changing composition of the flow in immigration, however, coupled with the troubled economy suffering from "stagflation" throughout the 1970s—a combination of high unemployment and high inflation due in part to the oil crisis of the decade—led to a growing political movement to again restrict immigration. The ending of the Bracero program in 1964, one of the compromises that President Kennedy had agreed to in order to move the Congress to increase the overall immigration level and end the national origins quota system, contributed to a dramatic increase in the number of illegal aliens crossing the nation's borders, mostly from Mexico. The 1965 law also coincided with the rise of affordable air travel. Millions of foreigners discovered that they could fly to the United States for a "vacation" and never leave. An estimated 30 to 40 percent of the 8 to 10 million illegal residents then believed to be in the country were "visa overstayers," that is, people who entered lawfully and "with documents," but stayed beyond the expiration date of their visas. Such overstayers are especially difficult to find and deport. Federal agents find it much easier to spot a Mexican slipping across the Rio Grande illegally (as an "undocumented alien") than to figure out which Irish bartender or Nigerian cabdriver no longer has a valid visa (Gorman: 383).

The coming-to-power of a conservative Republican Administration with the election of President Ronald Reagan in 1980, plus the most severe economic recession since the end of World War II during the initial years of that administration, heightened public awareness of and concern over the "illegal immigration issue." Public opinion polls spiked from 42 percent of the population saying that immigration levels should be decreased in 1977 to 49 percent saying so by 1986 and 65 percent saying so by 1993 (see Figure 6.2).

Public opinion was in large measure responding to a growing sense that the nation faced a crisis in national security; namely, that it had lost control of its borders; that it was experiencing a literal flood of illegal aliens. Figure 5.4 graphs the number of illegal or undocumented aliens apprehended by the Immigration and Naturalization Service (INS) at U.S. borders from 1960 to 1988. As can be seen in the figure, in 1984 alone the INS apprehended 1.3 million undocumented aliens (many of them more than once), and the agency estimated that two to three times as many slipped through. Various estimates as to the number of illegal aliens in the country ranged from 2 to 6 million. By anyone's estimates, about two-thirds of them were Mexicans driven by poverty and unemployment across the highly porous 2,000 miles of the Mexican/U.S. border (LeMay, 1989: 6).

Even for those who entered legally, often with student or temporary (vacation) visas, the INS seemed unable to keep track of them and ensure that they obeyed the terms of their visas. The nation was greatly embarrassed by the inefficiency of the INS record-keeping brought to light during the Iranian hostage crisis. The administration intended, as a measure of national security,

Number of apprehensions
(millions)

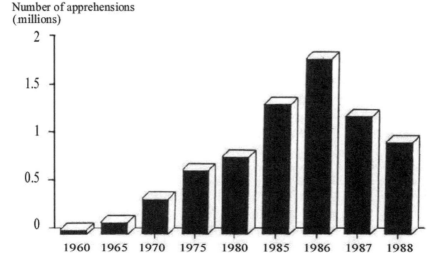

FIGURE 5.4. Immigration and Naturalization Service Apprehensions at U.S. Borders, 1960–1988

Source: Adapted from graph and data in GAO, Immigration Reform: Status of Implementing Employer Sanctions after One Year. Washington D.C.: U.S. Government Printing Office (1987a), 8; with 1987 data added from U.S. Department of Justice, INS Reporter. Washington D.C.: U.S. Government Printing Office (1988) 21; and updated to 1988 by INS data cited in Border Attacks Worry INS Agents. Washington Post, 16 October 1988: A18.
LeMay, 1994: 22.

to deport Iranian students with temporary (student) visas. President Carter and the nation were shocked to learn that the INS did not know how many Iranian students were living here, let alone how many were doing so illegally. Many of the Iranians who the INS was able to identify as being subject to deportation simply failed to attend deportation hearings or to leave when told to do so. This fed the "national security crisis" perceptions in public opinion.

The sense that such immigration-related problems, especially the "illegal alien" one, had reached a "crisis" stage forced first the administration and then the Congress to confront anew the need to revise immigration laws. The nature of how the immigration problem was perceived meant that the approach in policy-making to solve the problem would take a new direction. The method of "employer sanctions" emerged as a consensus view on the best method to "demagnetize" the pull of the U.S. economy that drew so many illegal aliens north across the borders.

The trend in the 1970s and 1980s raised serious questions among the American public. Should we or how could we absorb so many new aliens and at what rate? How many unskilled laborers were needed in an increasingly high-tech economy? Do illegal aliens drain the economy or enrich it? Do newcomers gain their footholds at the expense of the poor and the black? How possible or desirable is it to incorporate large numbers of such diverse racial, language, and cultural backgrounds? Do the advantages of such diversity outweigh the potential dangers to national security from the specter of separatism and intercultural conflict?

The Reagan administration responded by appointing a special task force on immigration and refugee policy within his administration, chaired by the Attorney General, William French Smith, to study the problems raised by the increased immigration flow, its changing complexion, and the issue of illegal aliens and how best to deal with them. Upon announcing the task force, President Reagan stated:

> ...we must ensure adequate legal authority to establish control over immigration; to enable us, when sudden influxes of foreigners occur, to decide to whom we grant the status of refugee or asylee; to improve our border control; to expedite (consistent with fair procedures and our Constitution) return of those coming here illegally; to strengthen enforcement of our fair labor standards and laws; and to penalize those who would knowingly encourage violation of our laws. The steps we take to further these objectives, however, must be consistent with our values of individual privacy and freedom [*The Papers of the Presidents, Ronald Reagan, 1981*, Vol. 1. Washington, D.C.: U.S. Government Printing Office (1982), 676].

The Reagan administration adopted six recommendations of the Task Force:

1. **Amnesty.** Aliens living in the U.S. illegally since January 1, 1980 would be permitted to remain and made eligible for resident-alien status after being there for ten years at which time they could seek naturalization (estimated number, 5 million).
2. **Guest workers.** A program allowing 50,000 Mexicans annually to come to work temporarily, increasing gradually over several years up to hundreds of thousands annually.
3. **Employer sanctions.** Employers with more than four employees who "knowingly hire" illegal aliens would be subject to fines up to 1,000 dollars per violation.
4. **Boat people.** Boats carrying Haitians would be intercepted. Detention camps would be established to hold as many as 6,000 people pending hearings on their deportation.
5. **Enforcement.** Increase the budget of the INS by 50 percent and add 1,500 officers to the Border Patrol to enhance enforcement of immigration and labor laws.
6. **Immigration limits.** Allow 610,000 new immigrants to the U.S. annually with a special preference to people from Canada and Mexico (LeMay, 1987: 138).

Of even greater importance than the views of the Task Force and of the Reagan administration was the report of the Select Commission on Immigration and Refugee Policy (SCIRP). Begun in the final days of the Carter administration, the commission was a joint presidential and congressionally appointed commission that began its work in 1979. It thoroughly studied immigration law and more particularly the problem of illegal immigration. It issued a final report in 1981. Its recommendations formed the basis of subsequent legislative action by the Congress throughout the 1980s and 1990s.

BOX 5.3. EXECUTIVE SUMMARY RECOMMENDATIONS OF THE SELECT COMMISSION ON IMMIGRATION AND REFUGEE POLICY, 1981

The Select Commission recommends that:

1. The United States work with other nations and principal international organizations to collect information and research on migratory flows and treatment of international migration.
2. The United States expand bilateral consultation with other governments, especially Mexico and other regional neighbors regarding migration.
3. Border patrol funding levels be raised to provide for a substantial increase in the number and training of personnel, replacement of sensor systems . . . and other needed equipment.
4. That regional enforcement posts be established to coordinate work with the INS, the U.S. Customs Service, the DEA, and the U.S. Coast Guard in the interdiction of both undocumented/illegal migrants and illicit goods, specifically narcotics.
5. That high priority be given to the training of INS officers to familiarize them with the rights of aliens and U.S. citizens and to help them deal with persons of other cultural backgrounds.
6. That legislation be passed making it illegal for employers to hire undocumented workers.
7. That a program to legalize illegal/undocumented aliens now in the U.S. be adopted.
8. That eligibility for legalization be determined by interrelated measurements of residence—date of entry and length of continuous residence—and by specified groups of excludability that are appropriate to the legalization program.
9. That voluntary organizations and community organizations be given a significant role in the legalization program.
10. An annual ceiling of 350,000 numerically limited immigrant visas with an additional 100,000 visas available for the first five years . . . to allow backlogs to be cleared.

11. That a substantial number of visas be set aside for reunifying spouses and unmarried sons and daughters and it should be given top priority in the numerically limited family reunification...
12. That country ceilings apply to all numerically limited family reunification preferences...
13. That "special" immigrants remain a numerically exempt group but be placed within the independent category.
14. Creating a small, numerically limited subcategory within the independent category to provide for the immigration of certain investors.
15. That specific labor market criteria should be established by the selection of independent immigrants...
16. A fixed-percentage limit to the independent immigration from any one country.
17. That U.S. allocation of refugee numbers include both geographic considerations and specific refugee characteristics...
18. That state and local governments be involved in planning for initial refugee resettlement and that...a federal program of impact aid [be established] to minimize the financial impact of refugees on local services.
19. That refugee achievement of self-sufficiency and adjustment to living in the U.S. be reaffirmed as the goal of resettlement.

Source: The Select Commission on Immigration and Refugee Policy, *Final Report.* Washington, D.C.: U.S. Government Printing Office (March 1, 1981), xv–xxxii.

Box 5.3 presents a brief summary of the major recommendations of the commission's final report.

In 1983, the U.S. Supreme Court rendered a decision in an immigration case that had importance beyond the immediate issue of immigration law. In *INS v. Chadha et al.* (462 U.S. 919, June 23, 1983), a class-action suit was filed against the INS over its deportation proceedings. The Supreme Court ruled that a House of Representative's use of the "legislative veto" to override the executive branch's rules and regulations (i.e., those promulgated by the INS) was unconstitutional. And in 1985 another class action suit was brought against the INS. This case, *Jean et al. v. Nelson* (472 U.S. 846, June 26, 1986), concerned denial of parole status by the INS to undocumented Haitian aliens who were ruled as "economic refugees" and therefore excluded from parole status. A federal district court ruled in favor of the Haitians on the basis that the decision by the INS to detain the aliens without parole was made on the basis of race and national origin and was thus in violation of the equal protection clause in the Fifth Amendment to the Constitution. The Supreme Court affirmed the judgment of the appeals court, which although rejecting the constitutional claim accorded relief on the basis of INS regulation, remanding the case to the district court to ensure that the INS exercised its discretion in parole decisions in a nondiscriminatory manner.

THE IMMIGRATION REFORM AND CONTROL ACT OF 1986

The approach of imposing employer sanctions and balancing that restrictionist provision with some sort of limited amnesty plan had first been proposed by Representative Peter Rodino (D.-NJ.) in the late 1970s. Organized labor had moved to deal with the threat of illegal aliens. They saw increasing unemployment and the recession with its resulting lower-wage jobs and poorer working conditions as the results of the market pressures from the increasingly large illegal alien influx. They felt illegal aliens were taking jobs that rightfully belonged to U.S. citizens. Led by the AFL-CIO and the International Ladies Garment Workers Union and joined in coalition by the National Association for the Advancement of Colored People (NAACP), which saw illegal immigration as threatening to the status and jobs of poor urban blacks, they moved Representative Rodino to propose an employer-sanctions amendment to the Immigration and Naturalization Act of 1965, essentially eliminating the "Texas Proviso." The Texas Proviso had favored growers and other employers of illegal aliens by exempting them from criminal action for hiring undocumented workers, although it was still illegal for workers to immigrate without documents (LeMay, 2004: 12).

Senator Edward Kennedy, Representative Rodino, and Representative Joshua Eilberg (D.-PA.) linked employer sanctions with limited legalization (amnesty) and antidiscrimination provisions. Their proposal, however, was opposed by Senator James Eastland (D.-Miss.), who was the chairman of both the Senate Judiciary Committee and its Subcommittee on Immigration and Naturalization at that time. Senator Eastland was an advocate of the growers who were opposed to the employer sanctions approach (led by the National Council of Agricultural Employers and the American Farm Bureau Federation). They insisted that any reform of immigration policy that did not have a foreign-worker program (i.e., a "guest-worker" program) would be unacceptable to growers. Senator Eastland effectively killed immigration reform bills in the committee.

After the SCIRP recommended closing the back door to undocumented immigration while opening slightly the front door to accommodate more legal immigration, immigration reform proposals were introduced again. In the early- to mid-1980s several bills were introduced that incorporated most of the SCIRP recommendations.

By the fall of 1981, the House and Senate Judiciary Subcommittees on Immigration were chaired, respectively, by Representative Romano Mazzoli (D.-Ky.) and Senator Alan Simpson (R.-Wyo.). They crafted the SCIRP and the Reagan Task Force recommendations into legislative proposals that they considered essential as incentives to cooperation among all the groups competing over the issue. The Simpson and Mazzoli bills were introduced into their respective chambers in March 1982. The Senate bill passed that body by a vote of 81 to 19, on August 17, 1982. The House bill, referred sequentially by Speaker of the House Tip O'Niell (D.-Mass.) to four committees (Education and Labor, Agriculture, Ways and Means, and Energy and Commerce) became saddled with several critical amendments (eventually 300 amendments had been filed). It died on the floor.

In 1983, with the Ninety-Eighth Congress, Simpson and Mazzoli renewed their efforts by reintroducing versions of their bills. Agricultural interests headed by the Farm Labor Alliance and advocated by Senator Hamilton Fish, Jr. (R.-N.Y.) developed a proposal for a guest-worker program. Representative Edward Roybal (D.-CA.), a leader of the House Congressional Hispanic Caucus, proposed an alternative bill that focused on tougher enforcement of existing labor laws and minimum-wage laws to clamp down on the hiring aspects of illegal immigration instead of the employer-sanctions approach.

The bills moved through their respective chambers once again. The Senate moved more readily to passage, with Senators Simpson and Kennedy working out compromises on employer-sanctions, amnesty, and asylum-adjudication provisions. In the House, the Mazzoli bill again moved sequentially by referral through the four committees. Representatives Mazzoli and Rodino, with the support of the Reagan administration and the House Republican leadership, pressed for quick floor action. The pending 1984 elections, however, once again led to obstructive amendments, and passage of the bill was delayed until June 20, 1984, when it finally passed by a slim margin of 216-211. With passage of different versions in the two chambers, the bills were sent to a House-Senate conference committee, where they failed to achieve an acceptable compromise, and it died in the conference.

In May 1985, Senator Simpson introduced a new version of his bill, without the co-sponsorship of a companion bill by Representative Mazzoli. In the House, Rodino introduced a bill similar to the version that had died in conference in 1984. Again, the two chambers eventually passed different versions of the proposed reform law. The White House strongly backed the Senate version, and the Senate Judiciary Committee rejected all attempts by the Senate Democrats to make the Senate version more akin to the House version. After the conference committee again seemed unable to reach a compromise, the issue seemed to be a corpse on its way to the morgue. A small group of legislators long committed to passage of immigration reform, however, refused to let it die. In October 1986, they fashioned a series of key compromises enabling passage of the law. Rep. Charles Schumer (D.-N.Y.) met with Reps. Rodino and Fish, Rep. Howard Berman (D.-CA.), Rep. Leon Panetta (D.-CA.), and Rep. Dan Lungren (R.-CA.). This group fine-tuned the bill's provisions, including numerous points designed to protect the rights of temporary workers. They secured Senator Simpson's approval of the compromises as well. After a decade of dealing with immigration reform policy, Congress was finally in a mood and in a position (with the mid-term elections over) to act. Further deterioration of the Mexican economy led to 1.8 million INS border apprehensions, a record high number. That fact, and the growing conservative mood of the country, seemed to convince opponents of the bill that continued resistance would probably lead to even more restrictive legislation in 1987. The Hispanic Caucus split on the bill, with five of its members supporting and six opposing it. The split in the Hispanic Caucus enabled the congressional Black Caucus to split on the bill as well: ten for and eight opposed. These developments are graphically portrayed in Figure 5.5. It views the enactment of Immigration Reform and Control Act (IRCA) as the resulting vector of change in the direction of an ongoing policy that is the *sum* of the contributions or influences of the involved policy factions. Figure 5.5 labels the various interest groups, administrative, and congressional factions involved in achieving the change in immigration policy resulting in the passage of IRCA in 1986.

The House passed the compromise conference bill by 238 to 173 on October 15, 1986. The Senate approved it 63 to 24 on October 17, 1986. The president signed it into law on November 6, 1986, as the IRCA of 1986.

Its main provisions are summarized in Box 5.4.

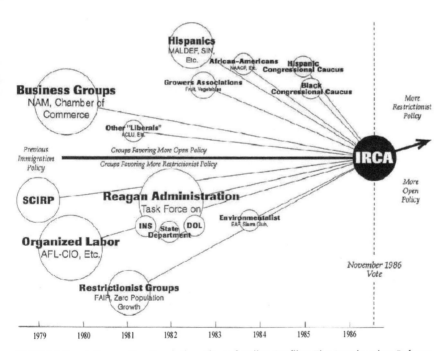

FIGURE 5.5.   A Cooperative Resolution View of Policy Conflict: The Immigration Reform and Control Act Case.

BOX 5.4.   ACT OF NOVEMBER 6, 1986—THE
IMMIGRATION REFORM AND CONTROL ACT (IRCA)

Title I – Control of Illegal Immigration

Sec. 101. Control of Unlawful Employment of Aliens

(a) In General
  (1) In General—It is unlawful for a person or entity to hire, or to recruit, or refer for a fee, for employment in the United States—
     (A) an alien knowing the alien is an unauthorized alien (as defined in subsection [RN1](h)(3)...
     (B) an individual without complying with the requirements of subsection (b).
  (2) Continuing employment—It is unlawful for a person or other entity, after hiring an alien for employment in accordance with paragraph (1), to continue to employ the alien in the United States knowing the alien is (or has become) an unauthorized alien with respect to such employment.
  (3) Defense—A person or entity that establishes that it has complied in good faith with the requirements of subsection (b) with respect to the hiring, recruiting, or referral for employment of an alien in the United States who has established an affirmative defense that the person or entity has not violated paragraph (1)(A) with respect to such hiring, recruiting, or referral.
  (4) Use of Labor Through Contract—For the purposes of this section, a person or other entity who uses a contract, subcontract, or exchange, entered into, renegotiated, or extended after the date of the enactment of this section, to obtain the labor of an alien in the United States knowing that the alien is an unauthorized alien... with respect to performing such labor, shall be considered to have hired the alien for employment in the United States in violation of paragraph (1)(A).
  (5) Use of State Employment Agency Documentation—For the purposes of paragraph (1)(B) and (3), a person or entity shall be deemed to have complied with the requirements of subsection (b) with respect to the hiring of an individual who was referred for such employment by a State employment agency...
(b) Employment Verification System—The requirements referred to in paragraphs (1)(B) and (3) are, in the case of a person or other entity hiring, recruiting, or referring an individual or employment in the United States, the requirements specified in the following three paragraphs:
  (1) Attestation After Examination of Documentation—
     (A) In General—The person or entity must attest, under penalty of perjury and on a form designed or established by the Attorney

General by regulation, that it has verified that the individual is
not an unauthorized alien be examining—
   (i) a document described in subparagraph (B), or
   (ii) a document described in subparagraph (C) and (D).
(B) Documents Establishing Both Employment Authorization and
   Indentity—A document described in this subparagraph is an
   individual's—
   (i) United States passport/
   (ii) Certificate of Unites States citizenship;
   (iii) Certificate of naturalization;
   (iv) Unexpired foreign passport, if the passport has an ap-
       propriate, unexpired endorsement of the Attorney Gen-
       eral authorizing the individual's employment in the
       United States; or
   (v) Resident alien card or other alien registration, if the
       card—
       (I) contains a photograph of the individual . . .
       (II) is evidence of authorization of employment in the
           United States.
(C) Documents Evidencing Employment Authorization—A document described . . . is [a]
   (i) Social Security account number card . . .
   (ii) Certificate of birth in the United States or establishing
       United States nationality at birth;
   (iii) Other documents evidencing authorization of employ-
       ment in the United States which Attorney General finds,
       by regulation, to be acceptable for the purposes of this
       section.
(D) Documents establishing identity of an individual—A document described in this subparagraph is an individual's
   (i) driver's license or similar document issued for the purpose
       of identification by a State, if it contains a photograph of
       the individual . . .
   (ii) in the case of individuals under 16 years of age or in a State
       which does not provide for issuance of an identification
       document . . . referred to in clause (i), documentation of
       personal identity of such type as the Attorney General
       finds, by regulation, provides a reliable means of identifi-
       cation . . .
(2) Definition of Unauthorized Alien—As used in this section, the term
   "unauthorized alien" means, with respect to the employment of an
   alien at the particular time, that the alien is not at that time (A) an
   alien lawfully admitted for permanent residence, or (B) authorized
   to be so employed by this Act or by the Attorney General . . .
Deferral of Enforcement with Respect to Seasonal Agricultural Services—
   (A) In General—Except as provided for in subparagraph (B), be-
       fore the end of the application period, it is unlawful for a

person or entity (including a farm labor contractor) or an agent of such person or entity, to recruit an unauthorized alien (other than an alien described in clause (ii) who is outside the United States to enter the United States to perform seasonal agricultural services).

(iii) Exception—Clause (i) shall not apply to an alien who the person or entity reasonably believes to meet the requirements of section 210(a)(2) of this Act (relating to the performance of agricultural services).

(j) General Accounting Office Reports—

(1) In General—Beginning one year after the date of enactment of this Act, and at intervals for one year thereafter for a period of three years after such date, the Comptroller General of the United States shall prepare and transmit to the Congress and to the taskforce established under subsection (k) a report describing the results of a review of the implementation and enforcement of this section during the preceding twelve-month period, for the purpose of determining if—(A) such provisions have been carried out satisfactorily;

(B) a pattern of discrimination has resulted against citizens or nationals of the United States or against eligible workers seeking employment; and

(C) an unnecessary regulatory burden has been created for employers hiring such workers.

(k) Review by the Taskforce—The Attorney General, jointly with the Chairman of the Commission on Civil Rights and the Chairman of the Equal Employment Opportunity Commission, shall establish a taskforce to review each report of the Comptroller General transmitted under subsection (j)(i).

(3) Recommendations to Congress—If the report transmitted includes a determination that the implementation of this section has resulted in a pattern of discrimination in employment (against other than unauthorized aliens) on the basis of national origin, the taskforce shall, taking into consideration any recommendations in the report, report to Congress recommendations for such legislation as may be appropriate to deter or remedy such discrimination.(1) Termination Date for Employer Sanctions—If Report of Widespread Discrimination and Congressional Approval—The provisions of this section shall terminate 30 days after receipt of the last report required to be transmitted under subsection (j), if—

(A) the Comptroller General determines, and so reports . . . that a widespread pattern of discrimination has resulted against citizens or nationals of the United States or against eligible workers seeking employment solely form the implementation of this section; and

(B) there is enacted, within such period of 30 calendar days, a joint resolution stating in substance that the Congress approves the findings of the Comptroller General contained in such report.

(2) Senate Procedures for Consideration—Any joint resolution refer-
eed to in clause (B) of paragraph (1) shall be considered in the
Senate in accordance with subsection (n)...

Sec. 111 (b). Increased Authorization of Appropriations for INS and
EOIR—In addition to any other amounts authorized to be appropriated,
in order to carry out this Act, there are authorized to be appropriated to
the Department of Justice—
  (1) for the Immigration and Naturalization Service, for fiscal year
  1987, $12,000,000 and for fiscal year 1988, $15,000,000...to
  provide for an increase in the Border Patrol personnel of the INS so
  that the average level of such personnel in each fiscal year 1987 and
  1988 is at least 50 percent higher that such level for fiscal year
  1986.

Title II—Legalization

Sec. 201. Legalization of Status.
Sec. 245A. (a) Temporary Resident Status—The Attorney General
shall adjust the status of an alien to that of an alien lawfully admitted for
temporary residence if the alien meets the following requirements:
  (1) Timely Application—(A) During Application Period—Except as
  provided in subparagraph (B), the alien must apply for such adjustment during the 12-month period beginning on a date (not later
  than 180 days after the date of enactment of this section) designated by the Attorney General...
  (2) Continuous Lawful Residence Since 1982—(A) In General-The
  alien must establish that he has resided continuously in the United
  States in an unlawful status since such date and through the date
  the application is filed under this subsection.
    (C) Non-immigrants—In the case of an alien who entered the
    United States as a non-immigrant before January 1, 1982, the
    alien must establish that the alien's period of authorized stay as
    a non-immigrant expired before such date through the passage
    of time of the alien's unlawful status was known to the Gov-
    ernment as of such date...
  (4) Admissible as Immigrant—
  For the purposes of this subsection, an alien in the status of a Cuban
  and Haitian entrant described in paragraph (1) or (2)(A) of section
  501(e) of Public Law 96-422 shall be considered to have entered the
  United States and to be in an unlawful status in the United States.
  (c) Subsequent Adjustment to Permanent Residence and Nature of Temporary Resident Status—
  (1) Adjustment to Permanent Residence. The Attorney General shall
  adjust the status of any alien provided lawful temporary status
  under subsection (a) to that of an alien lawfully admitted for permanent residence if the alien meets the following requirements:

(A) Timely Application After One Year's Residence—The alien must apply for such adjustment during the one-year period beginning with the nineteenth month that begins after the date the alien was granted such temporary status.

(B) Continuous Residence—The alien must establish that he—
   (i) is admissible to the United States as an immigrant, except as otherwise provided under subsection (d)(2), and
   (ii) has not been convicted of any felony or three or more misdemeanors committed in the United States.

(C) Admissible as Immigrant—The alien must establish that he—
   (i) is admissible to the United States as an immigrant, except as otherwise provided under subsection (d)(2), and
   (ii) has not been convicted of any felony or three or more misdemeanors committed in the United States.

(D) Basic Citizenship Skills—The alien must demonstrate that he—
   (I) meets the requirements of section 312 (relating to minimal understanding of ordinary English and a knowledge and understanding of the history and government of the United States . . .
   (II) is satisfactorily pursuing a course of study (recognized by the Attorney General) to achieve an understanding of English and such knowledge and understanding of the history and government of the United States . . .

(h) Temporary Disqualification of Newly Legalized Aliens from Receiving Certain Public Welfare Assistance—

(1) In General—During the five year period beginning on the date an alien was granted temporary resident status under subsection (a), and not withstanding any other provision of the law—

(A) except as provided in paragraphs (2) and (3), the alien is not elibible for—
   (1) many programs of financial assistance furnished under Federal law . . .
   (ii) medical assistance under a State plan approved under Title XIX of the Social Security Act; and
   (iv) assistance under the Food Stamp Act of 1977; and

(B) a State or political subdivision therein may, to the extent consistent with paragraph (A) and paragraphs (2) and (3), provide that an alien is not eligible for the programs of financial assistance or for medical assistance described in subparagraph (A) (ii) furnished under the law of that State or political subdivision . . .

Unless otherwise specifically provided by this section or other law, an alien in temporary lawful residence status granted under subsection (a) shall not be considered (for purposes of any law of a State or political subdivision providing for a program of financial assistance) to be permanently residing in the United States under color of law.

    (2) Exceptions—Paragraph (1) shall not apply—

        (A) to a Cuban and Haitian entrant...

Title III—Reform of Legal Immigration, Part A— Temporary Agricultural Workers

Sec. 301. H-2A Agricultural Workers

(a) Providing New 'H-2A' Nonimmigrant Classification for Temporary Agricultural Labor—Paragraph (15)(H) of section 101(a) (8 U.S.C. 1101(a)) is amended by striking out "to perform temporary services or labor," in clause (ii) and inserting in lieu thereof, "(a) to perform agricultural labor or services, as defined by the Secretary of Labor in regulations and including agricultural labor as defined in section 3121(g) of the Internal Revenue Code of 1954 and agriculture as defined in section 3 (f) of the Fair Labor Standards Act of 1938...or a temporary or seasonal nature, or (b) to perform other temporary service or labor."

(b) Involvement of Departments of Labor and Agriculture in H-2A Program—Section 214(c) (8 U.S.C. 1184(c)) is amended by adding to the end of the following: "For purposes of this subsection with respect to non-immigrants as described in section 101(a)(15)(H)(ii)(a), the term 'appropriate agencies of Government' means the Department of Labor and includes the Department of Agriculture. The provisions of section 216 shall apply to the question of importing any alien as nonimmigrant under section 101(a)(15)(H)(ii)(a)."

(c) Admission of H-2A Workers—Chapter 2 of Title II is amended by adding after section 215 the following new section: "Sec. 216(a) Conditions for Approval of H-2A Petitions—

    (1) A petition to import an alien as an H-2A worker may not be approved by the Attorney General unless the petitioner has applied to the Secretary of Labor for a certification that (A) there is not sufficient workers who are able, willing, and qualified, and who will be available at the time and place needed, to perform the labor or services involved in the petition, and (B) the employment of the alien in such labor or services will not adversely affect the wages and working conditions of workers in the United States similarly employed.

(Title IV of the act specifies various reports to Congress over the next three years dealing with the comprehensive reports on immigration, unauthorized alien employment, the H-2A program, the legalization program, evidence of discrimination, and the visa waiver pilot program.)

Source: 100 Stat. 3360.

The amnesty provisions in IRCA ultimately allowed nearly 3.5 million previously undocumented immigrants to become permanent resident aliens who, after five years in residence beyond the transition period to legalization, qualified to seek naturalization. They did so, as we will see more fully in the next chapter, in unprecedented numbers. Figures 5.6 and 5.7 show the dramatic increase in naturalization petitions. Figure 5.6 graphs the number of petitions for naturalizations filed from 1907 to 2000. The significant spike after mid-1980 is evident in the graph. Figure 5.7 graphically shows the percent of people naturalized by decade and selected region of birth for the years of this cycle, 1961 to 1990.

CONCLUSION

The long and rocky road to enactment of IRCA was followed by an equally bumpy effort to implement the complex and often contradictory law. The very compromises enabling its enactment sowed the seeds for difficulties in

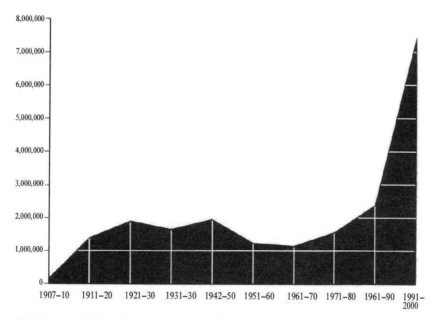

FIGURE 5.6. Petitions for Naturalization Filed, 1907–2001.

Source: Adapted from "Table 34, Petitions for Naturalizations Filed, Persons Naturalized, and Petitions for Naturalizations Denied: Fiscal Years 1907–2002," in *Fiscal Year 2002 Yearbook of Immigration Statistics*, U.S. Department of Homeland Security, Bureau of Citizenship and Immigration Services, Washington D.C. Online: http://www.bcis.gov/graphics/shared/aboutus/statistics/NA_TZ2002yrbk/NATZ2002list.htm (accessed July 17, 2003).

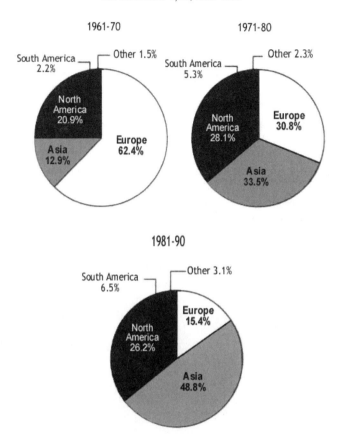

FIGURE 5.7.   Persons Naturalized by Decades, Selected Region of Birth, 1961–1990.
Source: "Chart M: Persons Naturalized by Decade and Selected Region of Birth: Fiscal Years 1961–2000," in *2000 Statistical Yearbook of the Immigration and Naturalization Service*, U.S. Department of Justice, Immigration and Naturalization Service, Washington D.C. Online: http://www.immigration.gov/graphicsshared/aboutus/statistics/00yrbk_NATZ/NATZ2000.pdf (accessed June 30, 2003).

implementation. Employer sanctions did not seem to work very well in its goal of "demagnetizing" the draw of the U.S. economy. A number of documents were accepted as valid demonstrations of a person's eligibility to work. These provisions simply fueled a phony-document industry enabling illegal aliens to continue coming to the United States and employers to continue hiring them without fear of legal penalty for "knowingly hiring" undocumented workers. Because of enforcement problems faced by the INS, the number of undocumented aliens successfully crossing the border declined for only a very brief period. Within a year after passage of IRCA, undocumented immigration was at the pre-IRCA levels.

Equally difficult was the implementation of the amnesty provisions. The program did result in the legalization of more than 3 million applicants. But the INS had no prior experience in dealing with such a program, which involved a 180-degree change in what had been the prevailing philosophy (or bureaucratic culture) and tradition of the agency. Illegal aliens who met the complicated criteria for legalization often distrusted the INS, and only after extensive involvement by nongovernmental organizations (called qualified designated entities, or QDEs), some of which became legal advocates against the INS' implementation of the legalization program, did the INS come to amend its procedural rules allowing extensive approval of applicants. The record of approval of applicants varied across the country and by type of category of applicant. There were essentially three legalization programs: the regular program referred to as Legalizing Authorized Workers (LAWs), a Seasonal Agricultural Worker program (SAWs), and a Cuban/Haitian Adjustment program (LeMay, 1994: 88–96).

IRCA authorized a 50 percent increase in the Border Patrol staff, but actual staff increases fell short of that due to difficulties in recruiting and expanding training staff and facilities. As the Border Patrol increased in staff, moreover, so did its duties. After 1986, the interdiction of drug traffic across the border became a prime focus (due in part to the 1986 Omnibus Anti-Drug Law). Border Patrol agents shifted their emphasis from alien apprehension and smuggling to work with the Drug Enforcement Agency (DEA) on Operation Alliance. The INS also expanded the number of staff being used to guard refugee camps and to identify, prosecute, and deport alien criminals (Bean, Vernez, and Keely, 1989: 44).

Another concern about IRCA was whether or not its employer sanctions provisions would result in increased discrimination against foreign-looking and foreign-sounding individuals, particularly those of Latino heritage. Several attempts to study whether IRCA increased job discrimination were conducted. The Department of Labor (DOL) did an exhaustive review of the research evidence on the impact of immigrants. DOL concluded that the market forces that characterize dynamic labor markets seem to effectively absorb and integrate immigrants, both legal and illegal, in a manner that makes their effects indistinguishable from those of other workers at the aggregate level. DOL found few instances of outright displacement of native workers.

The most important studies on the impact of discrimination were a series of three annual post-IRCA ones conducted by the General Accounting Office (GAO). The GAO's third and final report found that there was, indeed, widespread discrimination that was the direct result of IRCA (GAO, 1990: 3). The report indicated that the law resulted in citizenship discrimination, estimation, based on employer responses, that because of the law, an additional 430,000 employers (9 percent) began hiring only people born in the United States and not those with temporary work eligibility documents. In all, the GAO estimated that 891,000 (19 percent) of the 4.6 million employers surveyed nationwide began one or more discriminatory practices as a result of IRCA (GAO, 1990: 7).

Further evidence of such discrimination came from charges filed with the Office of Special Counsel (OSC) in the Department of Justice. A report by the Mexican American Legal Defense Fund (MALDEF) and the American Civil Liberties Union (ACLU) released in November 1989 found that IRCA was a source of increased discrimination against foreign-looking or -sounding people, as did a New York State Assembly Task Force on New Americans study released in November 1988 (LeMay, 1994: 122).

The continued problems with a huge influx of illegal immigrants (i.e., both undocumented and visa overstayers) resulted in renewed efforts in the 1990s to reform legal immigration and to tackle once again legislation that would impact the undocumented influx. These forces involved new groups, state government action, and renewed pressures on Congress to "fix the problem." A new cycle in immigration policy-making can be categorized as beginning in 1990: the "Storm-Door Cycle." That era is the focus of the next chapter. Events during the first decade of the twenty-first century propelled national security issues to become the preeminent concern of proposals to reform immigration policy, and the very concept of national security morphed into a new term, homeland security, which characterizes the "storm-door" nature of immigration policy dominant in the new era.

NOTES

1. Cited in Chiswick: 41. See also Rosemary Stevens, *The Alien Doctors* (New York: Wiley and Sons, 1978); and Patricia Mamot, *Foreign Medical Graduates in America* (Springfield, IL: Charles Thomas, 1974). Philippine nurses entered in significant and comparable numbers to those of medical doctors as well.

2. See LeMay, 1985: 358–359. See also Darrell Montero, *Vietnamese Americans* (Boulder, CO.: Westview Press, 1979). For a broader discussion of the entire refugee aid programs, see Grant McClellan, *Immigrants, Refugees, and U.S. Policy* (New York: H. W. Wilson, 1981). For aid to Soviet Jews, see William Oerback, *The American Movement to Aid Soviet Jews* (Amherst: University of Massachusetts Press, 1979).

3. LeMay, 1985: 359–362. See also, McClellan, op. cit.; and John Crewdson, *The Tarnished Door: The New Immigrants and the Transformation of America* (New York: Time Books, 1983); Harry Cross and James Sandos, *Across the Border* (Berkeley: Institute of Government Studies, 1981); and Nathan Glazer (ed.), *Clamor at the Gates: The New American Immigration* (San Francisco: ICS Press, 1985); and Bean, King, and Passel, 1985.

4. See Muller and Espanshade, 1985: 17; Cheng and Nitz, 1989: 12; and two *Governing* articles, 1989 and 1992.

─────── 6 ───────

The Storm-Door Cycle, 1990–?

INTRODUCTION: THE MAKING OF FORTRESS AMERICA—
IMMIGRATION POLICY-MAKING IN AN ERA OF
INTERNATIONAL TERRORISM

As we have seen in Chapter 5, IRCA heavily emphasized the issue of *illegal* immigration. It was passed only after protracted struggle and by including several key compromises that resulted in unintended consequences when IRCA was implemented. Congress soon took up proposals for immigration reform that were intended to refine its approach or that addressed issues of *legal* immigration.

On March 15, 1988, the Senate passed another Kennedy-Simpson bill by a vote of 88 to 4. This measure addressed a number of aspects of legal immigration not included in IRCA. It identified separate tracks for family and nonfamily immigrants, called for an increase in total legal immigration, tipped the ratio of independent to family-related immigrants, and separated refugees from family-related immigrants. The bill called for establishing eligibility for entrepreneurs who created at least ten new jobs and investing at least $1 million in the new jobs. It created separate avenues of entrance for immigrants with needed job skills and also doubled the number of such visas—from 54,000 to 150,000, aimed at drawing more skilled and better-educated workers.

The Kennedy-Simpson bill was a slightly modified version of the one passed by the Senate in 1988 but not voted on in the House, a bill sponsored by Senator Paul Simon (D.–Ill.). Simon's bill addressed some problems associated with the implementation of IRCA. It contained an amendment to end direct federal benefits to undocumented immigrants and a provision to grant stays of deportation to immediate relatives of individuals in the process of legalizing under IRCA. It was not uncommon for some family members of persons

qualifying for legalization (such as wives and children) who would have entered after the January 1, 1982 effective date of IRCA and thus would not be
eligible for the amnesty program. This had the effect of splitting families which
countered the overall goal of immigration policy at the time which was to
reunite families. Simon's bill attempted to rectify that split-family issue. In
addition, Simon's measure reflected a response to repression of the pro-
democracy movement in mainland China. The bill allowed for an increase in
the annual immigration level from Hong Kong, from 2 to 3.5 percent of the
worldwide total, and allowed Chinese students already in the United States to
remain for four years and be qualified for legal residency (Bean, Vernez, and
Keely, 1989: 1006–1107).

Senator Dennis DeConcini (D.-AZ.) introduced a bill halting the deportation of Salvadorans and Nicaraguans, a companion bill to one in the House
sponsored by Representative Joseph Moakley (D.-MA.). They had originally
launched their antideportation bills during the struggle to enact IRCA, but
their provisions were deleted in the compromises worked out in the conference committee. The manner in which IRCA was implemented aggravated the
problems facing Salvadorans and Nicaraguans, prompting Senator DeConcini
to sponsor the new Senate measure to deal with the situation (Church World
Service, 1987: 131–132).

Representative Berman (D.-CA.) introduced a companion bill to that of
Senators Simpson, Kennedy, and Simon. The Berman bill also exempted immediate relatives of permanent residents from the current family-preference
limit. Under the 1965 law, the maximum visa allotment per country was
20,000. The new Senate measure set that at 7 percent of the total, and the
Berman bill set it at 22,000.

Still another measure was introduced by Representatives Rodino and
Mazzoli. Their bill differed from the Kennedy-Simpson-Simon bill in that it
neither imposed a ceiling on annual admissions of immediate relatives of U.S.
citizens nor offset such admissions against other family-sponsored immigration (Benda, 1989: 72).

Congress passed several laws in 1987–1989 that modified the fringes of
existing law. In 1987, it passed the Amerasian Homecoming Act, which was an
appropriations bill providing for the admission of children born in Vietnam
between specified dates to Vietnamese mothers and American fathers, together
with their immediate relatives. Though admitted as nonquota immigrants, they
received refugee-program benefits.

In 1988, as part of the U.S.–Canada Free Trade Agreement Implementation
Act, Congress facilitated temporary entry of Canadians on a reciprocal basis
with Canada accepting U.S. emigrants. In November 1988, Congress amended
the 1965 act by providing for the extension of stay for certain nonimmigrant
H-1 nurses. In a 1989 appropriations bill, the Foreign Operations Act of 1989
(*Statutes at Large,* 1989b: 3908), Congress adjusted to permanent resident
status certain Soviet and Indochinese nationals who were paroled into the

United States between certain dates after denial of refugee status by the INS. Finally, in December 1989, Congress again amended the 1965 act by passing the Immigration Nursing Relief Act of 1989. It adjusted to permanent resident status without numerical limitations for certain nonimmigrants employed as registered nurses for three years (this in response to a severe nursing shortage in the United States).

The introduction of the various measures in 1987–1989 and the passage of a few others that nibbled at the fringes of immigration problems continuing despite the IRCA, coupled with the soon apparent failure of IRCA to stem the tide of undocumented aliens entering the United States, built up pressure for Congress to enact additional measures in the 1990s. The thrust of these laws, as we shall see later, was to signal a new cycle in immigration policy-making— that of the Storm-Door Era. Collectively, laws passed in the 1990s and the first decade of the twenty-first century reflected an atmosphere of "fortress-America." National security concerns over international terrorism rose to become *the* element of immigration policy that dominated the process and characterized the new era.

Some traditionally involved and new interest groups entered the arena of the battles over immigration policy. An impressive number of nongovernmental organizations played an advocacy role regarding immigrants and refugees or pressed for less restrictive policy as the government moved toward stricter policy.[1] Among the more visible and important were the following: Human Rights Watch, International Immigrants Foundation, American Immigration Law Foundation, American Immigrant Lawyers Association, American Refugee Committee, Catholic Charities USA, Center for Human Rights and the Constitution, Central American Refugee Center, Church World Service, Episcopal Migration Ministries, Hebrew Immigrant Aid Society, Humane Borders, League of United Latin American Citizens, Lutheran Immigration and Refugee Service, Mexican American Legal Defense Fund, National Council of La Raza, National Immigration Forum, National Immigration Law Center, National Network for Immigrant and Refugee Rights, New York Association for New Americans, U.S. Catholic Conference's Migration and Refugee Services, the Council on American–Islamic Relations, and the U.S. Committee for Refugees.

Among the more notable organizations advocating more limited immigration and restrictive immigration policy are the American Immigration Control Foundation, the Federation for American Immigration Reform, Numbers USA, Americans for Immigration Control, Inc., the Alliance for Immigration Reform, the Minutemen, Coalition for a Closer Look, Citizen Outreach, and the Congressional Immigration Reform Caucus.

Several noted "think-tank" centers have studied the immigration issue and have produced important reports and held conferences on the issue informing public opinion as well as influencing public policy-makers on the same: The Cato Institute, the Center for Immigration Studies, the Center for Migration Studies, the Migration Policy Institute, the National Immigration Forum, the

PEW Hispanic Center, the Prejudice Institute, the Rand Corporation, and the Urban Institute.

State governments entered the arena as well, placing new pressures on Congress to respond in ways to "fix-the-problem" of illegal immigration and border control which so adversely impacted the ten or so states that received the vast bulk of new legal and illegal immigration flows (Arizona, California, Colorado, Florida, Illinois, New Jersey, New Mexico, New York, and Texas). New and more restrictive powers were granted to the executive branch to enforce control of the borders and to protect the homeland from the threat of international terrorism.

THE IMMIGRATION ACT OF 1990

The first major law of the new era was passed by Congress on November 29, 1990 as the Immigration Act of 1990 (IMMACT) (104 Stat. 4981). This act was the culmination of the efforts to reform legal immigration that began with SCIRP and it plugged some IRCA-related loopholes. The law contained elements of virtually all the bills discussed earlier. Its major authors in the Senate were Kennedy, Simpson, and Simon; and its chief author in the House was Representatiave Bruce Morrison (D.-Conn.). Its major provisions are summarized in Box 6.1. Senator Kennedy described the bill as follows:

This bill, like all major legislation, represents many years of work, and many efforts at compromise. This measure is the culmination of a decade-long effort which began in 1979 with the Select Commission on Immigration and Refugee Policy. This commission's work laid the basis for the most comprehensive reforms of the nation's immigration laws in our history. This effort as been a two-step process. In 1986 we enacted a far-reaching measure to deal with illegal immigration. In this bill, an equally far-reaching reform of legal immigration will be achieved ... Our goal has been to reform the current immigration system—which has not changed in 25 years—so that it will more faithfully serve the national interest, and be more flexible and open to immigrants from nations which were so short-changed by current law ... This compromise creates two separate preference systems for immigrant visas—one for close family members, another for independent immigration. This two-track system was first recommended by the Select Commission (*Congressional Record—Senate,* October 26, 1990, S-17106).

Co-author Senator Simpson stressed yet another aspect of the measure:

But the bill provides, for the very first time, a mechanism through which the national level of immigration in the United States will be reviewed by the President and by the Congress every three years. So never again will we go 25 to 30 years without carefully reviewing immigration levels, how they should be adjusted to bring our immigration policy more into line with our national interests (*Congressional Record—Senate,* October 26, 1990, S-17109).

**BOX 6.1.   MAJOR PROVISIONS OF IMMIGRATION ACT
OF 1990 (IMMACT)**

1. It increased total immigration under a flexible "cap" of 675,000 beginning in 1995. The 675,000 immigrants were to consist of 480,000 family-sponsored immigrants, 140,000 employment-based immigrants, and 55,000 "diversity" immigrants.
2. It revised grounds for exclusion and deportation.
3. It authorized the attorney general to grant temporary protected status to undocumented alien nationals from designated countries subject to armed conflict or natural disaster (e.g., El Salvador, Nicaragua).
4. It revised nonimmigrant admission categories by redefining the H-1B temporary-worker category and creating new temporary-worker admission categories, revised and extended to 1994, the Visa Waiver Pilot Program, and revised naturalization authority by transferring jurisdiction from the courts to the attorney general and amending substantive requirements for naturalization.
5. It revised enforcement activities in several ways, which includes broadening of the definition of "aggravated felony" and imposing new legal restrictions on aliens convicted of crimes; it revised employer-sanctions provisions of IRCA; and it authorized funds to increase, by 1,000, the personnel level of the Border Patrol.
6. It revised criminal and deportation provisions by recodifying thirty-two grounds for exclusion into nine categories and revising or repealing some grounds for exclusion (including some health grounds).
7. It established a commission to do mandatory regular and continued study of immigration.

The measure passed in the House by a vote of 264 in favor to 118 against, with 50 not voting. In the Senate, it was adopted more comfortably, by a vote of 89 to 8, with 3 not voting. The Immigration Act of 1990, also referred to as IMMACT, split voting blocs much like how the IRCA did, but with more unanimity among some of the caucus blocs. Table 6.1 shows the roll call vote on the measure by political party affiliation, total Congress.

Although hailed as the most extensive reform of immigration law since 1965, IMMACT hardly solved all the problems nor marked the end of demands for immigration reform. The annual studies mandated by the 1990 act further documented the effects of the push side of the immigration process. Attempts to cope with drug smuggling and human trafficking contributed to a growing sense of the need for bilateral and multilateral agreements that pressured U.S. immigration policy-making toward a multinational approach. In 1993, Congress passed the North American Free Trade Agreement (NAFTA), which was seen as a step in that direction. Proponents of NAFTA emphasized that its benefits to the Mexican economy would have a beneficial impact on illegal

TABLE 6.1. Roll-Call Vote, Immigration Reform Act of 1990, by Political Party Affiliation, U.S. Congress

Party	Favored	Opposed	Not Voting	Total
Democrats	218 (62%)	58 (46%)	35 (66%)	311
Republicans	131 (38%)	68 (54%)	18 (34%)	217
Total	349 (100%)	126 (100%)	53 (100%)	528
Chi Square = 9.206 .01 level of significance				

Source: Table by author.

immigration pressures. To the extent that the Mexican economy expanded, jobs were created and the Mexican standard of living rose, then a corresponding reduction in pressure to emigrate north was predicted. Even NAFTA's proponents estimated that the treaty would cause up to 500,000 jobs to drain south of the border, conceding that point.

A recession in the U.S. economy in 1991–1993 added pressures for further action. The resulting federal budget crisis meant that authorization to substantially increase the Border Patrol's personnel and budget would remain unfunded. The Border Patrol continued to suffer from poor training, high turnover, little supervision, and a fortress mentality. As two scholars of the border patrol noted: "You could say that the Border Patrol is the bastard orphan stepchild of the immigration service" (Krauss and Pacheco: 155). The INS came under fire by allegations of discrimination, mismanagement, misconduct, and gross ineptitude. In 1993, the Clinton administration proposed legislation to significantly restructure the INS. Senator Dianne Feinstein (D.-CA.) advocated a controversial one dollar per-person border-crossing fee to fund improvements to the Border Patrol. The IMMACT's study commission proposed merging the INS, the Border Patrol, U.S. Customs, and certain divisions of the Departments of Treasury and Health and Human Services into one federal agency responsible for admitting, processing, and resettling immigrants (Caulen 1993: 49).

Asylum problems continued to fester and a tremendous rise in the number of asylum cases created backlogs that the INS could not handle. The asylum cases were highlighted to public opinion attention in 1993 when several boatloads of Chinese attempting to enter the United States illegally were seized off the shores of both California and New York. The renewed visibility of the illegal alien influx issue and the highly publicized cases of attempts to smuggle in asylum seekers fueled public opinion opposition to immigration generally (see Figure 6.2). The Clinton administration proposed new measures to tighten defense against undocumented aliens, including proposals for quick settlement of asylum cases, a beefed-up Border Patrol, and prosecution of alien smuggling rings under the racketeering laws. It proposed funding those measures by a five

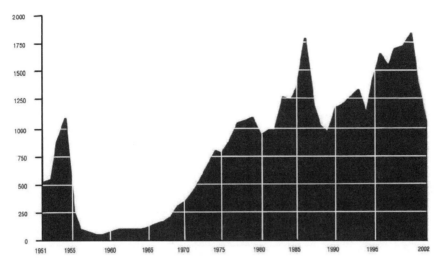

FIGURE 6.1. Aliens Apprehended at U.S. Borders, 1951–2002

Source: "Chart M Aliens Apprehended: Fiscal Years 1951–2002" in *Yearbook of Immigration Statistics*, Office of Immigration Statistics, Office of Management, Department of Homeland Security, Washington, D.C. [online] http://www.immigration.gov/graphics/shared/aboutus/statistics/ENF2002list.htm (accessed July 31, 2003).

to six dollar international airport inspection fee and by increasing fees for various benefits such as naturalization adjustment of immigrant status.

Despite the intention of national legislation to curb illegal immigration (i.e., IRCA and IMMACT), as the size and flow continued unabated, political pressure to do more increased by the mid-1990s. Figure 6.1 shows the number of aliens apprehended at the U.S. borders for selected fiscal years, 1951–2002. Note the spike in the level even after IRCA and building up again after 1995.

Public opinion varied up and down on whether or not immigration should be kept steady, increased, or decreased. These data are shown in Figure 6.2, which graphically presents their levels for selected years, 1965 through 2003.

CALIFORNIA'S PROPOSITION 187 (1994)

States that received the largest numbers of both legal and illegal immigrants, such as California, Florida, and Texas, sued the federal government in their respective federal district courts for the estimated billions of dollars the states had to bear for costs related to illegal immigrants and their children. The states argued that the federal government, by its failure to adequately control the nation's borders, was thereby responsible for these costs imposed on the states by its failure.

More significantly, in 1994 California attempted legislatively to reduce the draw of its economy and services to illegal immigrants and to send a message to

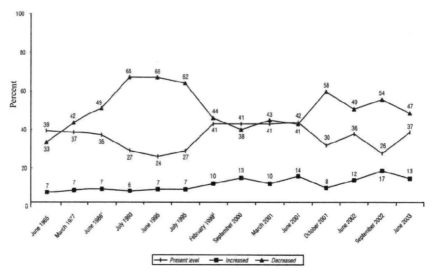

FIGURE 6.2. Public Opinion on U.S. Immigration Policy, 1965–2003
Note: CBS/New York Times poll.
Based on 514 national adults, margin of error 4/-5 percentage points.
Source: The Gallup Organization, Princeton, NJ, (June 2003), http://www.gallup.com

Congress by passing an anti-immigration measure—Proposition 187. Using the initiative process, California's voters passed the measure, officially entitled the "Save Our State Initiative," by nearly 60 percent. The measure required state and local agencies to report to the INS any person "suspected of being illegal," to prevent illegal aliens from receiving benefits or public services in the State of California. Among its several provisions: it restricted children of aliens from attending public schools; increased punishments for the manufacture, sale, or distribution of false citizenship or resident alien documents; increased criminal penalties for alien smuggling; made it a crime to use false documents; established verification requirements for state and local officials; excluded illegal aliens from most public social services, including health services except in cases of emergency or communicable diseases; and excluded illegal aliens from postsecondary education. Its authors anticipated the act being challenged in federal court and so they included a provision, Section 10, Amendment and Severability, which stated:

> In the event that any portion of this act or the application thereof to any person or circumstance is held invalid, that invalidity shall not affect any other provision or application of the act, which can be given effect without the invalid provision or application, and to that end the provisions of this act are severable.

The last provision of Proposition 187 anticipated a federal court challenge as to the law's constitutionality. They were correct in their anticipation. It was immediately brought to court by the League of United Latin American Citizens (LULAC). And the federal district court did rule that most of the law was unconstitutional (see *LULAC et al. v. Wilson et al.*, 908 F. Supp. 755 C.D. Cal. 1995: 787–791 as summarized in LeMay and Barkan, Document 147: 299–301).

California Governor Pete Wilson (R.) was running for reelection in 1994. The state was especially slow in emerging from the recession, and Governor Wilson initially trailed his Democratic challenger, Kathleen Brown, by a wide margin in the polls. As a U.S. Senator in the 1980s, Pete Wilson had favored guest-worker programs and similar measures to ensure a supply of cheap agricultural labor. He was fighting for his political life in his 1994 reelection bid, and he seized on the anti-immigration sentiment and the "Save Our State" initiative (Proposition 187) as the horse to ride back into the governor's mansion. He became its leading spokesman. The measure declared that citizens of the state suffered economic hardship from the presence of several illegal aliens in the state and were suffering injury and damage by the criminal conduct of such illegal aliens. In order to protect themselves from such illegal immigrants, the initiative required all state and local government agencies, with the federal government, to establish a system for identifying suspected illegal aliens and denying them benefits or public services in California. Governor Wilson won an easy victory in his reelection bid. Proposition 187 became *the* critical issue in the campaign and as the margin of the vote in favor of the proposition swelled, it provided him his dramatic electoral success (before the campaign he trailed his Democratic challenger by nearly 15 points in the early public opinion polls, but on election day defeated her by nearly 10 percent). His easy reelection and the 60 percent vote in favor of Proposition 187 did not go unnoticed by the U.S. Congress. The proponents of Proposition 187 had urged its adoption as a method "to send a message to Congress." The message was sent and received.

THE ACTS OF 1996

The federal district court ruled many of Proposition 187's provisions as unconstitutional in that they constituted state infringements of the national government's sole authority to enact immigration law or were state actions preempted by existing federal law. Congress nonetheless got the message sent by Proposition 187. It began efforts to address the "illegal immigration problem" once again. The data on INS apprehensions at the border were collected by the studies mandated by IMMACT, and the continued rise in those numbers, as was shown in Figure 6.1, created mounting public pressure on Congress.

In 1996, the Congress passed and President William Clinton signed into law two measures that essentially enacted into national law and policy the major provisions of Proposition 187. Congress enacted a welfare reform act that contained several immigrant-related provisions concerning both legal and illegal immigrants that had restrictions similar to those in Proposition 187. These immigrant-related provisions are summarized briefly in Box 6.2.

A sufficient consensus to enact broad-scale legal immigration reform could not be reached. Instead, many issues concerning legal immigration were separated from those regarding illegal immigration and were passed only after

---

BOX 6.2. IMMIGRATION-RELATED PROVISIONS OF THE PERSONAL RESPONSIBILITY AND WORK OPPORTUNITY ACT OF AUGUST 22, 1996

1. *Restrictions.* The act restricted the federal benefits for which illegal aliens and legal nonimmigrants (such as travelers and students) could qualify, denying the use of federal funds for any grant, loan, professional or commercial license, or retirement, disability, food assistance, or unemployment benefits.
2. *Exceptions.* It allowed legal and illegal immigrants to receive emergency medical assistance (but denied coverage for prenatal care or for delivery assistance that was not an emergency); short-term noncash emergency disaster relief; immunizations and testing for treatment of communicable diseases; noncash programs identified by the attorney general, such as soup kitchens, counseling, and short-term shelter; certain housing benefits; license and benefits directly related to work for which a nonimmigrant had been authorized to enter the United States; and certain Social Security retirement benefits protected by treaty or statute.
3. *State and local programs.* It prohibited states from providing state or local benefits to most illegal aliens, except that illegal aliens who were eligible for free public education under state or local law were entitled to school lunch or breakfast programs, and it permitted a state to opt to provide certain other benefits related to child nutrition and emergency food assistance.
4. *Current immigrants.* It made most legal immigrants ineligible for Supplemental Security Income (SSI) and food stamps until they became citizens, except for refugees and those granted asylum whose deportation was being withheld, those who had worked in the United States for ten years, veterans, or those on active duty and their spouses and unmarried children.
5. *Future immigrants.* It barred legal immigrants arriving after 1996 from receiving most federal benefits for low-income persons for five years, with some exceptions.
6. *State options.* It allowed states to deny benefits from the welfare block grants, Medicaid, and social service block grants to most legal immigrants, with exemptions for the SSI and food stamps; future immigrants would be subject to the five-year ban as for federal benefits.

7. *Sponsors.* It expanded the circumstances under which an immigrant's sponsor would be financially responsible for that individual.
8. *Reporting and verifying.* It required agencies that administer SSI, housing assistance, and welfare block grants to report quarterly to the INS the names and addresses of people they knew were unlawfully in the United States.

Source: Summary by author: HR 3734—PL 104-193. See also the discussion of the law and summary of provisions in *1996 Congressional Quarterly Almanac*, Vol. 52. Washington, D.C.: Congressional Quarterly (1997), 6-17, 6-18. We somewhat differently summarize it in LeMay and Barkan, Document 148: 301–304.

folding the provisions into the omnibus fiscal 1997 spending bill (H.R. 3610, P.L. 104-208), which President Clinton signed into law on September 30, 1996. The full measure covers more than 200 pages. The immigration-related provisions of the Omnibus Spending bill became the Illegal Immigration Reform and Immigrant Responsibility Act (IIRIRA) and numbered some sixty provisions. Some of the more major ones are detailed in Box 6.3.

Together, these laws enacted virtually all of the restrictive measures contained in Proposition 187. They had at best but a temporary impact on the numbers of legal and illegal immigrants entering the country. By the middle to the end of the decade, their influx reached levels matching the previous peak years of 1900 to 1910. Figure 6.3 presents graphically the amount of legal immigration, by region of birth, for fiscal years 1925 to 2001. Figure 6.4 shows in similar graphic form the non-immigrants admitted to the United States, 1975 to 2002. Both figures demonstrate the dramatic spike in the years 1990–2000. Figure 6.5 presents a bar graph depicting the source countries with high numbers of INS apprehensions, excluding Mexico, in 2001 and 2002.

Although the new laws did not appreciably slow the influx, as we have seen, they did make for some real strains on families in the United States split in their status (with one or more members here legally, but others illegally). As economic conditions improved by 2000, Congress eased up a bit by passing, on December 21, 2000, the Legal Immigration and Family Equity Act (LIFE) (See Information Plus, *Immigration and Illegal Aliens: Burden or Blessing?* Wylie, TX: Information Plus, 2001: 28). It covered about 640,000 undocumented aliens who had to be sponsored by a lawfully resident relative or by an employer. Naturalized citizens could apply on behalf of their spouses, children, parents, or siblings. Lawful permanent residents could apply on behalf of their spouses and unmarried children. The applicant had to file prior to April 30, 2001 for visas that could be granted there without them first having to leave the United States. When the visas became available, the applicant was required to pay a $1000 penalty fee and other filing fees.

BOX 6.3.   ILLEGAL IMMIGRATION REFORM AND IMMIGRANT
RESPONSIBILITY ACT, SEPTEMBER 30, 1996

1. It authorized a doubling of the Border Patrol (from 5,000 to 10,000 agents) by 2001.
2. It authorized funding of 900 additional INS agents to investigate and prosecute cases of smuggling, harboring, or employing illegal aliens and 300 new agents to investigate visa overstayers.
3. It authorized a three-tier border fence along a fourteen-mile strip of the U.S.–Mexican border south of San Diego and required that INS border-crossing cards include a biometric identifier and that future cards use devices such as retina scanners.
4. It granted increased wire-tap authority to the Justice Department for immigration document fraud, increased the penalties for smuggling, and granted broad authority to the INS to conduct underground operations to track organized illegal immigration rings.
5. It increased the penalties for document fraud from five to ten years and created a criminal penalty of up to five years for falsely claiming U.S. citizenship and up to one year in prison for unlawfully voting in a federal election.
6. It allowed courts to seize the assets of immigration law violators, greatly revised detention and deportation provisions by expanding the authority of the attorney general in such proceedings, and created a pilot program to use closed military bases as INS detention centers.
7. It modified employment verification programs and ordered the attorney general to create three pilot programs and to develop a program to use machine-readable documentation.
8. It made it harder for the government to sue employers who use immigration laws to discriminate against certain workers or job applicants.
9. It included a dozen provisions concerning public benefits, amended certain parole and asylum provisions, and denied visas to immigrants whose intent was to attend public elementary or secondary schools for more than one year.
10. It made female genital mutilation a crime punishable by prison.
11. It required the INS to report by the end of 1996 whether or not the United States had an adequate number of temporary agricultural workers.
12. It required the Social Security Administration to develop a prototype tamper-proof identify card.

Source: Summary by author: HR 3610—PL 104-208. See also a summary in *1996 Congressional Quarterly Almanac*, Vol. 52. Washington, D.C.: Congressional Quarterly (1997), 5-8–5-10. See also the discussion and summary excerpts in LeMay and Barkan, Document 149: 304–310.

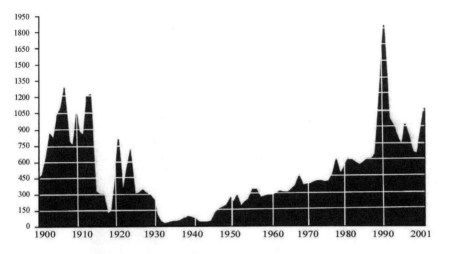

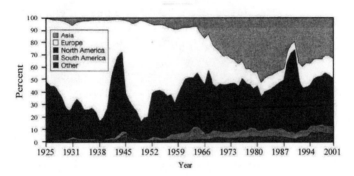

FIGURE 6.3. Legal Immigration to United States by Region of Birth, Fiscal Years 1925–2001

Source: "Chart A. Immigrants Admitted: Fiscal Years 1900–2001" in *2001 Statistical Yearbook of the Immigration and Naturalization Service*, U.S. Department of Justice, Immigration and Naturalization Service, Washington, D.C. Online: http://www.im migration.gov/graphics/shared/aboutus/statistics/yearbook2001.pdf (accessed June 30, 2003).

The combination of increased restrictions and denial of benefits to illegal aliens (mostly undocumented immigrants) and even to some legal resident aliens in the two 1996 acts, plus the over 3 million persons who had earlier been given amnesty in 1986 and were, by 1997, qualified to seek naturalization, and a strong reaction to Proposition 187 and its negative impact on noncitizens combined to dramatically increase the number of persons naturalized during the final years of the twentieth century. Figure 6.6 shows graphically the tremendous upsurge in naturalizations. It presents the number

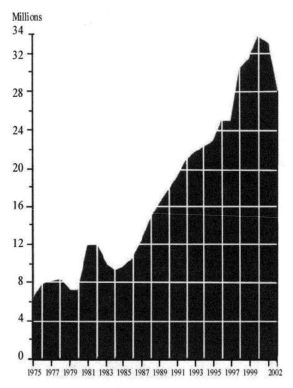

FIGURE 6.4. Nonimmigrants Admitted to United States, 1975–2002
Note: Data estimated for last quarter of 1979 and no data available for 1980 and 1997.
Source: "Chart F. Nonimmigrants Admitted: Fiscal Years 1975–2002," in *2002 Yearbook of Immigration Statistics.* U.S. Department of Homeland Security. Bureau of Citizenship and Immigration Services, Washington D.C. Online: http://www.immigrat ion/gov/graphics/shared/aboutus/statistics/TEMP02yrbk/Temp2002.pdf (accessed June 30, 2003).

of persons naturalized for the fiscal years 1908 to 2001. The dramatic spike to nearly 1.2 million in 1999, and over 1 million in 2001 is evident in the graph.

Those being naturalized shifted, since 1970, in their region of birth. The shift was toward those from Mexico, Asia, and South America, with a dramatic decline in those from Europe. In 1990, Mexico was the top sending country, with 22 percent of the total foreign-born. By 2000, Mexican immigrants ac-counted for 30 percent of the total foreign-born population, and Mexico alone accounted for 43 percent of the growth in the immigration population between 1990 and 2000. Figure 6.7 presents a bar graph showing the total foreign-born population and percent of total population, 1850–2000. It also shows a pie-chart indicating the foreign-born by region of birth, in percent, as of 2002.

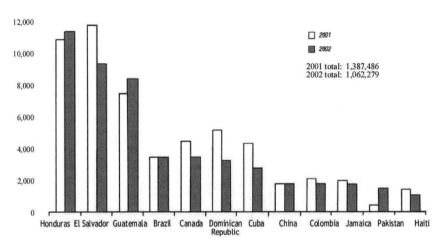

FIGURE 6.5. Source Countries with High Numbers of Immigration and Naturalization Service Apprehensions, Excluding Mexico, 2001–2002

Source: Adapted from "Table 53, Deportable Aliens Located by Status at Entry and Region and Country of Nationality, Fiscal Year 2001." *in 2001 Statistical Yearbook of the Immigration and Naturalization Service,* U.S. Department of Justice. Immigration and Naturalization Service, Washington D.C., (February 2003). Online: http://www.immigration. gov/graphics/shared/aboutus/statistics/Yearbook2001.pdf (accessed June 30, 2003), and "Table 58, Deportable Aliens. Located by Status of Entry and Region and Country of Nationality, Fiscal, Year 2002," in *Yearbook of Immigration Statistics,* Office of Immigration Statistics, Office of Management Department of Homeland Security. Washington, D.C. Online: http://www.Immigration.gov/graphics/shared/aboutus/statistics/ENF2002list.htm (accessed July 2, 2003).

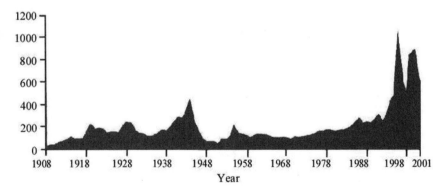

FIGURE 6.6. Persons Naturalized, Fiscal Years 1908–2001

Source: Statistical Yearbook of the Immigration and Naturalization Service (2002), 200. Online: http://www.immigration.gov/graphics/.

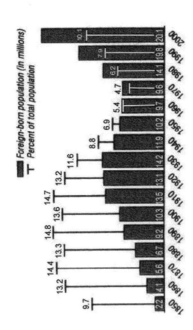

FIGURE 6.7. Foreign-Born Population in the United States as Percent of Total Population and by Region of Birth, 2002

Note: For 1850–1990, resident population. For 2000, civilian noninstitutional population plus Armed Forces living off post or with their families on post.

Source: Dianne Schmidley, "Figure 1-1, Foreign-Born Population and Percent of Total Population for the United States: 1856–2000," in *Profile of the Foreign-Born Population in the United States: 2000—Current Population Reports Special Studies*, P23–206, U.S. Census: Bureau, Washington D.C., (December 2001). Online: http://www.census.gov/prod/2002/pubs/p23-206.pdf (accessed July 2, 2003).

Source: Dianne Schmidley. "Figure 1. Foreign-Born by Region of Birth: 2002," in *The Foreign-Born Population in the United States: Mardi 2002.* Current Population Reports, P20-539, U.S. Census Bureau, Washington D.C., February 2003. Online: http://www.census.gov/prod/2003pubs/p20-539.pdf (accessed July 2, 2002).

Several states in which Mexican immigration is especially pronounced registered significant increases. In Arizona, for example, immigrants from Mexico grew from 5 to 67 percent of the foreign-born, and in Texas they went from 59 to 65 percent of the total. As Steven Camarota, the Director of Research for the Center for Immigration Studies, noted in a 2003 report: "In one sense today's immigration is more diverse than ever because people now arrive from every corner of the world. However, in another, and perhaps more important sense, it is less diverse. Allowing in so many people from one country and region of the world may significantly slow the assimilation process by creating the critical mass necessary for linguistic, cultural, and residential isolation" (http://www.cis.org/articles/2003/back1203.html).

Concentrations of foreign-born, not just Mexican-born, can be readily seen in Figure 6.8. It presents a map of the United States designating the degree of concentration of foreign-born population, by state, as of the 2000 census. The concentration in the southwest (California, Nevada, Arizona, and Texas), in Florida, and in New York, New Jersey, and Massachusetts is evident.

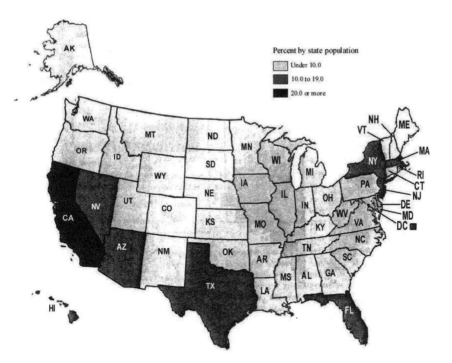

FIGURE 6.8.   Foreign-Born Population in the United States, by State, 2000

Source: "Figures 3. Foreign-Born Population by State: 2000," in Coming to America: A Profile of the Nation's Foreign Born (2000 Update), Census Brief: Current Population Survey, CENBR/01-1, U.S. Census Bureau, Washington D.C. (February 2002). Online: http://www.census.gov/prod2002pubs/cenbr01-1.pdf (accessed July 7, 2003).

The attacks of September 11, 2001 on the New York City World Trade Center Twin Towers and on the Pentagon in Washington, D.C. led Congress and the president to take actions in issuing executive orders and in passing several laws that are nearly without precedent in the speed of their passage and in the sweeping nature of the powers they grant to the government, and to the extent of change they involve for immigration policy-making and implementation. In part, the disarray at the INS made apparent by the attacks of September 11 sped up the process. After September 11th, Attorney General John Ashcroft issued an order to strictly enforce a rule requiring foreign visitors to file change of address forms that the government supposedly used to keep track of the visitors. The INS had an existing backlog of some 2 million documents piled up in boxes and shipped them to its warehouse in Kansas City. After Attorney General Ashcroft's announcement, the INS began receiving 30,000 such change of address forms per day and the backlog quickly increased to 4 million documents. An INS report indicated that an estimated 4 million foreigners were in the country with expired visas. Then it was revealed that the INS had sent a letter to the Florida flight school approving student visas for two of the September 11th attackers six months after the attacks. A government report on overall management in the Government Executive's 2002 Federal Performance Report, which had ranked the Coast Guard at an A, gave the INS a D. Border Patrol officers at the INS were quitting faster than they could be replaced. INS immigration investigators were viewed as undertrained, overworked, and overstressed, and its information management was assessed as abysmal. Drastic restructuring seemed to be needed.

Almost immediately after the attacks, President Bush issued Executive Order 13228 of October 8, 2001. It established the Office of Homeland Security and the Homeland Security Council within the Executive Office of the President (Relyea: 613). In Congress, Secretary Joseph Liberman (D-Conn.) introduced his initial proposal (S. 1534) to establish a Department of Homeland Security as a cabinet-level department. He and Representative Mac Thornberry (R-Texas) later introduced a more elaborate version, in early May 2002 (S. 2452 and H.B. 4660). While at first opposing the idea of creating a new department, President Bush responded to political pressures to do more than what EO 13228 could accomplish. He secretly had a team from his administration to begin drafting a response and an alternative to Senator Lieberman's bill: Mitchell Daniels, Jr., Director of the OMB, Tom Ridge, appointed to head up the OHS, Andrew Card, Jr., White House Chief of Staff, and Alberto R. Gonzales, White House Counsel. They began drafting the president's departmental plan on April 23. It was formally introduced as HR 5005 on June 24, 2002 (Relyea: 617).

More than any other action, the two laws passed as the response to September 11th mostly characterize this period as the "Storm-Door Era." More than any other Congressional action, they symbolize "Fortress America."

The USA Patriot Act (PL 107-56)

Within six weeks of the September 11th terrorist attacks, a jittery Congress, then virtually exiled from their offices by an anthrax contamination incident and confronted by warnings that more terrorist attacks were soon to come, responded to the Bush administration's demands for a new arsenal of anti-terrorism weapons. For nearly three weeks, from the initial outbreak of anthrax contamination on October 4, 2002, Congress and the public were unable to obtain clear information about the attack from the CDC. The fear and threat, however, far exceeded the actual damage. As *Fighting Bioterrorism* notes:

> The fall of 2001 anthrax outbreak was a far cry from the apocalyptic scenerios envisioned in the movies and government simulations. A mere twenty-one persons caught the disease, and only five died. Nonetheless, this handful of individuals changed Americans' world view forever because they were far from the only casualties of the still untracked attacks, also severely stricken were the already-shaky economy, the U.S. postal system, and, perhaps must telling of all, the public's confidence that "it can't happen here" (9).

Despite vigorous objections from civil liberties organizations at both ends of the political spectrum, Congress overwhelmingly approved of the USA Patriot Act. In the House, the vote was 356 to 66, and in the Senate, the vote was 98 to 1.

The hastily drafted, complex, and far-reaching legislation spans 342 pages. Yet it was passed with virtually no public hearings or debate, and it was accompanied by neither a conference nor a committee report. On October 26, 2001 the act was signed into law by a triumphant President George W. Bush (Torr: 43–44).

Proponents of the new law argued that it was needed to catch terrorists and deter further acts of terrorism. Advocates called for coercive interrogation of suspected terrorists to control "enemy cells" in their midst. "The danger that a preventive-detention regime for suspected terrorists would take us too far down the slippery slope...is simply not as bad as letting would-be mass murderers roam the country" (Stuart Taylor of the *National Journal* in Torr: 29). They argued that its sweeping new powers granted to the Department of Justice were essential to penetrate al-Qaeda cells. These included expanded surveillance, the use of informants, revisions to the use of search and seizure, use of wiretaps, arrests, interrogations, and detentions of suspected terrorists, uninhibited by the prior web of laws, judicial precedents and administrative rules proponents argued had hamstrung law enforcement officials in dealing with the new terrorist threat.

The USA Patriot Act removed many restrictions on law enforcement's ability to gather intelligence through physical searches, wiretaps, electronic surveillance, and increased access to criminal records (Stuart Taylor of the *National Journal* in Torr: 29).

Soon after its passage, the Department of Justice announced it had broken up terrorist cells in Portland, Detroit, and Buffalo, and charged seventeen individuals with terrorism-related activities. The Department of Justice (DOJ) targeted terrorist financing.

Critics, however, argued that the law was too sweeping and too dangerous an intrusion on civil-liberty protections. One critic characterized the Patriot Act as a threat to constitutional checks and balances, to open government, and to the rule of law that was greater than the threat posed by the terrorists. "Not since the World War II internment of Japanese-Americans have we locked up so many people for so long with so little explanation" (Nancy Chang, cited in Torr: 16). They maintain that the Patriot Act evades the Fourth Amendment by letting federal agents conduct "sneak and peek" searches or covert searches of a person's home or office that are conducted without notice to the person (Torr: 49). The mass arrests accomplished with secrecy and a lack of judicial oversight outraged many civil libertarians. They fear that the administration exercised unilateral authority to establish secret tribunals and breach attorney–client communications without a court order. To them, the USA Patriot Act is a threat to patriotic dissent, liberty, and equality. In the words of one such critic, David Cole, the legal affairs correspondent of *Nation*:

It appears the greatest threat to our freedoms is posed not by the terrorists themselves but by our own government's response . . . Administration supporters argue that the magnitude of the new threat requires a new paradigm. But so far we have seen only a repetition of the old paradigm—broad incursions on liberties, largely targeted at unpopular noncitizens and minorities, in the name of fighting a war. What is new is that this war has no end in sight, and only a vaguely defined enemy, so its incursions are likely to be permanent (in Torr: 12).

And another such critic, Nancy Chang, states:

But we should remember the words of German Pastor Martin Niemoller said after spending seven years in [the Nazi death camp at] Dachau. "In Germany, they came first for the communists, and I didn't speak up because I wasn't a communist." He went on to lament his failure to speak up for Jews, trade unionists and others, and concluded . . . "Then they came for me, and by that time there was no one left to speak up" (Torr: 67).

And in point of fact, the nonterrorists that have been most affected by the act have been immigrants. In the months immediately after September 11, some 1,200 immigrants, mostly Muslims, were rounded up by the police and the immigration officials across the nation. Some were held for months without access to lawyer or even having charges brought against them before an immigration judge. While some were deported, only a few have been charged with any crime, and most have subsequently been released as totally innocent but swept up in the postattack hysteria.

The fear of international terrorism was palpable and a powerful political force was driving national security policy. As Eli Lehrer notes:

> When a nation seeking to protect itself finds diplomacy, war, and foreign intelligence gathering insufficient, it can undertake three other types of activities to defend itself. It can control the movement of potential terrorists entering the country or traveling within it; it can capture or neutralize terrorist plotters within its borders; and when all else fails, it can mitigate damage from terrorist attacks. These three activities—access control, law enforcement, and disaster mitigation—comprise the essentials of homeland security. Congress and the Bush administration have consolidated many federal efforts to accomplish these three tasks in the Department of Homeland Security (DHS). In doing so, they hope to protect the nation from future terrorists attacks (71).

The Patriot Act makes aliens deportable for wholly innocent association with a terrorist organization because it defines a "terrorist organization" so broadly, as any group that has used or threatened to use violence, the proscription on political association potentially encompasses every organization that has been involved in a Civil War or a crime of violence, from a pro-life group that once threatened workers at an abortion clinic to the African National Congress, the Irish Republican Army, or the Northern Alliance in Afghanistan (our allies there). An estimated 1,500 to 2,000 persons were detained under the act. Their identities are still kept secret. Their number can only be estimated as the government stopped issuing a daily number after November 2001 when it was at 1,182. No one of those detained was ever charged for any involvement in the September 11th acts and most were cleared by the FBI of any involvement in terrorism (Etzioni and Marsch: 37–38).

Scholars of terrorism have more specifically defined it, such as the following:

> Terrorism is defined as the deliberate creation and exploitation of fear through violence or the threat of violence in the pursuit of political change. All terrorist acts involve violence or the threat of violence. Terrorism is specifically designed to have far-reaching psychological effects beyond the immediate victim(s) or object of terrorist attack. It is meant to instill fear within, and thereby intimidate, a wider 'target audience' that might include a rival ethnic group or religious group, an entire country, a national government or political party, or public opinion in general. Terrorism is designed to create power where there is none or to consolidate power where there is very little. Through the publicity generated by their violence, terrorists seek to obtain the leverage, influence, and power they otherwise lack to effect political change on either a local or an international scale ... Timothy McVeigh ... when asked by his defense lawyer why he could not have aired his grievances without killing anyone, said: 'that would not have gotten the point across. We need a body count to make our point' (Cooper: 31–33).

And as Thomas Dixon notes so well: "after 9/11 we've realized, belatedly, that our societies are wide-open targets for terrorists. As technological changes make it easier to kill, societies are more likely to become locked into perpetual cycles of attack and counter attack that render any normal trajectory of political and economic development impossible (53–54). He goes on to list the sorts of "soft-targets" that the U.S. society provides to international terrorists such as al Qaeda:

> True, the terrorists used simple box cutters to hijack the planes, but the box cutters were no more than the 'keys' that allowed the terrorists to convert a high tech means of transport into a high-tech weapon of mass destruction. Once the hijackers had used those keys to access and turn on their weapons, they were able to deliver a kiloton of explosive power to the World Trade Center with deadly accuracy... Complex terrorism operates like jujitsu—it redirects the energies of our intricate society against us (Thomas Dixon: 55, 58).

Creating the Department of Homeland Security and Dissolving the INS

The administration-backed bill to establish a new department of homeland security was introduced into the Congress and passed quickly in the House. The Senate debated the bill through early November, ending debate on a Thompson substitute bill (SA 4901) by a 65-26 vote. Four days later, it was adopted on a 73-26 vote, and the Senate then passed the House bill (HR 5005) as amended on a 90-9 vote. The House agreed to the Senate-amended version on November 22, and sent it onto the president for his signature (Relyea: 622).

When President George W. Bush signed the nearly 500-page bill creating the Department of Homeland Security (DHS; HR 5005) on Monday, November 25, 2002, he initiated the largest federal government reorganization since 1947. When it became fully operational on March 1, 2003, the newest cabinet-level department of the federal government was the third largest of the federal executive branch, having merged twenty- two agencies with over 190,000 employees. With that merger into the new department (i.e., the DHS), the INS ceased to exist, closing an often controversial history of over 100 years. President Bush stated:

> Today I have signed into law H.R. 5005, the "Homeland Security Act of 2002." This Act restructures and strengthens the executive branch of the Federal Government to better meet the threat to our homeland posed by terrorism. In establishing a new Department of Homeland Security, the Act for the first time creates a Federal department whose primary mission will be to help prevent, protect against, and respond to acts of terrorism on our soil (http://www.dhs.gov/dhspublic/dispaly?content=191, accessed 12/09/04).

When the 36,000 men and women of the INS were absorbed into the new department, they left the only entity within it that was abolished. The aftermath of the attacks of September 11, 2001 provided the "coup de grace" to the INS; a finale to the longstanding efforts within the Congress to eradicate an agency hampered by notorious mismanagement and a string of failures including backlogs in the millions of citizenship and naturalization applications, more millions of lost paperwork, a backlog of change-of- address forms in the millions, the failure to keep track of an estimated 4 million foreigners in the country with expired visas, and the outrageous approval of student visas, six months after the attacks, for two of the hijackers (September 11 Commission Report: 80–82).

In part, the failures of the INS to adequately control the nation's borders was seen as a major factor in the attacks, and the agency was blamed for them in measure. Even though none of the hijackers who participated in the attacks on September 11, 2001 had actually gained entry into the United States by illegally crossing the border, they very well could have done so. Prior cases of terrorists crossing the U.S.–Canada border were recalled. In 1996 a Palestinian emigrant, Ghazi Ibrahim Abu Maizar was caught crossing illegally in a bombing plot aimed at New York City. In 1999, Ahmed Ressan, a weapons expert and member of al Qaeda was caught smuggling explosives across the U.S.–Canada border intent on using them in Los Angeles during the millennium festivities (Krauss and Pacheco: 173–174). The INS and its border patrol were viewed as unable to control the border. Prior to September 11, there were fewer than 400 border patrolmen guarding the 4,000-mile U.S.–Canada border, stretching from Washington to Maine, meaning there was only about one patrolman for every ten miles of often rugged terrain with many obstacles limiting its methods of travel for enforcement purposes. As one border patrolman noted:

If you're halfway smart, and have any ambition at all, you can walk across the border between ports of entry and not have to deal at all with inspections, documents, or passports. This creates a problem when trying to fight terrorism, but it is not a new problem. Back in the eighties the Immigration Service was concerned about Middle-Easterners who were part of these small groups. We call them terrorists now, but they were just developing cells in those days. The Immigration Service was not totally unaware of that, but we lacked any public support. We lacked political support for doing anything about it because the U.S. government was heavily involved in developing the Middle East" (Joe Hardin, cited in Krauss and Pacheco: 175).

And so the INS was among the agencies merged into the new department, and like a merging of corporations in the private sector, this merger of twenty-two agencies into a new federal behemoth entails many administrative problems and unanticipated consequences for policy implementation. The reduced emphasis on immigration and citizenship matters is evident in the DHS's mission statement, where citizenship services seem to be almost an afterthougtht:

> The mission of the Department of Homeland Security (DHS) is to prevent terrorist attacks within the United States, reduce America's vulnerability to terrorism, and minimize the damage and recovery efforts from attacks that occur. DHS is also dedicated to protecting the rights of American citizens and enhancing public services, such as natural disaster assistance and citizenship services" (http://www.dhs.org).

That same lack of emphasis on immigration and citizenship services is apparent in the new department's budget priorities as well.

As we have seen here, the battles between proponents and opponents of more open or more restrictive immigration reform were often depicted in terms of a conflict to settle once-and-for-all "the immigration problem." The history of immigration reform demonstrates, however, that the battle is never really over, never finally won or lost, and measures are never enacted without some unanticipated consequences. The immigration reforms enacted since the attacks of 2001 (provisions within the USA Patriot Act and the Department of Homeland Security Act) are no exceptions.

In times of war, the federal government has always attempted to manipulate the discourse of patriotism to rally political support and limit dissent, and it has been no different in the aftermath of September 11. After only two days of debate and in an atmosphere of national hysteria, Congress passed the "United and Strengthening America by Providing Appropriate Tools Required to Intercept and Obstruct Terrorism" (USA Patriot Act, PL-107-56) (Platt and O'Leary 2003: 7).

Box 6.4 presents excerpts that summarize the USA Patriot Act of 2001 (HR 3162). Its key immigration-related provisions broadened the definition of terrorism, expanded grounds for admissibility to include aliens who were suspected of terrorist activity or who publicly endorsed such, and required the attorney general to detain aliens whom he certified as threats to national security.

Restructuring the INS

At first glance, the restructuring of the INS into two bureaus within the new DHS seems to reflect restructuring proposals predating enactment of the Immigration Reform and Control Act (IRCA) of 1986 (LeMay, 1994). Title IV, Section 402 of the Homeland Security Act transfers the responsibilities of the INS from the DOJ to the DHS. Within DHS, those former INS activities are divided between the Bureau of Citizenship and Immigration Services (BICS), responsible for processing visas and petitions for naturalization, asylum, and refugee status; and the Bureau of Immigration and Customs Enforcement

BOX 6.4.   EXCERPTS OF THE USA PATRIOT ACT
OF 2001 (HR 3162)

Sec. 102. Sense of Congress Condemning Discrimination against Arab and Muslim Americans.

(a) Findings, Congress makes the following findings:
   (1) Arab Americans, Muslim Americans, and Americans from South Asia play a vital role ... and are entitled to nothing less that the full rights of every American.
   (2) The acts of violence ... taken against [them] since September 11, 2001 ... should be condemned by all Americans who value freedom.

(b) Sense of Congress. It is the sense of Congress that—
   (1) the civil rights and civil liberties of all Americans, including Arab Americans, Muslim Americans, and Americans from South Asia, must be protected, and every effort made to preserve their safety.
   (2) Any acts of violence or discrimination against any Americans be condemned;
   (3) The Nation is called upon to recognize the patriotism of fellow citizens of all ethnic, racial, and religious backgrounds.

Title IV—Protecting the Border goes on to the following sections:
Subtitle A—Protecting the Northern Border
Sec. 401—Ensures adequate personnel on the northern border.
Sec. 403—Grants access by the Department of State and the INS to certain identifying records of visa applicants and applicants for admission to the United States.
Secion 405—Establishes an integrated automated fingerprint identification system for ports of entry and overseas consular posts.
Subtitle B—Enhanced Immigration Provisions
Sec. 411—Defines definitions of terrorism.
Sec. 412—Mandates detention of suspected terrorists; suspends habeas corpus under certain conditions; and limits judicial review.
Sec. 413—Ensures multilateral cooperation against terrorists.
Sec. 414—Provides for increased integrity and security of visas.
Sec. 415—Mandates participation of the Office of Homeland Security on the Entry-Exit Task Force.
Sec. 416—Establishes a foreign student monitoring program.
Sec. 417—Calls for machine-readable passports.
Subtitle C—Preservation of Immigration Benefits for Victims of Terrorism
Sec. 421—Grants special immigration status to victims of the 9/11 attacks.

Sec. 423—Grants humanitarian relief for certain surviving
spouses and children.
Sec. 427—Denies such benefits to terrorists or family members
of terrorists.
Title X –Miscellaneous
Sec. 1006—Provides for the inadmissibility of aliens engaged in money
laundering.

Source: Electronic Privacy Information Center (EPIC) Website. Available: http://www.epic
.org/privacy/terrorism/hr3162.html; accessed April 20, 2003.

(referred to as the Bureau of Border Security in the act), responsible for immigration enforcement (http://www.dhs.gov/interweb/assetlibrary/reorganization_plan.pdf; accessed November 29, 2004).

During the Carter Administration, when the INS could not establish even how many Iranian students were in the United States, some in Congress called for its restructuring. The more considered proposals emerged in the 1990s. The 1990 act (IMMACT) established a Commission on Immigration Reform (CIR). The Commission issued a report in 1997 calling for a restructuring of the INS. If it had been enacted, the plan would have: (1) maintained a single agency to coordinate immigration policy, (2) eliminated INS regional and district offices and replaced them with ones focused on either immigration service delivery or on law enforcement; (3) established new geographic operational areas based on workload, enforcement priorities, and service delivery considerations; (4) increased accountability to set clear roles and responsibilities for both INS missions, eliminating conflicting priorities for field managers and improving lines of authority from Washington, D.C. to the field; (5) placed senior managers with specialized skills and backgrounds in charge of the immigration enforcement chains of command and held those managers responsible for performance; (6) established Customer Service Advocates throughout the country; (7) consolidated asylum and oversees refugee and humanitarian programs; (8) expanded the new community-based fingerprinting sites to 150; (9) created Community Advisory Panels at national and area levels; and 10) centralized detention programs at the national level (see Meissner, 2000: 3; Gardner, 2000: 7–8; LeMay, 2004: 55–58, 63–64).

The Clinton Administration's proposals, reflecting several of those concerns, would have centralized INS functions by establishing national offices for: legal functions and representation; policy and strategy; financial management; professional responsibility and review; Congressional and intergovernmental relations; community relations and outreach; and public information.

Over five years, the Jordan Commission, as it came to be known, held hearings, consultations, and roundtable discussions. It defined four core functions of government in implementing immigration policy: (1) enforcement of laws at the border and in the interior; (2) adjudication and administration of immigration and citizenship benefits; (3) worksite enforcement of labor standards; and (4) administrative review of agency decisions. It felt the INS had two major systemic flaws in carrying out those functions—mission overload; and fragmentation and diffusion of responsibility. Its final recommendations for structural reform included the following: (1) immigration enforcement and investigation within a new Bureau of Immigration Enforcement remaining within the DOJ; (2) immigration and citizenship services within the State Department under a new Undersecretary for Citizen, Immigration, and Refugees; (3) worksite enforcement of immigration-related standards within the Wage and Hour Division of the Department of Labor; and (4) administrative review of all immigration-related decisions within a newly created Independent Agency for Immigration Review (Gardner, 2000: 17–21).

After the Jordan Commission report, several congressional representatives introduced, in 1998, variations to restructure the INS, but these measures were put on hold when the House Judiciary Committee undertook its impeachment referral. In 1999, a new bill was introduced by Representatives Rogers, Reyes, and the Chaiman of House Subcommittee on Immigration and Claims, Lamar Smith. This bill also called for creating two bureaus housed in the DOJ: a Bureau of Immigration Services and a Bureau of Immigration Enforcement. Each bureau was to be headed by a Director, appointed by the President with the Senate's consent, and each would have reported directly to the Attorney General.

The Smith bill called for the transfer from the INS Commissioner to a new Director of the Bureau of Immigration Services all functions, personnel, infrastructure, and funding provided to support: adjudication of nonimmigrant and immigrant visa petitions, of naturalization petitions, of asylum and refugee applications, adjudications performed at Service Centers, and all other adjudications under the Immigration and Naturalization Act performed by the INS. It would have transferred to the Director of the Bureau of Immigration Enforcement all functions, personnel, infrastructure and funding in support of the following programs: the Border Patrol, the Detention and Deportation program, the Intelligence program, the Investigations program, and the Inspections program. The bill would have created within each of the two bureaus a Chief Financial Officer (Ries, 2001: 101).

Yet another perspective on and proposal to restructure the INS came from the International Migration Policy Program of the Carnegie Endowment for International Peace (Papademetriou, Aleinkoff, and Meyers, *Reorganizing the U.S. Immigration Function: Toward a New Framework for Accountability.* Washington, D.C.: Carnegie Endowment for International Peace, 1999). There were several areas of consensus among the proposal emerging from the INS itself, the Jordan Commission, and the Carnegie Endowment report. All agreed that a dramatic structural change of the INS was necessary. All agreed in a separation of enforcement and service functions and chain of command. All agreed on the need for drastic improvement in management. Finally, all agreed that the detention function, like asylum, needed to be separated out. The Carnegie plan proposed two options: one to establish an independent agency, along the lines of the Environmental Protection Agency, with separate enforcement and service divisions, and a second one to elevate its functions within the Department of Justice (Aleinkoff, 2000: 22–27).

The Carnegie Plan for a new independent agency would have combined immigration work of the Justice Department: the visa, passport, and most of the asylum and refugee functions; the migration functions of the State Department; the labor certification functions of the Labor Department; and the refugee functions of the Department of Health and Human Services. Establishment of such an agency would have, for the first time ever, fully focused the resources of the Executive Branch on the important and difficult issues of immigration and citizenship.

The second option of the Carnegie Plan, in the event that Congress rejected the idea of a separate independent agency, was to elevate the immigration functions within the DOJ by establishing an Office of the Associate Attorney General for Immigration. All functions then performed by the INS were to be folded into the DOJ, with separate chains of command: the Executive Office for Immigration Review and the Office of Immigration Litigation would each report to the Attorney General. This concept kept separate the service and enforcement activities but placed them within the hierarchy of the DOJ. Such restructuring called for an upgrading in pay and benefits for immigration officers, much needed agency cultural change in how immigration laws are implemented and enforced, and substantial cost savings and increased efficiency by cutting several layers of overlapping bureaucracy (Alienikoff, 2000: 27–31).

The terrorist attacks of September 11 made these proposals moot. The failure of the INS to prevent the terrorists from entering the country, combined especially with their announced approval, some six months after the attack, of visa applications for several of the hijackers to come to the United States to attend flight-training schools, raised the level of rhetoric and the political demand that some action be taken. After some initial misgivings, the Bush administration developed and announced its plan to establish a new cabinet-level DHS. The House approved the final measure, modifying only to some extent the Bush administration's plan to establish a DHS by a margin of 295-132. In November, the Senate approved creation of the DHS by a vote of 90-9. As mentioned, the measure moved twenty-two agencies and some 190,000 employees into the new department, the most massive reorganization since the Department of Defense was established after World War II. The Congressional Budget Office placed the number of affected workers even higher—at 225,000. It pegged the cost of simply creating the new department at $3 billion. That would just be the cost of the reorganization itself, not the increased cost of additional security technology and so on (http://www.dhs.gov/interweb/

assetlibrary/reorganization_plan.pdf; accessed November 29, 2004). It creates within the new cabinet-level department two bureaus, each headed by an undersecretary: The Directorate of Border Transportation Security is headed by an undersecretary for border and transportation security; and a Bureau of Citizenship and Immigration Services is headed by the undersecretary for citizenship and immigration services. These key provisions from Title IV of the Act are highlighted in Box 6.5.

BOX 6.5. SUMMARY EXCERPTS OF THE HOMELAND SECURITY ACT OF 2002 (HR 5005)

Title IV—Border and Transportation Security
Subtitle A—General Provisions
Sec. 401. Creates the Under Secretary for Border and Transportation Security.
Sec. 402—Responsibilities –Transfers functions of the INS to the DHS. The Secretary, acting through the Under Secretary for Border and Transportation Security, shall be responsible for the following:

(1) Preventing the entry of terrorists and the instruments of terrorism into the U.S.
(2) Securing the borders, territorial waters, ports, terminals, waterways, and air, land and sea transportation systems of the United States, including managing and coordinating those functions transferred to the Department at ports of entry.
(3) Carrying out the immigration enforcement functions vested by statute in, or performed by, the Commissioner of Immigration and Naturalization (or any officer, employee, or component of the Immigration and Naturalization Service) immediately before the date on which the transfer of functions is specified under section 441 takes effect [March 1, 2003].
(4) Establishing and administering the rules, in accordance with section 428, governing the granting of visas or other forms of permissions, including parole, to enter the United States to individuals who are not citizens or an alien lawfully admitted for permanent residence in the United States.
(5) Establishing national immigration enforcement policies and priorities.

Subtitle B—Immigration and Nationality Functions
Sec. 411—Details the transfer of functions of the Border Patrol, INS to the Under Secretary for Border and Transportation Security in the DHS.
Sec. 412—Establishes a Bureau of Border Security headed by a Director.

Sec. 415—Calls for a report to Congress on improving enforcement functions.

Chapter 2—Citizenship and Immigration Services

Subchapter A—Transfer of Functions

Sec. 421—Establishes a Bureau of Citizenship and Immigration Services headed by a Director.

Sec. 422—Establishes a Citizenship and Immigration Services Ombudsman office.

Sec. 425—Establishes an Office of Immigration Statistics within the Bureau of Justice Statistics.

Sec. 426—Concerns preservation of the Attorney General's authority.

Subchapter B—Other Provisions

Sec. 431—Concerns funding for citizenship and immigration services.

Sec. 432—Calls for elimination of backlogs.

Sec. 433—Requires a report to Congress of efforts at improving immigration services.

Sec. 435—Calls for the application of Internet-based technologies.

Chapter 3—General Provisions

Sec. 41—Abolishes the INS as of March 1, 2003.

Sec. 45—Requires reports and implementation plans to Congress.

Sec. 46—Details immigration functions.

Source: Summary drawn from LeMay, 2004: 177–179.

Groupthink Aspects of the Decision to Create DHS

At second glance, the decision to dissolve the INS and merge its functions into the massive new bureaucracy of the DHS portends significant problems for immigration policy-making and implementation. The failures of the INS related to the attacks of September 11 clearly indicate the need for more innovative practices in implementing immigration policy. But for large, complex organizations, simply managing policy, yet alone innovation, is related to and dependent upon the organization's ability to comprehend and decide how potential future technologies and organizational impacts would be affected. Innovation requires *insightful* ways of achieving breakthroughs. It also requires that those insightful ideas be considered and synthesized in its organizational procedures and practices. Innovation requires strategic foresight (Mitchell, 2003: 16).

The decision to establish the DHS shows evidence of several aspects of decision-making behavior called *groupthink* (Janis, 1972, 1982; Chen et al., 1996; Kowert, 2002; Reich, 2004; Sneider, 2004; t'Hart, Stern, and Sundeluis, 1997; aYefiv, 2003), Congress clearly perceived the post-September 11 situation to be an emergency. And "emergencies" often cry out for drastic and expensive changes in public policy that later, on reflection, seem ill-conceived

(Roots, 2003: 503). According to Irving Janis, under conditions of stressful decision-making, groups can become excessively concerned with concurrence seeking that leads to groupthink and subsequently to foreign policy fiascoes. "Groupthink describes the failure to challenge assumptions, the pressure to interpret ambiguous evidence to back the collective wisdom and to ignore or minimize information that challenges it" (Sneider, 2004: pk4246). Janis (1972) defined *groupthink* as:

> "a mode of thinking that people engage in when they are deeply involved in a cohesive in-group, when the members' strivings for unanimity override their motivation to realistically appraise alternative courses of action . . . Groupthink refers to a deterioration of mental efficiency, reality testing, and moral judgment that results from in-group pressure" (9).

The very nature of organizational decision-making is decisions made by groups rather than individuals deciding alone. Organizational decision-making is inherently a social process (Chen et al., 1996: 581).

Janis argues that a cohesive group when coupled with directive leadership gives rise to three observable group decision features: a defective decision-making process, a low quality of decision outcome, and five groupthink symptoms. He characterizes groupthink symptoms as the illusions of invulnerability and unanimity, collective rationalization, self-censorship, and direct pressure on dissenters. Janis defines directive leadership as promoting a particular decision alternative coupled with ignoring rather than pursuing other decision alternatives. A directive leadership style gives rise to more groupthink symptoms and more observable defects in the group decision-making process than groups with a participative leadership style that encourages a wide variety of alternatives and member participation (Chen et al., 1996: 582).

There are several aspects of apparent groupthink behavior evident in the decision to create the DHS. For such an extensive reorganization of the federal bureaucracy, the law was passed in a very short time—just over two years after the September 11 attacks—as it sped through nearly a dozen committees.[2] Following the September 11 attacks, by April 25, 2002, the House passed an INS restructuring bill that would have dismantled the agency, and the proposal garnered the Bush administration's support. On October 8, 2001 the president issued an Executive Order establishing an Office of Homeland Security and a Homeland Security Council, to develop and implement a comprehensive domestic antiterrorism strategy and appointed former Pennsylvania Governor Tom Ridge as its Director. On October 26, 2001 President Bush signed the USA Patriot Act into law, providing law enforcement with sweeping new powers to conduct searches, employ electronic surveillance and detain suspected terrorists. It preserved immigration benefits for noncitizen victims of the attacks. It also provided for additional personnel along the northern border, added new grounds for inadmissibility for representatives of foreign terrorist organizations,

streamlined procedures for the Department of State designation of terrorist organization, and authorized the Attorney General to certify and detain aliens with
terrorist ties. It further permitted the detention of foreign nationals for up to
seven days while the government decided whether to bring charges against
them.

> ... By June 2002, President Bush abandoned his initial resistance to the idea of
> elevating Homeland Security to the status of a cabinet department. After months
> of wrangling with the Senate over his proposal to weaken civil service protections
> of employees in the new department (on the grounds that on matters of spying
> and terror, senior managers could not afford to battle "red tape"), and in the
> aftermath of the 2002 election, which returned control of the Senate to the GOP,
> Bush got his department. Ridge became the first Secretary of Homeland Security"
> (Walcott and Hult, 2003: 151).

On January 6, 2002 President Bush announced his administration's plan to
create a cabinet-level DHS, introducing it in the House as the Homeland Security Act of 2002 (H.R. 5005) on June 18, 2002. By July 26, 2002, the House
adopted H.R. 5005. On September 3, 2002, following the August recess, the
Senate resumed debate on Homeland Security legislation (S. 2452). The House
approved the final version of the measure on November 14, 2002. The Senate
approved the final version on November 19, 2002, and President Bush signed
the bill into a law on November 25, 2002.

In addition to the relative speed of its adoption, there was considerable
congressional unanimity in congressional voting, especially considering the
massive and complex nature of the nearly 500-page bill and the reshuffling of
many agencies with their accompanying "turf" considerations. The vote in the
Senate was 90-9; in the House it was 299 to 121. Among Republicans in the
House, the vote was 212 in favor and only six opposed. In the months leading
to passage of the bill, there was little or no debate about the dissolving of the
INS and the transfer of its functions to two separate bureaus in the DHS. Most
of the debate over the bill, as stated here, centered on unionization and civil
service protections of employees of the new department. Initially some of the
committees wanted to leave the Coast Guard, the Federal Emergency Management Agency, and half of the INS out of the new department. A select
committee set up by the House Republican leadership undid most of the
committees' handiwork (O'Beirne, 2002).

The following section discusses some discernable problems and potential
unanticipated consequences of the massive reorganization plan. They involve
the "behemoth" nature of the new department and some management issues
arising from the sheer size of the department and from the complexities of
merging twenty-two agencies into a cohesive and coherent department. As
critic Eli Lehrer notes in his insightful article, *The Homeland Security Bureaucracy,*

Certainly, much good work has been accomplished. But thus far, not enough thought has been given to the considerable structural impediments to serious reform. DHS's vast reach coupled with its lack of bodies on the ground, the checkered history of American bureaucratic reform, and the difficulty DHS's constituent agencies have encountered defining new missions all suggest that homeland security is at best a work in progress. DHS's various bureaus are still too limited in scope, too committed to the legacy missions, and too unlikely to change for the existence of a Department of Homeland Security to modify the way America confronts terrorists (2004: 71).

Critic Nancy Chang further observes: "Added bureaucracies will only cause agile terrorists glee as they outmaneuver sluggish government attempts to counter them" (in Torr: 61).

Problems and Consequences of Building a Behemoth

As referred to earlier, on March 1, 2003 all responsibility for providing immigration-related services and benefits, such as naturalization and work authorization, were transferred from the INS to the U.S. Citizenship and Immigration Services (USCIS) bureau of DHS. The new department also set up the US-VISIT Program with the goal to secure the borders and expedite the entry/exit process while enhancing the integrity of the immigration system and respecting the privacy of visitors to the United States. US-VISIT programs were deployed at 115 airports and fourteen seaports. The FY 2005 proposed budget for the program increased by $12 million over the FY 2004 budget, to a requested $340 million (http://www.whitehouse.gov/omb/budget/fy2005/over view.html; accessed November 17, 2004). It also established within DHS a Citizenship and Immigration Services Ombudsman (CIA Ombudsman) to provide recommendations for resolving individual and employer problems with the USCIS. Investigative and enforcement responsibilities for federal immigration laws, customs laws, and air security laws was transferred to the U.S. Immigration and Customs Enforcement (ICE), which assumed responsibilities for protecting the borders within the DHS.[2] How successful the merger will be is the issue.

...the behemoth known as the DHS is less than what it seems. Guided by advisors from the Defense and Justice departments and the CIA, the administration ensured that the DHS has quite limited authority. So now, while the DHS oversees a number of areas—everything from federal airline safety to federal responses to hurricanes and floods—it has no authority to oversee the counter-terrorism activity and priorities of other agencies. These include the Defense Department, the Justice Department, and the CIA, the very agencies that are crucial to homeland defense. Instead of streamlining our domestic preparedness strategy, the DHS has simply become another agency added to the mix, equal but not primary (Kayyem, 2003: 46).

The agenda of the DHS still seems to be a compendium of conventional wisdom to beef up the preparedness system with a limited sense of critical priorities. Critics note its strategy seems to be to "try anything and everything." Its most notable attempt to guide the nation in terrorism response was its color-coded threat scheme, now seen to be largely unworkable, forcing jurisdictions to respond to vague threats, pay police overtime, and wait it out.

The four "directorates" at the highest level of the Department's organizational chart carry out varied missions. The Border and Transportation Directorate is the most visible and has the largest budget. Its agencies include the Transportation Security Administration (TSA) and two border agencies created from pieces of the old INS's Border Patrol, Customs Service, Agriculture Inspection Service, and Immigration and Naturalization Service. The first agency, Immigration and Customs Enforcement (ICE), enforces immigration law within the United States and is charged with catching undocumented illegal aliens and visa overstayers. The second agency is the Customs and Border Protection which secures the borders. About half of all DHS employees work for this directorate, the largest portion of who work as baggage screeners. The Federal Emergency Management Agency (FEMA) dominates the Emergency Preparedness and Response Directorate. FEMA serves four basic functions: funding rebuilding efforts after disasters, offering expert advice on preparing for disasters, giving operating and capital assistance to local emergency response agencies (known as "first-responders"), and managing some secret facilities aimed at helping the federal government survive a catastrophic attack. FEMA's all-hazards approach to emergency management enables local government officials to prepare comprehensive plans to deal with a wide variety of potential hazards, both natural and man-made. This directorate also administers a vaccine stockpile program transferred to DHS from the Department of Health and Human Services and programs intended to mitigate nuclear, chemical, and biological attacks transferred from the FBI and the Department of Energy. The Science and Technology Directorate is the department's smallest. It funds university research of various types and manages four laboratories aimed at developing countermeasures for weapons of mass destruction involving nuclear, chemical, or biological weapons. FEMA established an Integrated Emergency Management System for Threat Analysis and Assessment. The Information Analysis and Infrastructure Protection Directorate attempts to coordinate information about terrorist threats. It combines six separate programs from agencies such as the FBI and the Department of Energy. It is responsible for the much-derided color-coded scheme for warnings about terrorist threats, produces the daily homeland security briefings for the president by analyzing information from the nominally independent Terrorist Threat Integration Center (TTIC) created by the president in January, 2003. The Center, a joint venture of the FBI, CIA, and DHS, is housed in the CIA headquarters and is largely staffed by the CIA. DHS's top officials are not always privy to the sources and methods used by the center to develop its reports (Lehrer: 72; Kemp: 52). The DHS seems equally poorly suited to the task of ensuring that whatever its homeland security strategy might be, it properly assesses the competing interests of security and liberty. The administration fought proposals to establish an Office of Civil Rights and Liberties within DHS to monitor the department's compliance with constitutional norms while it conducts the "war on terrorism." Few agencies, however, are likely to have as significant an impact on civil rights and liberties as the DHS. While the law establishing the DHS created an Office of Inspector General (OIG) to "prevent and detect fraud, abuse, mismanagement, and waste" within DHS programs, Republican-led congressional efforts have resulted in the OIG having less power than it needs. The law permits the DHS secretary to prohibit the OIG from continuing any investigations that might disclose sensitive national security information. Fears that DHS agencies have used racial profiling and abused noncitizens in their zeal to find and detain terrorist or suspected terrorists have been widespread (Aizenman, 2003; Alderstein, 2003; Banks, 2004; Brown, 2003; Chesney, 2003; Dahl, 2004; Gourevitch, 2003a; Hentoff, 2003; Hoffman, 2003; Judis, 2003; Robertson, 2003; Taylor, 2003).

The merger of so many agencies into such a huge department is more likely to create challenges to a federal government that is more responsive, more effective, and more efficient—the supposed values for creating the DHS (Crotty, 2003; GAO, 2003; Haynes, 2004; Hyong, 2003; O'Beirne, 2002; Stana, 2003). Indeed, one critic noted well the *management case* against this type of reorganization which simply adds additional obstacles to achieving those very values (Krauss, 2003: 51–58). These obstacles include the following.

1. **Mission complexity.** The DHS monitors nearly 5.7 million cargo containers and 600 million passengers on American aircraft every year, in addition to patrolling 95,000 miles of coastline and 430 major airports. It is also responsible for preparing for and preventing terrorist attacks, coordinating first responders at state and local levels for emergencies, and monitoring intelligence to protect against threats to the homeland.

2. **Cultural incompatability.** Mission complexities lead to major problems of trying to combine disparate organizational cultures, competing technologies used in day-to-day operations (such as integrating different infrastructure platforms, software applications for e-mail databases, networking, and security protocols), while maintaining good communication (internal, between federal agencies, vertically with state and local first responders, and with the general public). The new DHS merges agencies like the Coast Guard and FEMA that had relatively high ratings on overall management (an A and B, respectively) with agencies notably notorious for their poor performance management (C and D) such as the Customs Service and the INS (Light, 2002). Creating a huge federal bureaucracy is likely to result in an organization

bogged down with red tape and waste, as illustrated by FEMA after the Katrina hurricane.

3. **Task obfuscation.** Reducing the threat to terrorist attack is no easy task. The challenge of the merger makes it even harder to tackle. It appears that the DHS is more concerned with making Americans *feel safe* than with the task of really improving the quality of internal security. Making Americans feel safe is commonly accomplished by the budgetary strategy of increasing funding for security (see the budget figures for FY 2003, 2004 and projected for 2005 later in this chapter). But contrary to conventional wisdom, more funding does not necessarily mean more resources, or even more money being spent in the field. Some agencies, notably the FEMA, the Coast Guard, and the Secret Service have more added responsibilities with lesser additional funding. The very "behemoth" nature of the organization is likely to result in greater levels of overhead and administrative costs.

4. **Symbolic versus real performance results.** The very creation of DHS may create a false sense of safety. The public perceives that "something is being done and that America is more secure" (Birkland, 2004; Broder, 2002; "Candidates Scorecard," 2003; Halperin, 2003; Jacobson, 2003). The reality is that for some years to come, top management in DHS will be more engaged in coordination of the merged bureaucracies than in gauging their actual performance to ensure they are making America a safer place to live. Comparable performance data will not be available for years to come (Krauss, 2003; Light, 2002).

As one critic of the merger noted recently:

Each of the twenty-two agencies brings its own array of existing management challenges and program risks to the new mega-agency. The US Comptroller General reported that many of the major components merging into the new department, including the TSA, already face considerable problems such as strategic human capital risks, information technology management challenges, and financial management vulnerabilities (GAO 2003). Informed observers fear that neither the president's requested budget . . . for the new department, nor the reorganization plan . . . come anywhere near providing the funds and the foresight to successfully implement the president's National Strategy for Homeland Security (July 2002) . . . Add to the mix the role complexities . . . , a bewildering array of congressional oversight and appropriations committees, the challenge of meeting a grueling implementation schedule, and the absence of a culture of cooperation within [the agencies], and a daunting homeland security agenda begins to look more like an impossible and potentially catastrophic dream. We will be witness to a mind-boggling demonstration of the complexity of joint action (Haynes, 2004: 369).

In preparation for the FY 2005 budget proposal, nine DHS programs were assessed using the Program Assessment Rating Tool (PART), which evaluated each programs' design and purpose, strategic planning efforts, how well they are managed, and whether they are generating positive results for taxpayers.

The lowest assessments among the nine programs were the following: (1) the U.S. Immigration and Customs Enforcement's Detention and Removal Programs, in which the assessment found that the programs were struggling to remove subject aliens; (2) the USICE's Federal Air Marshal Service, where the assessment found the program did not yet have measurable results; and (3) the Border Patrol program of the US Customs and Border Protection, where the results were not demonstrated and where the assessment found a need for improving outcome and cost-effectiveness-based measures[3] (http://www.white house.gov/omb/budget/ fy2005/homeland.html; accessed November 29, 2004).

The overall funding level for the new DHS increased significantly in FY 2003 to 2005. Congress funded the new DHS by a dramatic 85 percent increase in 2003. Significant increases continued in FY 2004 and FY 2005. The administration requested and Congress approved funding for the DHS budget authority in billions of dollars for both mandatory and discretionary funding. While these amounted to impressive gains in terms of overall funding and funding increases for the DHS, the *internal* priorities of the department present a less impressive situation for the immigration-related services of the department. The very agencies that merged with the DHS are those that clearly needed the most attention and improvement and they are the ones with the least percentage improvement in discretionary budget funding. Immigration and Customs Enforcement received the lowest percent of the total discretionary funding in the department for FY 2003 and 2004, and the second lowest in FY 2002, and are again the lowest in FY 2005.

It is clear that DHS's scope is far smaller than the entire task of homeland security. Given that DHS does not have direct control over much of what it is supposed to do, it comes as no surprise that a number of tasks DHS promised to perform remain undone. A national assessment of critical infrastructure—a disaster mitigation function—may take as long as five years but was promised in one year. A repeated promise to create a single unified terrorist watch list, likewise, may never come to fruition. DHS has decided to build a complex terrorist tracking computer system instead. Access control tasks, which DHS does have more complete control over, does appear to have proceeded more smoothly: TSA, for example, has met goals to screen every airline passenger and perform X-rays or CT scans of checked luggage, and Customs and Border Protection will eventually be tracking foreigners visiting the United States, albeit several years behind schedule ... Some of these failings stem from the growing pains in starting a new federal agency. But their roots are likely deeper than that: DHS simply does not have the breadth of control necessary to mandate that state and local emergency managers or even other federal police agencies do what it says (Lehrer: 74).

This section closes with two tables, and a figure. Table 6.2 presents the numbers of immigrants admitted by major category of admission for 1998–2001. Table 6.3 details the number of immigrants coming into the United

TABLE 6.2. Immigrants Admitted by Major Category of Admission, 1998–2001

Category of Admission	2001 Number	2001 Percent	2000 Number	2000 Percent	1999 Number	1999 Percent	1998 Number	1998 Percent
Total	1,064,318	100.0	849,807	100.0	646,568	100.0	654,451	100.0
New Arrivals	411,059	38.6	407,402	47.9	401,775	62.1	357,037	54.6
Adjustments of Status	653,259	61.4	442,405	52.1	244,793	37.9	297,414	45.4
Family-sponsored immigrants	676,107	63.5	584,159	68.7	476,445	73.7	475,750	72.7
Family-sponsored preferences	232,143	21.8	235,280	27.7	216,883	33.5	191,480	29.3
Unmarried sons/daughters of U.S. citizens	27,098	2.5	27,707	3.3	22,392	3.5	17,717	2.7
Spouses and children of alien residents	112,260	10.5	124,595	14.7	108,007	16.7	88,488	13.5
Married sons/daughters of U.S. citizens	24,878	2.3	22,833	2.7	24,040	3.7	22,257	3.4
Siblings of U.S. citizens	67,907	6.4	60,145	7.1	62,444	9.7	63,018	9.6
Immediate relatives of U.S. citizens	443,964	41.7	348,879	41.1	259,562	40.1	284,270	43.4
Spouses	270,545	25.4	197,525	23.2	127,988	19.8	151,172	23.1
Parents	80,964	7.6	67,619	8.0	61,483	9.5	61,724	9.4
Children	91,526	8.6	82,726	9.7	69,113	10.7	70,472	10.8
Children born abroad to alien residents	929	0.1	1,009	0.1	978	0.2	902	0.1
Legalization dependents	37	Z	55	X	Z	Z	1	Z
Employment-based preferences	179,195	16.8	107,024	12.6	56,817	8.8	77,517	11.8
Priority workers	41,801	3.9	27,706	3.3	14,898	2.3	21,408	3.3
Professionals with advanced degree or of exceptional ability	42,620	4.0	20,304	2.4	8,581	1.3	14,384	2.2
Skilled workers, professionals, unskilled workers	86,058	8.1	49,736	5.9	27,966	4.3	34,317	5.2
Special immigrants	8,523	0.8	9,052	1.1	5,086	0.8	6,584	1.0
Investors	193	Z	226	Z	286	Z	824	0.1

224

Diversity	42,015	3.9	50,945	6.0	47,571	7.4	45,499	7.0
Other categories	166,964	15.7	107,624	12.7	65,735	10.2	55,664	8.5
Amerasians	376	Z	943	Z	239	Z	346	0.1
Parolees, Soviet, and Indochinese	5,468	0.5	3,163	0.4	1,827	0.3	1,225	0.2
Refugees and asylees	108,506	10.2	65,941	7.8	42,852	6.6	52,193	8.0
Refugee adjustments	97,305	9.1	59,083	7.0	39,495	6.1	44,645	6.8
Asylee adjustments	11,201	1.1	6,858	0.8	3,357	0.5	7,548	1.2
Subject to annual limit	10,111	0.9	4,567	0.5	2,532	0.4	7,546	1.2
Not subject to limit	1,090	0.1	2,291	0.3	825	0.1	2	Z
Cancellation of removal[a]	22,506	2.1	12,349	1.5	9,032	1.4	428	0.1
Subject to annual limit	3,157	0.3	4,334	0.5	8,459	1.3	428	0.1
Not subject to limit (NACARA, Sec. 203)	19,349	1.8	8,015	0.9	573	0.1	X	Z
IRCA legalization	263	Z	421	Z	8	Z	955	0.1
NACARA Sec 202[b]	18,926	1.8	23,641	2.8	11,267	1.7	1	Z
HRIFA[c]	10,111	0.9	X	Z	X	Z	X	Z
Other	808	0.1	1,166	0.1	510	0.1	516	0.1

[a] Includes immigrants admitted under Section 203 of the Nicaraguan Adjustment and Central American Relief Act of November 1997 (19,349 in fiscal year 2001, 8015 in fiscal year 2000, and 573 in fiscal year 1999) who are exempt from the 4000 annual limit.

[b] Section 202 of the Nicaraguan Adjustment and Central American Relief Act of November 1997.

[c] Haitian Refugee Immigration Fairness Act of 1998.

X: not applicable; Z: rounds to less than 0.05 percent.

Source: "Table 1. Immigrants Admitted by Major Category: Fiscal Years 1998–2001," in *Legal Immigration, Fiscal Year 2001,* U.S. Department of Justice, Immigration and Naturalization Service, Washington, DC. August 2002 (Online)— http://www.immigration.gov/graphics/shared/aboutus/statistics/IMM2001 .pdf (accessed June 30, 2003).

TABLE 6.3. Immigration by Region and Selected Country of Last Residence, 1991–2001

Region and Country of Last Residence	1991–2000	1998	1999	2000	2001
All countries	9,095,417	654,451	646,568	849,807	1,064,318
Europe	1,359,737	92,911	94,373	133,362	177,833
Austria-Hungary	24,882	1,435	1,518	2,024	2,318
Austria	15,500	610	727	997	1,004
Hungary	9,382	825	791	1,027	1,314
Belgium	7,090	557	522	827	1,002
Czechoslovakia	9,816	931	895	1,415	1,921
Denmark	6,079	447	387	556	741
France	35,820	2,961	2,664	4,093	5,431
Germany	92,606	6,923	7,442	12,372	22,093
Greece	26,759	1,183	4,061	5,138	1,966
Ireland	56,950	907	806	1,279	1,550
Italy	62,722	1,966	1,681	2,695	3,377
Netherlands	13,308	1,036	881	1,466	1,895
Norway-Sweden	17,893	1,344	1,284	1,977	2,561
Norway	5,178	327	358	513	588
Sweden	12,715	1,017	926	1,464	1,973
Poland	163,747	8,202	8,487	9,773	12,355
Portugal	22,916	1,523	1,078	1,402	1,654
Romania	51,203	4,833	5,417	6,521	6,224
Soviet Union	462,874	28,984	32,740	43,807	55,099
Spain	17,157	1,185	1,074	1,406	1,889
Switzerland	11,841	1,090	885	1,349	1,796
United Kingdom	151,866	10,170	8,663	14,532	20,258
Yugoslavia	66,557	7,264	7,077	12,213	21,937
Other Europe	57,651	9,970	6,811	8,517	11,766
Asia	2,795,672	212,799	193,061	255,860	337,566
China	419,114	41,034	29,579	41,861	50,821

India	363,060	34,288	28,355	39,072	65,916
Iran	68,556	4,945	5,042	6,505	8,063
Israel	39,397	2,546	2,538	3,893	4,925
Japan	67,942	5,647	4,770	7,730	10,464
Korea	164,166	13,691	12,301	15,214	19,933
Philippines	503,945	33,176	29,590	40,587	50,870
Turkey	38,212	4,016	2,472	2,713	3,477
Vietnam	286,145	16,534	19,164	25,340	34,648
Other Asia	735,356	49,543	52,717	65,746	78,142
America	**4,486,806**	**298,156**	**312,324**	**397,201**	**473,351**
Canada & Newfoundland	191,987	14,295	12,948	21,475	30,203
Mexico	2,249,421	130,661	146,436	171,748	204,844
Caribbean	**978,787**	**72,948**	**70,386**	**85,875**	**96,958**
Cuba	169,322	15,415	13,289	19,322	26,073
Dominican Republic	335,251	20,267	17,745	17,441	21,256
Haiti	179,644	13,316	16,459	22,004	22,535
Jamaica	169,227	14,819	14,449	15,654	15,099
Other Caribbean	125,343	9,131	8,444	11,454	11,995
Central America	**526,915**	**35,368**	**41,441**	**62,708**	**73,063**
El Salvador	215,798	14,329	14,416	22,332	31,054
Other Central America	311,117	21,039	27,025	40,376	42,009
South America	**539,656**	**44,884**	**41,112**	**55,392**	**58,279**
Argentina	26,644	1,649	1,578	2,485	3,459
Colombia	128,499	11,618	9,769	14,191	16,333
Ecuador	76,592	6,840	8,903	7,658	9,694
Other South America	307,921	24,777	20,862	31,058	38,793
Other America	40	—	1	3	4
Africa	**354,939**	**37,494**	**33,740**	**40,969**	**50,2090**
Oceania	**55,845**	**4,403**	**4,299**	**5,962**	**7,253**
Not Specified	**42,418**	**8,688**	**8,771**	**16,453**	**18,106**

States from the major regions and selected countries of last residence for the period of years covering this cycle—1991–2001.

The National Container Security Act

In addition to creating the DHS discussed here, the administration and Congress engaged in a number of other policies to increase homeland security that impact the immigration process. For example, the president authorized creation of the United States Northern Command to provide integrated homeland defense and coordinated Pentagon support to Federal, state, and local governments. The president made countering and investigating terrorist activity the number one priority of federal law enforcement and intelligence agencies. The 2005 budget reflects a 780 percent increase in funding to support the first responders. The president signed into law Project BioShield, a $5.6 billion effort to develop vaccines and other medical responses to biological, chemical, nuclear, and radiological weapons, and invested more than $7 billion in all aspects of biodefense. A BioWatch program monitors major cities for any suspected biological release, increased funding to procure smallpox vaccine for all citizens, and significantly increased the stocks of antibiotics against anthrax, and state and local health systems have been provided more than $4.4 billion to bolster their ability to respond to public health crises. Aviation security was improved by such measures as hardened cockpit doors, training of flight crews in handguns, and deploying thousands of air marshals. One such additional measure involved a multilateral approach—the Container Security Initiative (CSI) (http://www.whitehouse.gov/infocus/homeland/index .html; accessed August 18, 2005).

CSI was developed to allow United States inspectors to screen high-risk shipping containers at major ports before they are loaded in ships bound for U.S. ports. This was significant in that 90 percent of the world's total cargo moves by container, with 46 percent of all U.S. imports arriving by ocean-going cargo containers. The CSI is an umbrella term for security initiatives such as the Customs-Trade Partnership Against Terrorism (C-TPAT), the 24 hour advance notification rule (which requires shippers to transmit by electronic means manifest information to customs 24 hours before the shipment leaves the foreign port), and CSI itself. CSI refers to the specific port-to-port shipping element and C-TPAT is the customs-to-business element. The four key elements of CSI are: identifying high-risk containers; prescreening containers before they are shipped; using technology to prescreen high-risk containers; and using smarter, more secure containers (Holmes: 15).

In implementing CSI rules under the Maritime Transportation Security Act, the Coast Guard took a "trust but verify" stance with foreign vessels making their first port call after July 1, 2004 when inspection teams boarded ships to make sure crews were carrying out ISPS implementation plans. The Coast Guard brought aboard some 500 reservists to augment the number of regulars to carry out the inspections of the International Ship Security Certificate (ISSC) number, which is transmitted ninety-six hours before arrival of the ship, as a means of notification of the same. Typically, the Coast Guard inspects ships at the pier. If the ship reports it does not have an ISSC, it is not allowed to come in. If a ship reports having an ISSC number, they check to verify the certificate and to see that the crew has implemented the measures required by the code. Failure to implement results in any of the three control actions: detention until they do comply; refusal to unload the cargo; or ordering them removed from port. The CSI plan also involves reviews of foreign-port plans for security measures, which by late 2004 were 99 percent complete. Ports not yet in full compliance were given a "punch list" of discrepancies to correct (Edmonson: 15). Unveiled in 2002, CSI began a program in which nineteen of the world's largest ports joined U.S. Customs to enhance the security of the world's maritime trading system. Since its inception, CSI has expanded beyond the initial twenty ports. In December 2003, the U.S. Bureau of Customs and Border Protection published its final rules requiring advance manifest information for screening, which took effect on January 5, 2004.

A number of members in Congress were not entirely satisfied that the CSI was sufficient to insure homeland security in cargo container matters. On April 1, 2004 a measure was introduced to amend the Maritime Transportation Security Act (S. 2279). The new Senate legislation—sponsored by three long-time advocates for cargo security, Senate Commerce Committee Chairman John McCain (R-Ariz), ranking minority member Senator Ernest Hollings (D-S.C.), and Senator John Breaux (D-La). The new law would impose a users' fee to help fund new port security measures. It requires Customs and Border Protection to establish goals and standards for voluntary cargo security programs such as the Customs-Trade Partnership Against Terrorism. It directs the DHS to evaluate the effectiveness of the systems customs currently employs to identify high-risk shipments, and to double within one year the number of containers it scans. It would widen (but not replace) the CSI, in effect expanding what was purely a maritime initiative to include other forms of transport. Traders would submit shipment data electronically in advance, as follows: for inbound to USA; by air, four hours rior to arrival, by vessel, twenty-four hours before loading, by rail, two hours before arrival, and by truck, thirty minutes for all FAST participants and one hour for everyone else (Edmonson: 15; http://www.sitpro.org.uk/policy/security/csitraact0903.html; accessed August 18, 2005).

Referred to as the Maritime Transportation Security Act of 2004, S. 2279 amends shipping law to grant U.S. district courts jurisdiction to restrain violations of certain port security requirements and authorizes the Secretary of Transportation to refuse or revoke port clearance of any owner, agent, master, officer, or person in charge of a vessel that is liable for a penalty or fine for violation of such requirements. The act directs the Secretary to require uncleared, unladen imported goods remaining on a wharf or pier for more than seven calendar days to be removed and deposited in a public storage or general warehouse for inspection, after which a delivery permit may be granted, and to impose an administrative penalty of $5,000 on the consignee for each bill on lading for general merchandise remaining on a wharf or pier in violation of such requirement. It shifts from the Secretary of Transportation to the responsibility of the administrator of the Maritime Administration for assessing antiterrorism measures in foreign ports and notifying foreign government authorities of deficiencies and the steps necessary to improve such measures. It requires the administrator to identify foreign assistance programs that could facilitate implementation of port security antiterrorism measures in foreign countries, and to utilize such programs that are capable of implementing port security antiterrorism measures at ports in foreign countries where the Secretary finds a lack of effective antiterrorism measures. It directs the Secretary of Homeland Security to report to specified congressional committees on the security of ports in the Caribbean Basin; to establish a curriculum to educate and instruct Federal and State officials on commercial maritime and intermodal transportation; and to coordinate with the Federal Law Enforcement Training Center in such curriculum development and the provision of training Federal and State law enforcement officials at appropriate law enforcement training facilities. It directs the DHS Secretary to report to specified congressional committees on recommendations to coordinate background checks for all people engaged in transportation activities and to develop a timeline for implementation of the Transportation Worker Identification Credential in seaports. It directs the DHS Secretary to report to specified congressional committees on the security of ships and facilities used in the cruise line industry. It amends federal shipping law to direct the Undersecretary of Homeland Security for Border and Transportation Security to establish a maritime transportation security plan grant program to help fund compliance with federal security plans among port authorities, facility operators, and state and local agencies required to provide security devices; and finally, for the DHS Secretary to report to specified congressional committees on the design of Maritime security grant programs (http://www.thomas.loc.gov/cgi-bin/bdquery/Z?d108:SNO@@&(:@@@L&summ2=m&; accessed August 18, 2005).

Immigration Provisions of the Intelligence Reform and Terrorism Prevention Act of 2004

Finally, a recent area of presidential/congressional action that was intended to have direct impact on national/homeland security but also has some immigration policy import was the enactment of the Intelligence Reform and Terrorism Prevention Act [PL-108-458]. As was the case with the law to establish the DHS, at first President Bush resisted the idea of creating an "intelligence czar" or of substantially restructuring U.S. intelligence operations. Pressure from the September 11 Commission and from the public aroused by the joint hearings held by the House and Senate intelligence on the intelligence "failures" that contributed to the attacks of September 11, however, gradually moved President Bush to accept the need for reform legislation. The new law enacted H.R. 5150 and S. 2845 introduced in late September, 2004, and passed in early October, 2004, the bill was signed into law by President Bush on December 17, 2004. Its leading Senate sponsors were Senator Susan Collins (R-Maine) and Senator Joseph Lieberman (D-CT). In the House, it was sponsored by Representatives Pete Hoekstra (R-Mich.), and Representative Jane Harman (D-CA).

The Act creates a Director of National Intelligence (DNI) to oversee the fifteen government agencies involved in intelligence and a National Counterterrorism Center (NCTC), among other sections. The new law gives the DNI authority to be sure there is adequate exchange of information, a condition obviously lacking before September 11, among the various agencies. President Bush quickly appointed John Negroponte, the United States Ambassador to Iraq as the first DNI ("Bush taps intelligence chief": 2-A).

The legislation includes an array of antiterrorism provisions, such as adding 2,000 additional Border Patrol agents each year for five years, improving baggage screening procedures, imposes new standards on information that must be contained in drivers' licenses, and making it easier to track suspected terrorists not tied to known terrorist groups ("Intelligence director will help define institution": A-8).

It aims to get the government thinking more strategically than operationally about intelligence. The creation of the NCTC presents a model for the way in which the government might organize itself to think more strategically about a variety of problems and it extends that model to weapons of mass destruction by also establishing a National Counter Proliferation Center that will be the primary organization in government for analyzing and integrating all intelligence pertaining to the proliferation of weapons of mass destruction; and it gives the DNI authority to establish other such intelligence centers focusing on new threats as the need arises (e.g., bioterrorism, chemical, and so on). While the law gives the DNI a role in the budget process, it does not endow the office with clear and absolute budget authority as was recommended by the September 11 Commission.

Box 6.6 presents a summary of President Bush's remarks upon signing the new law.

Critics of the new law are skeptical of its "czar" approach: "Any time we create csars who are essentially bureaucratically orphaned from any control of any large organization, in the past there was not a real strong reason to think they [would] become powerful in Washington budget wars" (Michael O'Hanlon, cited in Marta Roberts, 2005: 78). Others note that with respect to intelligence collection, the act is suspect, in that while it addresses analysis and integration of intelligence through the creation of the NCTC, it does not make similar structural changes in the collection process. It simply directs the DNI

BOX 6.6. PRESIDENT BUSH'S REMARKS ON SIGNING THE INTELLIGENCE REFORM ACT

In a few minutes, I will sign into law the most dramatic reform of our nation's intelligence capabilities since President Harry S. Truman signed the National Security Act of 1947. Under this new law, our vast intelligence enterprise will become more unified, coordinated and will enable us better to do our duty, which is to protect the American people... We're staying on the offensive against the enemy to take the fight to terrorists abroad so we do not have to face them here at home. And here at home, we're strengthening our homeland defenses. We created the Department of Homeland Security. We have made the prevention of terror attacks the highest priority of the Department of Justice and the FBI... We have strengthened the security of our nation's borders and ports of entry and transportation systems. The bill I sign today continues the essential reorganization of our government. Those charged with protecting us must have the best possible intelligence information, and that information must be closely integrated to form the clearest possible picture of the threats to our country.

A key lesson of September 11th, 2001 is that America's intelligence agencies must work as a single, unified enterprise. The Intelligence Reform and Terrorism Prevention Act of 2004 creates the position of Director of National Intelligence, or DNI, to be appointed by the President with the consent of the Senate.

The Director will lead a unified intelligence community and will serve as the Principle advisor to the President on intelligence matters. The DNI will have authority to order the collection of new intelligence, to ensure the sharing of information among agencies and to establish common sharing among the intelligence community's personnel. It will be the DNI's responsibility to determine annual funds for all national intelligence agencies and offices and to direct how those funds are spent. These authorities vested in a single official who reports directly to me will make our intelligence efforts more coordinated, more efficient, and more effective...

The many reforms in this act have a single goal: to ensure that the people in Government responsible for defending America have the best possible information to make the best possible decisions. The men and women of our intelligence community give America their very best every day, and in return we owe them our full support. As we continue to reform and strengthen the intelligence community, we will do all that is necessary to defend its people and the nation we serve.

Source: http://www.whitehouse.gov/news/releases/2004/12/20041217-1.html; Accessed August 18, 2005.

to establish objectives, priorities, and requirements for the timely collection, processing, analysis, and dissemination of national intelligence. The current system of collection is rooted in the Cold War paradigm based on the notion we could target certain individuals who had secret information that we needed and could recruit them to cooperate with us. But facing amorphous organizations not tied to enemy states and officials, it will be much harder to recruit. Terrorist cells are not so easily penetrated. They do not come to embassy receptions. Proponents of the new law hope that new amendments to the Foreign Intelligence Surveillance Act that expand foreign intelligence gathering through physical searches, pen registers, and track-and-trace devices, along with greater access to certain business records will allow better collection.

The latest change grants the government broader authority to surveil anyone who is a noncitizen and suspected of being a threat even if they are not tied to a terrorist group. This gets at the so-called lone-wolf terrorist who is perhaps inspired by, but not associated with, a group such as al Qaeda. (The power does not extend to surveillance of U.S. citizens, however.) (Marta Roberts, 2005: 78).

Critics also question whether the new DNI structure will impact one aspect of the way intelligence analysis management approaches information. There is a strong need to have minority views on analysis being appropriately voiced and heard. Before September 11, the CIA basically ignored the State Department's analyses on Iraq having weapons of mass destruction. Whether or not a strong DNI at the top of the intelligence community will make it more likely that minority views are heard depends on whom you ask. Proponents believe it will. Critics of the DNI approach think it will not do so.

Another potential flaw in the new law noted by some critics is the translation issue. The intelligence community lacks sufficient numbers of trained translators in some languages like Arabic, Farsi, Korean, and so on. It will take five or more years to build up the needed language strengths across the board.

With respect to the dissemination of information that is collected and analyzed, the next issue is whether it is properly disseminated. The Intelligence Reform Act does create an Information Sharing Council and directs the president to establish what is called an information sharing environment that allows users to share information among agencies, between levels of government, and as appropriate, with the private sector. The law retains the DHS as the agency responsible for disseminating information about threats to state and local government officials and private sector entities.

The new law contains several provisions clearly aimed at the "illegal alien" issue, and thus impacting on immigration policy-making. These are briefly summarized in Box 6.7.

Finally, in March of 2006 the Congress enacted a law renewing, with very minor amendments aimed at civil liberty concerns, the USA Patriot Act. The 2006 law has been referred to as Patriot Act II.

BOX 6.7.   SOME IMMIGRATION-RELEVANT PROVISIONS OF THE INTELLIGENCE REFORM LAW

1. It requires the Secretary of Health and Human Services (HHS) to promulgate standards for birth certificates in consultation with the DHS and the Commissioner of Social Security.
2. Standards for the birth certificates would include a requirement for proof and verification of identity as a condition for issues of a birth certificate.
3. Requires HHS, in coordination with SSA, to award grants to states to assist them in computerizing their birth and death records; developing the capability to match birth and death records within and among the States, and noting the fact of death on birth certificates of deceased persons.
4. Beginning two years after promulgation of regulations, prohibiting federal agencies from accepting, for any official purpose, a driver's license or identification card newly issued by a State to any person unless the driver's license or personal identification card conforms to such minimum standards required by the 2004 law.
5. Such standards would include, among other things, a requirement for documentation of proof of identity of an application for such a license/card and a standard for the verifiability of documents used to obtain such license/card.
6. It requires the SSA to issue regulations to restrict the issuance of multiple replacement cards not later than 180 days after enactment.
7. Requires SSA to verify records provided by an applicant for an original Social Security card, other than for purposes of enumeration at birth, within one year of enactment.
8. Requires the SSA to add death, fraud, and work authorization indicators to the Social Security number verification system within 18 months after enactment.
9. Requires SSA, in consultation with the DHS, to form an interagency task force for the purpose of further improving the Social Security cards and numbers. Not later than one year after enactment, the task force will establish security requirements, including standards for safeguarding cards from counterfeiting, tampering, alteration, and theft; for verifying documents submitted for the issuance of replacement cards, and actions to increase enforcement against the fraudulent use or issuance of Social Security numbers and cards.
10. Authorizes, for each fiscal year 2005–2009, appropriations to the Commissioner of Social Security of such sums as are necessary to carry out the requirements of the law.

CONCLUSION

The merger of the multiplicity of agencies into the DHS is an elephantine problem. Immigration policy-making and implementation is more likely to be more difficult to describe and assess in the near future as the management of the new federal behemoth struggles with coordinating and managing the merging of such disparate entities into a commonly functioning whole. Rather than being the culmination of the reforms suggested in the 1990s, particularly by the Carnegie Report, the restructuring of the INS into two separate bureaus, but within a new huge federal agency, that is, the DHS, is a much more problematic restructuring. Instead of a new and relatively simple independent agency devoted to immigration and citizenship services and policy implementation, or two separate divisions within the DOJ, as the reformers of the 1990s called for, the dissolving of the INS and merger of its functions into the DHS suggests continued problems for decision-making. It is a merger fraught with management problems and a likely source of unanticipated consequences that will keep the issue of immigration reform on the front burner of the congressional agenda for some years to come.

The changing regulations making it easier for the DHS to remove aliens, as well as conditions inducing more voluntary departures, contributed to a rather substantial increase in the number of aliens expelled or who voluntarily departed since 2000. The number of aliens expelled (all deportations, exclusions, and removals) and the total number of voluntary departures (aliens under docket control required to depart and voluntary departures not under docket) increased substantially and steadily during the past few decades. From 1961 to 1970, for example, there were a total of 101,205 formal removals, and 1,334,528 voluntary departures. From 1971 to 1980 these increased to 240,217 removals and 7,246,812 voluntary departures. From 1981 to 1990, there were 232,205 formal removals and 9,961,912 voluntary departures. Those numbers really sky-rocketed during the most recent decade of 1991–2000, when there were 939,749 formal removals and 13,587,684 voluntary departures (Annual Report, BCIS, accessed online at http://www.immigration.gov/graphics/: 17).

Despite the crackdowns and the increased restrictions discussed in this chapter, illegal immigration, complex refugee issues, and the continued pressure for high levels of legal immigration to the United States make immigration policy-making more complex and less predictable. The total Hispanic population in the United States has continued to surge, as has illegal immigration, because federal sanctions against employers who hire illegal (undocumented or visa overstayers) immigrants are at best poorly enforced, and because IRCA's amnesty provisions and continued discussion of possible amnesty programs developed the expectation that asylum will eventually be granted to anyone who settles in the United States. According to the 2000 census, roughly 10 million Mexican immigrants are living in the United States, about half of whom are here illegally. Every year, 150,000 to 200,000 Mexicans arrive legally, and estimates are that a similar number also enter illegally. Tighter border controls since September 11 seem to have done little to staunch the flow. Those controls have shifted more of the traffic to dangerous routes. In fiscal 2003, for example, more than 150 would-be immigrants died in the Arizona desert (Gorman: 384).

One critic of the old INS notes an aspect of immigration policy-making that is no less appropriate to the immigration function as being implemented within the new DHS. The new law, as that of the old, suffers from the fact that immigration issues have been clouded by emotion.

> Although substantial resources and manpower are directed to enforcement policies, such as patrolling the border, it is the bureaucrats who process and have significant impact on Mexican immigrations. Second, many of the policies assigned to the agency in the past two decades are not based on realistic approaches to curbing immigration. Rather, immigration policies are motivated by the political and popular sentiments of the moment . . . Popular and emotional reactions to undocumented immigration develop at the local levels. When these sentiments eventually reach politicians at the federal level, Congress responds with new policy, which only creates more responsibilities for the INS. When these immigration policies are eventually assigned to the INS without appropriate improvements in the budget and the organizational infrastructure, the overall morale and quality of service suffers. The agency appears inefficient, and new policies are created to improve agency performance (Magana: 1, 9).

In so far as the establishment of the new DHS will actually increase homeland security and that the measures described in this chapter will be an improvement in the way national policy interweaves the issues of national security and immigration policy, the jury is decidedly still out. No less a qualified critic of the effort than Richard Clarke is pessimistic in his assessment. He is critical that Secretary Tom Ridge was a politician rather than a manager or security expert and was simply not up to the task of effectively managing the new department. Moreover, he faults the administration for not doing things that needed to be and should have been done because it wasted enormous attention and resources that should have been directed domestically at the war on terrorism in what he labels the wrong war—because they were devoted to Iraq (Clarke: 247–287). He says:

> The [Bush] Administration has squandered the opportunity to eliminate al Qaeda . . . A new al Qaeda has emerged and is growing stronger, in part because of our actions and inactions. It is in many ways a tougher opponent than the original threat we faced before September 11, and we are not doing what is necessary to make America safe from that threat (Clarke: 247).

Immigration control issues remain on the agenda of Congress. President George Bush has floated a plan to fulfill Americans' shared vision of what the nation is and should continue to be:

By tradition and conviction, our county is a welcoming society. America is a stronger and a better nation because of the hard work, and the faith, and entrepreneurial spirit of immigrants. Every generation of immigrants has reaffirmed our ability to assimilate newcomers, which is one of the defining strengths of our country (cited in Gorman: 384).

But public opinion is far less welcoming than President Bush's comments would lead one to believe. As Figure 6.2 shows, Gallop Polls indicate that a majority of Americans believe the government should enact policy to decrease immigration. In June, 2003 only 13 percent thought immigration should be increased. A 2003 Gallop poll found 73 percent of Americans thought the government *should not make it easier* for illegal immigrants to become citizens (and 67 percent felt that way in August 2001). After President Bush announced his plan, 55% of the American public said they opposed it (Gorman: 384).

No less an expert than former Senator Alan Simpson asserted that it was virtually impossible for Congress to deal rationally with immigration. In his words: "Every time you get a sensible provision, it is overcome by emotion, fear, guilt, or racism" (cited in Gorman: 384). He is equally skeptical about one cornerstone of President Bush's proposal, an expanded "guest-worker" program. Simpson doubts that the potential millions of foreign workers would be persuaded to go home, arguing that experience indicates there is no such thing in immigration law as "temporary." Guest workers would come here, supposedly on a temporary basis, but would put down roots. They marry, have children, and otherwise invest their future here. When the BCIS agent came to deport the guest worker who overstays, it will make headlines in the local paper.

Other critics question how well the nation's "melting-pot" tradition fits with asking millions to come to labor here, but only to stay three years. Would they be able to refrain from becoming emotionally invested in making the United States their permanent home?

President Bush not only supports a large-scale temporary worker program, he would see that as a "first-step" towards boosting the number of green cards (legal work authorizations) to help reduce illegal immigration, especially if today's illegal immigrants could earn points toward permanent legal residence for what they offer the nation—education, skills, and family ties.

In 2004, then Senator Tom Daschle (D.-S.D.) and Representative Chuck Hagel (R.-Neb.) introduced an alternative plan to that of President Bush that offers illegal immigrants a faster route to citizenship, and a number of House Democrats introduced bills to legalize undocumented immigrants. All have died in committee so far, but the issue will likely remain on the agenda of the administration and of the Congress for the remainder of the reelected Bush term. President Bush has promised a bipartisan effort and hopes for such an agreement about doing something fairly soon to stem the tide of illegal immigration.

238 GUARDING THE GATES

Should such a large-scale temporary worker program (as many as 8 million has been mentioned) be enacted, it would undoubtedly reshape American society. As this review of immigration policy-making over so many decades has demonstrated, U.S. policy-makers are poor at forecasting the demographic changes that result from rewriting immigration law. A large-scale temporary worker program would likely make the stream of future immigrants even more diverse. People in Africa or Central Asia may discover that they have skills suddenly marketable in the United States. An influx of people from the far corners of the globe would only accelerate current trends toward America's multiracial society.

It is difficult to predict future policy-making in any policy area, and especially so in immigration policy. How long will this new cycle of more restrictive policy last? Past cycles of three to four or more decades would suggest that the era of fortress America will prevail for another decade or two at a minimum. What will be the future changes in immigration policy-making? We can expect more of the same—increased restriction—for the foreseeable future. Congress may well ban state governments from issuing driver's licenses to illegal immigrants. Increased "expedited removal" is probable for the remainder of this decade. Increased funding for the DHS is likely as well, and a portion of that will go to increase the implementation ability of the BCIS. Technology enabling better tracking and control of immigrants and nonimmigrants alike is on the near horizon. It will likely take another half decade to do so, but improvements in the management of the DHS and particularly of the BCIS are likely as well.

It is to these current trends, ideas, and proposals for dealing with the nexus of national security, homeland security, and immigration policy-making that the next and concluding chapter of this volume is devoted.

NOTES

1. For a discussion and description of the organizations, groups, and "think tanks" involved in immigration policy-making issues, see LeMay, 2004: 181–210. Those mentioned here and others are identified and their approach and role summarized, along with contact information.

2. For a succinct yet thorough chronology of post-Sptember 11 events, see: "The Aftermath of September 11: A Chronology" in Appendix I, Information Plus, *Immigration and Illegal Aliens: Burden or Blessing?* Farmington Hills, MI: Gale/Thomson Learning, 2003: 125–128. This brief summary of events is drawn from their chronology.

3. See http://www.dhs.gov/dhspublic/themehome.4.jsp; accessed November 29, 2004. See also, "Program Analysis Findings and Addressing Shortcomings," at http://www.dhs.gov/interweb/assetlibrary/reorganization.plan.pdf; accessed November 29, 2004.

_____ 7 _____

Conclusion

INTRODUCTION: THE CONTINUING INTERPLAY OF NATIONAL SECURITY CONCERNS AND IMMIGRATION POLICY-MAKING

For two centuries, geography has been America's biggest security asset. With oceans to the east and west and friendly neighbors to the north and south, the United States has been untrammeled by enemy boots on our ground. Inhabiting the most peaceful corner of the world has meant that captains of industry and urban planners have been able to treat security as a marginal issue. Those carefree days are now gone and unfortunately, we have inherited infrastructures so open that they offer terrorists a vast menu of soft targets (Flynn: x).

This review of two centuries of the United States' immigration policy-making and the intertwining of national security issues and concerns with that of immigration policy has shown some continuous patterns and changing cycles. Many groups in favor of fairly open immigration policy have persisted throughout the years, generally advocating similar reasons for maintaining America's long tradition as a nation of immigrants, of a welcoming stance to newcomers from all over the world, and of the value of relatively open immigration to the U.S. economy and society. Such groups have consistently valued America as the refuge for asylum seekers and as the beneficiary of their talents and the national strength arising from diversity and multliculturalism. Decade after decade, the American history has echoed with the words of proimmigration groups sounding the same themes.

Likewise, many other groups have consistently and persistently pushed for strict restriction of immigration. Such groups have for hundreds of years feared the negative impact that is many and varied, which other-nationality loyalties may portend for a national population comprised of tens of thousands to even millions of immigrants from 170 nations of the world. Very similar groups over those years have feared the impact of "cheap labor" from what they view as excessive immigration rates and levels. They have persistently argued high levels of immigration results in low wages and poor working conditions, as both legal and illegal immigrants steal jobs from American workers and drive the labor market downward in a spiral toward the bottom. Still others have argued such "excessive multiculturalism" will destroy the "unum" in our "E Pluribus Unum." They fear the development of a separatist movement akin to Quebec Province in Canada. And for nearly four decades now, many similar such "nativist-oriented" groups have riled against illegal immigration and the loss of control over borders. That concern over the loss of border control reached its zenith after the attacks of September 11. "National security" concerns morphed into "homeland security" and a palpable fear that international terrorists would enter the country via the illegal immigration flow, establish terrorist cells, and wreck havoc on the nation—killing hundreds to hundreds of thousands and causing untold billions of dollars of cost to our economy. Our political leaders and the general public accept the fact that we cannot secure our nation if we cannot secure our borders.

Proimmigration and anti-immigration groups come and go, but their arguments remain remarkably consistent. Their perspective on what should be "proper" immigration policy to best achieve national security persists over the decades. Indeed, even their views as to what constitutes "the immigration problem" are perennial issues seeking attention on the agenda of federal government policy-making.

This final chapter will discuss continuing trends and issues that affect the nexus of national security and immigration policy-making—two inherently "intermestic" areas of policy-making. It will review current proposals before the U.S. Congress that addresses those issues. It will conclude with some final thoughts on what the future portends for immigration policy-making as the cycle of the "Storm-Door Era" matures and then once again changes, as have such cycles so often done in the past.

CONTINUING TRENDS AND ISSUES OF NATIONAL SECURITY AND IMMIGRATION POLICY-MAKING

For approximately the past four decades, several trends and issues have dominated the attention of the political leadership and national policy-makers with respect to what is the best policy to promote national security, and what is the best balance in national immigration policy between more open or more restricted levels of immigration. How do we best control our borders? What is the optimum level of immigration that we can safely and effectively absorb into our economy and into our culture and society? Who should we let in? Who can assimilate into our national "melting pot"? How do we guard against the incursion of international terrorist bent on harm and intent of mass destruction?

Sovereignty—Unilateral versus Collective Security

At the very heart of the issue of national security policy is the concept of sovereignty. An issue with the concept of sovereignty is how best to maintain it—through mostly unilateral action or through depending more on a collective approach to sovereignty and security.

Unilateral Approach to Sovereignty and National Security

A unilateral perception of national security arises from the traditional sense and definition of sovereignty. A nation-state has the power and the rightful authority to govern its territory and to secure its borders. The late Senator Alan Cranston, while advocating a more collective approach to security, defined the traditional idea of sovereignty as follows:

> Sovereignty is one, indivisible, unalienable, and imprescriptible; it belongs to the Nation; no one group can attribute sovereignty to itself, nor can any individual arrogate it to himself (Cranston: 30).

Another scholar defines the traditional idea of sovereignty as:

> The emergence of the territorial state (a governing system for a specific territory with a stable population and a functioning government) was accompanied by the notion that the state was sovereign. Accordingly, the sovereignty of all other social groupings was legally subordinated to the sovereignty of the state. Political and legal theorists argued that sovereignty resided in territorial states' rulers; they had ultimate authority to make policy within a state's borders. Those who negotiated the two treaties making up the Peace of Westphalia [in 1648] wanted to stop the religious wars that brought such destruction to Europe; they specified that whoever ruled a certain territory could determine the religion of that territory (Weiss: xliii).

But in a democratic republic, such as is the United States, national sovereignty arises from the people who grant it to the states. As George Soros, in his article, "The People's Sovereignty," published in a recent issue of *Foreign Policy* puts it:

> But true sovereignty belongs to the people, who in turn delegate it to their government. If governments abuse the authority entrusted to them and citizens have no opportunity to correct such abuses, outside interference is justified. By specifying that sovereignty is based on the people, the international community can penetrate nation-states' borders to protect the rights of citizens. In particular, the principle of the people's sovereignty can help solve two modern challenges: the obstacles to delivering aid effectively to sovereign states, and the obstacles to global collective action dealing with states experiencing internal conflict (cited in Cranston: 87).

The traditional and unilateral approach to nation-state sovereignty lodged firmly in a national government underlies the changing nature of national security in the United States, which is now defined more as "homeland security." Such perception of sovereignty justifies the primacy of the national government in security policy-making. The Bush administration can justify the requirement, for example, that the new DNI, John Negroponte, be allowed to help choose a powerful new intelligence chief at the FBI. It trumps the FBI's traditional "turf" protection. The appointment, for the first time in the bureau's history, gives an outsider a significant role in the selection of a high-level official at the FBI, an agency long regarded by its critics fiercely protective of its turf and resistant to change (The Denver Post, 6/12/05: 27A).

Unilateral national sovereignty, however, is complicated when the nation-state involves a federal system, as does the United States. In a federal system, national sovereignty is divided and in some respects shared with the constituent units, in this case the fifty states. Authority for dealing with the threat of international terrorism may reside with the national government ultimately, but in a federal system can only be implemented by a sharing with state and local governments who are so often the "first responders" to any terrorist attack, like those of September 11.

Federal and state officials have made substantial progress in the field of homeland security since September 2001. City and county managers and their elected officials, however, are at the forefront of this movement. After all, local governments were the first responders to the terrorist acts of September 11. Although national and state leadership are essential, the future of homeland security depends on preparedness initiatives at the local level. Local public officials have developed new emergency management practices, applied new computer software to this field, and begun to make local codes to enhance safeguards to protect citizens. All of these new measures fall into one or more of the four phases of emergency management: mitigation, preparedness, response, and recovery. In less than two years, states have standardized many of their practices of emergency management for those cities and counties within their respective boundaries (Kemp, *National Civic Review*, 2003: 45).

Threat analysis and assessment in order to better manage and mitigate against terrorist threats are aided by a number of federal grant programs, largely administered by FEMA, to assist state and local governments to properly analyze and assess the level of possible terrorist acts by individuals or groups within their jurisdictions. To do so, city and county officials must work with state and federal agencies, placing a premium on collaboration among government agencies, and challenging efforts to build the capacity for joint action. Such a more comprehensive approach to emergency management fits well FEMA's Integrated Emergency Management System, which provides an all-hazards approach to emergency preparedness. The mitigation of the effects of terrorist attacks also depends on state and local governments taking nonstructural measures to improve building safety, and the development of pedestrian and vehicular evacuation routes from buildings and neighborhoods or even entire cities, depending on the type and size of a particular disaster, including man-made disasters perpetrated by terrorists. Police and fire departments typically have mutual aid agreements with neighboring communities that can be integrated into emergency responses when local resources have been exhausted. As Kemp notes:

> In the case of an arson fire or terrorist bombing, people must be evacuated immediately from all affected buildings and surrounding areas. Procedures should exist to facilitate the smooth evacuation of large numbers of people in the shortest possible time. In case of fire or the imminent collapse of a building, a prompt response does save many lives. Vehicles owned by the local government, such as buses and vans, should be used to facilitate such evacuation. The number of vehicles available, as well as issues relating to their accessibility, should be known in advance of an incident. Proper exit signs and evacuation routes should be conspicuously posted in all buildings, both public and private. The location of safety equipment and first aid supplies should also be known and posted in advance of an emergency (48).

After the September 11 terrorist attacks, the federal government coined the phrase "homeland security" to describe the actions of *all levels of government* to internally and unilaterally protect citizens from future acts of violence by terrorists. Although the emergency management practices, procedures, and techniques that evolve during the coming years will necessarily differ from the civil defense measures of the past, the goal of such initiatives will be the same: to minimize the loss of life and property. The field of emergency management has come full-circle in the past half-century. External threats have focused the attention of emergency planners on man-made disasters.

The federal department taking the point for a unilateral approach to national security, as we have seen in Chapter 6, is the DHS. The merging of the many agencies into the new department poses many challenges for the management of that department. In *Taming the Spending Beast*, Greg Rothwell, the acquisitions manager of the new department, notes his top three challenges as: "merging cultures, supporting customers, and satisfying stakeholders" (10). The merging of cultures is no small task. While nine of the twenty-two agencies merged into DHS had their own procurement offices, thirteen received it from the new centralized office. Merging twenty-two stove-piped, mostly law enforcement, organizations into a single department is a huge management hurdle. And the new department faced new mission needs. Buying the right commodities which were the right things and having them delivered on time is a huge challenge. Developing new goods and services, as well as new procedures for procurement required developing "strategic sourcing"— understanding needs across the entire (and in this case, vast) organization to obtain a certain commodity or service in the best way to acquire those goods or services. It sounds simple, but strategic sourcing is complex, and the merging of the cultures of so many and sometimes so disparate agencies to agree on requirements and reaching a consensus on how to conduct the acquisition is difficult to say the least. The DHS established councils for commodity areas identified as strategic sourcing targets, ranging from ammunition to boats and from office supplies to uniforms. Each council is co-chaired by an acquisition person and someone familiar with the commodity, or a "user." Each council sets up measures and metrics specific to its mission, and also participates in enterprise-wide metrics. The councils are governed by the Strategic Sourcing Group, consisting of the Director of Procurement, and representatives from the Office of the Chief Financial Officer, General Counsel, Chief Information Officer, Small Business Office, and a member of the DHS Investment Review Board, and they respond to the Secretary of the DHS's Management Council.

The establishment of the huge DHS offers not only the challenge of merging twenty-two agencies, but also an opportunity, given its size, to use the advantages of scale. The sheer mass of the department's purchasing power opens many doors. The DHS uses the DOD's e-Mal, an array of vendors and catalogs that took the DOD years to build up. A similar area of challenge and potential involves the information technology. It is a daunting task to merge the components of DHS into a single enterprise architecture. Twenty-two agencies each had their own infrastructure. Even those agencies that had first-class networks had to change somewhat in becoming one DHS. And when the merger included agencies such as the former INS, with its notoriously poor information infrastructure, the challenge was not to have the INS drag more efficient agencies down to their level. Three of the commodity councils in the DHS focus on the information technology endeavor (Rothwell: 13).

The United States is a world power and much of world politics consists of managing the contradictions between conceptions of state sovereignty on the one hand, and the desire for improved security, human rights, and sustainable human development on the other hand (Weiss: xlvii).

The Collective Approach to Sovereignty and Security

The sovereignty issue is further complicated by an increasing need for a more multilateral, or collective, approach to security. Collective security means not only the security of the territorial state, but the security of the community of nations from war and most recently, from international terrorism.

With the signing of the UN Charter on June 26, 1945, the world undertook a new experiment in organizing states to control war . . . Two world wars within two decades, the Holocaust, and the advent of the nuclear age produced a political will to improve on the League of Nations. The international community rejected isolationism and committed itself to trying to safeguard the peace that had been won at great cost (Weiss: 3).

The "war" on terrorism declared by the Bush administration after the September 11 attacks necessarily engaged the U.S. in global conflict. Alan Cranston described it as a war about sovereignty after the first attack on the World Trade Center in 1993:

> The bombing of the World Trade Center in New York was a direct and ominous import into our country of the terrorism creating so much havoc elsewhere, carried out by militant and fanatic Islamic fundamentalists in retaliation for various perceived grievances including our intervention in the sovereignty struggles of the Middle East. Its toll was six dead, 1,000 injured. There are dark warnings of worse to come as terrorists proclaim they will wage a holy war against the United States and its citizens wherever they may be as long as we keep our "infidel" forces in Islamic lands in what they view as irreverent violation of their sacrosanct sovereignty by the Great Satin (Cranston: 71–72).

A global conflict necessarily requires a more multilateral approach, although many policy-makers in the national security arena resist a multilateral perspective. Senator Cranston addressed that aspect of the sovereignty issue debate as well, when he stated:

> The dubious concern about putting national sovereignty in jeopardy that has deterred us from following globally the course chosen regionally in the U.S. and the E.U. is having unintended consequences. It is leading, in a perverse way, to the very withering away of national sovereignty that those possessed by the concern would avoid, as nations fail to control and even influence and guide many world trends and events that impact the lives of everyone (Cranston: 50).

The United States, being a global power, needs to involve a multilateral and unilateral approach to security. The Cold War extended the U.S.' "blanket of security" to cover much of the world. With the end of the Cold War and the demise of the Soviet Union as a superpower, the United States has retained and even expanded its already extended defense perimeter. Perimeter defense inherently involves policy related to immigration and international trade and commerce. It refers, for example, to such things as: airport security, cargo security, seaport security, road and rail security at ports of entry, unmanned border monitoring, visa processing, document integrity enhancement, and document checks (O'Hanlon et al, 2002: 14).

And as Ivan Eland notes about the ever-expanding role of the United States as the sole global superpower:

> Profligate U.S. interventions around the world could also prompt rogue states to obtain nuclear, biological, chemical, or missile technologies to forestall U.S. meddling in their affairs. The Saddam Husseins and Kim Jong Il's of the world have found that they cannot hope to defeat the powerful U.S. military in a conventional war. Thus, they have an incentive to obtain and threaten the U.S.

homeland with weapons of mass destruction, to give the United States pause before an intervention (Eland: 3).

The United States has to respond to the threat of international terrorism aided, encouraged, or inspired by rogue states, with a collective-security approach. Rogue states are described as states that engage in either terrorism or the proliferation of weapons of mass destruction—they enter the "rogues gallery" of nations in the world such as Iran, Iraq, Libya, Syria, Cuba, and North Korea (Tanton: x). Rogue states cannot confront U.S. military might directly, so they do so by sponsoring nonstate groups (such as al Qaeda) who employ terrorism for political gains.

The idea of collective security can be traced through a long history of proposals to deal with war and peace. The central threat has remained the same: all states would join forces to prevent one of their number from using coercion to gain advantage. Under such a system, no government could conquer another or otherwise disturb the peace for fear of retaliation from all other governments. Any attack would be treated as if it were an attack on each of them. The notion of self-defense, universally agreed on as a right of a sovereign state, was expanded to include the international community's right to prevent war (Weiss et al: 7).

During the 1990s, the United States was the primary force behind the UN campaign to repel Iraqi aggression against Kuwait; to pressurize Iraq into complying with various UN resolutions after Desert Storm; to deliver humanitarian aid to Civil War-torn countries, such as Somalia; and to make other UN security operations succeed. Indeed, historically, no UN security operation was undertaken against the wishes of the United States, and whenever the UN was less than fully effective in UN-sponsored collective security matters, such as the early years in Bosnia or in Haiti, it was largely a reflection of the unwillingness of the United States to engage fully (Weiss et al: 328).

When the UN appeared reluctant to follow the lead of the United States in how it perceived collective security should be pursued, the United States used its tremendous financial pressure to induce UN compliance. During the first two years of the Bush administration, it delayed paying its UN dues in an effort to force certain "reforms" on UN operations. That approach changed after Spetember 11 and when the administration decided to launch a "preemptive strike" or war against Iraq.

The UN's chronic financial difficulties were only partially improved with the U.S.' payment of past dues in the wake of the attacks in New York and Washington on September 11, 2001, by al Qaeda. Washington, wanting UN endorsement for its security concerns, quickly showed what had been true all along regarding its payments to the UN—namely, that the issue was less about money and more about symbolic politics. In general, the United States had withheld UN payments because it objected to UN independent policies that deviated from Washington's preferences and challenged its unfettered sovereignty.

When the UN failed to support its incursion into Iraq, the United States went in nearly alone, cobbling together its own "multinational" coalition without UN endorsement. When the war bogged down with an entrenched insurgency, the U.S. once again sought UN involvement and backing. Despite the reluctance of many in the administration for using the UN and a UN-backed multilateral approach to collective security, the realities of the war in Afghanistan and Iraq, and the continuing effective use of international terrorism by groups associated with al Qaeda, has forced U.S. policy-makers to use a more collective approach.

> A preference for multilateral diplomacy is not idealistic at the start of the twenty-first century. On the contrary, unilateralists promoting an image of unbridled state control over events are the real utopians of the twenty-first century... In this first decade of the current millennium, it is difficult to conceive of a world without multilateralism (Weiss: xxvii, xxxix).

International Terrorism

The attacks of September 11 on New York City and Washington, the train bombings in Madrid, Spain, and the suicide and related train-bus bombings in London have very clearly demonstrated that international terrorism can strike almost anyone and almost anywhere. Far from being weakened by "taking the war to them in Afghanistan and Iraq," al Qaeda and other similar terrorist groups operating on the international scene seem to be growing in their size and capabilities, and evolving in their tactics. The nature of their threat is clear:

> Terrorism will remain a threat to Americans at home and abroad. But even as the United States engages in isolated strikes against terrorists and their sponsors, it will also fortify the homeland and reign in its overseas commitments in an attempt to cordon itself off from such threats (Kupchan: 160).

The first decade of the new century has amply demonstrated the force of the threat arising from international terrorism. It is a threat that is difficult to combat precisely because by its very nature it is elusive and sporadic. That means the "war" against it (a concept or movement, rather than a nation-state as in our wars of the past) will be more long-term than the past wars, and will likely involve much that will erode liberal internationalism rather than rebuilding it. As Kupchan puts it:

> And should attacks on American targets continue abroad and in the U.S., the voices in favor of retrenchment may well grow stronger. As the founding fathers vigorously and repeatedly asked, why should America involve itself in distant lands and their troubles if doing so ultimately brings harm to America's shores (200–201).

Table 7.1 presents a listing of attacks on the U.S. homeland versus attacks on other regions from 1993 through 1999. The table shows that the threat until then was clearly aimed at targets abroad than in the homeland, which changed, of course, after September 11.

In addition to these actual attacks, there were reported at least fifty-two incidents of terrorist threats to use WMD between 1968 and 1994 (Kupchan: 14).

The increased violence and effectiveness of such attacks in the first few years of the twenty-first century, in New York, Washington, Spain, London, and so on focused the attention of policy-makers on the threat for such violence implicit in fairly liberal immigration and visa policy (for nonpermanent residence travel to the United States). The foreign threat includes the potential threat from foreign students and immigrants—although it should be stressed that native-born Americans have posed a much more serious threat (prior to 2001) than any posed by foreign visitors or residents that are not directly involved with terrorist groups. The National Commission on Terrorism identified foreign students studying in the U.S. as potential threats in its June 2000 report (Cordesman: 74–75).

Since September 11, the fight against international terrorism has expanded policy-making to include taking the battle to the offensive, as well as deterrence, denial (of opportunity), defense, and retaliation as essential parts of homeland defense. Policy-makers modified their views and concerns as to what constitutes the enemy in international terrorism—expanding that to include not only state-sponsored terrorism (asymmetric warfare), but also the threat from organizations such as al Qaeda, and now from independently acting groups not directly linked or affiliated with groups such as al Qaeda, but inspired by the group and its tactics and generally espousing its philosophy as to the use of terrorism against its ideological foes. What is increasingly clear is that homeland defense, to be effective, must respond to ever-changing threat,

TABLE 7.1. Attacks on U.S. Homeland versus Other Regions, 1993–1999

Total International Terrorist Attacks by Region	1993	1994	1995	1996	1997	1998	1999
Africa	6	25	10	11	11	21	52
Asia	37	24	16	11	21	49	72
Eurasia	5	11	5	24	42	14	35
Latin America	97	58	92	84	128	110	116
Middle East	100	116	45	45	37	31	25
Western Europe	185	88	272	121	52	48	85
North America	1	0	0	0	13	0	2
Worldwide totals	431	322	440	296	304	272	387

Source: Cordesman: 17.

particularly in forms or tactics that are harder to predict and defend against. The emergence of new patterns of attack is likely to go on for some years to come. Such attacks may involve threats from rogue states backing groups that make it difficult to trace the origin of the attack back to that state, or from independent terrorist groups that are international in scope and loosely knit in organizational structure (Cordesman: 9–10).

Given these developments, the responsible course of action for national security policy-makers is to seek new governmental powers that are aimed at improving homeland security, yet to set such boundaries on those new powers so as to prevent their overuse and abuse. That requires a difficult policy balancing act.

> How can we avert catastrophe and hold down the number of lesser mass murders? Our best hope is to prevent al-Qaeda from getting nuclear, biological, or chemical weapons and smuggling them into this country . . . Ultimately, we can hold down our casualties only by finding and locking up (or killing) as many as possible of the hundreds of thousands of possible al-Qaeda terrorists whose strategy is to infiltrate our society and avoid attention until they strike (Torr: 24).

The use of sleeper cells and suicide bombers in Western Europe and the United States has been articulated by advocates of the use of terrorism. Dr. Ramadan Shalah, the Secretary General of the Palestinian Islamic Jihad, for example, forecast those developments and justified such acts well before the attacks of September 11:

> Our enemy possesses the most sophisticated weapons in the world and its army is trained to a very high standard . . . We have nothing with which to repel killings and thuggery against us except the weapon of martyrdom. It is easy and costs us only our lives . . . human bombs cannot be defeated even by nuclear bombs (cited in Sprinzak: 68).

Table 7.2 demonstrates the global reach of suicide attacks by terrorist organizations between 1983 and 2000. It lists the terrorist organization using the tactic and the number of suicide bombing attacks launched by the group during those years.

One critic of U.S. security (and homeland security) defense policy to date reflects on the very fact that our military might encourage that strategy by terrorists.

> Ironically, our overwhelming military capabilities make it attractive to target the nonmilitary backbone of our power. We spend more on conventional military muscle than the next thirty countries combined. Never in human history has such a disproportionately large amount of force been concentrated in the hands of one nation. In the face of this reality, our adversaries must become creative Davids to our Goliath (Flynn: 5).

TABLE 7.2. Martyrdom's Global Reach—Suicide Attacks
by Assorted Terrorist Organizations, 1983–2000

Terrorist Organization	Number of Attacks
Liberation Tigers of Tamil Eelan	171
Lebanese Hezbollah and Amal	25
Other Lebanese groups	25
Palestinian Hamas	22
Kurdistan Worker's Party	21
Palestinian Islamic Jihad	8
Chechen Separatists	7
Al Qaeda (Osama bin Laden)	2
Kuwaiti Dawa	2
Egyptian Islamic Jihad	1
Egyptian Islamic Group	1
Algerian Armed Islamic Group	1

Source: Sprinzak, 2000: 69.

He argues persuasively that our very military strength means that they will increasingly seek "soft targets" that are much easier to strike and much harder to defend against.

From water and food supplies, refineries, energy grids, and pipelines; bridges, tunnels, trains, trucks, and cargo containers; to the cyber backbone that under-pins the information age in which we live, the measures we have taken and have been cobbling together are hardly fit to deter amateur thieves, vandals, and hackers, never mind determined terrorists. Worse still, small improvements are often sold as giant steps forward, lowering the guard of the average citizens as they carry on their daily routine with an unwarranted sense of confidence (Flynn: 2).

Policy designed to counter that threat has used the major institutions of the government, including the FBI and the military. The FBI recently announced a terror probe that uncovered an alleged sleeper-cell in Lodi, California, made up of Pakistani-Americans who the FBI claims are connected to al-Qaeda and have attended terrorist training camps (*The Denver Post*, 6/9/05: 4A). The Northern Command, established in 2002 to handle homeland defense, and housed at Peterson AFB in Colorado Springs, developed fifteen secret crisis scenarios for responding to terrorist attacks in the United States. These involve using the military (active and national guard) as a domestic police force in the event of an attack here. The plans call for such use of the military as that would lessen chaos after an attack; they already have and are experienced in setting up field hospitals; have the ability to feed, shelter, and transport large numbers of people; are experienced and equipped to set up communications, repair bridges and water systems and roads. Northcom's role is "in support of a federal agency, such as FEMA, when directed by the president or secretary of defense. But to some critics of such plans, that is the scary part. The ACLU and the Center for Defense Information (a D.C. "think-tank") warn: "We don't need generals telling state or city authorities what to do" (Marcus Corbin of the Center for Defense Information quoted in the *Denver Post*, Monday, August 15, 2005: B-7).

Part of the Bush administration's response to the threat involves taking the fight abroad rather than on our shores. Such a policy approach includes not only the wars in Afghanistan and Iraq, but also in negotiating international agreements. The administration recently successfully had passed in the Senate ratification of the Central America Free Trade Agreement (CAFTA), designed "to integrate more closely with 34 hemispheric neighbors, thus furthering the Free Trade Agreement of the Americas, 2001 Quebec Resolution to bring about hemispheric integration." Similarly, the administration has backed a Council of Foreign Relations plan called a "Security and Prosperity Partnership" in which the United States, Mexico, and Canada will integrate their economies and create an economic space with a more open border for the movement of people and goods within a "common security perimeter"—the North American Community. The CFR is made up of leaders from transnational corporations, academia, government, and the mass media.

The Bush administration's approach to fighting terrorism through international agreements and the wars in Afghanistan and Iraq is being criticized from both the political left and the political right. Opposition from the left will be discussed more fully later in this chapter. Opposition from the political right is highlighted in Box 7.1, which summarizes a viewpoint from a political column written by Pat Buchanan in a recent *Middle America* issue.

A particularly feared form of international terrorism concerns the issue of *bioterrorist* attacks. While the likelihood of a bioterrorist attack officially remains rated as extremely low, the potential for high numbers of possible fatalities remains high—with estimates up to 1 million (O'Hanlon, 2002: 6). The public is especially fearful of an efficient biological attack employing a contagious agent like ebola, smallpox, or anthrax. In part, the extra-edge to this fear of biological attack results from a realization that a suicide-terrorist could infect him or herself with one of these dreaded pathogens whose incubation period is several days or longer, then simply fly to the United States on a tourist visa. The travel time is so short that symptoms would not yet be visible upon arrival at a U.S. airport. If the individual while in a contagious stage then traveled extensively, purposely passing through bus or train terminals or airport terminals, the potential spread could be significant and extremely difficult to guard against.

The idea that disgruntled individuals or small groups as well as rogue governments might employ bioterror weapons also began to circulate around the start of the new century. Some writers called bioterror weapons "the poor man's atom

BOX 7.1. WHY ARE THEY KILLING US?

Few Americans have given more thought to the motivation of suicide bombers than Robert Pape, author of "Dying to Win: The Logic of Suicide Terrorism." His book is drawn from an immense database of every suicide-bomb attack from 1980 to early 2004. Conclusion: The claim that 9-11 and the suicide-bombings in Iraq are done to advance some jihad by "Islamofascists" against the West is not only unsubstantiated, it is hollow.

"Islamic fundamentalism is not as closely associated with suicide terrorism as many people think," Pape says. Indeed, the world's leader in suicide terror was the Tamil Tigers of Sri Lanka. This secular Marxist group "invented the famous suicide vest for their suicide assassination of Rajiv Ghandi in May 1991. The Palestinians got the idea of the vest from the Tamil Tigers."

"Suicide terrorist attacks are not so much driven by religion as by a clear strategic objective: to compel modern democracies to withdraw military forces from the territory that the terrorists view as their homeland. From Lebanon to Sri Lanka to Chechnya to Kashmir to the West Bank, every major suicide terrorist campaign—over 95 percent of all incidents—has had as its central objective to compel a democratic state to withdraw."

Before the U.S. invasion, says Pape, "Iraq never had a suicide attack in its history. Since our invasion, suicide terrorism has been escalating rapidly, with 20 attacks in 2003, 48 in 2004, and over 50 in just the first five months of 2005. Every year since the U.S. invasion, suicide terrorism has doubled . . . Far from making us safer against terrorism, the operation in Iraq has stimulated suicide terrorists and has given suicide terrorism a new lease on life."

The good news? "The history of the last 20 years," shows that once the troops of the occupying democracies "withdraw from the homeland of the terrorists, they often stop—and stop on a dime."

Between 1982 and 1986, there were 41 suicide attacks on U.S., French, and Israeli targets in Lebanon. When U.S. and French troops withdrew and Israel pulled back to a six-mile buffer zone, suicide bombings virtually ceased. When the Israelis left Lebanon, the Lebanese suicide-bombers did not follow them to Tel Aviv.

"Since suicide terrorism is mainly a response to foreign occupations and not Islamic fundamentalism," says Pape, "the use of heavy military force to transform Muslim societies . . . is only likely to increase the number of suicide terrorists coming at us." . . . .

Bush's cure for terrorism is a cause of the epidemic. The doctor is spreading the disease. The longer we stay in Iraq, the greater the number of suicide attacks we can expect. The sooner we get our troops out, the sooner terrorism over there and over here will end.

How would we defend our vital interests in the Gulf? Answers Pape: By getting our troops out, removing the cause of suicide-terror, leaving behind stocked bases and putting U.S. carrier and air forces over the horizon to ensure the Gulf oil flows. But unless and until American troops are withdrawn from the Middle East, the suicide attacks continue.

Source: Summarized by author from: Viewpoint, *Middle America*, August 2005: 13.

bomb," because they were easier and cheaper to produce than nuclear weapons. Experts pointed out that these small groups might not be deterred by factors that might limit the activities of national governments, such as fear of massive retaliation (Yount: 7).

Moreover, under some circumstances, a pathogen could be effectively introduced into the United States without the perpetrators even entering the country—by infecting cargo and such. Think of the economic devastation to the beef industry in Great Britain as a result of a relatively few cases of mad cow disease. Infecting U.S. cattle, pigs, sheep, or other animals with diseases such as foot and mouth or mad cow is unlikely to cause a great many deaths in humans. Such outbreaks are likely to erode public confidence in food safety and would devastate the U.S. agricultural industry, which relies heavily upon exports (Yount: 41).

Ongoing health care crises in cities such as Las Vegas and Atlanta, as well as reactions to the terrorist attacks in late 2001 (the anthrax outbreak), reveal dangerous flaws in the healthcare system and in government communication that must be addressed if the nation is to be truly protected against bioterror (Yount: 51).

The Center for Disease Control (CDC) is the front line agency to protect against bioterror attacks. It works with state and local governments to identify, contain, and control outbreaks of contagious diseases. In planning for bioterrorism, for example, it has provided Smallpox Response Team guides to the Department of Health in every state of the union, as well as embassy missions abroad. Once a suspected case is reported to the State Health Department and confirmed, a state of emergency will be declared. In such an outbreak, schools and businesses will be closed until the situation is declared safe, after the affected population is properly vaccinated, and all cases are confined and treated. The CDC will ship the vaccination supplies within twenty-four hours of notification (Bertollli: 12).

Fortunately, spreading diseases is not an easy task. The sarin attacks in Tokyo, for example, resulted in only a few deaths. But if terrorist organizations should ever get their hands on toxins or viruses, such as that which caused the Spanish Influenza outbreak in 1917–1918 that resulted in a pandemic and killed millions worldwide, the potential for another such pandemic is, indeed, terrifying and could cause millions to be infected. Even the CDC has no known cure or vaccine for that particular strain of virus, and the danger of mutations in flu viruses is well known and justifiably feared by agencies such as the CDC.

Still other critics contend that our political leadership is simply grossly exaggerating the danger of terrorism. For example, they note that the odds of dying in a terrorist attack are miniscule. According to the U.S. Center for Disease Control, the odds are about 1 in 82,000, while the odds of falling off a ladder are 1 in 10,010. Even in 2001 with its huge losses in the attacks on September 11, car crashes killed fifteen times the number of Americans than did the terrorists. Heart disease, cancer, and strokes are the leading cause of death in the United States, not terrorism (Friedman, 2005: 22). Such critics note that the destruction of al Qaeda's Afghan sanctuary and the capture or killing of many of the original leadership has weakened the capability of al Qaeda.

> Some experts and policy-makers call this collage of al Qaeda fellow travelers and wannabes a network—and treat it as some form of higher organization. But the fact that this collection of fundamentalists is the primary national security threat to the United States should be a cause for celebration. These groups are dangerous, but, thankfully, they lack the geographic reach and organizational capacity that al Qaeda had in 2001 (Friedman: 27).

These critics also contend that the danger through our ports is also exaggerated. While it is true that in excess of $600 billion in goods and nearly 50 percent of U.S. imports annually flow through American ports, and that U.S. ports are vulnerable to both weapons being smuggled into the United States and attacks on U.S. ships are possible, there is little indication that such attacks are likely. Since September 11, the nation has greatly increased investment in port security and the Coast Guard's budget has grown to $6.3 billion in four years. Although only 5 percent of containers entering the United States are inspected by U.S. custom agents, the measure of success to increased port security is not in the percentage searched, but which containers are searched. Intelligence to identify risky cargo has been greatly improved with the Container Security Initiative instituted by the Customs and Border Protection Agency in 2002. The initiative aims are identifying suspect cargo before it sails by stationing agents in foreign ports, requiring a manifest prior to a ship's arrival, determining the origin of containers, and developing electronic, tamper-proof container seals. While far from perfect, this system is better than spending vast sums to inspect every shipment. Additional port security must respond to known threats, not to any and all vulnerability (Friedman: 24).

Still other critics contend that Washington has little appetite to move beyond government reorganization and color-coded alerts. While airport security has been visibly increased, the other "soft targets" that are critical to our way of life remain largely unprotected. As Stephen Flynn notes in *America the Vulnerable*:

> Throughout our history, Americans have displayed an extraordinary degree of resolve, nimbleness, and self-sacrifice in times of war. Today we are breaking with that tradition. Our nation faces grave peril, but we are unwilling to mobilize at home to confront the threat before us. Managing the danger that al Qaeda poses cannot be achieved by relying primarily on military campaigns overseas... The 9/11 attacks highlighted the fact that our borders offer no effective barrier to terrorists intent on bringing their war to our soil (x).

Illegal Immigration

The presence of such a large number of illegal immigrants in the United States keeps it a perennial issue of concern in American politics and on the agenda of Congress since the 1970s. It continues to be so into the twenty-first century. Despite enactment of legislation aimed at solving the "illegal immigration problem," such as the Immigration Reform and Control Act of 1986 (IRCA), the Immigration Act of 1990 (IMMACT), the Personnel Responsibility and Work Opportunity Act of 1996 (PRWO), and the Illegal Immigration Reform and Immigrant Responsibility Act of 1996 (IIRIRA), (LeMay and Barkan: 282–310), the number of illegal immigrants in the United States ranges from an estimated 8 to 12 million. The Pew Center for Hispanic Studies puts the number at 10.3 million (cited in the *Denver Post*, 5/31/05: A-1). The number remains so high in part because past legislation has had little impact on the flow. Illegal immigration results from both push and pull factors. U.S. policymakers can do little in their policy-making to reduce the pressure to emigrate caused by push factors. And the U.S. borders, with over 2,000 miles in the south with Mexico and over 4,000 miles to the north with Canada, are very porous and easy to penetrate by illegal aliens, many coming across with the aid of "coyotes"—human smugglers.

This continued influx of both legal and illegal immigration from Latin America, coupled with their higher birth rates, has a profound effect on the demographics of the United States. A recent U.S. Census Bureau study reported that one of every seven people in the United States is now of Latino heritage. Now the nation's largest minority group, Latinos accounted for one-half of the overall population growth of 2.9 million between 2003 and 2004. The Census Bureau estimates there were 41.3 million Latinos in the United States as of July, 2004, with the Asian population growth running a close second. Most immigrants to the United States arrive while in their twenties, and thus are people more likely to have children than is the average white population here. A far greater percentage of whites than Latinos are sixty-five years old or older. The opposite is true among those under eighteen years of age. The Latino growth rate from July 2003 to July 2004 was 3.6 percent. The overall population growth was but 1 percent. Asian growth rate in the same year was 3.4 percent, compared to 1.3 percent for black Americans and only 0.8 percent for whites. That meant that as of July 2004, the population of the United States was estimated at 294 million with the following racial and ethnic breakdown: 240 million whites, 39.2 million blacks, 14 million Asians, 4.4 million native Americans and Alaskans, 980,000 native Hawaiins and other islanders; with 4.4 million listing themselves as having more than one race. The bureau estimates that by the year 2050 whites and minorities will be of equal size. While some consider these demographics a serious problem, Lewis Goodman of American University and an expert on U.S–Latin American relations points out that the increased fertility among the young Latino and Asian population makes for a more sustaining social structure for economic production and enables older people in the culture to have their retirements continue to be financed (*The Denver Post*, 6/09/05: A-2).

The United States has something of a schizophrenic attitude toward immigration, particularly illegal or undocumented immigration. While public opinion surveys report high rates of approval to crack down on illegal immigration, when asked if "family reunification" should be a major part of immigration policy, nearly equally high numbers support that idea.

> The relevance of the "profamily" political rhetoric is that it struck at the Achilles heel of the restrictionist argument. Virtually all public opinion polls show that most Americans want to decrease immigration, and they agree with restrictionists that immigrants burden the social welfare system, displace American workers, and balkanize the country. Yet . . . most Americans are lenient when it comes to family reunification. Because the family enjoys a sacrosanct position in the hearts of Americans, most people want the families of all ethnicities to be reunited. Indeed, people are more likely to support visas for family reunification than for business/economic reasons or for refugees (Lee, 1998: 134).

Moreover, the social and economic impacts of the demographic shifts noted earlier may be surprising to the general public. Numerous studies have shown, for example, that the mere presence of immigrants in the economy results in a net gain in tax revenue, both federal and local, as well as overall spending in consumption. Their presence creates jobs for American workers and does not seem to be related to a rise in unemployment. Foreign workers are, however, more susceptible to wage and employment exploitation. They are imported and repatriated in times of high unemployment, and they serve as scapegoats during periods of economic crisis (Magana: 7).

The two major political parties are split on questions of immigration, both legal and illegal. Republicans usually are less united than Democrats on the issue and a slight majority of Republicans in Congress voted to restrict immigration. Democrats are more united and are more likely to favor immigration and amnesty-type proposals. The current high levels of immigration, legal and illegal, can be partly attributed to labor unions and state governments refraining from strenuously lobbying against immigration. Their position strengthened the political clout of the proimmigration forces (Lee: 122). The post-1965 era of liberal immigration policy can be attributed to an unusual but powerful Left–Right interest group coalition. The coalescing of conservatives and liberals was facilitated by two major developments in recent decades: the civil rights movement and the ascendancy of conservative economics in a globalized economy, which empowered ethnic groups and strengthened Republican support for immigration, respectively (Lee: 122).

Since September 11, the federal government has been pressuring state and local law enforcement agencies toward taking more of a role in immigration enforcement. While a few departments have obliged, many are reluctant to do so. The costs to local departments can be significant. In order to avoid civil rights lawsuits, local officers need to receive special training. Being in the United States illegally is a civil violation and historically the purview of federal immigration officials. Many local departments have policies and procedures on their books prohibiting officers from checking the immigration status of people they pull over. There is also a concern that local officers, in questioning persons suspected of being illegal, may be charged with racial profiling. There is also the question of whether or not federal immigration officers will show up if persons are detained and the local police call them. In New Ipswich, New Hampshire, failure to do so has resulted in the police chief charging undocumented immigrants with tresspassing and being in his city unlawfully. Immigration and Customs Enforcement (ICE) is stretched thin. For example, only 200 agents cover all of Colorado, Idaho, Montana, and Wyoming. They are responsible, as well, for more than immigration control matters—for instance, child pornography, money laundering, and narcotics smuggling. With undocumented immigrants estimated at over 10 million, and climbing, ICE often finds itself at loggerheads. Their failure or inability to respond when local departments do call regarding apprehended illegal aliens contribute to the problems localities have with increasing their involvement. They often lack the funds, their officers lack the training, and they lack the detention facilities to keep those held for much longer than overnight. Anything longer than that becomes onerous. Los Angeles and Orange County California have reached agreements with federal agencies on getting training for their officers and will begin to catch illegal immigrants with criminal convictions, and will begin reviewing the citizenship status of inmates and those being held for criminal investigations for felony crimes. Florida and Alabama have entered into agreements with the federal government to train members of their state patrols to identify and detain undocumented drivers. Several bills have been proposed in Congress that would force local governments to enforce civil immigration laws, but have been unsuccessful so far in part because groups like the National League of Cities have lobbied against such proposals as being unfunded mandates for cities and that they would divert local resources to federal obligations (Crummy, 2005: A-12).

There are similar divisions with respect to guest worker programs and the granting of driver's licenses to undocumented aliens. Some hold that guest worker programs would be beneficial in decreasing illegal immigration and allowing those currently here to come forward from the shadows and the underground economy if they could work here legally. Some argue that creating a program to legalize them would help homeland security by allowing law enforcement agencies to concentrate on border security and tracking down criminals and potential terrorists instead of chasing after millions of ordinary undocumented aliens, especially Hispanics, who are here simply to find work. Proponents of guest worker programs point to serious studies that show that immigrants are a net asset to the country, taking menial jobs that American workers will not take, and paying taxes. When they work illegally, they are subject to exploitation by unscrupulous employers (Kondrake: Metro 5).

While millions of Mexicans here in the United States send billions of dollars back home, studies have shown that it all comes back to the U.S. economy. Money transfers, called remittances, are expected to total $19.5 billion by the end of 2005, surpassing foreign investment as the second most important source of revenue for Mexico after oil. But all remittances return to the United States every year, plus a few billion more. Remittances become the main source of income for many Mexican families. These monies contribute to an increase in the economic well-being of Mexico's poor and working class who then buy more consumer goods from the United States.

Restrictionist charge that such guest worker programs constitute an amnesty that simply encourages illegal immigration. House Judiciary Chairman Jim Sensenbrenner (R-Wis) is sponsoring a measure that would bar states from giving driver's licenses to illegal aliens, arguing that because some of the September 11, 2001 terrorists gained access to aircraft using driver's licenses as identification, all illegal aliens should be denied them. The measure, called the Real ID Act was passed recently in the House of Representatives by a vote of 261-161. The act allows completion of a fence along the U.S–Mexican border south of San Diego, California by waiving environmental hurdles. Currently, ten states do not require proof of citizenship or legal residency by license applicants: Hawaii, Maryland, Michigan, Montana, New Mexico, North Carolina, Oregon, Washington, Wisconsin, and Utah. Tennessee issues "driving certificates" to people who cannot prove that they are legal residents. The Bush administration supports the bill, but it faces stiff opposition in the U.S. Senate and draws criticism from Mexico and among many Democrats who view it simply as "a backdoor effort to impose immigration restriction." Proponents argue that the act addresses recommendations of the September 11 commission and implements a common-sense reform to strengthen border security and better protect the homeland by disrupting terrorist travel, containing important border and document security provisions crucial to interrupting terrorist travel by implementing much-needed driver's license reforms, and closing loopholes in the asylum system (Rep. Bob Beauprez, R-Colorado, in *The Denver Post*, 2/19/2005: 12-C; and 2/11/2005: A-2). Opponents of the act, such as Rep. Mark Udall, D-Colorado, charge it has serious constitutional issues, that it raises the bar for persons seeking asylum from religious and political persecution, and grants to the Secretary of Homeland Security unprecedented powers to circumvent the judicial branch in matters pertaining to border security. They fear that rather than closing the door to those who would exploit our asylum laws to do us harm, it more likely will close the door on real refugees fleeing political and religious persecution precisely when we need allies in the fight against international terrorism. Passage of the Real ID Act, they claim, would make America less popular and sympathetic in the world, something we can ill-afford at this time. It is also opposed by the National Governors Association and the National Conference of State Legislatures for its top–down approach and unfunded mandate aspects.

Building a fence near San Diego has the effect of inducing undocumented immigrants to try crossing elsewhere—through Arizona, Texas, and New Mexico, for example, where the climate and terrain can be much more dangerous and has led to a number of deaths. A recent notorious incident highlights that impact. A smuggler bringing seventy-four people across Texas in an eighteen-wheeler, having charged them $7000 each, lost its refrigeration. Tempuratures reached an estimated 173 degrees in the back of the truck. Seventeen people, including a five-year-old boy, died in the trailer and two others died later, marking it as the deadliest human-smuggling attempt in U.S. history (*The Denver Post*, 3/25/2005: A-1, 16).

Vigilante Groups and State Emergency Declarations

The flood of illegal immigration across the southern borders, has inspired some citizens to act as do-it-yourself immigration enforcers. A number of vigilante groups have become activists patrolling the borders for migrants. Groups like the American Border Patrol, Ranch Rescue, the Minuteman Project, and the Colorado Minutemen have begun patrolling the deserts of Texas, New Mexico, and Arizona and claim that they only seek to report migrants to the U.S. Border Patrol. But the groups use high-tech equipments such as home-made drones, sophisticated listening devices, and at least sixteen light aircrafts. A proimmigrant group in Tuscon, Border Action Network, argues that this is an inherently dangerous mix—people motivated by racism and xenophobia clashing with undocumented immigrants. The Arizona desert has become the main entry crossing point for illegals, accounting for more than half of the 1.1 million border crossers apprehended in 2004. For the vigilante groups, the 350-mile Arizona–Mexico border has become the very symbol of the government's lack of enforcement of the country's borders and immigration laws. One such vigilante estimated he will spend $1,500 for his time in the desert, including the price of night-vision equipment, a directional microphone, and body armor capable of withstanding a round fired from an AK-47 assault rifle. The Minuteman Project has been highlighted by the Aryan Nation websight, and the National Alliance, a neo-Nazi organization, has been handing out flyers in support of the movement (*The Denver Post*, 3/31/2005: A-6).

The situation in the border states of Arizona and New Mexico has become critical enough that their governors have declared a state of emergency. Governor Bill Richardson (D-NM) declared such in four New Mexican border counties crippled by the burgeoning effects of illegal immigrants. He called for national reform. His executive order declares that the four counties "are devastated by the ravages and terror of human smuggling, drug smuggling, kidnapping, murder, destruction of property and death of livestock." His order frees up $750,000 in state emergency funding and the governor pledged an extra $1 million in aid. He cited the total inaction and lack of resources from the federal government and the Congress. Part of the money will be used to build and staff a field office for the New Mexico Office of Homeland Security. By linking immigration to homeland security, Richardson is attempting to at least partially reframe the debate over America's borders, given the thousands of illegal aliens who cross the border each year. Near the city of Columbus, New Mexico, 300,000 undocumented immigrants were apprehended in 2004. In July 2005, someone shot at the Columbus police chief, and area ranchers witnessed the attempted kidnapping of three female undocumented immigrants by three masked and armed men on his ranch land. Governor Jane Napolitano (D-Ariz) declared a state of emergency in Arizona's border counties, pledging $1.5 million in aid for extra sheriffs' deputies and other officers, overtime costs, and more equipment.

The immigration issue rose to a near boiling point and Governor Richardson's voice added weight to the issue in that as an Hispanic, a Democrat, and a possible vice-presidential or even presidential candidate in 2008, his is an important addition to the calls for immigration reform. Representative Tom Tancredo (R-Colorado), an ultra-Conservative Republican who is a leading voice for immigration restriction and illegal immigration reform and also testing the waters for a possible presidential candidacy in 2008, praised the governors' declaration and chided President Bush and the administration to get serious about border security (*The Denver Post*, 9/16/2005: 6-B).

The Americans for Immigration Control, Inc. (AIC) launched a state-by-state campaign seeking to enact legislation that would reverse the trend to ever-increasing levels of immigration to the United States. Their focus is to build public awareness in every state in order to restore, in their words, traditional limits on America's immigration policy. Using "surveys," talk-radio, newspapers, and television stations across the country, they are attempting to gain support for an "immigration moratorium" that would cease *all* immigration for a three- to five-year period. They hold this as necessary to give the current immigrant population time to assimilate and for the Border Patrol

(ICE) the opportunity to regain control over the borders. In any event, they advocate cutting legal immigration to no more than 300,000 per year.

Representative Tom Tancredo (R-Col), chairman of the Congressional Immigration Reform Caucus, and organizer of an anti-immigration group, *Citizen Outreach*, bewailed the porous nature of our borders that allowed terrorists, drug smugglers, and criminals to cross into the United States completely undetected. He noted that an estimated 300,000 people who have been ordered deported remain in the United States because their deportation orders were not enforced, despite the ICE having spent $31.2 million on a computer tracking system to track whether visa holders overstay their visas. The system, he states, does not work and the DHS is asking for $57 million more to fix it. Tancredo calls for: eliminating local level "sanctuary policies," quick processing and deportation of apprehended illegals, an end to nonemergency public assistance for illegals, the abolishment of discounted tuition for illegal aliens, and a bar to states to issue driver's licenses for illegal aliens (Citizen Outreach Flyer, August 2005).

Civil Liberties versus National Safety

A value conflict at issue in national security policy and immigration policy-making involves striking a balance between civil liberty on the one hand and national safety on the other. Loss of civil liberties due to the fight against international terrorism most often focuses upon the powers granted to the federal government by and the way it is implementing The USA Patriot Act and the DHS Act. Congress renewed the Patriot Act by enacting the Domestic Security Enforcement Act, referred to as the Patriot Act II. Battle lines were drawn over its counterterrorism powers by an unlikely coalition of liberal civil rights groups and conservative libertarians, gun-rights supporters and medical privacy advocates. Led by former Republican Congressman Bob Barr, who had voted for the USA Patriot Act but has since become a sharp critic, the new coalition, called Patriots to Restore Checks and Balances, joined conservative groups, such as the American Conservative Union, the Center for Privacy and Technology Policy, and Free Congress, with the American Civil Liberties Union, the American Librarians Association, and so on. The nationwide grassroots coalition claims that 383 communities and seven states have enacted anti-Patriot Act laws, called "civil liberties safe zones," and have pressurized Congress to amend the law. The coalition focused on efforts to urge Congress to scale back in particular three provisions of the law: one that allows federal agents to conduct "sneak and peek" searches without notification; one that demands records from institutions, such as libraries and medical offices, and one that uses a sweepingly broad definition of terrorism in pursuing suspects (*The Denver Post*, 3/23/05).

Critics argue that the approach of the USA Patriot Act to fighting the war on terrorism domestically involves a cure that is worse than the disease.

Three principles in particular should guide our response to the threat of terrorism. First, we should not overreact in a time of fear, a mistake we have made
all too often in the past. Second, we should not sacrifice the bedrock foundations
of our constitutional democracy—political freedom and equal treatment—absent
a compelling showing of need and adoption of narrowly tailored means. And
third, balancing liberty and security, we should not succumb to the temptation to
trade a vulnerable minority's liberties, namely, the liberties of immigrants in general, or Arab and Muslim immigrants in particular, for the security for the rest of
us . . . The USA Patriot Act violates all three of those principles (David Cole, cited
in Etzioni and Marsch, 2003: 35).

Proponents of the primacy of the public safety value, in contrast, argue that
foreign citizens in our midst have no entitlement to enter or to remain here,
and that prudence dictated measures that did not curb the civil liberties of
citizens but merely changed the terms under which we allowed guests from
overseas to remain in the United States.

It would be unfortunate if, in our effort to prevent another 3,000 American
deaths—or 30,000 or 300,000—we were inadvertently to deport some foreign
citizens who pose no threat to us. But their presence here is a privilege we grant,
not a right they have exercised, and we may withdraw that privilege for any
reason (Mark Krikorean, in Etzioni and March: 33–34).

Advocates for passage of Patriot Act II argued that the separation of powers
was impeding the ability of the government to capture terrorists and that is
why the law was changed. They pointed to the break-up of the alleged cell in
Portland, Oregon. Then Attorney General John Ashcroft credited the act's elimination of the wall of separation as critical in allowing all the dots to be
connected, and criminal charges to be fully developed in the case against the
so-called "Portland Six," launched when a deputy sheriff in rural Washington
state spotted a group of Middle Eastern men with a cache of automatic weapons
target-shooting at a gravel pit and called the FBI (*Los Angeles Times*, September
2, 2003: A-15).

Critics counter by pointing to an October 2004 raid by the FBI on the offices
of a small charity called the Islamic-American Relief Agency (IARA). Its attorney stated the charity was effectively shut down under a little-known provision of the Patriot Act that expanded the International Emergency Economic
Powers Act to allow the government to seize the assets of organizations while
it investigates for links to terrorism. The government has not presented one
shred of evidence linking IARA to funding for terror, but by seizing their funds
and interviewing their donors, they have effectively destroyed the charity and
created a chilling effect in the Muslim community in Columbia (Lindorff,
"Patriot Act II?": 1). Akeel states the government may have confused IARA,
founded two decades ago as the Islamic African Relief Agency and which
changed its name during the Bosnia conflict when demands for aid expanded

beyond the Africa focus, with a Sudan-based charity called the Islamic African Relief Agency, which the U.S. government claims has links to terrorists. The targeting, some charge it as racial profiling, of some minorities who become "suspect" merely because of their looks or names is of particular concern to the civil libertarians. They note the unfortunate slaying by police in London of a Latin American who was mistakenly shot in the head and killed after the London bombings apparently simply because he looked Middle Eastern and did not stop when challenged by the police. They also look skeptically at programs like the Total Information Awareness (TIA) Project of the Department of Defense, which focuses on people who speak certain languages—Afghanese languages, Arabic, Farsi, Korean, and Mandarin (Torr: 61).

The federal government's reluctance to give out information of the implementation of the USA Patriot Act, as well as stealthy actions to expand its powers have further raised civil liberty concerns. For example, on December 13, when U.S. forces captured Saddam Hussein and public attention was focused on that development, President Bush signed into law a dramatic expansion of the USA Patriot Act's powers.

The Bush administration and its Congressional allies tucked away these new executive powers in the Intelligence Authorization Act for Fiscal Year 2004, a legislative behemoth that funds all the intelligence activities of the federal government. The Act included a simple, yet insidious, redefinition of "financial institution," which previously referred to banks, but now includes stockbrokers, car dealerships, casinos, credit card companies, insurance agencies, jewelers, airlines, the U.S. Post Office, and any other business "whose cash transactions have a high degree of usefulness in criminal, tax, or regulatory matters (Martin, "With a Whisper, Not a Bang": 1).

The federal government is also using its expanded "expedited removal" powers to deport illegal aliens convicted of a crime. During FY 2004, U.S. Immigration and Customs Enforcement (ICE) deported a record 157,281 immigrants, more than half of which had criminal records, a reflection on its emphasis on booting out such people from the country. ICE agents have swept up a record number of undocumented immigrants whose sole crime involves violation of visa limits or related immigration laws. This campaign boosted the total number of deportations by more than 45% from 2001 to 2004. About 70 percent of those deported returned to Mexico, while most of the rest were sent back to Central or South America and the Dominican Republic. In 2004, ICE used four jets it owns and operates to make 317 flights that returned more than 18,500 immigrants to their native countries. Those deportations are but a small faction of the 8 million illegal immigrants that the ICE estimates are in the country. Most, of course, are unknown to U.S. immigration officials and only those who are caught or otherwise reveal themselves, for example, by committing crimes, applying for asylum or seeking government benefits, become targets of the ICE for deportation. Despite the record numbers of deportations, the DHS struggles to reduce the number of illegal aliens who have disobeyed orders to leave the country or have failed to appear at deportation hearings. That number has remained at about 400,000 because new illegal immigrants continue to flow into the United States, particularly along the southwest border, and illegal aliens continue to defy orders to appear at deportation hearings. Agents also track noncitizens who are serving time for serious crimes and bring their cases to a immigration judge. If the judge orders them to be deported, they can be sent to their home country as soon as they are released from prison (http://www.aolsvc.news.aol.com/news/article.adp? accessed 2/17/05).

Among the 400,000 persons ordered out of the country who continue to defy those orders and remain here, some are from countries known to harbor terrorists. Conservative Republicans are skeptical about creating any guest worker program or the granting of amnesty until substantial progress is made to boost enforcement. From the homeland security perspective, the threat of those ordered to be deported, however, may be small. A 2003 staff report of the September 11 commission noted that only 5,000 of the 400,000 were from countries with ties to al Qaeda. And of the 1,100 people from that group captured in the program's first year, none were charged with terrorism-related offenses (*The Denver Post,* 1/16/05: A-15).

CURRENT CONGRESSIONAL PROPOSALS

Virtually all of these issues and concerns over national security and immigration policy-making are addressed in dozens of bills currently before the U.S. Congress. Some of the major such proposals are discussed here. They focus on guest-worker programs, identification programs, financial aid to immigrant students, border security enhancement, a congressional reapportionment amendment, a proposal to encourage state and local law enforcement agencies to become involved in immigration law enforcement, and a proposal to end the "visa lottery" provision in current law. These proposals, like the struggle to balance national security and immigration policy-making, often take dramatically different approaches to the problems and issues discussed here. Immigration reform is among the most ticklish and difficult tasks facing Congress, with social and economic ramifications along with diplomatic and domestic security impacts.

Guest-Worker Proposals

In order for immigration reform legislation to pass the Congress, a comprehensive bill would seem to need three essential components: a guest-worker program pairing willing employers with willing employees; a new and more punitive round of criminal penalties for employers who knowingly hire illegal aliens; and a tamper-proof identification card.

There are a number of bills likely to receive serious attention by the Congress that deal with what is referred to as a guest-worker program. The

Comprehensive Enforcement and Immigration Reform Act of 2005 is a temporary worker program bill proposed by Senators Jon Kyle (R-Ariz) and John Cornyn (R-TX). It would establish a new visa category to allow foreign workers to enter the United States to work temporarily (up to two years). Workers could reapply to participate for a total of six years (*The Denver Post*, Tuesday, August 9, 2005: 7-B).

Another bill on the topic likely to have even greater consideration is the McCain-Kennedy bill. Sponsored by Senators John McCain (R-Ariz) and Ted Kennedy (D-Mass), the "odd-duck" sponsorship represents a need to forge a broad consensus and is basically in synchrony with many of the ideas for immigration reform floated by President Bush. That increases the bill's likelihood of successful passage. The bill proposes legitimizing (an euphemism for an amnesty program) the status of illegal workers currently working in the United States. It would require them to pay a $2,000 fine, as well as back taxes, and pass criminal background checks and medical exams. These immigrants could then apply for three-year guest-worker visas (without having to first return to their country of origin), renewable once. After six years, they would be eligible to apply for permanent resident status for themselves and their families, and after an additional five years, could then apply for U.S. citizenship. McCain-Kennedy would allow U.S. employers to hire up to 400,000 workers the first year, upon showing that no residents would take the jobs, eventually qualifying for permanent resident status. Despite its bipartisan support, it faces an uphill battle on both sides of the aisle. Republicans tend to oppose its amnesty provision while favoring its guest-worker provisions. In sharp contrast, Democrats favor an amnesty program, but fear the guest-worker program will simply result in cheap labor that will depress domestic wages.

The Bush administration favors a guest-worker bill as well. As originally drafted, the temporary workers would allow foreign citizens to apply for work permits good for one year that could be renewed (for up to six years). At the end of three years the person would have to return to his or her country of origin, but could apply for a visa under improved status. Subsequently, the White House has let it be known in Congress that President Bush would accept a revision not requiring the return to the country of origin.

Representative Tom Tancredo (R-CO) is sponsoring legislation that would allow guest workers for a finite period to fill jobs for which there are no American workers. It would reduce legal immigration to 300,000. It calls for a secure border utilizing the U.S. military until the U.S. Border Patrol is up to full strength. It strengthens penalties for immigration law violations by employers. Although his bill went no where in 2003–2004, he has been campaigning nationally using his Team America, a political action group he founded, and is gearing up for a possible presidential candidacy in 2008. Although he was only elected to the Congress in 1998, and has a reputation as a maverick in the Congress, his growing national reputation and visibility on the immigration issue and his possible presidential run could give him added clout in the new

Congress. His appeal to nativist groups on the threat of the "balkanization" of the United States and the "dire threat of multiculturalism" has given him wide appeal in the public.

All the proposals to establish some sort of a guest-worker program face the hurdle of their being characterized as a return to the disasterous "Bracero program" of the 1940s and 1950s, which had a notorious reputation for human rights abuses, exploitation of the workers, and resulting in an enormous incentive for illegal immigration once the program ended. Critics of the approach maintain there is no such thing as "temporary" workers; that these proposed programs would effectively expand permanent legal immigration by the hundreds of thousands. Moreover, guest workers, when here legally and having children, would add to the number of citizens who were "native-born," and they, on becoming legal resident aliens or citizens, would draw additionally higher numbers of family members who would qualify for legal immigration under the family reunification preferences.

Other Proposals

Representative James Sensenbrenner, Jr. (R-WIS) is the sponsor of the Real ID Act, which claims to be an antiterrorist measure, but it has elements that are intended to have an impact on illegal immigration. It passed the House in 2005. It passed again and if it also were passed in the Senate, the bill would set new federal standards for driver's licenses. If states opted not to adopt the federal standards, licenses from those states could not be used for federal identification purposes, such as boarding an airplane. The measure would also require people applying for a driver's license to prove their citizenship or legal resident status. It requires driver's licenses for foreigners to expire on the same day as their temporary visas expire, and such date would be displayed on the card. It would make it easier for the government to deny entry to foreigners and to deport those in the country by broadening the definition of "terrorist activity." Giving any kind of support to a terrorist organization would constitute a terrorist activity, and that could be applied retroactively to any one who gives support now to an organization deemed a terrorist group by the Department of State in the future. The measure allows the Secretary of Homeland Security to waive any local laws that would impede the building of physical barriers (fences) along U.S. borders. Finally, it tightens definitions for asylum by requiring applicants to prove through a police report or other means that they are victims of persecution.

Representative Candice Miller (R-MI) has proposed a bill for a constitutional amendment that requires congressional districts to be apportioned on the basis of resident citizens. Currently, illegal aliens and other noncitizens are counted in the population for the purpose of apportionment. The current arrangement takes representation in Congress away from states with small populations of illegal aliens and increases representation from states with large illegal populations. Language in the Constitution specifies apportionment on the basis of "persons." Representative Miller's amendment would replace "person" with "citizen."

Representative Charles Norwood (R-GA) introduced a bill, the CLEAR Act (H.R. 3137) that encourages local and state police agencies to become involved in immigration law enforcement. In 2004, his measure was co-sponsored by 125 legislators. While promoting local and state cooperation with the federal government to enforce immigration laws, it would require federal reimbursement to the localities for the costs of their efforts. It further contains a provision that increases the civil penalties against foreigners who reside illegally in the United States.

Representative Bob Goodlatte (R-VA) introduced a bill (H.R. 1219) that ends the "visa lottery." This program (from the IMMACT of 1990) admits 55,000 immigrants per year on the basis of a random lottery drawing. The lottery provision requires no skills or abilities. It allows for illegal immigrants residing in the United States to participate in the lottery. The Inspector General of the State Department reported that the visa lottery "poses significant threats to national security from entry of hostile intelligence officers, criminals and terrorists."

In sharp contrast to these measures that increase restrictions or are aimed at national security and the international terrorism threat directly, Senators Orrin Hatch (R-Utah) and Richard Durbin (D-Ill) have introduced a bill in 2003, 2004, and 2005 that will likely be reintroduced again. This measure would allow universities that receive federal funding to provide financial aid to illegal immigrants; and would allow immigrant students "of good moral character" to apply for legal residency.

CLOSING THOUGHTS

If the past 200 years of U.S. history with respect to immigration policy and national security issues reviewed here are any guide to the future, than we can expect that both policy areas will remain on the front burner of the policy agenda of the U.S. Congress and of political party and interest group leaders for at least the remainder of this first decade of the twenty-first century. But we can anticipate, as well, that there will be pressures building toward yet another shift by the end of the second decade. Perhaps such pressures will be associated with the election of a new president, more likely from the Democratic Party, who is of Hispanic-American descent and who will thus be politically more able to lead the way toward some new direction. The current high level of fear of Arab and Muslim Americans will more likely decrease in a decade or two. Perhaps by the end of his second term, President Bush will again declare victory in Iraq (Mission Accomplished) and bring the troops home. By the end of 2010, the war on "international terrorism" may be declared won. Such developments would ease pressure for restrictionist immigration policy. The currently weak recovery of the U.S. economy might strengthen considerably as well, indicating an increased need for an expanded labor force with the talents that immigrants can bring to it. The Social Security crisis might well justify increased immigrant laborers (legal or temporary) who would pay into the system and likely not draw on it ever or for decades at least.

Of course, no scholar of national security or of immigration policy can predict exactly when such a shift in policy direction may occur, nor what the precise nature of that shift might entail. But, this examination of more than 200 years of U.S. policy-making surely argues that such a shift will come. This review of immigration policy-making and its inherent nexus with national security concerns and issues demonstrates a relatively constant struggle with the immigration process and its periodic or cyclical attempts to achieve a politically acceptable balance to procedural justice with respect to immigration. Which of the four basic elements underlying immigration policy will come to the fore in the next decade or two? One cannot now say which one, but one can predict that a new balance among those four underlying elements will be sought and enacted, ushering in some new direction in immigration policy-making. Given the current heavy emphasis upon national security matters, it is likely to be in a direction that downplays those concerns in favor of another element, although national security concerns will always be part of the mix in any balanced immigration policy.

New groups and new political coalitions will gain new power as others lose some of their power, and the new coalitions will assert that political power in the arena of immigration policy-making. As in the past decades, it will be the interplay among such groups that will demonstrate in the 2020s and 2030s how wide open or how closed will be the doors to the United States, and how, who, and how many of outsiders we allow to enter the United States will impact our sense of national identity and national security.

After this chapter is a selected bibliography identifying the copious sources used in writing this volume. Finally, a section "About the Author" briefly describes the academic and past scholarly work of the author as demonstration of his qualifications to write this comprehensive study of the nexus of national security concerns and their intertwining with U.S. immigration policy-making during the past 200 years.

Glossary

Adjustment to Immigrant Status a procedure whereby a nonimmigrant may apply for a change of status to a lawful permanent resident if an immigrant visa is available for his or her country. The alien is counted as an immigrant as of the date of adjustment.

Alien a person who is not a citizen or a national of a given nation-state.

Amicus curiae a "friend of the court" legal brief submitted by a state or an interest group that is not a party to a case but which has an interest in the outcome of the case in which it argues its position on the case.

Amnesty the granting of legal relief or pardon; in Immigration Reform and Control Act (IRCA), granting legal temporary resident status to a previously illegal (undocumented) alien.

Asia-Pacific Triangle an area encompassing countries and colonies from Afghanistan to Japan and south to Indonesia and the Pacific Islands. Immigration from the area was severely limited to small quotas established in the McCarran-Walter Act (1953). The Asian-Pacific Triangle replaced the Asiatic Barred Zone.

Asiatic Barred Zone established by the Immigration Act of 1917, it designated a region from which few natives could enter the United States.

Asylee a person in the United States who is unable or unwilling to return to his/her country of origin because of persecution or fear of persecution. The person is eligible to become a permanent resident after one year of continuous residence in the United States.

Asylum the granting of temporary legal entrance to an individual who is an asylee.

Border card a card allowing a person living within a certain zone of the U.S. border to legally cross back and forth for employment purposes without a passport or visa.

Border patrol the law enforcement arm of the Immigration and Naturalization Service.

Bracero program a temporary farm worker program that allowed, from 1942 to 1964, migrant farm workers to come to the United States for up to nine months annually to work in agriculture.

Certiorari a writ issued by the U.S. Supreme Court to send up for its review, upon appeal, the records of a lower court case.

Cuban-Haitian entrant status-accorded Cubans who entered the United States illegally between April 15, 1980 and October 10, 1980, and Haitians who entered illegally before January 1, 1981. Those who were in residence continuously for one year were allowed to adjust their status to legal immigrants by the IRCA of 1986.

Debarkation leaving a ship or airplane to enter the United States.

Deportation a legal process by which a nation sends an individual back to their country of origin after refusing them legal residence.

Diversity immigrants a special category of immigrants established by the 1990 IMMACT to allow a certain number of visas to be issued to immigrants from countries, which previously had low admission numbers.

Due process of law the constitutional limitation on governmental behavior to deal with an individual according to prescribed rules and procedures.

Emigrant an individual who voluntarily leaves his/her country of birth for permanent resettlement elsewhere.

Emigration the act of leaving one's place of origin or birth for permanent resettlement.

Employer sanctions a restrictive device of IRCA, it imposes penalties (fines or imprisonment, or both) for knowingly hiring an illegal immigrant.

Equal protection of the law the Constitution guaranteed right that all persons be treated the same before the law.

Escapee an individual fleeing persecution from a (Communist or Communist-dominated) government usually for racial, religious, ethnic, social organization, or political opinion reasons.

Eugenics a pseudoscientific theory of racial genetics.

EWIs entered without inspection—another term for undocumented or illegal aliens, those who came without proper documentation or a visa.

Excluded categories a listing in immigration law of those persons specifically denied entrance to the United States for stated reasons for the purpose of permanent settlement.

Exclusion the denial of legal entrance to a sovereign territory.

Exempt an individual or class or category of individuals to whom a certain provision of the law does not apply.

Expulsion the decision of a sovereign nation to legally compel an individual to leave permanently its territory.

Green card a document issued by the INS that certifies an individual as a legal immigrant entitled to work in the United States.

Guest worker program a program enabling the legal importation of workers for temporary labor in specified occupations.

Identity papers legal documents recognized by government as establishing a person's identity.

Illegal alien an individual who is in a territory without the documentation permitting permanent residence.

Immediate relatives in recent immigration law, spouses, minor children, parents (of a citizen or resident alien over twenty-one years of age), and brothers or sisters of a U.S. citizen or permanent resident alien.

Immigrant an alien admitted to the United States as a lawful permanent resident.

Investor immigrant an individual permitted to immigrate based upon a promise to invest $1 million in an urban area or $500,000 in a rural area to create at least ten new jobs.

Legalized alien an alien lawfully admitted for temporary or permanent residence under the Immigration and Nationality Act of 1965 or under the IRCA of 1986.

Literacy test a device imposed upon immigrants by the 1917 immigration act to restrict immigration to persons who are able to read and write.

Mortgaging the legal device to "borrow" against future fiscal year immigration quotas to allow entrance of immigrants, for refugee or humanitarian purposes, after their national origin fiscal quota had been filled.

Naturalization the legal act of making an individual a citizen who was not born a citizen.

Net EWIs estimates of the total number from each country who entered without inspection and established residency in the United States, a large majority of whom are from Mexico. Net EWIs are computed by adjusting the count of undernumerated aliens and subtracting the estimated legal resident population and subtracting the estimated number of visa overstays.

NGOs nongovernmental organizations. Term used to refer to organizations involved in immigration matters, usually advocacy or immigrant assistance, which are not government agencies.

Nonimmigrant an alien seeking temporary entry into the United States for a specific purpose other than permanent settlement—such as a foreign government official, tourist, student, temporary worker, or cultural exchange visitor.

Nonpreference a category of immigrant visas apart from family and employment-based preferences that was available primarily between 1966 and 1978, but eliminated by the Immigration Act of 1990.

Nonquota immigrant people allowed entrance by specific reason who were not charged against a nation's annual quota.

Pacific Triangle an area in Southeast Asia from which immigration was specifically excluded during most of the quota era that was ended by a provision of the McCarran-Walter Act (1952).

Parolee an alien, appearing to be inadmissible to the inspecting officer, allowed to enter the United States under urgent humanitarian reasons or when that alien's entry is determined to be for significant public benefit.

Passport a legal identification document issued by a sovereign nation-state attesting to the nationality of an individual for international travel purposes.

Permanent resident a noncitizen who is allowed to live permanently in the United States and who can travel in and out of the country without a visa and can work without restriction. This person also is permitted to accumulate time toward becoming a citizen.

Preferences specific categories of individuals to be awarded visas for permanent immigration.

Preference system a device used in immigration law to establish rules and procedures to determine the order in which annual limits of immigration visas were to be issued.

Protocol an international agreement governing the understanding and procedures that Member States who are parties to a treaty agree upon for a given purpose, as in the UN Protocols regarding the status and treatment of refugees.

Pull factor characteristics of a country that attract immigrants for permanent resettlement.

Push factor a reason that compels an individual to emigrate from their nation of origin and seek permanent resettlement elsewhere.

Quota immigrant an individual seeking entrance to the United States or coming under the system that fixed an annual number of visas to be awarded to a person from a particular nation or territory.

Refugee-parolee a qualified applicant for conditional entry between 1970 and 1980 whose application for admission could not be approved because of inadequate numbers of seventh preference visas. The applicant was paroled into the United States under the parole authority granted to the attorney general.

Relocation camps a number of places established by Executive Order for holding Japanese aliens or Japanese-American citizens during World War II on their way to the ten permanent internment camps.

Special Agricultural Workers aliens who performed labor in perishable agricultural crop commodities for a specified period of time and were admitted for temporary and then permanent residence under the IRCA of 1986.

Transit alien an alien in immediate and continuous transit through the United States, with or without a visa. Transit aliens are principally aliens and their families who serve at the UN headquarters and foreign government officials and their family members.

Unauthorized alien an individual who is in a territory without documentation—an illegal immigrant.

Undocumented alien an individual in a sovereign territory without legal authorization to be there—an illegal alien.

Visa a legal document issued by a consular or similar State Department official allowing a person to travel to the United States for either permanent or temporary reasons—such as immigrant, student, tourist, government representative, business, or cultural exchange.

Withdrawal an alien's voluntary removal of an application for admission in lieu of an exclusion hearing before an immigration judge.

Xenophobia an unfounded fear of the foreigner.

Bibliography

Abbey, Sue Wilson. "The Ku Klux Klan in Arizona, 1921–25," *Journal of Arizona History*, 1973, 14(1): 10–30.

Abrams, Elliott and Abrams, Franklin S. "Immigration Policy—Who Gets In and Why?," *Public Interest*, 1975 (38): 3–29.

Adamic, Louis. *Nation of Nations*. New York: Harper and Brothers, 1945.

Aizenman, Nurith C. "A Rude Awakening from the American Dream," *The Washington Post National Weekly Edition* (January 27–February 2, 2003): 29.

Alderstein, Jo Anne Chernev. "Anarchy, Amnesty, and the Demise of the INS," *New Jersey Law Journal*, March 17, 2003, 171(12): 23+.

Aleinkoff, Thomas A. *Immigration and Nationality Laws of the United States*. St. Paul, Minnesota: West Publishing, 1990.

Aleinkoff, T. Alexander and Douglas Klusmeyer, eds. *Citizenship Policies for an Age of Migration*. Washington, D.C.: Brookings Institution Press, 2002.

———. *Citizenship Today: Global Perspectives and Practices*. Washington, D.C.: Brookings Institution Press, 2001.

———. *From Migrants to Citizens: Membership in a Changing World*. Washington, D.C.: Brookings Institution Press, 2000.

"Aliens Become More Diverse Over Decades," *The Washington Post*, Sunday, June 10, 1984: A1, 16.

Allen, Leslie. *Liberty: The Statue and the American Dream*. New York: Statue of Liberty, Ellis Island Foundation, National Geographic Society, 1985.

"Amnesty Program Means Phony Document Business Will Flourish," *The Cumberland Sunday Times*, Sunday, November 2, 1986: A-16.

Anbinder, Tyler. *Nativism and Slavery: The Northern Know Nothings and the Politics of the 1850s*. New York: Oxford University Press, 1992.

Anderson, James. *Public Policy-Making*, 2nd edn. New York: Holt, Rinehart and Winston, 1979.

Andreas, Peter and Timothy Snyder, eds. *The Wall Around the West: State Borders and Immigration Controls in North America and Europe*. Lanham, MD: Rowman and Littlefield, 2000.

Annals of the American Academy of Political and Social Science, 1979, 441: 55–81.

Archdeacon, Thomas. *Becoming Americans: An Ethnic History*. New York: Free Press, 1983.

"A Refugee's Despair," *Newsweek*, November 17, 1986: 12.

"Asian Indians Operating Many U.S. Hotels, Motels," *The Cumberland Times-News*, Thursday, September 12, 1985: 36.

Associated Press. *INS Is Years Behind in Processing Records*, Washington, D.C., August 5, 2002

———. *House Panel Approves Homeland Security Agency*. Washington, D.C., July 20, 2002.

———. *More Seek Citizenship, But Fewer Get It*. Washington, D.C., July 17, 2002.

AuCoin, Les. "Strengthening National Security," *Arms Control Today*, March 2005, 35(2): 4.

Auerbach, Carl A. "Freedom of Movement in International Law and United States Policy," in McNeill and Adams, eds., *Human Migration*. Bloomington, Ind.: Indiana University Press, 1978: 317–335.

Babcock, Kendrick C. *The Scandinavian Element in the United States*. Urbana: University of Illinois Press, 1914.

Bach, Robert L. "Looking Forward: New Approaches to Immigration Law Enforcement," in Lydio Tomasi, ed. *In Defense of the Alien, XXII*. New York: Center for Migration Studies, 2000.

———. "Mexican Immigration and the American State," *International Migration Review*, Winter 1978, 12: 536–558.

Bacon, David. "In the Name of National Security: Bush Declares War on Unions," *The American Prospect*, October 21, 2002, 13 (19): 15–18.

Bailey, Thomas H. *Voices of America*. New York: Free Press, 1976.

Baker, Susan Gonzales. *The Cautious Welcome: The Legalization Program of the Immigration Reform and Control Act*. Santa Monica, CA: Rand Corporation; Washington, D.C.: Urban Institute, 1990.

Balderrama, Francisco E. *In Defense of La Raza: The Los Angeles Mexican Consulate and the Mexican Community, 1929–1936*. Tuscon: University of Arizona Press, 1982.

Balderrama, Francisco E. and Raymond Rodriguez. *Decade of Betrayal: Mexican Repatriation in the 1930s*. Albuquerque: University of New Mexico Press, 1995.

Baldwin, Carl R. *Immigration Questions and Answers*. New York: Allworth Press, 1995.

Banks, R. Richard. "Racial Profiling and Anti-terrorism Efforts," *Cornell Law Review*, July 2004, 89(5): 1201–1218.

Barbour, Scott, ed. *Immigration Policy*. San Diego: Greenhaven Press, 1995.

Barkan, Elliott, ed. *Asian and Pacific Islander Migration to the United States: A Model of New Global Patterns*. Westport, CT: Greenwood, 1992.

———. *And Still They Come: Immigrants and American Society, 1920–1990*. Wheeling, IL: Harlan Davidson, 1996.

———. ed. *A Nation of Peoples: A Sourcebook on America's Multicultural Heritage*. Westport, CT: Greenwood, 1998.

Barringer, Herbert, Robert Gardner, and Michael Levin. *Asians and Pacific Islanders in the United States*. New York: Russell Sage Foundation, 1995.

Baylor, Ronald. *Neighbors in Conflict*. Baltimore, MD: The Johns Hopkins University Press, 1978.

Baum, Dale. "Know Nothingism and the Republican Majority in Massachusetts: The Political Realignment of the 1850s," *Journal of American History*, 1978, 64(4): 959–986.

Beals, Carleton. *Brass Knuckle Crusade.* New York: Hasting House, 1960.

Bean, Frank, Georges Vernez, and Charles B. Keely. *Opening and Closing the Doors.* Santa Monica, CA.: The Rand Corporation; Washington, D.C.: The Urban Institute, 1989.

Bean, Frank B. and Stephanie Bell-Rose, eds. *Immigration and Opportunity: Race, Ethnicity and Employment in the U.S.* New York: Russell Sage Foundation, 1999.

Bean, Frank B., Barry Edmonston, and Jeffrey Passell. *Undocumented Migration to the U.S.* Santa Monica, CA: The Rand Corporation; Washington, D.C.: The Urban Institute, 1990.

Beck, Roy H. *The Case Against Immigration.* New York: Norton, 1996.

Benda, Susan. "The Unfinished Business of Immigration Reform," in Lydio Tomasi, ed., *In Defense of the Alien, XII.* New York: Center for Migration Studies, 1989: 70–72.

Bennett, David. *The Party of Fear: From Nativist Movements to the New Right in American History.* Chapel Hill, NC: University of North Carolina Press, 1988.

Bennett, Douglas C. "The Enforcement of Immigration Policy and the Meaning of Citizenship," Paper delivered at the 1985 Annual Meeting of the APSA, New Orleans, August 29, 1985.

Bennett, Marion. *American Immigration Policies: A History.* Washington, D.C.: Public Affairs Press, 1963.

Bernard, William S., ed. *Immigration Policy: A Reappraisal.* New York: Harper, 1950.

Bertolli, E. Robert and Constantine Forkiokiotis. "Smallpox: Response Team Review," *The Forensic Examiner*, November—December 2003, 12(11): 7–13.

Betten, Neil A. "Nativism and the Klan in Town and City: Valparaiso and Gary, Indiana," *Studies in History and Sociology*, 1973, 4(2): 3–16.

Billington, Ray A. *The Origins of Nativism in the United States, 1800–1844.* New York: Arno Press, 1974.

"Bilingual Education's Dilemmas Persist," *The Washington Post*, Sunday, July 7, 1985: A1, 12–13.

Birkland, Thomas A. "The World Changed Today: Agenda-setting and Policy Change in the Wake of 9/11 Terrorists Attacks," *The Review of Policy Research*, March 2004, 21(2): 179–201.

Bleckman, Barry M. and Stephen S. Kaplan. *Force Without War: U.S. Armed Forces as a Political Instrument.* UBC Press, 2005.

Bleckman, Barry M. and W. Philip Ellis. *The Politics of National Security: Congress and U.S. Defense Policy.* Twentieth Century Fund Book, 1992.

Bleckman, Barry M., William Durch, David Graham, and John Henshaw. *The American Military in the 21st Century.* New York: Palgrave Macmillan, 1993.

Bleda, Sharon E. "Intergenerational Differences in Patterns and Bases of Ethnic Residential Dissimilarity," *Ethnicity*, 1978, 5(2): 91–107.

Bodner, John E. "The Procurement of Immigrant Labor: Selected Documents," *Pennsylvania History*, 1974, 4(2): 189–206.

Boeri, Tito, Gordon H. Hanson, and Barry McCormick, eds. *Immigration Policy and the Welfare State.* New York: Oxford University Press, 2002.

Bogue, Alan G. "United States, the 'New' Political History," *Journal of Contemporary History*, January 1968, 11: 5–27.

Bonacich, Edna. "Advanced Capitalism and Black/White Relations: A Split-Labor Market Interpretation," *American Sociological Review*, February 1976, 41: 34–41.

"Borders and Reason," *Rocky Mountain News/Denver Post*, Saturday, August 20, 2005: C-12, 13.

Borjas, George. "The Economics of Immigration," *Journal of Economic Literature*, 1994, 32: 1667–1717.

————. *Friends and Strangers: The Effect of Immigration on the U.S. Economy*. New York: Basic Books, 1997.

Boulden, Jane and Thomas G. Weiss, eds. *Terrorism and the U.N.: Before and After September 11*. Bloomington: Indiana University Press, 2004.

Bouvier, L.F. *The Impact of Immigration on U.S. Population Size*. Washington, D.C.: Population Reference Bureau, 1981.

Bradley, Carla. "Not Just One Tool in the Toolbox: Utilizing Various Tools to Improve Airport Security," *The Forensic Examiner*, May–June 2003: 20–22.

Breitman, Richard and Alan M. Kraut. *American Refugee Policy and European Jewry, 1933–1945*. Bloomington: Indiana University Press, 1987.

Briggs, Vernon M., Jr. *Mass Immigration and the National Interest*, 2nd edn. Armonk, NY: M.E. Sharpe, 1996.

Briggs, Vernon M. Jr. and Stephen Moore. *Still an Open Door?: U.S. Immigration Policy and the American Economy*. Washington, D.C.: American University Press, 1994.

Broder, David S. (editorial), "Security in the Homeland," *The Washington Post National Weekly Edition*, September 2–8, 2002: 4.

Brown, Cynthia, ed. *Lost Liberties: Ashcroft and the Assault on Personal Freedom*. New York: The New Press, 2003.

Brubaker, William R., ed. *Immigration and the Politics of Citizenship in Europe and North America*. New York: University Press of America; German Marshall Fund of the United States, 1989.

Bryce-LaPorte, R.S., ed. *A Scrapbook on the New Immigration*. New Brunswick, NJ: Transaction Books, 1981.

Brye, David L., ed. *European Immigration and Ethnicity in the United States and Canada: A Historical Bibliography*. Santa Barbara, CA: CLIO Press Inc.,1983.

Burgess, Thomas. *Greeks in America*. Boston: Sherman, French and Co., 1913.

Burke, Jason. "Think Again: Al Qaeda," *Foreign Policy*, May/June 2004.

Burke, John. "The Neutral/Honest Broker Role in Foreign-Policy Decision Making: A Reassessment," *Presidential Studies Quarterly*, June 2005, 35(2): 403–408.

Burke, Melissa Nana. "Homeland Security Nominee Chertoff Long in Law Enforcement Experience," *New Jersey Law Journal*, January 17, 2005.

"Bush Signs Homeland Measure," *The Press Enterprise*. Riverside, CA: November 26, 2002, A-1, A-5.

"Bush Taps Intelligence Chief," *The Denver Post*, Friday, February 18, 2005: 2-A.

Butz, William et al. "Demographic Challenges in America's Future," R-2911-RC. Santa Monica, CA: The Rand Corporation, May 1982: 40pp.

Calavita, Kitty. *Inside the State: The Bracero Program, Immigration, and the INS*. New York: Routledge, 1992.

Camarota, Steve A. *Immigrants in the United States—1998: A Snapshot of America's Foreign-Born Population*. Washington, D.C.: Center for Immigration Studies, 1999.

Candeloro, Dominic. "Louis F. Post and the Red Scare of 1920," *Prologue*, 1979, 11(1): 41–55.

"Candidate Scorecard," *The American Prospect*, July/August 2003, 14I(7): 1.

Caulen, Brae. "San Diego Burning," *California Lawyer*, August 1993: 44–49.

"Census: 1 in 7 U.S. Residents Latinos," *The Denver Post*, Thursday, June 9, 2005: A-2.

Center for Immigration Studies, "News Backgrounder." Washington, D.C.: Center for Immigration Studies, June 2002.

————, "Guestworkers," On-Line; available: http://www.cis.org/topics/guestworkers .html; accessed July 14, 2003.

Cerny, Philip G. "Terrorism and the New Security Dilemma," *Naval War College Review*, Winter 2005, 58(1): 9–34.

Chan, Sucheng, ed. *Entry Denied: Exclusion and the Chinese Community in America, 1882–1943*. Philadelphia: Temple University Press, 1991.

Chang, Gordon H., ed. *Asian Americans and Politics: Perspectives, Experiences, Prospects*. Palo Alto, CA: Stanford University Press, 2001.

Chang, Leslie. *Beyond the Narrow Gate: The Journey of Four Chinese Women from the Middle Kingdom to Middle America*. New York: Penguin Putnam, 2002.

Chavez, Leo R. *Shadowed Lives: Undocumented Immigrants in American Society*. New York: Harcourt Brace Jovanovich, 1992.

Chen, Shehong. *Being Chinese, Becoming Chinese American*. Champaign: University of Illinois Press, 2002.

Chen, Zenglo, Robert B. Lawson, Lawrence R. Gordon, and Barbara McIntosh. "Groupthink: Deciding with the Leader and the Devil," *The Psychological Record*, Fall 1996, 46(4): 581–591.

Cherry, Robert. "Radical Thought and the Early Economic Profession in the U.S.A.," *Review of Social Economics*, 1976, 34(2): 147–162.

Chesney, Robert M. "Terrorism and the Constitution," *Michigan Law Review*, May 2003, 101(6): 1408–1453.

Chiswick, Barry R., ed. *The Gateway: U.S. Immigration Issues and Policies*. Washington, D.C.: American Enterprise Institute, 1982.

Church World Service. *Fulfilling the Promise: Church Orientation Guide to the New Immigration Law*. New York: Church World Service, 1987.

Claghorn, Kate H. *The Immigrants Day in Court*. New York: Arno Press, 1969.

Clark, Malcolm, Jr. "The Bigot Disclosed: 90 Years of Nativism," *Oregon Historical Quarterly*, 1974, 75(2): 108–190.

Clarke, Richard. *Against All Enemies: Inside America's War on Terror*. New York: Free Press, 2004.

"Closing the Golden Door," *Time*, May 18, 1981: 24.

Cohen, Steve, Beth Humphries, and Ed Mynott, eds. *From Immigration Controls to Welfare Controls*. New York: Routledge, 2001.

Commission on the Wartime Internment and Relocation of Civilians. *Personal Justice Denied*. Washington, D.C.: United States Government Printing Office, 1982.

Commission Report—9/11. *Final Report of the National Commission on Terrorist Attacks on the United States*. New York: W.W. Norton, nd.

"Conferees Agree on Vast Revisions in Laws on Aliens," *The New York Times*, Wednesday, October 15, 1986: A-1, B-11.

"Congress Appears Ready to Go Its Own Way on Immigration," *The Denver Post*, Sunday, February 13, 2005: A-6.

Congressional Quarterly Weekly Report, October 18, 1986: 2595–2598, 2612–2613.

Congressional Record, 101st Congress, 2nd Session, 136(149), Part IV, October 26, 1990: H-13203–H-13240.

Congressional Research Service, The Library of Congress, "Alien Eligibility Requirements for Major Federal Assistance Programs." Washington, D.C.: The Library of Congress, January 9, 1981.

———, "Illegal/Undocumented Aliens," Issue Brief No. IB74137. Washington, D.C.: The Library of Congress, September 14, 1981.

———, "Immigration and Refugee Policy," IP0164. Washington, D.C.: The Library of Congress, October 1981.

———, "Immigration and Refugee Policy," MB81244. Washington, D.C.: The Library of Congress, September 16, 1981.

———, "The Immigration and Nationality Act—Questions and Answers," Report No. 81–65 EPW. Washington, D.C.: The Library of Congress, March 10, 1981.

———, "Refugees in the United States: The Cuban Emigration Crisis," Issue Brief No. IB80063. Washington, D.C.: The Library of Congress, August 6, 1981.

———, "U.S. Immigration and Refugee Policy: A Guide to Sources of Information," Research Guide JV6201. Washington, D.C.: The Library of Congress, February 26, 1982.

Cook, Robin. *Contagion*. New York: G. P. Putnam's Sons, 1995.

Cooper, Barry. *New Political Religions, or an Analysis of Modern Terrorism*. Columbia: University of Missouri Press, 2004.

Cordesman, Anthony. *Terrorism, Asymmetric Warfare, and Weapons of Mass Destruction: Defending the U.S. Homeland*. Westport, CT: Praeger, 2002.

———. *Strategic Threats and National Missile Defense: Defending the U.S. Homeland*. Westport, CT: Praeger, 2003.

Cordero-Guzman, Hector, Robert C. Smith, and Ramon Grosfoguel, eds. *Migration, Transnationalization, and Race in a Changing New York*. Philadelphia: Temple University Press, 2002.

Cornelius, Wayne and Ricardo Montoya. *America's New Immigration Law: Origins, Rationales, and Potential Consequences*. San Diego: Center for U.S.–Mexican Studies, 1983.

———. "Illegal Mexican Migration to the United States: Recent Research Findings and Policy Implications," *Congressional Record*, July 13, 1977: H7061–H7068.

Couch, Leslie F. "The Extent of Constitutional Protection Afforded Resident Aliens," *Albany Law Journal*, January 1955, 19: 62–73.

Craig, Richard. *The Bracero Program: Interest Groups and Foreign Policy*. Austin: University of Texas Press, 1971.

Crane, Keith, Beth Asch, Joanna Zorn Heilbrunn, and Danielle Cullinane. *The Effects of Employer Sanctions on the Flow of Undocumented Immigrants to the United States*. Santa Monica, CA: The Rand Corporation; Washington, D.C.: The Urban Institute, 1990.

Cranston, Alan. *The Sovereignty Revolution*. Stanford: Stanford University Press, 2004.

Crewdson, John. *The Tarnished Door*. New York: N.Y. Times Books, 1983.

Crotty, William. "Presidential Policymaking in Crisis Situations: 9/11 and Its Aftermath," *Policy Studies Journal*, August 2003, 31 (3): 451–465.

Crum, John. "After the Fall: Making the New Federal Personnel Changes Work," *The Public Manager*, Spring–Summer 2004, 33(1): 60–62.

Crummy, Karen E. "A Reluctant Enforcer," *The Denver Post*, Tuesday, May 31, 2005: A-1, 12.

Cuddy, Edward. "Are Bolsheviks any Worse than the Irish?," Ethno-Religious Conflict in America During the 1920s, *Eire-Ireland*, 1976, 11(3): 13–32.

Curran, Thomas. *Xenophobia and Immigration, 1820–1930*. Boston: Twayne, 1975.

Daader, Iro H. and I.M. Destler. "Behind America's Front Lines: Organizing to Protect the Homeland," *Brookings Review*, Summer 2002, 20(3): 17–20.

Dahl, Robert. "Does Secrecy Equal Security?," *Environmental Health Perspectives*, February 2004, 112(2): 104–108.

Daniels, Deborah J. "The Challenge of Domestic Terrorism to American Criminal Justice," *Corrections Today*, December 2002, 64(7): 66–70.

Daniels, Roger. "American Historians and East Asian Immigrants," *Pacific Historical Review*, November 1974: 449–472.

———. *The Asian American*. Santa Barbara, CA: CLIO Books, 1976.

———. *The Politics of Prejudice: The Anti-Japanese Movement in California and The Struggle for Japanese Exclusion*, 2nd edn. Berkeley: University of California Press, 1977.

———. *Coming to America: A History of Immigration and Ethnicity in American Life*. New York: Harper, 1990.

———. *Not Like Us: Immigrants and Minorities in America, 1890–1924*. Chicago: Ivan R. Dee, 1997.

———. "No Lamps were Lit for Them: Angel Island and the Histography of Asian-American Immigration, *Journal of American Ethnic History*, Fall 1997, 17(1): pp. 3–18.

Daniels, Roger and Harry Kitano. *American Racism*. Englewood Cliffs, NJ: Prentice-Hall, 1970.

Daniels, Roger and Otis L. Graham. *Debating American Immigration, 1882–Present*. Lanham, MD: Rowman and Littlefield, 2003.

Davis, Jerome. *The Russian Immigrant*. New York: Arno Press, 1969.

DeLeon, Arnoldo. *They Called Them Greasers: Anglo-American Attitudes Towards Mexicans in Texas, 1821–1900*. Austin: University of Texas Press, 1983.

Demmer, Valerie R. "Civil Liberties and Homeland Security," *The Humanist*, January—February 2002, 62(1): 7–10.

"Department of Homeland Security Proposes and Finalizes Changes to TSA Regulations," *Hazardous Waste Consultant*, January 2005, 23(1): 2.

Department of Homeland Security. "Program Analysis Findings and Addressing Shortcomings," @http://www.dhs.gov/interweb/assetlibrary/reorganization_plan.pdf. Accessed November 29, 2004.

———. "Reorganization Plan, November 25, 2002," @ http://www.dhs.gov/interweb/assetlibrary/reorganization _plan.pdf. Accessed November 29, 2004.

Department of Justice. "The Immigration and Naturalization Service's Removal of Aliens Issued Final Orders," Report Number I-2003–004. Washington, D.C.: Department of Justice, 2003.

Department of Justice/GAOffice. "Major Management Challenges and Program Risks," DOJ/GAO-03–105. Washington, D.C.: U.S. Government Printing Office, 2003.

DeSipio, Louis. "The New Urban Citizen: Political Participation and Policy Attitudes of The Newly Naturalized," Paper presented at the American Political Science

Association Meeting, Boston, 2000, and in Lydio Tomasi, ed. *In Defense of the Alien, XXII*. New York: Center for Migration Studies, 2000: 79–100.

"Developments in the Law—Immigration Policy and the Rights of Aliens," *Harvard Law Review*, 1983, 96: 1268–1465.

Dimmitt, Marius. "The Enactment of the McCarren-Walter Act of 1952." Ph.D. Dissertation, University of Kansas, 1970.

Dinnerstein, Leonard. *Anti-Semitism in America*. New York: Oxford University Press, 1994.

Dinnerstein, Leonard and Frederick Jaher. *Uncertain Americans: Readings in Ethnic History*. New York: Oxford University Press, 1977.

Dinnerstein, Leonard and David M. Reimers. *Ethnic Americans*, 3rd ed., New York: Harper and Row, 1988.

DiNunzio, Mario and Jan T. Galkowski. "Political Loyalty in Rhode Island, a Computer Study of the 1850s," *Rhode Island History*, 1977, 36(3): 93–95.

Divine, Robert A. *American Immigration Policy: 1924–1952*. New Haven: Yale University Press, 1957.

Dixon, Thomas H. "The Rise of Complex Terrorism," *Foreign Policy*, January/February 2002.

Duleep, Harriot O. and Wunnava Phanindra. *Immigrants and Immigration Policy*. Greenwich, CT: JAI Press, 1996.

Dummett, Michael. *On Immigration and Refugees*. New York: Routledge, 2001.

Dunlevy, James A. and Henry Gemery. "Economic Opportunity and the Response of Old and New Migrants to the United States," *Journal of Economic History*, 1978, 38(4): 901–917.

Dye, Thomas. *Understanding Public Policy*, 5th edn. Englewood Cliffs, NJ: Prentice-Hall, 1984.

Edmonson, R.G. "On Course for July 1: Coast Guard Expects Little Disruption from ISPS, Maritime Transportation Security Act," *The Journal of Commerce*, June 7, 2004, 5(23): 15.

Edmonston, Barry and Jeffrey S. Passel, eds. *Immigration and Ethnicity: The Integration of America's Newest Arrivals*. Washington, D.C.: Urban Institute, 1994.

Edwards, Carl N. "The Mind of the Terrorist," *The Forensic Examiner*, May–June 2003: 22–27.

Eggen, Dan. "Big Brother on Campus," *Washington Post National Weekly Edition*, February 3–9, 2003: 29.

Eisinger, Peter K. "Ethnic Political Transition in Boston: 1884–1933: Some Lessons for Contemporary Cities," *Political Science Quarterly*, 1978, 93(2): 217–239.

Eland, Ivan. *Putting Defense Back into U.S. Defense Policy: Rethinking U.S. Security in the Post-Cold War World*. Westport, CT: Praeger Press, 2001.

Elles, Diana. *International Provisions Protecting the Human Rights of Non- Citizens*. New York: The United Nations, 1980.

Enders, Walter and Todd Sandler, "Transnational Terrorism, 1968–2000: Thresholds, Persistence, and Forecasts," *Southern Economic Journal*, January 2005, 71(3): 467–483.

English, Larry D., "Information Quality: Critical Ingredient for National Security," *Journal of Database Management*, January–March 2005, 16(1): 18–33.

Espenshade, T. J. and H. Fu, "An Analysis of English-Language Proficiency Among U.S. Immigrants," *American Sociological Review*, 1997, 62: 288–305.

Etzioni, Amitai and Jason H. Marsch, eds. *Rights vs. Public Safety After 9/11: America in the Age of Terrorism*. Lanham, MD.: Rowman and Littlefield, 2003.

Fairchild, Henry Pratt. *Greek Immigration*. New Haven: Yale University Press, 1911.

———. *Immigration*. New Haven: Yale University Press, 1925.

Faist, Thomas. *The Volume and Dynamics of International Migration and Transnational Social Spaces*. New York: Oxford University Press, 2000.

"Feds Face Daunting Task in Push to Deport Illegals," *The Denver Post*, Sunday, January 16, 2005: A-15.

Feingold, Henry. *The Politics of Rescue: The Roosevelt Administration and the Holocaust, 1938–1945*. New Brunswick: Rutgers University Press, 1970.

Feldstein, Stanley and Lawrence Costello, eds., *The Ordeal of Assimilation: A Documentary History of the White Working Class, 1830–1970*. Garden City, NJ: Doubleday, 1974.

Ferguson, Charles D., William C. Potter, Amy Sands, Leonard S. Spector, and Fred L. Wahling. *The Four Faces of Nuclear Terrorism*. New York: Routledge, 2005.

Fermi, Laura. *Illustrious Immigrants: The Intellectual Migration from Europe, 1930–1941*. Chicago: University of Chicago Press, 1968.

Ferris, Elizabeth G., ed., *Refugees and World Politics*. New York: Praeger Publisher, 1985.

Fine, Sidney, "Mr. Justice Murphy and the Hirabayashi Case," *Pacific Historical Review*, May 1964: 195–209.

Fitzgerald, Keith. *The Face of the Nation: Immigration, the State, and the National Identity*. Stanford, CA: Stanford University Press, 1996.

Fix, Michael. *Immigration and Immigrants: Setting the Record Straight*. Washington, D.C.: The Urban Institute, 1994.

Fix, Michael and Jeffrey S. Passel. *The Door Remains Open: Recent Immigration to the United States and a Preliminary Analysis of the Immigration Act of 1990*. Washington, D.C.: The Urban Institute, 1991.

Flynn, Stephen. *America the Vulnerable: How Our Government is Failing to Protect Us from Terrorism*. New York: Harper-Collins, 2004.

Foner, Nancy, Ruben Rumbant, and Steven J. Gold, eds., *Immigration Research for a New Century: Multidisciplinary Perspectives*. New York: Russell Sage Foundation, 2000.

Fragomen, Austin T., Jr. "Alien Employment," *International Migration Review*, 1979, 13(3): 527–531.

———. "Permanent Resident Status Redefined," *International Migration Review*, 1975, 9(1): 63–68.

Franklin, Frank G. *The Legislative History of Naturalization in the United States*. New York: Arno Press, 1969.

Freedman, Morris and Carolyn Banks. *American Mix: The Minority Experience in America*. New York: J.B. Lippincott, 1972.

Freeman, Gary P. "Restructuring the INS: Draft Design Proposal," in Lydio Tomasi, ed., *In Defense of the Alien XXII*. New York: Center for Migration Studies, 2000: 223–235.

Fried, Charles, ed. *Minorities: Community and Identity.* New York: Springer-Verlag New York, Inc., 1983.

Friedman, Benjamin. "Homeland Security: Think Again," *Foreign Policy,* July–August 2005, (149): 22–27.

————. "Leap Before You Look: The Failure of Homeland Security," *Breakthrough,* Spring 2004.

Friis, Erick J., ed., *The Scandinavian Presence in North America.* New York: Harper and Row, 1976.

Fuchs, Lawrence. *American Ethnic Politics.* New York: Harper, 1968.

————. *The American Kaleidoscope: Race, Ethnicity, and Civil Culture.* Hanover, NH: University Press of New England, 1990.

Fullilove, Michael. "All the President's Men—the Role of Special Envoys in U.S. Foreign Policy," *Foreign Affairs,* March 2005, 84(2): 13+.

Gabaccia, Donna R. and Colin Wayne Leach, eds. *Immigrant Life in the U.S.* New York: Routledge, 2003.

Gallaway, Lowell E. et al. "The Distribution of the Immigrant Population in the United States: An Economic Analysis," *Explorations in Economic History,* 1974, 11(3): 213–226.

Gardner, Robert. "Restructuring the INS: Draft Design Proposal," in Lydio Tomasi, ed., *In Defense of the Alien, XXII.* New York: Center for Migration Studies, 2000: 6–10.

Garza, E. (Kika) de la et al. "Should People Stay Home? Regulation and Free Movement and Rights of Establishment Between the U.S., Canada, and Mexico," *American Society of International Law,* 1974, 68: 38–58.

General Accounting Office, "Information on the Enforcement of Laws Regarding Employment of Aliens in Selected Countries." Washington, D.C.: U.S. Government Printing Office, August 31, 1982.

————. *Immigration Reform: Employer Sanctions and the Question of Discrimination.* Washington, D.C.: U.S. Government Printing Office, 1990.

————. *Illegal Aliens: National Net Cost Estimates Vary Widely.* Washington, D.C.: U.S. Government Printing Office, 1995.

————. *Illegal Aliens: National Cost Estimates Vary Widely.* Washington, D.C.: U.S. Government Printing Office, 1995.

————. *Illegal Aliens: Extent of Welfare Benefits Received on Behalf of U.S. Citizen Children.* Washington, D.C.: U.S. Government Printing Office, 1997.

————. *Illegal Aliens: Significant Obstacles to Reducing Unauthorized Alien Employment Exists.* Washington, D.C.: U.S. Government Printing Office, 1998.

————. *Welfare Reform: Public Assistance Benefits Provided to Recently Naturalized Citizens.* Washington, D.C.: U.S. Government Printing Office, 1999a.

————. *Welfare Reform: Many States Continued Some Federal or State Benefits for Immigrants.* Washington, D.C.: U.S. Government Printing Office, 1999b.

————. *Illegal Immigration: Status of Southwest Border Strategy Implementation.* Washington, D.C.: U.S. Government Printing Office, 1999c.

————. *Illegal Aliens: Opportunities Exist to Improve the Expedited Removal Process.* Washington, D.C.: U.S. Government Printing Office, 2000a.

————. *H-1B Foreign Workers: Better Controls Needed to Help Employers and Protect Workers.* Washington, D.C.: U.S. Government Printing Office, 2000b.

————. *Alien Smuggling: Management and Operational Improvements Needed to Address Growing Problem.* Washington, D.C.: U.S. Government Printing Office, 2002.

————. *Homeland Security, DHS Is Taking Steps to Enhance Security at Chemical Facilities, but Additional Authority Is Needed*, GAO-06-150. Washington, DC: U.S. Government Printing Office, 2003.

Gerstle, Gary and John Mollenkopf, eds. *E Pluribus Unum? Contemporary and Historical Perspectives on Immigrant Political Incorporation.* New York: Russell Sage Foundation, 2001.

Geschwender, James R. *Racial Stratification in America.* Debuque, Iowa: William C. Brown, 1978.

Gibney, Matthew J. *The Ethics and Politics of Asylum: Liberal Democracy and the Responses to Refugees.* New York: Cambridge University Press, 2004.

Gibson, William. *Aliens and the Law.* Chapel Hill, NC: University of North Carolina Press, 1940.

Gjerde, Jon, ed. *Major Problems in American Immigration and Ethnic History.* Boston: Houghton Mifflin, 1998.

Glazer, Nathan, ed. *Clamor at the Gates: The New American Immigration.* San Francisco: ICS Press, 1985.

Glazer, Nathan and Daniel P. Moynihan. *Beyond the Melting Pot.* Cambridge, MA: Harvard University Press, 1973.

Goldstein, Bruce. "Recent Temporary Worker Proposals in Agriculture." In Lydio Tomasi, ed., *In Defense of the Alien, XXIII.* New York: Center for Migration Studies, 2001: 69–85.

Goldstein, Robert J. "The Anarchist Scare of 1908: A Sign of Tensions in the Progressive Era," *American Studies*, 1974, 15(2): 55–78.

Goodenow, Ronald K. "The Progressive Educator, Race and Ethnicity in the Depression Years: An Overview," *History of Education Quarterly*, 1975, 15(4): 365–394.

Gordon, Charles. "The Alien and the Constitution," *California Western Law Review*, Fall 1971, 9: pp. 1–36.

————. "The Need to Modernize Our Immigration Laws," *San Diego Law Review*, 1975, 13: 1–33.

Gordon, Charles E. and Harry Rosenfield. *Immigration Law and Procedure.* New York: Matthew Bender, 1980.

Gordon, Michael. "Labor Boycott in New York City: 1880–1886," *Labor History*, 16(2): 184–229.

Gorman, Robert F. *Historical Dictionary of Refugee and Disaster Relief.* Metuchen, NJ: Scarecrow Press, 1994.

Gorman, Siobhan. "The Endless Flood," *National Journal*, February 7, 2004, 6: 378–384.

Gotanda, Neil., "Critique of 'Our Constitution is Colorblind,'" *Stanford Law Review*, November 1991, 44(1): 1–68.

Gotcham, Benjamin and Rutilio Martinez. "Mexicans in the U.S. Send Billions Home—and It All Comes Back," *The Denver Post*, Saturday, February 19, 2005: C-13.

Gourevitch, Alex. "Alien Nation," *The American Prospect*, January 13, 2003a, 13(24): 15–17.

————. "Asylum Interrupted: Is America Still a Safe Haven?" *The American Prospect*, April 2003b, 14(4): 20–22.

Grant, Madison. *The Passing of the Great Race.* New York: Arno, 1916.

Green, Stephen, "Immigration Politics," *The Cumberland Times News*, November 1, 1984: 13.

Greenway, H.D.S. "Unwatched Ships at Sea: The Coast Guard and Homeland Security," *World Policy Journal*, Summer 2003, 20(2): 73–79.

Guerin-Gonzales, Camile. *Mexican Workers and the American Dream: Immigration, Repatriation, and California Farm Labor, 1900–1939.* New Brunswick: Rutgers University Press, 1994.

Guillet, Edwin C. *The Great Migration: The Atlantic Crossing by Sailing Ships: 1770– 1860.* Toronto, London, New York: Thomas Nelson and Sons, 1937.

Gutman, Herbert. *Work, Culture and Society in Industrializing America.* New York: Alfred A. Knopf, 1977.

Hakim, Joy. *War, Peace, and All That Jazz.* New York: Oxford University Press, 1995.

Halich, Vasyl. *Ukranians in the United States.* Chicago: University of Chicago Press, 1933.

Halperin, Morton H. "Safe at Home," *The American Prospect*, November 2003, 14(10): 36–40.

Halperin, Morton H., Priscilla Clapp, and Arnold Kanter. *Bureaucratic Politics and Foreign Policy.* Washington, D.C.: Brookings Institute, 1974.

Ham, Peter van. *Managing Non-Proliferation Regimes in the 1990s: Power, Politics and Policies.* New York: Council on Foreign Relations, 1994.

Hamermesh, Daniel S. and Frank Bean, eds. *Help or Hindrance? The Economic Implications of Immigration for African Americans.* New York: Russell Sage Foundation, 1998.

Hammamoto, Darrell Y. and Rodolfo Torres, eds. *New American Destinies: A Reader in Contemporary Asian and Latino Immigration.* New York: Routledge, 1997.

Handlin, Oscar. *The Problem of the Third Generation Immigrant.* Rock Island, ILL: Augustana Historical Society, 1938.

———. *The Uprooted.* Boston, MA: Little Brown, 1951.

———, ed. *Immigration as a Factor in American History.* Englewood Cliffs, NJ: Prentice-Hall, 1959.

———. *The Americans.* Boston: Little, Brown, 1963.

———. *The Uprooted*, 2nd edn. Boston: Little, Brown, 1973.

———. *Boston's Immigrants.* Cambridge: Harvard University Press, 1979.

Hansen, Marcus Lee. *Atlantic Migration, 1601–1860.* New York: Harper Torchbooks, 1961.

Harney, Robert F. "The Padrone and the Immigrant," *Canadian Review of American Studies*, 1974, 5(2): 101–118.

Harper, Elizabeth. *Immigration Laws of the United States*, 3rd edn. Indianapolis: Bobbs-Merrill, 1975.

Hart, Jeffrey, "Illegal Immigration." *The Cumberland Evening Times*, Monday, July 22, 1985: 8.

Harwood, Edwin, "Can Immigration Laws Be Enforced?," *The Public Interest*, Summer 1983, 17: 105–123.

Haynes, Wendy. "Seeing Around Corners: Crafting the New Department of Homeland Security," *The Review of Policy Research*, May 2004, 21(3): 369–396.

Hayslip, Le Ly and Jay Wurts. *When Heaven and Earth Changed Places: A Vietnamese Woman's Journey from War to Peace.* New York: Penguin Putnam, 2002.

Hentoff, Nat. "The Patriot Whistleblower," *Free Inquiry*, Summer 2003, 23(3): 20–22.

Helbush, Terry J. "Aliens, Deportation and the Equal Protection Clause," *Golden State University Law Review*, Fall 1975, 6: 23–77.

Herberg, William. *Protestant, Catholic, Jew*. Garden City, NJ: Doubleday, 1955.

Hewlitt, S. "Coping with Illegal Aliens," *Foreign Affairs*, 1981, 60: 358–378.

Higham, John. *Strangers in the Land: Patterns of American Nativism, 1860–1925*. New Brunswick: Rutgers University Press, 1955.

———. *Send These to Me*. New York: Athenium, 1975.

———. ed. *Ethnic Leadership in America*. Baltimore: Johns Hopkins University Press, 1978.

"Hill Revises Immigration Law," *The Washington Post*, Saturday, October 18, 1986: A-1, 7–8.

Hillyard, Michael J., "Organizing for Homeland Security," *Parameters*, Spring 2002, 32(1): 75–86.

Himes, Kenneth R. "Intervention, Just War, and U.S. National Security," *Theological Studies*, 2004, 65(1): 141–158.

Hing, Bill Ong. *Making and Remaking Asian America Through Immigration Policy, 1850–1990*. Stanford, CA: Stanford University Press, 1993.

Hirschman, Charles, Josh DeWind, and Philip Kasinitz, eds. *The Handbook of International Migration*. New York: Russell Sage Foundation, 1999.

"Hispanic Americans Haven't Found Their Pot of Gold," *The Washington Post National Weekly Edition*, May 28, 1984: 9–10.

Hoerder, Dirk, ed. *American Labor and Immigration History: 1877–1920*. Urbana, Illinois: University of Illinois Press, 1982.

Hoffman, Frank G. *Homeland Security: A Competitive Strategies Approach*. Washington, D.C.: Center for Defense Information, 2002.

Hoffman, Grayson A. "Litigating Terrorism," *American Criminal Law Review*, Fall 2003, 40(4): 1655–1683.

Hofstadler, Richard, ed., *U.S. Immigration Policy*. Durham, NC: Duke Press Policy Studies, 1984.

Hofstadler, Richard and Michael Wallace. *American Violence*. New York: Knopf, 1971.

Holmes, Jeffrey L. "The Container Security Initiative," *Fleet Equipment*, August 2004, 30(8): 15.

Holt, Michael. "The Politics of Impatience: The Origins of Know-Nothingism," *Journal of American History*, 1973, 60(2): 309–333.

"Homeland Security Gets OK," *Press-Enterprise*. Riverside, CA: November 20, 2002, A-1, A-5.

Hosokawa, William. *The Quiet Americans*. New York: William and Morrow, 1969.

"House Approves Compromise Immigration Bill," *The Washington Post*, Thursday, October 16, 1986: A-5.

"House Approves License Ban for Illegal Immigrants," *The Denver Post*, Friday, February 11, 2005: A-2.

"House of Cards? Point-Counterpoint Commentary," *The Denver Post*, Saturday, February 19, 2005: C-12.

Howe, Irving. *World of Our Fathers*. New York: Simon and Schuster, 1976.

Huddle, Donald. *The Cost of Immigration*. Washington, D.C.: Carrying Capacity Network, 1993.

Hundley, Norris, ed. *The Asian-American: The Historical Experience*. Santa Barbara, CA: American Bibliography Center, CLIO Press, 1976.

Hussain, Rashad. "Security with Transparency: Judicial Review in 'Special Interest' Immigration Proceedings," *Yale Law Journal*, April 2004, 113(16): 1333–1341.

Hutchinson, Edward. *Legislative History of American Immigration Policy, 1798–1965*. New Brunswick: Rutgers University Press, 1970.

———. *Immigrants and Their Children*. New York: Wiley, 1956.

Hyong, Y. "Building a Department of Homeland Security: The Management Theory," *The Public Manager*, Spring 2003, 32(1): 55–57.

"Illegal Aliens: Invasion Out of Control," *U.S. News and World Report*, January 29, 1979: 38–43.

"Illegals Going Back by the Planeload," http://www.aolsvc.news.aol.com/news/article .adp?ids=2005. Accessed February 17, 2005.

Illich, Richard. *The Human Rights of Aliens in Contemporary International Law*. Manchester: Manchester University Press, 1984.

"Immigrants in Washington," *The Washington Post Magazine*, April 10, 1983.

"Immigrants: The Changing Face of America," *Time*, July 8, 1985 (special edn.).

Immigration and Naturalization Service. *An Immigration Nation: United States Regulation Of Immigration, 1798–1991*. Washington, D.C.: U.S. Government Printing Office, 1992.

———. *INS Statistical Yearbook, 1996*. Washington, D.C.: U.S. Government Printing Office, 1997.

———. *INS Statistical Yearbook, 1997*. Washington, D.C.: U.S. Government Printing Office, 1998.

———. Interpreter Releases. "Homeland SecurityDebate on Hold," August 5, 2002a.

———. Interpreter Releases. "INS Proposes Requiring Aliens to Acknowledge Advance Notice of Change of Address Requirements: 200,000 Cards Remain Unfiled," August 5, 2002b.

———. "Legal Immigration, Fiscal Year 2001: Annual Report, Office of Policy and Planning, Statistical Division," Washington, D.C.: U.S. Government Printing Office, no. 7, August 2002c.

"Immigration Bill Approved: Bars Hiring Illegal Aliens, But Gives Millions Amnesty," *The New York Times*, Saturday, October 18, 1986: A-1, 8.

"Immigration Bill: How 'Corpse' Came Back to Life," *The New York Times*, Monday, October 13, 1986: A-16.

"Immigration Bill Mixed Blessing for Aliens," *The Washington Post*, Sunday, June 24, 1984: C-1, 7.

"Immigration Briefs," *Middle America News*, August 2005: 9.

"Immigration Issues Heats Up Again," *The Washington Post*, Sunday, July 28, 1985: A-15.

"Immigration," *Law and Contemporary Problems*, Duke University School of Law, Spring 1956, 21: 211–426.

"Immigration Legislation Voted Down," *The Cumberland Times/News*, Saturday, September 14, 1985: A-1.

"Immigration Measures Produces Sharp Division in House Hispanic Caucus," *The Washington Post*, Sunday, March 18, 1984: A-2.

"Immigration Reform and Control Act," HR 1510, 98th Congress, First Session (The Simpson-Mazzoli Bill). Washington, D.C.: U.S. Government Printing Office.

"Immigration Reform Plan Must Embrace Three Key Ideas," *The San Diego Union-Tribune*, June 1, 2005: Editorial page.

Information Plus. *Immigration and Illegal Aliens: Burden or Blessing?* Wylie, Texas: Information Plus, 1999, 2001, 2003.

Ingraham, Patricia W. "Towards a More Systematic Consideration of Policy Design," *Policy Studies Journal*, 1987, 15(4): 610–628.

"INS Should Put Its House in Order," *Atlanta Journal-Constitution*, August 9, 2002. Available online at http://www.cis.org; accessed August 12, 2002.

"Intelligence: First Director Will Help Define the Institution," *The Gazette*, Colorado Springs, Friday, February 18, 2005: 8-A.

Iorizzo, Luciano and Salvatore Mondello. *The Italian-Americans*. New York: Twayne Publishing, 1971.

"Is Hatred of Japanese Making a Comeback?," *The Washington Post*, Sunday, July 7, 1985: B-1, 4.

Isbister, John. *The Immigration Debate: Remaking America*. West Hartford, CT: Kumarian Press, 1996.

Jacobson, Gary C. "Terror, Terrain and Turnout: Exploring the 2002 Midterm Elections," *Political Science Quarterly*, Spring 2003, 18(1): 1–23.

Janis, Irving. *Victims of Groupthink*. Boston: Houghton-Mifflin, 1972.

———. *Groupthink*, 2nd ed. Boston: Houghton-Mifflin, 1982.

Janis, Ralph. "Flirtation and Flight: Alternatives to Ethnic Confrontation in White Anglo-American Protestant Detroit, 1880–1940," *Journal of Ethnic Studies*, 1978, 6(2): 1–17.

Jasso, G., D.S. Massey, M.R. Rosenzweig, and J.P. Smith. "The New Immigrant Pilot Survey (NIS-P): Overview and New Findings about U.S. Legal Immigrants at Admission," *Demography*, 2000, 37: 127–138.

Jones, Charles O. *An Introduction to the Study of Public Policy*, 3rd edn. Monterey, CA: Brooks, Cole, 1984.

Jones-Correa, Michael, ed. *Governing American Cities*. New York: Russell Sage Foundation, 2001.

Jones, Maldwyn Allen. *American Immigration*. Chicago: University of Chicago Press, 1960.

Jones, Susanne and Catherine Tactaquin, "Latino Immigrants Rights in the Shadow of the National Security State: Responses to Domestic Preemptive Strikes," *Social Justice*, Spring–Summer 2004, 31(2): 67–92.

Jordan, Amos A., William J. Taylor, Jr., Michael J. Mazarr, and Sam Nunn. *American National Security*. Baltimore, MD: Johns Hopkins University Press, 1984.

Jordan, Philip D. "Immigrants, Methodists and a 'Conservative' Social Gospel, 1865–1908," *Methodist History*, 1978, 17(1): 16–43.

Judis, John B. "Strategic Disinformation," *The American Prospect*, September 2003, 14(8): 44–47.

Kamin, Leon J. "The Science and the Politics of I.Q.," *Social Research*, 1974, 41(3): 387–425.

Kayyem, Juliette N. "The Homeland Security Muddle," *The American Prospect*, November 2003, 14(10): 46–49.

Keefe, Thomas M., "The Catholic Issue in the Chicago Tribune Before the Civil War," *Mid-America*, 1975, 57(4): 227–245.

Keely, Charles, "Illegal Migration," *Scientific American*, March 1982, 246: 31–37.
————. *U.S. Immigration: A Policy Analysis*. New York: Population Council, 1979.
Kellas, James G. *The Politics of Nationalism and Ethnicity*. New York: St. Martin's Press, 1991.
Keller, Morton. *Affairs of State*. Cambridge, MA: Harvard University Press, 1977.
Kemp, Roger L. "Homeland Security: Trends in America," *National Civic Review*, Winter 2003, 92(4): 45–53.
Kennedy, John F. *A Nation of Immigrants*, Rev. Ed. New York: Harper and Row, 1986.
Kerwin, Donald. "Family Reunification and the Living Law: Processing, Delays, Backlogs, and Legal Barriers," in Lydio Tomasi, ed. *In Defense of the Alien, XXIII*. New York: Center for Migration Studies, 2001: 107–116.
Kettner, James H. *The Development of American Citizenship: 1608–1870*. Chapel Hill, NC: University of North Carolina Press, 1978.
Kiernan, James Patrick. "Shaping Security Beyond Borders," *Americas*, January–February, 2004, 56(1): 56–58.
Kilpatrick, James J. "Looking at 'Immigrant,'" *United Press Syndication*, Tuesday, February 21, 1984: A-2.
Kim, Hyung Chan, ed. *Asian Americans in Congress: A Documentary History*. Westport, CT: Greenwood Press, 1995.
Kim, Won, "On U.S. Homeland Security and Database Technology," *Journal of Database Management*, January—March 2005, 16(1): 1–18.
Kinzer, Donald. *An Episode in Anti-Catholicism: The American Protective Movement*. Seattle, Washington: University of Washington Press, 1963.
Kiser, George and David Silverman, "Mexican Repatriation During the Great Depression," *Journal of Mexican American History*, 1973, 3(1): 139–164.
Kitano, Harry. *Japanese Americans: The Evolution of a Subculture*. Englewood Cliffs, NJ: Prentice-Hall, 1969.
————. *Race Relations*. Englewood Cliffs, NJ: Prentice-Hall, 1984.
Knickrehm, Kay M. "Congress, the Executive, and Immigration Policy," Paper Delivered at the Annual APSA Meeting, New Orleans, August 29, 1985.
———— and G. Hastedt. "State Terrorism, Development and Refugee Flows," in G. Lopez and M. Stohl, eds., *Development, Dependence, and State Repression*. Westport, CT: Greenwood Press, 1985.
Knobel, Dale. *America for Americans: The Nativist Movement in the United States*. New York: Twayne, 1996.
Koehan, Peter. *Refugees from Revolution: U.S. Policy and Third World Migration*. Boulder, CO: Westview Press, 1991.
Kondrake, Morton. "Guest Worker Program Could Add to Our Safety," *The Colorado Springs Gazette*, Saturday, December 18, 2004: Metro-5.
Kontorovich, Eugene. "Liability Rules for Constitutional Rights: The Case of Mass Detentions," *Stanford Law Review*, February, 2004, 56(4): 755–834.
Konvitz, Milton R. *The Alien and the Asiatic in American Law*. Ithaca, NY: Cornell University Press, 1946.
————. *Civil Rights in Immigration*. Ithaca, NY: Cornell University Press, 1953.
————. *First Amendment Freedoms, Select Cases on Freedom of Religion, Speech, Press, Assembly*. Ithaca, NY: Cornell University Press, 1963.

Kowert, Paul A. *Groupthink or Deadlock: When Do Leaders Learn from Their Advisors?* Albany: SUNY Press, 2002.

Kramer, Jane M. "Due Process Rights for Excludable Aliens Under U.S. Immigration Law and the United Nations Protocol Related to the Status of Refugees: Haitian Aliens, A Case in Point: The *Pierre* and *Sannon* Decisions," *New York Journal of International Law and Policy*, 10(1): 203–240.

Kranick, Nancy. "The Impact of the U.S. Patriot Act: An Update," The Free Expression Policy Project, http://www.frepproject.org/commentaries/patriotactupdate.html. Accessed August 23, 2005.

Krauss, Elishia. "Building a Bigger Bureaucracy: What the Department of Homeland Security Won't Do," *The Public Manager*. Spring, 2003, 32(1): 57–59.

Krauss, Erich with Alex Pacheco. *On the Line: Inside the U.S. Border Patrol*. New York: Citadel Press, Kensington Publishing Corp., 2004.

Kraut, Alan. *Silent Travelers: Germs, Genes and the 'Immigrant Menace'*. Baltimore: Johns Hopkins University Press, 1994.

Kritz, Mary M. *U.S. Immigration and Refugee Policy: Global and Domestic Issues*. Lexington: Lexington Books, 1983.

Kyle, David, and Rey Koslowski. *Global Human Smuggling: Comparative Perspectives*. Baltimore: Johns Hopkins University Press, 2001.

Kupchan, Charles A. *The End of the American Era: U.S. Foreign Policy and the Geopolitics of the Twenty-First Century*. New York: Alfred A. Knopf, 2003.

Labov, T. "English Acquisition by Immigrants to the United States at the Beginning of the Twentieth Century," *American Speech*, 1998, 73: 368–398.

Lai, Him Mark, Genny Lim, and Judy Yung. *Island: Poetry and History of Chinese Immigrants on Angel Island, 1910–1940*. San Francisco: Hoc Doi—Chinese Culture Foundation, 1980.

Lamm, R. D. and G. Imhoff. *The Immigration Time Bomb*. New York: Truman Tally Books, 1985.

Lane, A. "American Labor and European Immigrants in the Late Nineteenth Century," *Journal of American Studies*, 1977, 11(2): 241–260.

Lansford, Tom. "Homeland Security from Clinton to Bush: An Assessment," *White House Studies*, Fall 2003, 3(4): 403–411.

Latham, Earl. *The Group Basis of Politics*. New York: Octagon Books, 1965.

Lazarowitz, Arlene. "Promoting Air Power: The Influence of the U.S. Air Force on The Creation of the National Security State," *Independent Review*, Spring 2005, 9(4): 477–500.

Lee, Erika. "Immigrants and Immigration Law: A State of the Field Assessment," *Journal of American Ethnic History*, 2000, 18(4): 85–114.

Lee, Kenneth K. *Huddled Masses, Muddled Laws: Why Contemporary Immigration Policy Fails to Reflect Public Opinion*. Westport, CT: Praeger Publishers, 1998.

Lehrer, Eli. "The Homeland Security Bureaucracy," *Public Interest*, Summer 2004, 1156: 71–86.

Leibowitz, A. "Refugee Act of 1980: Problems and Concerns," *Annals of the American Academy of Political and Social Science*, 1983: 163–171.

LeMay, Michael. *The Struggle for Influence*. Lanham, MD: University Press of America, 1985.

————. *From Open Door to Dutch Door: An Analysis of U.S. Immigration Policy Since 1820.* New York: Praeger Press, 1987.

————, ed. *The Gatekeepers.* New York: Praeger Press, 1989.

————. "Assessing the Impact of IRCA's Employer Requirements and Sanctions," in Lydio Tomasi, ed. *In Defense of the Alien, XII.* New York: Center for Migration Studies, 1990: 146–169.

————. *Anatomy of a Public Policy.* New York: Praeger Publishers, 1994.

————. "Recent Immigration Reform: Using Commissions for Agenda Setting," in Lydio Tomasi, ed. *In Defense of the Alien, XIX.* New York: Center for Migration Studies, 1997: 17–24.

————. "Assessing Assimilation: Cultural and Political Integration of Immigrants and Their Descendants, in Lydio Tomasi, ed. *In Defense of the Alien, XXIII.* New York: Center for Migration Studies, 2001: 163–176.

————. *U.S. Immigration.* Santa Barbara, California: ABC-CLIO, 2004.

————. *The Perennial Struggle,* 2nd ed. Upper Saddle River, NJ: Prentice-Hall, 2005.

———— and Elliott R. Barkan. *U.S. Immigration and Naturalization Laws and Issues.* Westport, CT: Greenwood Press, 1999.

Leventman, Seymour. *The Ghetto and Beyond.* New York: Random House, 1972.

Levine, Edward M. *The Irish and the Irish Politician.* Notre Dame: University of Notre Dame Press, 1996.

Levitt, Peggy and Mary C. Waters, eds. *The Changing Face of Home: The Transnational Lives of the Second Generation.* New York: Russell Sage Foundation, 2002.

Levy, Mark and Michael Kramer. *The Ethnic Factor.* New York: Simon and Schuster, 1972.

Lewis, James A. "Three Reforms to Make America More Secure," *World and I,* October 2002, 17(10): 32.

Lieberson, Stanley. *A Piece of the Pie.* Berkeley: University of California Press, 1980.

Light, Jennifer S. "Urban Planning and Defense Planning: Past and Future," *Journal of the American Planning Association,* Autumn 2004, 70(4): 399–410.

Light, Paul C. *Homeland Security Will Be Hard to Manage.* Washington, D.C.: Brookings Institution's Center for Public Service, August 25, 2002.

Lindorff, Dave, "Patriot Act II? Alternet, http://www.alternet.org/rights/22134. Accessed August 23, 2005.

Lineberry, Robert L. *American Public Policy.* New York: Harper and Row, 1977.

Linkh, Richard M. *American Catholicism and European Migration.* New York: Center for Migration Studies, 1975.

Litt, Edgar. *Ethnic Politics in America.* Glenview, Illinois: Scott, Foresman, 1970.

Litwak, Robert S. *Rogue States and U.S. Foreign Policy: Containment After the Cold War.* Baltimore, MD: Johns Hopkins University Press, 2000.

————. "The Imperial Republic After 9/11," *Wilson Quarterly,* Summer 2002: 76–82.

Loescher, Gil and Ann Dull Loescher. *The Global Refugee Crisis.* Santa Barbara, CA: ABC-CLIO, 1994.

Lopata, Helena Znaniecki. *Polish Americans.* Englewood Cliffs, NJ: Prentice-Hall, 1976.

Lopez-Garza, Marta and David R. Diaz, eds. *Asian and Latino Immigrants in a Restructuring Economy: The Metamorphosis of Southern California.* Palo Alto, CA: Stanford University Press, 2001.

Lopez, Ian F. Haney. *White Law: The Legal Construction of Race.* New York: New York University Press, 1996.

Lowe, Lisa. *Immigrant Acts: On Asian American Cultural Politics*. Durham, NC: Duke University Press, 1997.

Luikart, Kenneth A. "Transforming Homeland Security," *Air and Space Power Journal*, Summer 2003, 17(2): 69–79.

Lungren, Daniel. "Immigration Reform: If Not Now, When?," *The Washington Post National Weekly Edition*, September 24, 1984: 28.

Lutton, Wayne and John Tanton. *The Immigration Invasion*. Petosky, Michigan: The Social Contract Press, 1994.

Lynch, James P. and Rita J. Simon. *Immigration the World Over: Statutes, Policies, and Practices*. Lanham, MD: Rowman and Littlefield, 2003.

Magana, Lisa. *Straddling the Border: Immigration Policy and the INS*. Austin: University of Texas Press, 2003.

Majaridge, Dale. *The Coming White Minority: California's Eruptions and America's Future*. New York: Random House, 1996.

Mamot, Patricia R. *Foreign Medical Graduates in America*. Springfield, ILL: Charles Thomas, 1974.

Mann, Arthur. *The One and the Many*. Chicago: University of Chicago Press, 1979.

Manning, B. "The Congress, the Executive, and Intermestic Affairs: Three Proposals," *Foreign Affairs*, 1977, 55: 306–324.

"Marcos' Filipinos Flock to America," *The Cumberland Times/News*, Wednesday, July 17, 1985: 7.

"Marriages of Convenience," *The Washington Post*, Sunday, October 21, 1984: A-1, 18–19.

Martin, David. "Expedited Removal, Detention, and Due Process," in Lydio Tomasi, ed., *In Defense of the Alien, XXII*. New York: Center for Migration Studies, 2000: 161–180.

———. "With a Whisper, Not a Bang: Bush Signs Parts of Patriot Act II into Law—Stealthly," *San Antonio Current*, http://www.saccurrent.com/site/news/cfm? Accessed August 23, 2005.

Martin, Philip. "Temporary Workers at the Top and Bottom of the Labor Market," in Lydio Tomasi, ed., *In Defense of the Alien, XXIII*. New York: Center for Migration Studies, 2001: 44–55.

Martinez, Oscar J. *Border People: Life and Society in US—Mexico Borderlands*. Tuscon: University of Arizona Press, 1994.

Massey, Douglas, Jorge Durand, and Nolan Malone. *Beyond Smoke and Mirrors: Mexican Immigration in an Era of Economic Integration*. New York: Russell Sage Foundation, 2002.

Mcbride, Paul. "Peter Roberts and the UMCA Americanization Program, 1907–World War I," *Pennsylvania History*, 1977, 44(2): 145–162.

McCarthy, Kevin, "Immigration and California: Issues for the 1980s," P-6846. Santa Monica: CA: The Rand Corporation, January 1983, 11 pp.

——— and R. Burciaga Valdez. *Current and Future Effects of Mexican Immigration in California*, R-3365-CR, Santa Monica, CA: The Rand Corporation, May 1986.

——— and George Vernez. *Immigration in a Changing Economy: California' Experience*. Santa Monica, CA: Rand, 1997.

McClain, Charles J. *In Search of Equity: The Chinese Struggle Against Discrimination in Nineteenth Century America*. Berkley, CA: University of California Press, 1994.

McClellan, Grant S., ed. *Immigrants, Refugees and U.S. Policy*. New York: H.W. Wilson, 1981.

McClemore, Dale S. *Racial and Ethnic Relations in America*. Boston: Allyn and Bacon, 1980.

McClymer, John F. "The Federal Government and the Americanization Movement, 1915–1924," *Prologue*, 1978, 10(1): 23–41.

McConnell, Eileen Diaz, and Felicia B. Leclere. "Selection, Context, or Both? The English Fluency of Mexican Immigrants in the American Midwest and Southwest," *Population Research and Policy Review*, 2002, 21(3): 159–178.

McDowell, Lorraine and Paul T. Hill. *Newcomers in American Schools*. Santa Monica, CA: Rand, 1993.

McGouldrick, Paul F. and Michael Tannen. "Did American Manufacturers Discriminate Against Immigrants Before 1914?," *Journal of Economic History*, 1977, 37(3): 723–746.

McKenna, George. *A Guide to the Constitution, That Delicate Balance*. New York: Random House, 1984.

McLemore, Dale S. *Racial and Ethnic Relations in America*, 2nd ed. Boston, MA: Allyn and Bacon, 1983.

McSeveny, Samuel T. "Ethnic Groups, Ethnic Conflicts, and Recent Quantitative Research in American Political History," *The International Migration Review, VII*, Spring 1973: 14–33.

Meissner, Doris. "Management Challenge and Program Risks," in Lydio Tomasi, ed. *In Defense of the Alien, XXII*. New York: Center for Migration Studies, 2000: 1–5.

Meister, Richard J. *Race and Ethnicity in Modern America*. Lexington, MA: D.C. Heath, 1974.

Miller, R.M. and T.D. Marzik, eds., *Immigrants and Religion in Urban America*. Philadelphia, PA: Temple University Press, 1977.

Miller, Stuart C. *The Unwelcome Immigrant: The American Image of the Chinese, 1785–1882*. Berkeley: University of California Press, 1969.

Minnite, Lorraine, Jennifer Holdaway, and Ronald Hayduk. "The Political Participation of Immigrants from New York," in Lydio Tomasi, ed., *In Defense of the Alien, XXIII*. New York: Center for Migration Studies, 2001: 192–228.

Mintz, John and Christopher Lee. "The Homeland Security Wish List," *The Washington Post National Weekly Edition*, February 3–9, 2003: 31.

Mitchell, Kenneth D. "The Other Homeland Security Threat: Bureaucratic Haggling," *The Public Manager*, Spring, 2003, 32(7): 15–19.

Mohl, Raymond A. "The Saturday Evening Post and the 'Mexican Invasion'," *Journal of Mexican-American History*, 1973, 3(1): 131–138.

Montero, Darrel. *Vietnamese Americans*. Boulder, CO: Westview Press, 1979.

Moore, Stephen. *Fiscal Impacts of the Newest Americans*. Washington, D.C.: National Immigration Forum/Cato Institute, 1998.

Morris, Milton. *Immigration—The Beleaguered Bureaucracy*. Washington, D.C.: The Brookings Institution, 1985.

Mosisa, Abraham T. "The Role of Foreign-Born Workers in the U.S. Economy," *Monthly Labor Review*. Washington, D.C.: U.S. Department of Labor, May 2002, 125: 3–14.

Moskos, Charles C. *Greek Americans*. Englewood Cliffs, NJ: Prentice-Hall, 1980.

Muller, Thomas and Thomas Espanshade. *The Fourth Wave*. Washington, D.C.: The Urban Institute, 1985.

Mundy, Alicia. "Iffy on Sacrifice: Americans' Attitude Towards National Security," *American Demographics*, July 1, 2004, 26(6): pNA.

Murphy, Caryle. "Sanctuary: How Churches Defy Immigration Law," *The Washington Post National Weekly Edition*, September 17, 1984: 8–9.

Nadig, Aninia. "Forced Migration," *Journal of Refugee Studies*, 2003, 16(4): 364+.

National Archives and Records Administration. NARA-RG-90, Central Files, 1897–1923, File 219, Box 38, Ellis Island.

National Geographic Society. *We Americans*. Washington, D.C.: National Geographic Society, 1975.

National Research Council. *The New Americans: Economic, Demographic, and Fiscal Effects of Immigration*. Washington, D.C.: National Research Council; National Academy Press, 1997.

Nelli, Humbert. *Italians in Chicago, 1830–1930*. New York: Oxford University Press, 1970.

Neely, Mark E. "Richard W. Thompson: The Persistent Know Nothing," *Indiana Magazine of History*, 1976, 72(2): 95–122.

Nenny, Barbara L. "Municipal Emergency Preparedness: The Local Face of Homeland Security," *The Public Manager*, Winter 2002, 32(4): 46–51.

Neuman, Gerald L. "The Lost Century of American Immigration Law, 1776–1875," *Columbia Law Review*, December 1993, 93(8): 1834, 1837–1838.

Nevins, Allan. *Ordeal in Union: A House Dividing*. New York: Charles Scribners Sons, 1947.

Nevins, Joseph. *Operation Gatekeeper*. New York: Routledge, 2001.

Newman, Edward and Van Selm, eds., *Refugees and Forced Displacement*, 2003.

Newman, William H. *Managing National Security Policy: The President and the Process*. Pittsburgh, PA: University of Pittsburgh Press, 2003.

Nord, Douglas C. "The Problem of Immigration: The Continuing Presence of the Stranger Within Our Gates," *American Review of Canadian Studies*, 1978, 8(2): 116–133.

North, David S. "The Growing Importance of Immigration to Population Policy," *Policy Studies Journal*, 1977, 6(2): 200–207.

―――. *Seven Years Later: The Experiences of the 1970 Cohort of Immigrants in the U.S. Labor Market*. Washington, D.C.: New Trans-Century Foundation, 1978.

North, David. *Immigration and Income Transfer Policies in the United States: An Analysis of a Non-Relationship*. Washington, D.C.: New Trans-Century Foundation, 1980.

North, David and Allen LeBel. *Manpower and Immigration Policies in the United States*. Washington, D.C.: U.S. National Commission for Manpower Policy, Special Report 20, The Commission, 1978.

Novak, Michael. "Just Peace and the Asymetric Threat: National Defense in Unchartered Waters," *Harvard Journal of Law and Public Policy*, Summer 2004, 27(3): 817–842.

―――. *The Rise of the Unmeltable Ethnics*. New York: Macmillan, 1972.

O'Beirne, Kate. "Bureaucratic Nightmare on the Way?," *National Review*, Opinion Page in *The Press Enterprise*. San Bernardino, CA: August 25, 2002: D-1.

O'Brien, Kenneth B., Jr. "Education, Americanization, and the Supreme Court: the 1920s," *American Quarterly*, XIII, Summer 1961): 161–171.

O'Brien, Tim, "Making Homeland Security a Niche," *New Jersey Law Journal*, July 18, 2005: pNA.

Obsatz, Sharyn. "INS Says Foreigners Required to Register," *Press-Enterprise*. Riverside, CA: December 7, 2002a: B-5.

———. "Vandals Turn Desert Deadly," *Press-Enterprise*. Riverside, CA: September 14, 2002b, A-1, 10.

O'Connor, Thomas. *The German Americans*. Boston: Little, Brown, 1968.

"Odd Cast Boosts Immigration Reform," *The Denver Post*, Sunday, June 12, 2005: E-4.

O'Gallagher, Marianna. *Grosse Ile: Gateway to Canada, 1832–1937*. Ste. Foy, Quebec, Canada: Livries Carraig Books, 1984.

O'Grady, Joseph D. *How the Irish Became Americans*. New York: Twayne, 1973.

O'Hanlon, Michael E. *Defense Strategy for the Post-Saddam Era*. Washington, D.C.: Brookings Institution Press, 2005.

O'Hanlon, Michael E., Peter R. Orszag, Ivo H. Daalder, I.M. Destler, David L. Gunter, Robert E. Latan, and James B. Steinberg, eds. *Protecting the American Homeland: A Preliminary Analysis*. Washington, D.C.: Brookings Institution Press, 2002.

O'Harrow, Robert Jr. "Who's Minding the Passengers?," *The Washington Post National Weekly Edition*, September 16–22, 2002: 29.

"1,000 Activists to Patrol Arizona Border for Migrants," *The Denver Post*, Thursday, March 31, 2005: A-6.

"One-time Internee Returns to Camp," *Cumberland Evening Times*, Thursday, August 15, 1985: 38.

O'Neill, Terry. *Immigration: Opposing Viewpoints*. San Diego, CA: Greenhaven Press, 1992.

Orback, William. *The American Movement to Aid Soviet Jews*. Amherst, MA: University of Massachusetts Press, 1979.

Orth, Ralph and Alfred Ferguson, eds., *The Journals and Miscellaneous Papers of Ralph Waldo Emerson*. Cambridge: Harvard University Press, 1971.

Overdyke, W. Darrell. *The Know Nothing Party in the South*. Gloucester, MA: Peter Smith, 1968.

Papadetriou, Demetrious and Mark Miller, eds. *The Unavoidable Issue*. Philadelphia: Institute for the Study of Human Issues, 1984.

Papademetriou, Demetrios, Alexander Aleinkoff, and D.W. Meyers. *Reorganizing the U.S. Immigration Function: Toward a New Framework for Accountability*. Washington, D.C.: Carnegie Foundation for International Peace, 1999.

"Paper Provides Homeland News to Indian Immigrants," *The Cumberland Times/News*, Wednesday, July 17, 1985: 7.

Parlin, Bradley W. "Immigrants, Employers, and Exclusion," *Society*, 1977, 14(6): 23–26.

Parrillo, Vincent. *Strangers to These Shores*. Boston: Houghton-Mifflin Co., 1980.

———. *Strangers to These Shores*. New York: Wiley, 1985.

Parry, Wayne. "Many Arrested, But Few Charged," *The Press-Enterprise*. San Bernardino, CA: Sunday, September 8, 2002: D-1, D-4.

Passel, Jeffrey. *Immigration and Taxes: A Reappraisal of Huddle's 'The Cost of Immigration*. Washington, D.C.: Urban Institute, 1994.

Passel, Jeffrey S. and Rebecca L. Clark. *How Much Do Immigrants Really Cost?* Washington, D.C.: Urban Institute, 1994.

Pearlstein, Deborah. "Rights in an Insecure World: Why National Security and Civil Liberty Are Complements," *The American Prospect*, October 2004, 15(10): A7–A11.

Peffer, George A. "Forbidden Families: Emigration Experiences of Chinese Women Under the Page Laws, 1875–1882," *Journal of American Ethnic History*, 1986 6: 28–46.

Perea, Juan F. *Immigrants Out!: The New Nativism and the Anti-Immigrant Impulses In the United States*. New York: New York University Press, 1997.

Perlmutter, Philip. "The American Struggle with Ethnic Superiority," *Journal of Intergroup Relations*, 1977, 6(2): 31–56.

Perotti, Rosanna. "Resolving Policy Conflict: Congress and Immigration Reform," Ph.D. Dissertation, University of Pennsylvania, 1989.

Peters, Ronald M. and Arturo Vega. "The Role of House Democratic Party Leaders on Non-Party Position Legislation with Partisan Consequences: The Immigration Bill," Paper Presented at the 1986 Meetings of the American Political Science Association, August 28–31, 1986, Washington, D.C.

Piore, Michael. *Birds of Passage: Migrant Labor and Industrial Societies*. New York: Cambridge University Press, 1979.

Piott, Steven L. "The Lessons of the Immigrants: Views of Immigrants in Muckraking Magazines, 1900–1909," *American Studies*, 1978, 19(1): 21–33.

Pitkin, Thomas. *Keepers of the Gate*. New York: New York University Press, 1975.

Platt, Tony and Cecilia O'Leary. "Patriot Acts," *Social Justice*, Spring 2003, 30(1): 5–22.

Podesta, John and Peter Swire. "Speaking Out About Wiretaps," *The Washington Post National Weekly Edition*, September 9–15, 2002: 27.

Portes, Alejandro and Ruben G. Rumbaut. *Immigrant America*. Berkeley: University of California Press, 1990.

———. *Legacies: The Story of the Immigrant Second Generation*. New York: Russell Sage Foundation, 2001a.

———. *Ethnicities: Children of Immigrants in America*. New York: Russell Sage Foundation, 2001b.

Post, Louis F. *The Deportation Delirium of Nineteen-Twenty*. Chicago: Charles H. Kerr, 1923.

Poulson, Barry W. and James Holyfield, Jr. "A Note on European Migration to the United States: A Cross-Spectral Analysis," *Exploration in Economic History*, 1974, 11(3): 289–310.

"Powers of the Patriot Act in Eye of the Beholder," *Los Angeles Times*, Tuesday, September 2, 2003: A-15.

Pozzetta, George, ed. *Contemporary Immigration and American Society*. New York: Garland Publishing, 1991.

"President Endorses Immigration Proposal," *The Washington Post*, Friday, October 17, 1986: A-4.

Preston, William, Jr. *Aliens and Dissenters: Federal Suppression of Radicals, 1903–1963*. Cambridge, MA: Harvard University Press, 1963.

Proper, Emberson Edward. "Colonial Immigration Laws: A Study of the Regulation of Immigration by the English Colonies in America," Ph.D. Dissertation, Department of Political Science, New York: Columbia University, 1900.

Pypic, George. *South Slavic Immigration in America*. Boston: Twayne, 1978.

"Quiz Traps Fraudulent Immigrants," *The Cumberland Sunday Times*, November 3, 1985: A-3.

"Raids Nab High-Pay Aliens, Make Jobs, Outrage Clergy," *The Washington Post*, May 2, 1982, A-10.

Rak, Mary Kidder. *Border Patrol*. Boston: Houghton Mifflin, 1983.

Razin, Lora. "An Update from Capitol Hill," in Lydio Tomasi, ed. *In Defense of the Alien, XXIII*. New York: Center for Migration Studies, 2001: 99–103.

"Reaction to Immigration Bill Is Sharply Split," *The New York Times*, Friday, October 16, 1986: B-15.

"Reagan Said to Favor Signing New Aliens Bill," *The New York Times*, Friday, October 17, 1986: A-2.

Reich, Robert B. "A Failure of Intelligence," *The American Prospect*, August 2004, 15(8):72–73.

Reimers, David. *Still the Golden Door: The Third World Comes to America*, 2nd edn. New York: Columbia University Press, 1985.

Relyea, Harold C. "Organizing for Homeland Security," *Presidential Studies Quarterly*, September 2003, 33(3): 602–625.

Renner, Richard W. "In a Perfect Ferment: Chicago, the Know-Nothings, and the Riot for Lager Beer," *Chicago History*, 1976, 5(3): 161–169.

Research Institute on Immigration and Ethnic Studies, "Recent Immigration to the United States: The Literature of the Social Sciences," *RIIES* Bibliographic Studies No. 1. Washington, D.C.: The Smithsonian Institution Press, 1976.

———, "Pacific Migration to the U.S.," *RIIES* Bibliographic Studies, No. 2. Washington, D.C.: The Smithsonian Institution Press, 1977.

———, "Quantitative Data and Immigration Research," *RIIES* Research Notes, No. 2. Washington, D.C.: The Smithsonian Institution Press, 1979.

———, "Female Immigrants to the U.S.," *RIIES* Occasional Papers No. 2. Washington, D.C.: Smithsonian Institution Press, 1981.

———, "Return Migration and Remittances: Developing a Caribbean Perspective," *RIIES* Occasional Papers No. 3. Washington, D.C.: The Smithsonian Institution Press, 1982.

———, "Caribbean Immigration to the United States," *RIIES* Occasional Papers No. 1. Washington, D.C.: Smithsonian Institution Press, 1983.

Ries, Lora. "An Update from Capitol Hill," in Lydio Tomas, ed. *In Defense of the Alien, XXIII*. New York: Center for Migration Studies, 2001: 99–103.

"Right Versus Right: Immigration and Refugee Policy in the United States," *Foreign Affairs*, Fall 1980.

Riis, Jacob. *How the Other Half Lives*. New York: Dover, 1971.

Ringer, Benjamin B. *"We the People" and Others*. New York: Tavistock Publications, 1983.

Ringle, Ken. "What Did You Do Before the War, Dad?," *The Washington Post Magazine*, December 6, 1981: 54–62.

Rippley, LeVern T. *The German Americans*. Chicago: Claretian Press, 1973.

Rischin, Moses, ed. *Immigration and the American Tradition*. Indianapolis: Bobbs-Merrill, 1976.

Rivera, Jose A. "Aliens Under the Law: A Legal Perspective," *Employer Relations Law Journal*, 3, Summer 1977: 12–37.

Roberts, Marta. "20-20 Spy Sight," *Security Management*, February 2005, 59(2): 76–80.

Roberts, Patrick S. "Shifting Priorities: Congressional Incentives and the Homeland Security Process," *The Review of Policy Research*, July 2005, 22(4): 437–450.

Roberts, Peter. *Immigrant Races in North America*. New York: Association Press, 1912.

Robertson, Lori. "High Anxiety," *American Journalism Review*, April 2003, 25(3): 18–26.

Roots, Roger. "Terrorized into Absurdity: the Creation of the Transportation Security Administration," *Independent Review*, Spring 2003, 7(4): 503–518.

Rosenblum, Gerald. *Immigrant Workers: Their Impact on American Labor Radicalism*. New York: Basic Books, 1973.

Rostow, Eugene. "The Japanese-American Cases—A Disaster," *Yale Law Journal*, June 1945: 489–533.

———. "Our Worst Wartime Mistake," *Harper's Magazine*, September 1945: 193–201.

Rothwell, Greg, "Taming the Spending Beast," *The Public Manager*, Spring/ Summer 2004, 33(1): 10–13.

Roucek, Joseph S. and Bernard Eisenber, eds., *America's Ethnic Politics*. Westport, CT: Greenwood Press, 1982.

Rubin, Jay. "Black Nativism: The European Immigrant in Negro Thought, 1830–1860," *Phylon*, 1978, 39(3): 193–202.

Rumbaut, Ruben G. *Immigrant Children in California Public Schools: A Summary of Current Knowledge*. Baltimore: The Johns Hopkins University Center for Research on Effective Schooling for Disadvantaged Students, 1990.

Rumbaut, Ruben G. "Transformations: The Post-Immigrant Generation in an Age of Diversity," in Lydio Tomasi, ed., *In Defense of the Alien, XXIII*. New York: Center for Migration Studies, 2001: 229–259.

Samuel, Joseph. *Jewish Immigration to the U.S., 1881–1910*. New York: Arno Press, 1969.

Sanchez, Rene. "Deadly Smuggling at the Border," *The Washington Post National Weekly Edition*, August 19–25, 2002: 17.

Satariano, William A. "Immigration and the Popularization of Social Science, 1920–1930," *Journal of History of the Behavioral Sciences*, 1979, 15(4): 310–320.

Saveth, Edward. *American Historians and European Immigrants, 1875–1925*. New York: The Free Press, 1938.

Saxton, Alexander. *The Indispensable Enemy: Labor and the Anti-Chinese Movement in California*. Berkeley: University of California Press, 1971.

Sayer, Lucy E. *Laws Harsh as Tigers: Chinese Immigrants and the Shaping of Modern Immigration Law*. Chapel Hill: University of North Carolina Press, 1995.

Scanlon, Joseph and G. Loescher. "Mass Asylum and Human Rights in American Foreign Policy," *Political Science Quarterly*, 1982, 97: 39–56.

Schander, Edwin R. "Immigration Law and Practice in the U.S.: A Selective Bibliography," *International Migration Review*, 1978, 12(1): 117–127.

Schlesinger, Arthur M. *The Disuniting of America: Reflections on a Multicultural Society*. New York: Norton, 1992.

Schmitt, Michael N. "U.S. Security Strategies: A Legal Assessment," *Harvard Journal of Law and Public Policy*, Summer 2004, 27(3): 797–816.

Schuck, Peter H. "The Transformation of Immigration Law," *Columbia Law Review*, January 1984, 84(1): 39–56.

Schwartz, Abba P. *The Open Society.* New York: William Morrow, 1968.

Scott, Franklin D. *The Peopling of America: Perspectives on Immigration.* Washington, D.C.: American Historical Association, Pamphlet #241, 1972.

Seamon, Richard Henry and William Dylan Gardner. "The Patriot Act and the Wall Between Foreign Intelligence and Law Enforcement," *Harvard Journal of Law and Public Policy*, Spring 2005, 28(2): 319–464.

Select Commission of Immigration and Refugee Policy. *Final Report.* Washington, D.C.: United States Government Printing Office, 1981.

"Senate Passes S. 2845, the National Intelligence Reform Act of 2004," http://www.ssa.gov/legislation/legis_bulletin_102704.html, accessed August 18, 2005.

Sharp, Nancy. "International Assignments and the Immigration Issues Surrounding Spousal Employment," in Lydio Tomasi, ed., *In Defense of the Alien, XXII.* New York: Center for Migration Studies, 2000: 59–63.

Shaw, Albert, ed., *Messages and Papers of Woodrow Wilson.* New York: 1924.

Shotwell, Lynn Frendt. "Comparison of the H-1B Bills," in Lydio Tomasi, ed., *In Defense of the Alien, XXIII.* New York: Center for Migration Studies, 2001: 87–95.

Shumsky, Neil L. *The Evolution of Political Protest and the Workingmen's Party of California.* Columbus: Ohio State University, 1991.

Sibley, Mulford Q. *The Transformation of American Politics, 1840–1860.* Englewood Cliffs, NJ: Prentice-Hall, 1967.

Siegel, Mark. "Ethnics: A Democratic Stronghold?," *Public Opinion*, September/October 1978.

Sieghart, Mary Ann. "Border Patrol: A Revolving Door Policy," *The Washington Post National Weekly Edition*, September 17, 1984: 7.

Siesseger, Marie E. "Conspiracy Theory: The Use of the Conspiracy Doctrine in Times of National Crisis," *William and Mary Law Review*, December 2004, 46(3): 1177–1219.

Simcox, David. *Measuring the Fallout: The Cost of the IRCA Amnesty After Ten Years.* Washington, D.C.: Center for Immigration Studies, 1997.

———. *U.S. Immigration in the 1980s: Reappraisal and Reform.* Boulder, CO: Westview Press; Washington, D.C.: Center for Immigration Studies, 1985.

Simon, Jonathan. "Parrhesiastic Accountability: Investigatory Commissions and Executive Power in an Age of Terror," *Yale Law Journal*, April 2005, 114(6): 1419–1458.

Simon, Julian. *The Economic Consequences of Immigration.* Cambridge, MA: Basil Blackwell, 1990.

Simon, Rita J. and Susan Alexander. *The Ambivalent Welcome: Print Media, Public Opinion and Immigration.* Westport, CT: Praeger Publications, 1993.

"Simpson Tackles Immigration Reform Again," *Minneapolis Star and Tribune*, Monday, June 24, 1985: A-10.

"Simpson: the 'Anglo' Behind the Immigration Bill," *The Washington Post*, Sunday, October 19, 1986: A-8-9.

Singh, Jaswinder and Kalyani Gopal. *Americanization of New Immigrants.* Lanham, MD: University Press of America, 2002.

Smith, Darrell Hevenor and H. Guy Herring. *Bureau of Immigration: Its History, Activities, and Organization.* Baltimore: Johns Hopkins University Press, 1924.

Smith, James M. *Freedom's Fetters: Alien and Sedition Laws.* Ithaca: Cornell University Press, 1956.

Smith, Theodore C. *Politics and Slavery*. New York: Negro University Press, 1969.

Smith, T. Lynn and Vernon J. Parenton. "Acculturation Among the Louisiana French," *American Journal of Sociology*, 44, November 1938: 130pp.

"Smuggling Deaths Net Conviction," *The Denver Post*, Thursday, March 25, 2005: A-1, 16.

Sneider, Daniel. "The Groupthink Failure: A Centralized Bureaucracy Won't Improve Intelligence," *Knight Ridder/Tribune News Service*, September 10, 2004: pk.4246.

Social Security Trust Fund (SSTF). *Board of Trustees Report*. Washington, D.C.: U.S. Government Printing Office, 1998.

Soloutos, Theodore. *The Greeks in the United States*. Cambridge: Harvard University Press, 1964.

Soros, George. "The People's Sovereignty," *Foreign Policy*, January/February 2004: 66–67.

Sowell, Thomas, ed., *Essays and Data on American Ethnic Groups*. Washington, D.C.: Urban Institute Press, 1978.

———. *Ethnic America: A History*. New York: Basic Books, 1981.

Sprinzak, Elund. "Rational Fanatics," *Foreign Policy*, September/October 2000.

Staley, Joseph. "Law Enforcement and the Border," in Erb, Richard D. and Stanley R. Ross, *United States Relations with Mexico*. Washington, D.C.: American Enterprise Institute, 1981: 106–120.

Stana, Richard M. *Homeland Security: Challenges to Implementing the Immigration Interior Enforcement Strategy*. GAO-03-660T, Washington, D.C.: U.S. Government Printing Office, 2003.

Stedman, Stephen J. and Fred Tanner, eds. *Refugee Manipulations: War, Politics, and the Abuse of Human Suffering*. Washington, D.C.: Brookings Institution Press, 2003.

Steinberg, Peter L. *The Great 'Red Menace', United States Prosecution of American Communists, 1947–1952*. Westport, CT: Greenwood Press, 1984.

Steiner, Edward. *On the Trail of the Immigrant*. New York: Fleming H. Revell Co., 1906.

Stephenson, George M. *The Religious Aspect of Swedish Immigration*. New York: Arno Press, 1969.

Stevens, Gillian. "U.S. Immigration Policy and the Language Characteristics of Immigrants," in Lydio Tomasi, ed., *In Defense of the Alien, XXIII*. New York: Center for Migration Studies, 2001: 177–191.

———. "Age at Immigration and Second Language Proficiency Among Foreign-Born Adults," *Language in Society*, 1999, 28: 555–578.

Stevens, Rosemary. *The Alien Doctors*. New York: Wiley and Sons, 1978.

Stipanovich, Joseph. "Immigration and American Social History," *Journal of Urban History*, 1978, 5(1): 133–142.

Stolzenberg, Ross M. "Occupational Differences Between Hispanics and Non-Hispanics," N-1889-NCEP. Santa Monica, CA: The Rand Corporation, July 1982, 107pp.

Stout, Harry H., "Ethnicity: The Vital Center of Religion in America," *Ethnicity*, June 1975, 2: 204–224.

Strange, Steven L. "Private Consensual Sexual Conduct and the 'Good Moral Character' Requirement of the Immigration and Nationality Act," *Columbia Journal of Transnational Law*, 1975, 14(2): 357–381.

"Study Shows Indochina Refugees Doing Well," *The Cumberland Times/News*, Wednesday, July 24, 1985: 5.

"Surge in Bogus Papers Predicted in Wake of Change in Alien Law," *The New York Times*, Monday, October 20, 1986: A-1, 24.

Swazo, Norman K., "The Duty of Congress to Check the President's Prerogative In National Security Policy," *International Journal on World Peace*, December 2004, 21(4): 21–63.

Szumski, Bonnie, ed. *Interracial America Opposing Viewpoints*. San Diego, CA: Greenhaven Press, 1996.

Takaki, Ronald. *Chinese America: History and Perspectives, 1990*. Brisbane, CA: Chinese Historical Society of America, 1990.

"Tancredo Working to Turn the Tide," *The Denver Post*, Sunday, June 5, 2005: A-1, 8.

Tanter, Raymond. *Rogue Regimes: Terrorism and Proliferation*. New York: St. Martin's Press, 1998.

Tanton, John. *Rethinking Immigration Policy*. FAIR Immigration Paper 1, Washington, D.C.: Federation for American Immigration Reform, 1980.

Taylor, Margaret. "Detained: Immigration Law and the Expanding INS Jail Complex," *International Migration Review*, Winter 2003, 37(4): 1306–1309.

Taylor, Philip. *The Distant Magnet: European Emigration to the U.S.A.* New York: Harper and Row, 1971.

Teitelbaum, M. "Rights versus Rights: Immigration and Refugee Policy in the United States," *Foreign Affairs*, 1980, 59: 21–59.

"Temporary Worker Bill Proposal," *The Denver Post*, Tuesday, August 9, 2005: B-7.

T'Hart, Paul, Eric K. Stern, and Bengt Sundeluis, eds., *Beyond Groupthink: Political Dynamics and Foreign Policymaking*. Ann Arbor, MI: University of Michigan Press, 1997.

"The Gatekeepers," *The Wall Street Journal*, Thursday, May 9, 1985: 1–2, 7.

"The New Immigrants," *Newsweek*, July 7, 1980: 26–31.

Thernstrom, Stephen. *Harvard Encyclopedia of American Ethnic Groups*. Cambridge, MA: Harvard University Press, 1980.

Thomas, William and Florian Znanicki, "The Polish American Community," in Leonard Dinnerstein and Frederick Jaher, *Uncertain Americans*. New York: Oxford University Press, 1977.

Thompson, James J., Jr. "Southern Baptists and Anti-Catholicism in the 1920s," *Mississippi Quarterly*, 1979, 32(4): 611–625.

"Thousands Eligible for Alien Amnesty Across Maryland," *The Cumberland Times/ News*, Tuesday, November 11, 1986: A-10.

Tindall, George Brown. *America: A Narrative History*, 2nd edn. New York: W.W. Norton, 1984.

Tomasi, S.M., ed., *Perspectives in Italian Immigration and Ethnicity*. New York: Center for Migration Studies, 1977.

Torr, James D., ed. *Homeland Security*. San Diego: Greenhaven Press, 2004.

"Tortilla Curtain Fails to Stem Tide of Illegal Aliens," *The Washington Times*, Monday, May 13, 1985: 8a.

Truman, David. *The Governmental Process*. New York: Knopf, 1951.

Tulak, Authur N., Robert W. Kraft, and Don Silbaugh, "State Defense Forces and Homeland Security," Parameters, Winter 2003, 33(4): 132–147.

Ueda, Reed. *Postwar Immigrant America: A Social History*. Boston: Bedford Books, St. Martin's Press, 1994.

"Unusual Coalition Pans Patriot Act," *The Denver Post*, Wednesday, March 23, 2005: A-5.

"U.S. Border Patrol Going 'High Tech'," *The Cumberland Times/News*, Thursday, October 17, 1985: 23.

U.S. Bureau of the Census. *The Foreign Born Population in the United States, March, 2000*. Current Population Reports. Washington, D.C.: U.S. Government Printing Office, 2001.

U.S. Congress, Senate, Committee on the Judiciary. *The Immigration and Naturalization Systems of the United States*. Washington, D.C.: U.S. Government Printing Office, 1950.

United States Commission on Civil Rights. *The Tarnished Door: Civil Rights Issues in Immigration*, Washington, D.C.: U.S. Government Printing Office, 1980.

United States Congress, House of Representatives, "Immigration Reform and Control Act of 1983, "[The Mazzoli Bill], HR 1510, 98th Congress, 1st Session, February 17, 1981: 1–63.

United States, Department of Health and Human Services. *Temporary Assistance for Needy Families (TANF) Program: Third Annual Report to Congress*. Washington, D.C.: U.S. Government Printing Office, 2000.

———, Department of Justice, Immigration and Naturalization Service, "1979 Statistical Yearbook of the INS." Washington, D.C.: U.S. Government Printing Office, 1980.

———, Department of Labor. *International Migration to the United States, 1999*. Washington, D.C.: U.S. Government Printing Office, 1999.

———, Department of State. *Proposed Refugee Admissions for Fiscal Year 2001: Report to Congress*. Washington, D.C.: U.S. Government Printing Office, 2000.

———, *U.S. Refugee Admissions for Fiscal Year 2000*. Washington, D.C.: U.S. Government Printing Office, 1999.

———. General Accounting Office. *Illegal Aliens: Extent of Welfare Benefits Received on Behalf of U.S. Citizen Children*. Washington, D.C.: U.S. Government Printing Office, 1997.

"U.S. Hispanics 'Melting' But Not Prospering," *The Washington Post*, Sunday, May 13, 1984: A-1, 8.

U.S. Immigration Commission. "Brief Statement of the Investigations of the Immigration Commission, with Conclusions and Recommendations and Views of the Minority," U.S. Senate Document 747, 61st Congress, 3rd Session. Washington, D.C.: U.S. Government Office, 1910–1911.

United States, Immigration and Naturalization Service. *An Immigrant Nation: United States Regulation of Immigration, 1798–1991*. Washington, D.C.: Immigration And Naturalization Service, 1991.

U.S. Interagency Task Force on Immigration Policy, *Staff Report*. Washington, D.C.: Departments of Labor, Justice, and State, March, 1979.

U.S. President's Commission on Immigration and Naturalization. *Whom Shall We Welcome: Report*. Washington, D.C.: U.S. Government Printing Office, 1953.

U.S. President's Select Commission on Immigration and Refugee Policy. *U.S. Immigration Policy and the National Interest: Final Report*. Washington, D.C.: U.S. Government Printing Office, March 1, 1981.

U.S. Statistics At Large, 101: 1329. Amerasian Homecoming Act, 1987.

————, 102: 1876. U.S.–Canada Free Trade Agreement Implementation Act, 1988.

————, 103: 3908. Foreign Operations Act, 1989a.

————, 103: 2099. Immigration Nursing Relief Act, 1989b.

Utley, Jon Basil. "Analyzing Al Qaeda and Protecting America," *World and I*, May 2004, 19(5): 34+.

Vecoli, Rudolph and Joy Lintelman. *A Century of American Immigration, 1884–1984*. Minneapolis, MN: University of Minnesota Continuing Education and Extension, 1984.

————. "Prelates and Peasants: Italian Immigrants and the Catholic Church," *Journal of Social History*, Spring 1969, 2: 217–268.

Vialet, Joyce. "A Brief History of U.S. Immigration Policy," *Report 80-223 EPW*. Washington, D.C.: Education and Public Welfare Division, INS, December 1980.

Vittoz, Stan. "World War I and the Political Accommodation of Transitional Market Forces: The Case of Immigration Restriction," *Politics and Society*, 1978, 8(1): 49–98.

Walcott, Charles E. and Karen M. Hult. "The Bush Staff and Cabinet System," *Perspectives on Political Science*, Summer 2003, 32(3): 150–156.

Walters, Robert. "Immigrants and Jobs," *The Cumberland Times/News*, Friday, October 25, 1985: 8.

Walton, Gary M. and Ross M. Robertson. *History of the American Economy*, 5th edn. New York: Harcourt, Brace, Jovanovich, Inc., 1983.

Wang, Peter H. "Farmers and the Immigration Act of 1924," *Agricultural History*, 1975, 49(4): 647–652.

————. "The Immigration Act of 1924 and the Problem of Assimilation," *Journal of Ethnic Studies*, 1974, 2(3): 72–75.

Wareing, J. "The Changing Pattern of Immigration into the United States, 1956–1975," *Georgraphy*, 1978, 63(3): 220–224.

Waugh, William L., Jr. "Securing Mass Transit: A Challenge for Homeland Security," *The Review of Policy Research*, May 2004, 21(3): 307–317.

Weinberg, Daniel E. "Ethnic Identity in Industrial Cleveland: 1900–1920," *Ohio History*, Summer 1971, 86, 13.

————. "Greek Americans Score Big in Carter/Mondale Campaign," *Greek World*, November/December 1976.

————. "The Ethnic Technician and the Foreign Born: Another Look at Americanization Ideology and Goals," *Societas*, 1977, 7(3): 2009–2227.

Weiser, Marjorie P. *Ethnic America*, 1978.

Weiss, Thomas, ed. *Collective Security in a Changing World*. Boulder, CO: Lynne Reinner Publisher, 1993.

Weiss, Thomas G., David Forsythe, and Roger Coate. *The United Nations and Changing World Politics*. Boulder, CO: Westview Press, 2004.

Weiss, Richard. "Ethnicity and Reform: Minorities and the Ambience of the Depression Years," *Journal of American History*, 1979, 66(3): 566–585.

Weissbrodt, David. *Immigration Law and Procedure*. St. Paul, MN: West Publishing, 1984.

Wellner, Alison Stein. "The Money in the Middle," *American Demographics*, April 2000, 22: 58–64.

"Where the Family Comes First," *Parade Magazine*, June 2, 1985: 4–6.

White, Jerry C. *A Statistical History of Immigration*. Immigration and Naturalization Reporter, 25. Washington, D.C.: U.S. Government Printing, Summer 1976.

Whittke, Carl. *We Who Built America*. Akron, OH: Case Western Reserve University Press, 1967.

Williamson, Jr., Charlton. *The Immigration Mystique: America's False Conscience*. New York: Basic Books, 1996.

Williamson, Jeffrey G. "Migration to the New World: Long-Term Influence and Impact," *Explorations in Economic History*, 1974, 11(4): 357–389.

Wolchok, Carole Leslie. "Where Do We Go From Here? The Future of the Expedited Removal Process," in Lydio Tomasi, ed., *In Defense of the Alien, XXII*. New York: Center for Migration Studies, 2000: 181–192

Wolfe, Alan. *One Nation, After All*. New York: Penguin Putnam, 2002.

Woll, Peter. *Public Policy*. Cambridge, MA: Winthrop, 1974.

Wong, Janelle E. "The Effects of Length of Residence and Community Context on Political Attitude Formation and Participation Among Asian and Latino Immigrants," in Lydio Tomasi, ed., *In Defense of the Alien, XXII*. New York: Center for Migration Studies, 2000: 123–157.

Wyman, David. *Paper Walls: America and the Refugee Crisis*. Amherst, MA: University of Massachusetts Press, 1968.

Wyman, Mark. *Round-Trip to America: The Immigrants Return to Europe, 1880–1930*. Ithaca: Cornell University Press, 1993.

Yang, Philip Q. *Post-1965 Immigration to the United States: Structural Determinants*. Westport, CT: Praeger Publications, 1995.

Yans-McLaughlin, Virginia, ed., *Immigration Reconsidered: History, Sociology, And Politics*. New York: Oxford University Press, 1990.

Yefiv, Steve A. "Groupthink and the Gulf Crisis," *British Journal of Political Science*, July 2003, 33(3): 419–443.

Yi, Hyong. "Building a Department of Homeland Security: The Management Theory," *The Public Manager*, Spring 2003, 32(1): 55–57.

Yoo, John. "War, Responsibility, and the Age of Terrorism," December 2004, 57(3): 793–824.

Yount, Lisa, ed., *Fighting Bioterrorism*. San Diego: Greenhaven Press, 2004.

Yzaquirre, Raul. "What's Wrong with the Immigration Bill," *The Washington Post National Weekly Edition*, December 12, 1983: 29.

Zhou, Lina. "Special Issue: Database Technology for Enhancing National Security," *Journal of Database Management*, January—March 2005, 6(1): i–iv.

Zhou, Min and Carl Bankston III. *Growing Up American: How Vietnamese Children Adapt to Life in the United States*. New York: Russell Sage Foundation, 1999.

Ziegler, Benjamin. *Immigration: An American Dilemma*. Lexington, MA: D.C. Heath, 1953.

Zolberg, Aristide, Astri Suhrki, and Sergio Aguayo. *Escape from Violence: Conflict and the Refugee Crisis in the Developing World*. New York: Oxford University Press, 1989.

Zucker, Norman L. and Naomi Flink Zucker. *The Guarded Gate: The Reality of American Refugee Policy*, San Diego: Harcourt Brace Jovanovich 1987.

Index

United States Public Health Service
(Marine Hospital Service), 72
Union Pacific Railroad, 57, 61
Urban Institute, 190
Urban Political Machine, 59, 80
USA Patriot Act of 2001, 4, 29, 38, 205–8,
210, 217, 233, 261–64, 266
USA Patriot Act II of 2006, 233,
261–64
U.S.-Canada Free Trade Agreement
Implementation Act, 188
U.S. Catholic Conference, Migration and
Refugee Services, 189
U.S. Citizenship and Immigration
Services (USCIS), 219
U.S. Committee for Refugees, 189
U.S. Customs Service, 192, 221, 254
U.S. Department of Defense, 29, 214,
219, 243–44, 263
U.S. Department of Energy, 220
U.S. Department of Health and Human
Services, 157, 192, 221, 234
U.S. Department of Homeland Security,
1, 9, 205–7; Homeland Security Act of
2002, 29, 207–10, 217; structure of,
208–9, 215–16, 218–23, 234, 236,
239, 243–44, 261, 263–64, 266
U.S. Department of Justice, 157, 185,
205–6, 212, 213–14, 219, 235
U.S. Department of Labor, 105–6, 184
U.S. Department of State, 106, 136, 157,
165, 213, 218, 233, 266
U.S. Department of the Treasury, 96,
101, 192
U.S. General Accounting Office (GAO),
178, 184, n184, n221
U.S. House Committee on the Judiciary,
156, 173–74, 258
U.S. v. Rousake Schwimmer, 132–33, 147
U.S. Senate Committee on the Judiciary,
173–74
U.S. Supreme Court, 18, 37, 60, 63,
93, 96, 97, 100–101, 113, 117, 132,
144, 146, 160, 172, 205–6, 212,
217–18
US-VISIT Program, 219
Utah, 61–62, 82–83, 258

Vasa Order of America, 118
Vaile, Rep. Colorado, 121–22, 128
Vietnamese immigrants, 157, 160,
163–65, 188
Vietnam War, 3, 4, 26, 164
Vigilante groups, 259–61
Vinson, Carl, representative, 120–21
Virginia, 58, 74
Visa Waiver Pilot Program, 191
Visas, 123, 164, 168; allotment of, 187;
application and processing backlogs of,
123, 214, 228–29; overstayers, 168,
185, 188, 245, 254, 261–62; T-visa,
264; visa lottery, 264–65, 267

Walker, Francis, general, 97
War-Brides Act of 1946, 24, 146
War of 1812, 34–35
War on Terrorism, 4, 220, 244–45
War Powers Act, 145
War Relocation Authority, 141–42
Warren, Earl, Attorney General of
California, 143
War with Mexico, 1847–1848, 36–37
Washington, George, president, 15, 18,
25, 34; letter regarding immigration,
18, 34, 57
Washington, DC, 84, 246–47, 254
WASPs, defined, 57
"Waves" of immigration, 6, 13–16, 39,
57, 67
Webb-Henry Bill, 99–100
Welsh, 52–53
Welfare Reform Act of 1996, 187–88
Western Europe, 37, 98, 249
Western Hemisphere, 15, 13, 73, 131–32,
148, 156, 163–64
Whig Party, 74
White-Slave Traffic Act, 104
Wilson, Pete, governor, 28, 195
Wilson, Woodrow: Executive Order
2932, of August 8, 1918, 106;
president, 22, 80, 100, 105–6, 107,
110, 114, 118; veto of literacy bill,
1915, 22, 106, 110, 118
Wisconsin, 50–52, 76, 258
Withdrawal, voluntary defined, 235

About the Author

Dr. Michael LeMay is Professor Emeritus from California State University-San Bernardino where he served as Director of the National Security Studies Program, an interdisciplinary Master's Degree Program, and as Chairman of the Department of Political Science and Assistant Dean of the College of Social and Behavioral Sciences. He has frequently written and presented papers at professional conferences on the topics of this book. He has authored numerous journal articles and book reviews on them. He has published in: *The International Migration Review, In Defense of the Alien, Journal of American Ethnic History, Southeastern Political Science Review, Teaching Political Science*, and the *National Civic Review*. Author of a dozen academic volumes, his prior books dealing with immigration policy are: *U.S. Immigration: A Reference Handbook* (2004, ABC-CLIO), *U.S. Immigration and Naturalization Laws and Issues: A Documentary History* (with Elliott Barkan, 1999, Greenwood Publishing), *Anatomy of a Public Policy: The Reform of Contemporary American Immigration Law* (1994, Praeger), *The Gatekeepers: Comparative Immigration Policy* (1989, Praeger), and *From Open Door to Dutch Door: An Analysis of U.S. Immigration Policy Since 1820* (1987, Praeger). He is author of the forthcoming volume: *Illegal Immigration: A Reference Handbook* (Santa Barbara: ABC-CLIO, anticipated release, spring 2007). Professor LeMay has authored two textbooks that have related material to these topics: *Public Administration: Clashing Values in the Administration of Public Policy*, 2nd edn., 2006, Wadsworth Publishing, and *The Perennial Struggle: Race, Ethnicity and Minority Group Relations in the United States*, 2nd edn. (2005, Prentice-Hall).

HARFORD COMMUNITY COLLEGE LIBRARY
401 THOMAS RUN ROAD
BEL AIR, MARYLAND 21015-1698